THE DORSEY SERIES IN PSYCHOLOGY

Advisory Editors

Wendell E. Jeffrey
University of California, Los Angeles

Salvatore R. Maddi
The University of Chicago

Behavior Modification in Applied Settings

ALAN E. KAZDIN

Professor of Psychology
The Pennsylvania State University

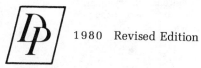 1980   Revised Edition

The Dorsey Press
Homewood, Illinois   60430

IRWIN-DORSEY LIMITED
Georgetown, Ontario   L7G 4B3

ISBN 0-256-02196-1

Library of Congress Catalog Card No. 79–53964

Printed in the United States of America

1 2 3 4 5 6 7 8 9 0 ML 7 6 5 4 3 2 1 0

To Eve, Joann, Nicole, and Michelle—
past, present, and future
sources of inspiration

Preface

The purpose of this book is to provide an introduction to behavior modification techniques in applied settings. The major focus is placed upon the application of operant principles, implementation of behavior modification techniques, and measurement and evaluation of program effectiveness. The applications include a variety of settings such as hospitals and institutions, schools, day-care centers, and the home, as well as outpatient applications. By emphasizing the application of operant procedures, details can be provided that ordinarily would be sacrificed in a cursory review of the entire domain of behavior modification.

A number of books on behavior modification have appeared, including introductory manuals designed for specific audiences such as teachers, parents, or mental health workers, and scholarly texts which present theoretical disputes and review the general field. The hiatus between "how-to-do-it" manuals and extensive scholarly reviews which deemphasize applied research in behavior modification is obvious. This is further reflected in the lack of resources available for undergraduate audiences of diverse disciplines who wish to learn about research and practice in behavior modification. In this book I attempt to emphasize applied research and clinical intervention techniques and achieve a balance not usually found in behavioral texts.

As with the first edition, major techniques for altering behavior and conditions that influence their effectiveness are discussed. The revised edition provides updated information for these techniques and issues that continue to reflect significant topics. For example, progress has been made in studying techniques to promote maintenance of behavior and transfer of that behavior to new settings once the behavioral program has been terminated; in developing self-control techniques for use in applied settings; and in training individuals such as parents and teachers to serve as behavior-change agents, and so on. Updating not only consisted of providing contemporary examples but new techniques and procedural variations as well. Advances have been made in various reinforcement and punishment techniques that reflect creative practices that were unavailable or not widely used only a few years ago.

The revised edition reflects a number of developments that have taken place within the field in ways that differ from merely updating important topics. First, applications have extended to many new areas since the preparation of the first edition. For example, applications of behavioral techniques to medical problems have accelerated and represent a fascinating focus illustrated throughout the text and highlighted in a separate section. Applications in many other areas, such as community work reflect the important work illustrated in the present edition.

Second, many issues within the field have received increased attention and are reflected in the book as well. Prominent among these are legal issues that present some of the conditions within which treatment must operate, and guidelines to ensure that client rights are protected. Also, behavioral applications reflect an increasing concern with evaluating the social context within which treatments operate. The views of people in everyday life increasingly are consulted to help design programs and to evaluate their impact. Although general issues can easily lead one astray, the purpose in raising these in the present book is their relevance to designing effective programs and evaluating their impact.

The overall organization of the book is similar to that of the previous edition. Additional chapters have been added and a few of the previous chapters have been expanded to reflect developments in techniques to assess behavior and evaluate behavioral programs, to use peers as therapeutic agents, to address ethical and legal issues, and to examine possible future directions. As in the previous edition, a glossary is included at the end of the book to help review concepts introduced within the text.

Many people have helped in various ways with completion of the book. Prominent among those who aided the final product are Michele Shawver who typed the manuscript and Nicole Kazdin, my six-year-old daughter who charged me a reasonable sum for alphabetizing some of the references. I am grateful for research support from the National Institute of Mental Health (Grant No. MH 31047) which was provided during the period in which this book was completed.

December 1979   **Alan E. Kazdin**

Contents

Introduction

The procedures used in psychological treatment, rehabilitation, education, and counseling depend heavily upon one's view of "human nature." Treatment strategies follow directly from assumptions and conceptions about normal and abnormal behavior, personality development, and human motivation. Given a particular set of assumptions and theoretical approach, vastly different interpretations can be made about events in the past or present that account for a particular person's behavior. Moreover, the interpretations that are made can serve as the basis for a variety of different procedures that might be applied to achieve therapeutic change. The present chapter provides an introduction to the behavioral approach and its assumptions and views about client problems and the procedures that can be used to alter behavior.

■ TRADITIONAL APPROACHES TOWARD PERSONALITY AND BEHAVIOR

Behavior modification as an approach is relatively new and represents a departure from traditional approaches. However, traditional conceptions of personality and behavior have dominated mental-health related fields such as psychiatry, clinical psychology, social work, education, and rehabilitation. Hence, to appreciate recent developments in behavior modification, traditional views of personality and behavior need to be discussed.[1]

Traditionally, personality had been viewed by many theorists as an assortment of psychological forces inside the individual (Hall & Lindzey, 1978). Although these forces vary depending upon specific theories of personality, they generally consist of such psychological factors as drives, impulses, needs, motives, conflicts, and traits. The traditional approach toward understanding behavior, both abnormal and normal behavior, can be referred to as *intrapsychic* because psychological forces within the individual are accorded the crucial role. "Normal" behavior generally represents a socially acceptable expression of intrapsychic forces. On the other hand, "abnormal" behavior reflects disordered personality development or a dysfunction that results in maladaptive behavior. Psychological processes that have somehow become disordered or have gone awry lead to abnormal behavior.

The intrapsychic approach is firmly entrenched in contemporary views about abnormal behavior. For example, children who are excessively active, horribly misbehaved, and generally obnoxious often are said to be "emotionally disturbed." The inference that one's emotions are disturbed, whatever that would mean, shows the focus of the intrapsychic approach. Similarly, persons who are severely withdrawn, have hallucinations and delusions, and seem generally irrational are regarded as severely "mentally ill." The disease process is implied to rest in their mental or psychological faculties. In each of these examples, the problem is attributed to the psychological processes that in someway are disturbed or diseased. Viewing the bases of behavioral problems as disturbed psychological processes has had remarkably important implications for treatment, rehabilitation, and education. The implications of the traditional approach encompass how to diagnose, assess, and treat abnormality. It is important to discuss the intrapsychic approach because it represents the dominant conceptual view from which the behavioral approach has departed.

Development of the Intrapsychic Approach

Over the course of history in psychiatry and clinical psychology, views about abnormal behavior have varied. At different points in history, abnormal behavior and mental disorders were considered to be caused by demons, evil spirits, and sin. Treatment was directed at these supposed causes. For example, physical punishment and torture were often used in treatment to drive away the evil spirits thought to cause abnormal behavior.

Biological causes for disordered behavior also were accorded a role in abnormal behavior at different periods. In the 19th century, the biological approach increased in importance because of the developments in science, especially the biological sciences. Many advances were made in identifying the organic bases of physical diseases, and breakthroughs in biology and medicine had a tremendous impact on psychiatry (Zilboorg & Henry, 1941).

Although the major developments were in diagnosis and treatment of physical disease, some of the specific breakthroughs had direct relevance for mental disorders. For example, in the early 19th century a bacteria (syphilitic spirochete) was discovered to be the cause of a disorder referred to as *general paresis*. General paresis is a late stage of syphilis and hence is a physical disease. However, the physical basis of the disease had not been known. Since the disease has important psychological symptoms such as impaired intellectual functioning and distorted thoughts and perception, it was viewed as a mental disorder. When the organic basis was found, the findings had very important implications. The breakthrough suggested that various forms of mental disorders might have an underlying organic basis. Essentially, mental illness might really be the result of a physical disease.

The success achieved with general paresis stimulated enthusiasm for finding an organic basis for mental illnesses and severely disordered behavior. However, for most disorders no evidence of an organic disease agent has been identified. In the late 19th century, many theorists abandoned the physical disease approach toward abnormal behavior and instead looked to psychological factors as the causal agents. Rather than organic disease, perhaps "psychological disease" processes might be the basis of abnormal behavior. The general *disease model* or approach toward physical disorders was extended to account for mental disorders (abnormal behavior). The disease model refers to the general approach that particular symptoms (e.g., fever, infection, discomfort) can be explained on the basis of underlying internal conditions (e.g., bacteria, virus, lesions, disease, organ dysfunction). In physical diseases, the symptoms are not the real problem but rather result from the underlying malfunction or disease process. Treating the symptom alone (e.g., chest pain) is not the real cure because the underlying condition causing the problem (e.g., heart disease) has to be remedied.

The general orientation of the disease model was extended to psychological disorders in cases where no organic factors could be identified. The underlying disease processes were considered to be internal motives and intrapsychic processes of the person. Behavior was considered to reflect basic underlying motives that form personality. A person's behavior might be abnormal because of some underlying defect or disturbance in personality. To understand abnormal behavior, it became important to consider the underlying psychological processes. Yet, what are these intrapsychic processes and how do they operate?

Psychoanalytic Theory

Sigmund Freud (1856–1939) developed a theory of personality called *psychoanalysis* that filled the theoretical void about intrapsychic processes. He explained virtually all behaviors by referring to manifestations of unconscious personality processes. Understanding behavior required a careful scrutiny of personality to determine the meaning of behavior, that is, what motives behavior represents. The psychological processes and motives behind behavior were regarded as existing in the individual. The Freudian view frequently is referred to as a *psychodynamic* view. Dynamics refers to a branch of mechanics in which phenomena are explained by referring to energy forces and their relation to motion, growth, and change in physical matter. Freud's dynamic view of personality describes behavior in terms of psychological energies or motivating forces, drives, and impulses, and their interrelation. Growth and psychological development are traced to the psychological impulses and their expression at various stages early in the child's development. Diverse behaviors can be traced to the expression of a few psychological forces to which they owe their origin.

Freud posed three structures of personality: The *id*, which houses instincts and provides the source of psychic energy (*libido*) for all psychological processes and behavior; the *ego*, which interacts with the demands of reality in fulfilling instinctual wishes; and, the *superego*, which represents the internalization of social and parental standards and ideals of behavior. These structures operate in constant conflict. Each personality structure contributes in determining whether an impulse will be expressed, and precisely when and in what form it will be expressed. The expression of psychic energy can be traced to different sources of instinctual gratification as the child develops. Freud delineated stages of psychosexual development through which everyone passes. At each stage, the source of pleasure or instinctual gratification is associated with different areas and functions of the body. As the child develops, the expression of psychic energy invariably leads to conflicts with reality and within the structures of personality. Anxiety reactions, defense mechanisms, and alternate modes of behaving result from instincts not obtaining direct and immediate expression. Impulses, such as attraction toward the opposite-sexed parent, may not be resolved and result in a breakdown of normal personality development. Normal behavior develops from the expression of impulses, wishes, and desires in socially appropriate ways. Abnormal behavior, according to the psychoanalytic view, is attributed to maldevelopment of personality, and the disruption of the normal unfolding and expression of drives and needs, and their gratification. Psychological drives can become blocked or fail to find expression in socially appropriate ways. Drives and unresolved conflicts may, however, find expression in psychological symptoms or aberrant behaviors.

The development of psychoanalytic theory provided several important contributions to understanding behavior. First, the view advanced the notion that behavior is *determined* and that the causes of even the most mundane behaviors (e.g., slips of the tongue) could be explained. Second, psychoanalytic theory stimulated theory and research about the psychological basis of behavior. Third, the theory stimulated the development of psychological treatments, beginning with psychoanalytic treatment but leading indirectly to other techniques as well.

Many criticisms have been levied against Freud's view including the difficulty in verifying many of its propositions empirically, inconsistencies within the theory itself and the therapeutic procedures derived from the theory, the neglect of social and cultural influences on behavior, and the lack of empirical support in many areas (such as aspects of child development) in which research has been conducted (see Kazdin, 1978b; Salter, 1952; Stuart, 1970). Psychoanalytic theory has evolved considerably over the years (Hall & Lindzey, 1978); however, the major view of underlying psychic influences determining disordered behavior has been generally retained.

Trait Theory

The Freudian view is not the only intrapsychic position. *Trait theory* also posits underlying personality structures which account for behavior (Mischel, 1971). Traits refer to consistent and relatively enduring ways of behaving which distinguish one individual from another. Traits are inferred from behaviors which seem to persist over time and across various situations. Although different trait theorists disagree on the traits which best explain behavior, they all adhere to the notion that there are behavioral patterns which are consistent and these patterns are expressions or signs of underlying traits. A trait position is familiar to virtually everyone. In everyday life, people frequently allude to traits as aggressiveness, kindness, carelessness, dominance, submissiveness, honesty, laziness, and others to explain behavior.

When traits are employed as summary labels to characterize apparent patterns of behavior, they may be quite useful. For example, if a person is referred to as being very kind (having the trait of "kindness"), this may be useful in describing that this individual, in fact, behaves or has behaved in a particular fashion. However, frequently traits are used to *explain* behavior. Traits are inadequate as explanations of behavior for at least three reasons.

First, traits are inferred from behavior. A person who behaves in an aggressive fashion is considered to have the trait "aggressiveness." The trait which has been inferred from behavior is used to account for behavior. For instance, the reason a person behaves aggressively is attributed to his trait "aggressiveness." Yet, how does one know there is a trait of aggressiveness without inferring it from behavior? The account of traits and behavior is circular. To be meaningful, the existence of traits would have to be determined independently of the behaviors they are supposed to explain. One possible rebuttal to this objection is that traits are not inferred from a single behavior performed in one situation but from different behaviors performed in a variety of situations. The behavior of individuals with various traits or a great amount of a given trait is consistent across situations and over time. This view brings us to the second criticism of traits as an explanation of behavior.

As a second point, evidence suggests that individuals do not always perform consistently across a variety of situations and over time, as would be predicted from a trait position (Mischel, 1968). Also, different behaviors which are considered to make up a general trait often are not highly correlated. For example, an individual might be labeled as honest or as having the trait of honesty. Yet evidence reveals that various behaviors which might make up such a personality trait are not performed consistently. An individual who performs honestly in one situation may not perform honestly in another situation. Much of behavior is situation specific. As situations change, a person's responses change as well. For example, children display different patterns of aggressive behavior (Bandura & Walters, 1959) and social behavior (Redd, 1969) depending upon the person with whom they are interacting. The consistency in behavior required to support a trait theory of personality often is lacking. The consistency that an individual *perceives* in the behavior of someone often comes from conceptions of the perceiver rather than the person observed (e.g., Dornbusch, Hastorf, Richardson, Muzzy, & Vreeland, 1965).

A third criticism of a trait explanation of behavior is that the antecedent conditions that explain traits are not explained. If traits account for behavior, what accounts for traits? How do traits originate? Skinner (1953) has noted that a behavior is not explained by relating it to an underlying trait or mental state until the trait or state has been accounted for. He refers to underlying concepts which are used to explain behavior in this way as "explanatory fictions" or "mental way stations." Instead of giving a complete account of behavior, the trait explanation only goes partially back in the causal chain of behavior. Very often, attributing behavior to a trait *appears* to provide an explanation of behavior. Yet, because the traits themselves are not explained, no actual explanation is provided.

Despite the criticisms of the psychoanalytic and trait theories—two popular versions of the intrapsychic model, the model has persisted in some form as the guiding view in mental health and education. The model pervades virtually all aspects of clinical lore including psychological assessment, diagnosis, and treatment of "psychological" problems.

Assessment and Diagnosis

The intrapsychic model has strongly influenced psychological assessment and diagnosis of behavioral disorders. Because people are assumed to have underlying psychological motives or traits which account for their behavior, emphasis is placed upon assessing underlying personality rather than observing behavior directly. Assessment, then, focuses upon underlying motives which are assumed to explain behavior. The overt behavior which may have caused the client to seek treatment or to be institutionalized is not of direct interest. For example, an individual may seek therapy to overcome anxiety which arises in social situations. The specific situations which appear to precipitate anxiety are not focused upon. Assessment is concerned with the client's psychodynamics or traits. Through psychodynamic assessment, the psychologist attempts to provide global descriptions of personality, to reconstruct the individual's psychological development, and to determine how the person reacted to important psychological impulses (e.g., sex and aggression) in his or her past, what defense mechanisms have developed, and what basic characteristic traits or psychic defects account for behavior. It is believed that once these psychological processes are revealed, the source of the behavioral problem will be evident.

Projective tests exemplify diagnostic tools of traditional personality assessment. These tests attempt to assess personality indirectly through behaviors such as reactions to inkblots, creative stories in response to ambiguous stimuli, free associations, or other unstructured tasks. Projective tests provide the client with an ambiguous situation on which he or she must impose meaning and structure. The responses are considered as signs which reveal personality structure, psychodynamics, and unconscious motivation. Conclusions are made by interpreting the meaning of the behavioral signs and inferring underlying processes. Interpretation of projective tests requires clinical judgment to extract meaning from the responses. There has been serious criticism of the reliability and validity of these interpretations in predicting behavior. Individuals who interpret the tests often disagree on the psychological processes or disorders to which test responses are attributed. On the basis of these and other reasons, the overall utility of projective tests has been questioned (Mischel, 1968, 1971; Peterson, 1968).

Many other types of assessment devices are available in addition to projective tests. A variety of measures can assess aspects of the client's personality, character traits, and psychological needs, deficits, or defects (e.g., tests of anxiety, extraversion, paranoid tendencies, impulsiveness, brain damage, and intelligence). Clients can complete various tasks, solve problems, or report on their own personality and behavior patterns to provide information to infer personality characteristics. Behaviors in "real life" situations usually are not observed directly. Because traditional assessment devices are assumed to assess general personality patterns, the results on assessment devices are considered to reflect performance in situations that are not observed directly.

A major task of diagnosis is to assign a label to an individual which implies the underlying condition or defect responsible for the behavioral problem. The labels include "schizophrenia," "neurosis," "mental retardation," "learning disability," "brain damage," "hyperactivity," "emotional disturbance," and numerous others which depict a motivational problem, or inherent deficit, defect, or disease. The major focus has been on identifying disorders and symptom patterns that go together. Once the disorders are clearly delineated, it is hoped that the etiology (cause) of the disorder will be more readily discovered. The rationale is that if the cause can be uncovered, knowledge of the treatment and prognosis of the disorder will follow.

The purposes of diagnosis are to describe the presenting problem, identify conditions related to its occurrence, suggest a therapeutic plan to alter the problem, and predict the outcome of treatment (Stuart, 1970). These purposes have been fulfilled with many disorders in medicine. However, there are several problems in extrapolating the traditional diagnostic approach to behavior problems (see Frank, 1975; Hersen, 1976; Kazdin, 1978b). Often there is little agreement between professionals who independently assign patients to diagnostic categories. Also, there are great differences in the behavior of persons ascribed the same diagnosis as well as similar behaviors among persons assigned diverse diagnoses. Diagnosis of a person seems to provide little information beyond the "symptomatology" which was already known when the diagnosis was made. Specifically, little information is given about the etiology, treatment of choice, and prognosis, which should be major advantages of using diagnosis and classification.

Treatment

One would expect that once assessment and diagnosis are completed, the information gained would be useful in treating the client. However, this is not the case. Traditional assessment is used minimally or is neglected entirely by practicing clinicians conducting therapy (e.g., Meehl, 1960; Rogers, 1951). Unfortunately, assessment of underlying personality provides little information that can be used for treatment or educational purposes (Arthur, 1969; Blanco, 1970; Goldfried & Kent, 1972; Peterson, 1968).

The treatments developed from the intrapsychic model of abnormal behavior have been a major source of dissatisfaction. For many years, the effectiveness of traditional forms of psychotherapy has been heavily debated. The effectiveness of psychological treatments with psychotics, neurotics, sociopaths, retardates, delinquents, emotionally disturbed children, and other populations has been seriously challenged (Dunn, 1971; Eysenck, 1966; Fairweather & Simon, 1963; Levitt, 1971; Rachman, 1971).

Although reviews suggest that psychotherapy can lead to positive changes in behavior (e.g., Bergin & Lambert, 1978; Meltzoff & Kornreich, 1970; Smith & Glass, 1977), the magnitude of treatment effects are not that large, and the clinical importance of the changes is difficult to evaluate. Also, treatments often are not specific to the problems that clients bring to therapy. Individual or group psychotherapy often is regarded as a general treatment strategy in outpatient and inpatient settings independently of the specific problems brought to treatment (London, 1964; Stuart, 1970).

Other sources of dissatisfaction have been associated with traditional forms of psychological treatment based upon an intrapsychic model. For example, psychotherapy with different types of patients and institutional care for such populations as psychiatric patients or the mentally retarded sometimes are associated with decrements in adaptive behavior (Bergin, 1971; Kaufman, 1967; Scheff, 1966). Institutional treatment in particular often fosters bizarre behaviors, dependency, apathy, and other characteristics that may compete with successful posthospital adjustment (Freeman & Simmons, 1963; Miller, 1967).

From the standpoint of the development of behavior modification, a major source of dissatisfaction with traditional treatment derives from assumptions about intrapsychic causes of behavior. Traditionally, problematic behaviors have been assumed to result from underlying psychological conflicts and processes. The problematic behaviors supposedly cannot be treated in their own right because they were viewed as symptoms of the "real" problem. Even if the problematic behavior were changed without treating the underlying disorder, the client might develop another problem as a substitute for the original symptoms. This notion is referred to as symptom substitution. Symptom substitution often was invoked as an argument against treating the specific problem behavior. If an impulse, drive or psychological conflict caused the symptom, it is important to get at the root of the problem. If the underlying cause is not resolved, it may be expressed in another form. Hence, according to the traditional intrapsychic approach, cures would be more readily achieved by treating the intrapsychic problem.

There has been a great deal of dispute about whether symptom substitution occurs, whether it can be assessed empirically, whether substitute symptoms can be predicted in advance, and whether their occurrence necessarily supports the intrapsychic model (Cahoon, 1968; Kazdin, 1978b; Stuart, 1970; Ullmann & Krasner, 1975). At present little evidence is available demonstrating deleterious effects follow from the treatment of specific behaviors. In fact, as discussed later, considerable evidence exists showing that beneficial side effects follow from behavioral treatment.

Role of the Professional

Since traditional approaches focus on the underlying personality problem or character disorder (e.g., neuroses and psychoses), defect (e.g., retardation), or emotional disturbance (e.g., hyperactivity), it is no surprise that professional training in assessment, diagnosis, and treatment is extensive. The complexity of the psychological problem or deficit warrants treatment from highly trained professionals. Yet, there are many undesirable consequences of this approach. First, professionals provide treatment or rehabilitation in situations which often remove the client from the environment in which the problem behaviors were performed. For example, often psychiatric patients, retardates, and emotionally disturbed children are withdrawn from the community in which their behavior has been deficient to a noncommunity situation where a special treatment or training service is provided. Analogously, children who show severe problem behaviors in the home or classroom are treated by counselors, social workers, and therapists in an office away from the situation in which the problem behaviors are performed. The resemblance of this approach to medical treatment is obvious. In medicine, patients frequently are taken out of their everyday life and placed in a special setting for treatment by someone who is trained to administer special procedures. Only when the patient is cured can he or she return to community life. In any case, psychological treatment, as dictated by the intrapsychic model, usually takes place in a situation (e.g., office or institution) different from that in which the problem was evident (e.g., the home). This is undesirable because behavior in the special situation is not likely to resemble the problematic behavior in the original situation. Moreover, the environmental conditions which contribute to the problem behavior may be present only in the original situation.

A second undesirable consequence is that there are too few professionals for the number of clients who need treatment and therapy, special training and education, and rehabilitation (e.g., Sobey, 1970). The shortage of professionals necessitates that numerous individuals with behavioral problems or psychological impairment go untreated and that others are treated en masse. Reliance upon professionals alone cannot resolve the "mental health crisis." A large reservoir of potential personnel which could be employed for treatment and rehabilitation purposes, namely, nonprofessionals (parents, teachers, peers, spouses, and friends) has not been utilized. Nonprofessionals can be used directly to provide treatment and to serve training functions. However, according to traditional views of therapy and training, there is little that nonprofessionals can do in the way of treatment because they cannot be easily trained to alter the underlying problems or basic defects in the individuals with whom they interact.

The main role of nonprofessionals has been to identify behavior problems and refer the clients to professionals rather than to do something directly to alter the problem. When recommendations are made to nonprofessionals, often they are nonspecific and provide little insight on how to alter problem behavior. For example, teachers of emotionally disturbed children are instructed to accept the child and convey understanding or to satisfy the child's demands so that a relationship can be established (cf. Hewett, 1968). These recommendations, however, do not lead directly to actions resolving the problems for which the child was identified and labeled "emotionally disturbed." By not actively employing nonprofessionals as therapeutic agents, a large resource is neglected.

A few investigators have responded to the problem by determining whether nonprofessionals can conduct tasks traditionally considered to require extensive training. In fact, persons who are not professional therapists or counselors, such as college students, homemakers, and aides, in rehabilitation settings have been as effective or in some cases more effective than professionals in administering treatment to adults and children (Guerney, 1969; Rioch, Elkes, Flint, Usdansky, Newman & Silber, 1963; Truax, 1967). Despite the favorable results with nonprofessional therapists, this resource has not made a substantial impact on traditional psychological treatment. The bulk of treatment still is administered in settings by professionally trained therapists. It is usually assumed that little impact can be achieved by persons who are not thoroughly trained to deal with psychological problems.

General Comments

Conceptualization of abnormal and deviant behavior from the standpoint of the intrapsychic disease model continues to dominate today. Indeed, it is difficult even to talk about abnormal behavior and its amelioration without quickly showing the pervasive medical orientation. For example, people whose behaviors are abnormal often are referred to as *patients*, and may receive *treatment* for their mental *illness*, in a psychiatric *hospital*, until they are *cured*. Each of these terms reflects the strong ties that abnormal behavior has had to a medical orientation.

The intrapsychic disease model of abnormal behavior has had tremendous beneficial impact on the conceptualization of abnormal behavior that should not be overlooked. First, prior to the model, deviant behavior often was treated harshly using such procedures as torture, flogging, and starvation. These "treatments" fit existing conceptions of deviance based upon wickedness, sin, and possession by evil spirits. Recasting deviant behavior as mental illness or disease has led to more humane treatment.

A related advantage is that a disease approach encouraged the study of abnormal behavior and its causes. Great advances have been made by assuming that behavior has identifiable causal factors within the individual or environment and that these can be known through research.

Although the disease model has had tremendous impact, over the years many sources of dissatisfaction began to develop. Specific aspects of major theories such as orthodox psychoanalysis, the difficulties in research to support assumptions and basic propositions of the theories, and dissatisfaction with psychiatric diagnosis, clinical assessment, and therapy techniques all provided the climate for new advances. The behavioral approach represented a convergence of influences that provided a new approach to conceptualize, diagnose, assess, and alter behavior.

■ BEHAVIORAL APPROACH

The behavioral approach departs from the traditional conception of behavior by rejecting inferred motives, hypothesized needs, impulses, and drives which supposedly explain behavior. Rather, emphasis is placed upon environmental, situational, and social determinants that influence behavior. The behavioral approach considers the majority of behaviors to be learned or alterable through learning procedures. The focus is placed upon behaviors that have been learned or need to be learned. Explicit attempts are made to train behaviors rather than to alter aspects in the person which, according to the disease model, underlie behavior.

Abnormal behavior is not regarded as distinct from normal behavior in terms of how it develops or is maintained. Abnormal behavior does not represent a dysfunction or disease process which has overtaken normal personality development. Rather, certain learning experiences or a failure to receive or profit from various learning experiences can account for behavior. Principles of learning explain how behavior develops, whether or not the behavior is labeled as abnormal.

Labeling behavior as abnormal often is based upon subjective judgments rather than objective criteria (Szasz, 1960; Ullmann & Krasner, 1975). A given behavior may be viewed by different people as abnormal or normal. For example, fighting among male children may be regarded as an expression of masculinity by peers and parents but regarded as a sign of emotional disturbance by teachers and school counselors. The individual who evaluates behavior plays a major role in deciding whether it is normal or deviant.

The social context is also important in determining whether a given behavior is regarded as deviant. For example, staring out into space with a fixed gaze is acceptable when one is traveling on a bus and looking out a window. Yet, staring into space while standing on a street corner may be taken as a sign of abnormal behavior. Behaviors which seem similar are differentially interpreted depending upon the social context. Abnormal behavior is inferred from the degree to which behavior deviates from social norms (Scheff, 1966). Since social norms vary across cultures and across groups within a given culture, it is difficult to objectively define criteria for abnormal behavior. For example, aggressive behaviors labeled as antisocial reflect patterns of behavior which are socially condoned and strongly supported in many peer groups where street fighting and crime are commonly accepted activities. Labeling the behavior as antisocial and indicative of psychological disturbance is based on value judgments rather than evidence of "diseased" psychological processes. The differences in behavior among individuals reflect differences on a continuum rather than differences in illness and health.

Often there is an objective basis for making a diagnosis as in cases of brain damage, organic psychosis, certain forms of mental retardation, and other disorders with evidence of physical aberrations. In such cases, there may be a clear basis for qualitatively distinguishing normality from abnormality with regard to a particular characteristic. Yet, even for persons with organic impairment, the problem from the standpoint of treatment and rehabilitation is in the behavior that is deviant rather than the impairment. Although the long-term goal is to prevent such impairment in future generations, the immediate need is to provide interventions to overcome deficits and inappropriate behaviors and to develop adaptive and prosocial behaviors to enhance a client's functioning in everyday situations. Behavior modification attempts to provide special learning experiences to develop appropriate and adaptive behavior.

Types of Learning

Three types of learning are considered important in developing and altering behavior: classical or respondent conditioning, operant conditioning, and observational learning.

Classical Conditioning. Classical conditioning, investigated by Pavlov (1849–1936), is concerned with stimuli which automatically evoke responses. Certain stimuli in one's environment such as noise, shock, light, and the taste of food *elicit* reflex responses. These stimuli are referred to as unconditioned stimuli. The reflex responses elicited by these stimuli are referred to as *respondents* or unconditioned responses. Respondents frequently are considered involuntary or automatic responses which are not under control of the individual. Examples of respondents include salivation in response to the presence of food in one's mouth, pupil constriction in response to bright light, flexion of a muscle in response to pain, or a startle reaction in response to loud noise. The connection between the unconditioned stimulus and the response is automatic, i.e., not learned. However, reflex behavior sometimes occurs in response to a stimulus which does not automatically elicit the response. Through classical conditioning, a stimulus which is neutral, that is, does not automatically elicit a particular reflex, is made to elicit a reflex response. To achieve this, the neutral stimulus (referred to as a conditioned stimulus) is paired with an unconditioned stimulus. Pairing a conditioned stimulus with an unconditioned stimulus eventually results in the conditioned stimulus alone eliciting the response (referred to as a conditioned response). The process whereby new stimuli gain the power to elicit respondent behavior is classical or respondent conditioning. In respondent conditioning, events or stimuli which *precede* behavior control the response.

A historical example that attempted to show the importance of respondent conditioning was provided by Watson and Rayner (1920) who conditioned a fear reaction in an 11-month-old boy named Albert. Albert freely played with a white rat without any adverse reaction. Prior to the study, the investigators noted that a loud noise (unconditioned stimulus) produced a startle and fear reaction (unconditioned response) in Albert. In contrast, a white rat given to Albert to play with did not elicit any adverse reaction. The investigators wished to determine whether the startle reaction could be conditioned to the presence of the white rat. To condition the startle reaction, the presence of the white rat (neutral or conditioned stimulus) was immediately followed by the noise. Whenever Albert reached out and touched the rat, the noise sounded, and Albert was startled. Over a period of one week, the presence of the rat and the noise were paired only seven times. Finally the rat was presented without the noise, and Albert fell over and cried. The conditioned stimulus elicited the fear response (conditioned response). Moreover, the fear generalized so that other objects he was not afraid of previously (e.g., a rabbit, dog, Santa Claus mask, seal-skin coat, and cotton wool) also resulted in the fear reaction. This demonstrated that fears can be acquired through respondent conditioning. Of course, whether fears evident in everyday experience in fact are acquired through respondent conditioning is difficult to say, since one rarely has access to an individual at the time fears develop. Other evidence suggests that fears may be acquired for objects with which the individual has had no direct personal contact (Bandura, 1971; Rachman, 1972). Independently of how fears are actually learned, respondent conditioning may be useful in ameliorating fears because the power of conditioned stimuli to elicit fear reactions can be altered.

Some behavior therapy techniques are derived from a respondent conditioning framework. A widely used treatment of enuresis (bed wetting) is based upon classical conditioning. Enuresis can be conceptualized as a failure of certain stimuli (bladder cues) to elicit a response (waking) so the individual can get up and urinate appropriately. To condition waking to the bladder cues (distension), a stimulus which elicits waking is required. O. H. Mowrer and W. A. Mowrer (1938) devised an apparatus to classically condition waking to the cues which precede urination while the child is asleep. The apparatus includes a liquid-sensitive pad which is placed in the child's bed. As soon as the child urinates, a circuit is closed and an alarm is activated. The alarm serves as an unconditioned stimulus for waking. Bladder distension which precedes the unconditioned stimulus eventually elicits waking prior to urination and sounding of the alarm. The procedure results in control of urination and permits the individual to sleep through the night without urinating. Although the procedure was originally derived from classical conditioning, its precise interpretation is a matter of dispute (Lovibond, 1964).

Another procedure derived from a classical conditioning framework is called *systematic desensitization* (Wolpe, 1958) and is used primarily for the treatment of anxiety reactions. Certain cues or stimuli in the environment elicit anxiety or fear reactions. The fear can be altered by conditioning an alternative response to those cues which is incompatible with fear responses. The procedure employs a nonanxiety response, usually deep muscle relaxation, which is considered to be incompatible with fear. The fear-eliciting cues, placed in an ascending order on the basis of their arousal value, are paired with the relaxation response. The client relaxes and imagines a scene which includes mildly anxiety-provoking cues. While being relaxed, the mild anxiety which might arise is inhibited by the deep relaxation. Gradually, as relaxation is paired with the mild anxiety cues, scenes with greater anxiety-eliciting cues can be imagined with little or no arousal. Relaxation becomes associated with each scene in the hierarchy of items which is imagined. Finally, the capacity of the stimuli to elicit anxiety is eliminated. Altering the valence of stimuli closely adheres to the respondent paradigm. Other behavior therapy techniques derived from respondent conditioning have been used to alter a variety of behaviors, including excessive eating, drinking, cigarette smoking, and deviant sexual behavior (Kazdin & Wilson, 1978b; Leitenberg, 1976; Rimm & Masters, 1979).

Operant Conditioning. A major portion of human behavior is not involuntary nor *elicited* by stimuli in the sense of reflexive reactions. Rather, many behaviors are *emitted* spontaneously and are controlled primarily by their consequences. Behaviors amenable to control by altering consequences which follow them are referred to as *operants* because they are responses which operate (have some influence) on the environment, and generate consequences (Skinner, 1953). Operants are strengthened (increased) or weakened (decreased) as a function of the events which follow them. Most behaviors which are performed in everyday life are operants. They are not reflex responses controlled by eliciting stimuli. Examples of operant behaviors include reading, walking, working, talking, nodding one's head, smiling, or any response freely emitted. Operants are distinguished by virtue of being controlled by their consequences. The types of consequences which control behavior will be elaborated in the next chapter.

Most of the behaviors altered in applied settings are operants. Clients engage or fail to engage in responses which could be controlled by altering consequences. Speech in mute individuals, academic, self-care, or social skills in retardates, aberrant behavior in psychotics, aggressive acts in delinquents, and similar responses are operants which can be modified by altering the consequences which follow behavior. It is for this reason, in part, that the book will be devoted to operant conditioning techniques.

It should be pointed out that the distinction between respondent and operant conditioning is blurred, and a sharp delineation is often difficult to make. Indeed, historically, differences between classical and operant conditioning methods were often confused (Hilgard & Marquis, 1940; Kazdin, 1978b). A number of reasons exist for the confusion. First, the responses that are operant and respondent are not always clearly different. For example, for many years operants were considered to be voluntary responses while respondents were considered to be involuntary. Yet, evidence has shown that responses considered to be involuntary such as heart rate, blood pressure, and intestinal contractions can be altered by operant consequences which follow them (e.g., Kimmel, 1974). Hence, the distinction between respondent and operant conditioning on the basis of responses is not entirely clear.

Even in practical situations the distinction between the types of responses is difficult to make. A response may be elicited (respondent conditioning), yet be controlled by consequences which follow it (operant conditioning). For example, crying may be elicited in a child in response to an aversive event (a look of anger from a parent which may have been associated previously with physical punishment). Once the crying begins, it may be maintained by its consequences (e.g., sympathy or cuddling). This may exemplify how crying episodes can develop into frequent tantrums. Independently of how the tantrums begin, they can be maintained or eliminated by altering their consequences.

A second reason for the ambiguity in distinguishing respondent and operant conditioning is that operant behaviors can be controlled by antecedent stimuli. Operant behaviors are performed in certain situations with various cues present. When the consequences which follow behavior consistently occur in the presence of a particular set of cues (a certain person or place), the cues alone increase the probability that the behavior is emitted. The stimuli which have preceded the response set the *occasion* for the response to be performed. For example, the sound of music may serve as a stimulus for singing or dancing. This is not an example of respondent conditioning because the antecedent stimulus (music) does not force the response (singing) to occur. In operant conditioning, the stimulus does not produce a response; it only occasions the response or increases the probability that the response will be performed.

Other reasons can be cited to show the basis of the difficulty in distinguishing respondent and operant conditioning. For example, to increase the frequency of operant behaviors, it has been thought that positively rewarding consequences usually need to follow behavior. However, in experimental laboratory research operant behaviors have been developed even without using special consequences to follow the behavior (Schwartz & Gamzu, 1977).

Even though these and other reasons point to the difficulties in distinguishing respondent and operant conditioning, it is important to keep the major difference in mind. In respondent conditioning, the primary result is a change in the power of a stimulus to elicit a reflex response. In operant conditioning, the primary result is a change in the frequency of the response emitted or a change in some other aspect of the response such as intensity, speed, or magnitude.

Observational Learning. Observational or vicarious learning, or modeling includes both types of responses discussed above (respondents and operants). Observational learning occurs when an individual observes a model's behavior but performs no overt responses nor receives direct consequences himself. The behavior is learned by the observer from merely watching a model. By observing a model, a response may be learned without actually being performed. Modeling can train new responses as well as alter the frequency of previously learned responses.

To clarify modeling effects, it is important to distinguish *learning* from *performance*. The only requirement for learning via modeling is the observation of a model. The modeled response is assumed to be acquired by the observer through a cognitive or covert coding of the events observed (Bandura, 1977). However, whether a learned response is performed may depend upon response consequences or incentives associated with that response. The importance of response consequences in dictating performance has been demonstrated by Bandura (1965). Children observed a film where an adult modeled aggressive responses (hitting and kicking a large doll). For some children, the model's aggression was rewarded, for others, aggression was punished, and for others, no consequences followed the model's behavior. When children had the opportunity to perform the aggressive responses, those who had observed the model punished displayed less aggression than those who observed aggression rewarded or ignored. To determine whether all children had *learned* the responses, an attractive incentive was given to children for performing aggressive responses. There were no differences in aggressive responses between the three groups. Apparently, all groups learned the aggressive responses, but consequences to the model and observer determined whether they would be performed.

The extent to which modeling stimuli influence performance also depends upon other factors such as the similarity of the model to the observer, the prestige, status, and expertise of the model, and the number of models observed. As a general rule, imitation of a model by an observer is greater when the model is similar, more prestigious, higher in status and expertise, and when several models perform the same behavior.

A frequently cited example of modeling in the history of behavior modification was reported by Jones (1924) who treated a young boy named Peter who was afraid of a rabbit and several other furry objects (e.g., fur coat, feather, cotton wool). Peter was placed in a play situation where three other children and a rabbit were present. The other children, selected because they were unafraid of rabbits, interacted with the rabbit in a nonanxious fashion. Peter touched the rabbit immediately after observing others touch it. Other procedures were employed with Peter to overcome his fear, such as associating the rabbit with the presence of food, so it is unclear what the precise contribution of modeling was in reducing his fear.

Modeling has been used extensively in treatment in behavior modification to alter a variety of behaviors (see Kirkland & Thelen, 1977; Rosenthal & Bandura, 1978). In many therapeutic applications, problems such as fear or lack of social skills have been treated effectively both with children and adults. Applications have encompassed outpatient therapy, as well as treatment in institutional and educational settings. Even in applications which rely upon other procedures, including operant conditioning techniques, modeling often plays a major role in conveying to the client exactly what the desired responses are.

Social Learning: An Integration of Learning Concepts

Each type of learning has developed largely on its own with extensive laboratory research, often with infrahuman subjects. Obviously, clinical problems that are evident in human behavior represent much more complex phenomena than those studied in animal research and based upon relatively simple interpretations. Also, animal research often does not reflect the complexity of processes that appear to be involved in human behavior such as language, thoughts, beliefs, and similar processes.

Several authors have provided theories of behavior that attempt to integrate aspects of different learning paradigms and take into account cognitive processes (thoughts, beliefs, perceptions) (e.g., Bandura, 1977; Rotter, 1954; Staats, 1975). For example, Bandura (1977) has developed a social learning theory that encompasses each type of learning and a wide range of influences that each type of learning entails. Thus, elements of classical, operant, and vicarious learning are utilized to explain behavior. Events in the environment and to a much greater extent cognitions (thoughts, beliefs, perceptions) about environmental events are integrated into a general framework that depends upon different learning experiences. A social learning approach emphasizes the multiple types of influences on behavior that occur in the context of social development and provides a framework from which behavior can be explained in general. The advantage of a social learning approach is that it can account for a broad range of behaviors to a greater extent than accounts based upon simplistic applications of one type of learning rather than another (Murray & Jacobson, 1978).

In behavioral treatment, knowledge of the different types of learning is important. Behavioral programs in applied settings such as the home, school, hospital, and institution have relied most heavily upon operant conditioning techniques to alter behavior. Nonetheless, knowledge of the other types of learning is essential for two reasons. First, respondent conditioning and modeling are valuable as behavior change techniques in their own right. Second, operant conditioning procedures as ordinarily practiced include aspects of other types of learning. For example, an operant program in a classroom setting may increase desirable student behavior (e.g., working on assignments) of one student by following it with a favorable consequence or event (e.g., praise from the teacher). Yet, modeling and respondent conditioning may be operative in the situation in addition to operant conditioning. Students other than the one who is praised may increase in desirable behavior because of modeling influences, i.e., observing peers (Kazdin, 1979c). Classical conditioning might also be involved in control of classroom behavior. For example, the teacher may shout (unconditioned stimulus) at a student which leads to a startle reaction (unconditioned response). The presence of the teacher within close proximity of the child (conditioned stimulus) may, through repeated association with shouting, eventually elicit anxiety and arousal (conditioned response). Of course, if proximity of the teacher to the child elicits anxiety, this might detract from the teacher's reinforcing properties. As is obvious by this point, the behavioral approach draws heavily on the psychology of learning to explain how behavior develops, is maintained, and is altered. The behavioral view, just as the traditional view of personality, has far-reaching implications for the assessment and treatment of behavior problems.

Assessment

The behavioral approach toward assessment of behaviors departs dramatically from traditional diagnostic assessment (Goldfried & Linehan, 1977). The major focus is on the behaviors that are to be altered rather than on the underlying personality considered to cause behavior. Although a problem may be described in vague or general terms (e.g., hyperactivity), the behavior modifier seeks to clarify these terms by observing the behavior that requires change and the events which precede and follow the behavior. For example, if an attendant claims an institutionalized retarded child has a "bad temper," the behavior modifier would want to measure the behaviors which prompted the attendant to make the statement, the frequency of these behaviors, and the antecedent and consequent events which are associated with any outbursts.

Two components of assessment are usually used by behavior modifiers: (1) assessment of behavior itself and (2) assessment of the events which precede and follow the behavior. In short, assessment focuses on the behavior of the client as well as environmental events. Assessment of the behavior to be changed (referred to as the target behavior) is essential to ascertain the extent of the "problem" or the extent of change that is required. Observed behaviors are of direct interest in their own right, rather than as reflections of underlying psychological problems. Assessment also is made of the factors which precede and follow behavior. These factors may be useful in altering the target behavior. Events which precede behavior may include the presence of a particular person, instructions, and other cues in the environments that affect the frequency with which a response is performed. Events which follow behavior include favorable events such as attention, praise, candy, prizes, or other "rewards" which may be useful in increasing behavior and undesirable events such as reprimands, isolation, and loss of privileges, which may be useful in reducing behavior. Assessment of such environmental events which go on outside of the person is unlike traditional assessment which attempts to measure processes inside the person.

Treatment

In applied settings where operant conditioning techniques are extensively implemented, emphasis is placed upon external events in the environment that can be used to alter behavior. Emphasis on external events does not necessarily mean that events within the individual do not influence behavior. Indeed, many behavioral techniques, discussed much later in the book, rely upon internal processes such as thoughts and self-statements to exert their influence. However, in most applied intervention programs, emphasis is placed on overt behaviors and on external situational determinants that can be altered to influence these behaviors.

Proponents of behavior modification are concerned with isolating events that maintain deviant behavior or develop adaptive behaviors where deficiencies exist. To this extent, the behavioral approach is concerned with events that determine or cause behavior. Yet, the determinants sought are not intrapsychic factors or underlying motives. Also, instead of considering early childhood events as responsible for present behavior, proponents of behavior modification tend to focus on current environmental events that affect and maintain performance. In a large percentage of cases in which behavioral programs are applied, the original cause of deviant behavior is not known. For example, the causal basis of major disorders such as hyperactivity, autism, many forms of retardation, and other conditions are not entirely known. Even though the causes of the conditions are not known, adaptive behaviors often can be learned to improve the client's functioning. Alternatively, there are many conditions in which the causes are known. Behaviors shown by a number of clients in treatment, rehabilitation, and educational settings often result from physical deficiencies, anatomical anomalies, or physical trauma, and the basis of the problem (e.g., brain damage) may be obvious. Whether the cause of deviant behavior is known or not, adaptive behaviors often can be trained to improve performance. The usual procedure to achieve change in behavior modification is direct manipulation of environmental events.

Proponents of behavior modification do not adhere to the notion of *symptom substitution* for which there is a paucity of clear support. Symptom substitution implies that overt behavior is a symptom of some other problem. Yet, maladaptive behavior can be viewed as the problem itself without recourse to underlying motives and intrapsychic processes. Thus, altering a problematic behavior would not be expected to result automatically in replacement by another problem behavior. In fact, once a particular problem behavior is altered for a client, other aspects of his or her life and behaviors might improve as well. The beneficial effects of treating one behavior may spread or generalize to other behaviors. For example, if the behavior of a "hyperactive" child is altered so that he or she can sit in class and pay attention to the lessons, it is likely that other behaviors (e.g., academic performance) may improve because the child can now learn his or her lessons. Also, socially desirable behavior on the part of a deviant student increases the probability that peers will develop greater interest in him or her and promote social interaction. Similarly, if a stutterer is trained to speak more fluently, additional positive changes might be expected to result. As the client can speak more fluently, he or she may become more confident, extraverted, and less shy in everyday situations.

Changing one problem behavior may begin to influence a variety of other behaviors in a person's life. In a large number of applications of behavioral techniques, treatment of one behavior has resulted in beneficial effects for behaviors or personality characteristics not included in treatment (Kazdin & Wilson, 1978b). In a few instances, reports have documented the appearance of new problem behaviors over the course of treatment. However, these instances appear to be exceptions, and even in these few instances, it is not easy to invoke symptom substitution as the most reasonable interpretation. It is possible that a person who has one behavior altered will still have additional problems or that other problems will assume increased importance.

An important aspect of behavior modification is that treatment usually is carried out in the settings in which the behavior requiring change is evident, such as the home and school. This is distinguished from traditional treatment where inpatient or outpatient services are provided similar to medical treatment. Numerous advantages accrue to treating problems in the situations in which they arise. First, since behavior is situation specific, isolating the individual from the situation in which a problem behavior arose may hide the behavior which needs to be changed. For example, if a hyperactive child is given individual counseling, it is unlikely that the behaviors which are a problem at home or at school will be evident in the counseling situation; it is the problem behaviors at home and at school which require alteration and not the behaviors in the counseling situation. Second, alteration of a response in a situation removed from the "real world" may not alter behavior in the situation in which behavior was originally a problem. Even if behavior is altered in the counseling setting, it is unlikely to carry over or generalize to other situations. A third advantage of altering behavior in the actual environment rather than isolating the individual from others is to avoid the deleterious effects of institutionalization, mentioned earlier. Moreover, there may be less stigma if the person is treated in the natural environment than if mental health professionals are sought for treatment (cf. Phillips, 1963).

Role of Professionals and Nonprofessional "Natural Agents" in Everyday Life

The behavioral approach requires the use of natural agents who normally are in contact with the clients in everyday life. Individuals who have the greatest contact with the client include teachers, relatives, spouse, peers, supervisors, and colleagues. Individuals who are in contact with the client play the major role in altering behavior because they have the greatest opportunity to regulate the consequences which control behavior. Moreover, individuals in contact with the client observe the behaviors in the actual situations in which they are performed so they are in the best position to focus on the behavior as it is actually occurring.

Utilizing individuals who are with the client is especially important since they often contribute to deviant behavior. Indeed, staff, teachers, and parents often contribute to or support those behaviors they wish to eliminate (Patterson & Reid, 1970; Wahler, 1976). To alter the behavior of the client requires that behavior of the agent responsible for the client is altered first. Thus, working with nonprofessionals is often the best way to guarantee change in the clients.

Professionals have a role in training and consulting with nonprofessionally trained individuals who carry out the procedures that are likely to alter client behavior. Ideally, training may include instruction in identifying problems, selecting treatment goals, and evaluating program effectiveness. Lectures, demonstration, feedback, practice, and incentives for actual performance are used to accomplish training of nonprofessionals (see Chapter 9). Nonprofessionals have included parents, teachers, attendants in institutions and day-care centers, peers, college students, spouses, and siblings. Operant conditioning techniques can be readily applied by nonprofessionals who learn to control antecedent and consequent events to alter client behavior.

■ MAJOR CHARACTERISTICS OF THE BEHAVIORAL APPROACH

Several characteristics distinguish behavior modification from traditional approaches (see Agras, Kazdin & Wilson, 1979; Rimm & Masters, 1979). These include a focus on observable behavior, careful assessment of the behavior that is to be altered, evaluation of the effect of the program in altering behavior, and concern for socially significant changes in behavior.

The direct focus on observable behavior is a salient characteristic of the behavioral approach. The behaviors that serve as "symptoms" for traditional intrapsychic approaches are the focus of the behavioral approach. Behavioral treatment should not be viewed as merely treating symptoms because this implies that there are underlying emotional concomitants that are responsible for the behavior. Evidence for underlying psychological causal agents is simply unavailable for most behaviors focused upon in applied settings. For example, the focus of treatment for persons diagnosed as psychotic is on observable maladaptive behaviors such as social interaction skills and expression of delusions or hallucinations that may interfere with living in the community (e.g., Paul & Lentz, 1977). For hyperactive children, obstreperous behaviors that led to applying that label will be focused upon directly (e.g., Ayllon & Rosenbaum, 1977). The hallmark of the behavioral approach is the focus on specific problem behaviors rather than global characteristics and psychological states.

It is important to note that behavioral techniques have been used with specific "behaviors" that are not publicly observable. For example, private events such as thoughts, ideas, and images that are not "observable" to anyone other than the person for whom they are occurring have been altered (Mahoney, 1974; Meichenbaum, 1977). Private events, however, have been considered to be *covert operants* (also called *coverants*) that respond to the laws of operant conditioning as do overt behavior (Homme, 1965). For example, Mahoney (1971) reported treating a young male adult with uncontrolled obsessional thoughts about being brain damaged, persecuted, and "odd." Punishment was used to suppress these covert responses. Whenever the individual obsessed, he snapped a heavy-gauge rubber band which was around his wrist. This self-punishment procedure effectively eliminated obsessions in a matter of a few weeks. Subsequently, positive self-thoughts were developed by having the person read a positive statement about himself whenever he smoked. Since smoking was a frequent response, this ensured that positive statements occurred frequently. Eventually, the statements were made spontaneously without being associated with smoking. The frequency of positive self-reference statements increased. Whether the focus is on covert or overt events, behavior modification focuses directly on the behaviors which are creating problems for the patient, client, or resident, rather than on constructs which have to be inferred from those responses.

A second characteristic of behavior modification, related to the emphasis on observable behavior, is *assessment* of the behavior that is to be altered, i.e., the target behavior. Rather than attempting to assess the client's responses to psychological tests or to reveal underlying personality organization, assessment is made of the behavior itself. The number of times a response occurs or the duration of a response may be assessed. For example, learning "problems" may be assessed by measuring the responses performed on academic tasks. Apathy of psychotic patients may be defined by the number of activities that are performed on the ward. Social interaction can be assessed by counting the number of social contacts made with peers. Similarly, anxiety or fear responses may be assessed by confronting the individual with an anxiety-provoking situation and objectively recording how close the individual can approach the stimulus.

A third characteristic of behavior modification is a careful *evaluation* of the effect of the program which is designed to change behavior. Emphasis is placed on demonstrating the effect of the program empirically. Traditional therapy, as practiced in most clinical settings, is rarely evaluated. When therapy is evaluated, the effect is assessed at the *end* of treatment to determine whether there is any change in personality. With behavior modification procedures, particularly in applied settings, the effect of the program on behavior usually is assessed *while* the program is going on as well as after the program is terminated. Data are gathered constantly to ensure the program is having its intended effect. If the program is not working, it can be altered rapidly in response to the client's behavior. Assessment and treatment are interwoven. There is constant feedback to the professionals and nonprofessionals working in the program.

A fourth characteristic, related to the above, is a concern for producing behavior change that is *socially significant*. The behavior focused upon in treatment should be clinically or socially important to begin with. The focus on problem behaviors or deficits illustrates the importance of the treatment focus. In numerous examples, marked changes have been achieved in self-destructive behavior in autistic and retarded children, social behaviors have been increased in severely withdrawn psychiatric patients, academic performance and achievement have been increased in "normal" and retarded children, among many other problems (Kazdin, 1977e; Leitenberg, 1976; Rimm & Masters, 1979). The behaviors focused upon are socially important because they often represent the characteristic problems that have led to clients being labeled as abnormal.

The social significance of behavior change is not only reflected in the specific behaviors that are treated but in the magnitude of change that is sought. The behavior change resulting from the program should make a difference that is noticeable to persons in the client's environment. The change should move the client appreciably closer toward the level of performance necessary for functioning in society (Kazdin, 1977b; Risley, 1970; Wolf, 1978). This is not to say that normality or conformity is a goal toward which all should strive. However, the populations for which behavioral techniques are often used engage in behaviors that make them deviant when evaluated by social standards held by the public. A socially significant change may be evident when the procedures markedly alter the target behavior so it is aligned with normative standards.

For example, in a school setting, a "hyperactive" child may run around the room 90 percent of the time during class whereas most students engage in this behavior less than 10 percent of the time. If a behavior modification program reduced the student's inappropriate behavior to 60 percent, the program would not be very successful in making a socially significant change in the student's behavior. A much larger reduction of running around the room would be required to make the child indistinguishable from his or her peers and to lead the teacher to regard the child as no longer "hyperactive." Because the behavioral approach often seeks large changes in behavior, special assessment procedures often are used to evaluate how the client performs before and after treatment relative to peers whose behaviors are not regarded as problematic and how people in contact with the client evaluate performance (see Chapter 5).

Remaining chapters will illustrate the characteristics of behavior modification. As noted earlier, the primary emphasis will be placed upon the principles of operant conditioning and a variety of behavior modification techniques that have been derived from them. Among behavior modification procedures, those derived from operant conditioning have been the most widely used in applied settings. Part of the reason for the extensive application of operant techniques is due to the focus of treatment in various settings in which problems arise and the relatively less training that may be required for the use of these techniques by nonprofessionals, relative to other behavioral techniques.

■ NOTE

[1] The traditional and behavioral approaches and many different theories and practices within each approach can only be highlighted here. Interested readers may wish to consult additional sources for more detail (Kazdin, 1978b; Rimm & Masters, 1979; Ullmann & Krasner, 1975).

2

Principles of
Operant
Conditioning

In the previous chapter, three kinds of learning—classical conditioning, operant conditioning, and observational learning—were discussed. Although all three types of learning are evident in behavior modification, programs in applied settings such as the classroom, hospitals, institutions, the home, and even in society at large have relied primarily upon the principles of operant conditioning. The present chapter briefly explains the basic principles. Later chapters will elaborate the major principles and the various procedures that have been developed from them.

The principles of operant conditioning describe the relationship between behavior and environmental events (antecedents and consequences) that influence behavior.[1] Developing effective programs depends upon understanding the types of antecedent events and consequences that influence behavior. In most programs, emphasis is placed on the *consequences* which follow behavior. One of the most basic requirements of using consequences effectively pertains to how they are applied to behavior. For a consequence to alter a particular behavior, it must be dependent or contingent upon the occurrence of that behavior. Stated another way, behavior change occurs when certain consequences are *contingent* upon performance. A consequence is contingent when it is delivered only after the target behavior is performed and is otherwise not available. When a consequence is not contingent upon behavior, this means it is delivered independently of what the person is doing. The noncontingent delivery of consequences ordinarily does not

27

result in systematic changes in a preselected target behavior because the consequences do not consistently follow that behavior.

For example, if a psychiatric patient receives attention (the consequence) from an attendant on the ward each time he or she speaks, attention is considered to be contingent upon speech. On the other hand, the patient may receive attention every so often from an attendant independently of what he or she is doing. Attention would be delivered noncontingently. To increase speaking systematically, attention should be delivered contingent upon instances of speaking. In everyday life, many consequences are contingent upon our behavior. Wages are contingent upon working, grades are contingent upon studying for exams, and health is contingent, to some extent, upon the care with which we treat ourselves. *A contingency refers to the relationship between a behavior and the events that follow the behavior.* The notion of contingency is important because behavioral techniques alter behavior by modifying the contingencies that influence behavior. The principles outlined below refer to different kinds of contingent relationships between behavior and the events which follow behavior. The major principles are reinforcement, punishment, and extinction.

■ REINFORCEMENT

The *principle of reinforcement* refers to an increase in the frequency of a response when it is immediately followed by certain consequences. The consequence which follows behavior must be contingent upon behavior. A contingent event which increases the frequency of behavior is referred to as a *reinforcer*. Positive and negative reinforcers constitute the two kinds of events which can be used to increase the frequency of a response (Skinner, 1953). *Positive reinforcers* are events which are presented after a response is performed and increase the frequency of the behavior they follow. *Negative reinforcers* (which will also be referred to as aversive events or aversive stimuli) are events which are *removed* after a response is performed and increase the behavior that preceded their removal.

Positive Reinforcement. *Positive reinforcement refers to an increase in the frequency of a response which is followed by a favorable event (positive reinforcer).* The positive or favorable events in everyday language frequently are referred to as rewards. However, it is desirable to distinguish the term "positive reinforcer" from "reward." A positive reinforcer is defined by its effect on behavior. If an event follows behavior and the frequency of behavior increases, the event is a positive reinforcer. Conversely, any event which does not increase the behavior it follows is not a positive reinforcer. An increase in the frequency or probability of the preceding behavior is the defining characteristic of a positive reinforcer. In contrast, rewards are defined merely as something given or received in return for doing something. Rewards are usually highly valued but they do not necessarily increase the probability of the behavior they follow. The distinction between rewards and reinforcers may seem subtle, but when trying to develop an effective treatment program, the distinction is exceedingly important.

Many rewards or events that are evaluated favorably when a person is queried may serve as reinforcers. However, the reinforcing value of an event cannot be known on the basis of verbal statements alone. An individual may be unaware of or not consider as rewards many events that are reinforcers. For example, occasionally verbal reprimands (e.g., "Stop that!") or physically restraining someone have served as positive reinforcers (e.g., Flavell, McGimsey, & Jones, 1978; Madsen, Becker, Thomas, Koser, & Plager, 1970). Even though reprimanding and physically restraining someone occasionally have served as positive reinforcers, it is unlikely that anyone would ever refer to them as rewards. Hence, a reward is not synonymous with a positive reinforcer. Whether an event is a positive reinforcer has to be determined empirically. Does the frequency of a particular behavior increase when the event immediately follows behavior? Only if the behavior does increase is the event a positive reinforcer.

Examples of positive reinforcement in everyday life would seem to be abundant. However, rarely does anyone actually measure whether a favorable event which followed behavior increases the frequency of that behavior. Nevertheless, it is useful to provide some examples of situations which probably depict positive reinforcement. A student who studies for an examination and receives an "A" probably is reinforced. Studying is likely to increase in the future because it was reinforced by an excellent grade. Alternatively, if an infant cries before going to sleep and is picked up by his parents, the frequency of crying before sleeping may increase. Picking up a child provides attention and physical contact which are likely to be positive reinforcers. (Of course, the risk involved in increasing crying in the future must be weighed against the possibility of the child crying because of pain or discomfort.) Winning money at a slot machine usually increases the frequency of putting money into the machine and pulling the lever. Money is a powerful reinforcer which increases performance of a variety of behaviors.

Positive reinforcers include any events which, when presented, increase the frequency of the behavior they follow. There are two categories of positive reinforcers, namely, *primary*, or unconditioned, and *secondary*, or conditioned, reinforcers. Events which serve as primary reinforcers do not depend upon special training to have acquired their reinforcing value. For example, food to a hungry person and water to a thirsty person serve as primary reinforcers. Primary reinforcers may not be reinforcing all of the time. Food will not reinforce someone who has just finished a large meal. However, when food does serve as a reinforcer, its value is automatic (unlearned) and does not depend upon a previous association with any other reinforcers.

Many of the events which control behavior are not primary reinforcers. Conditioned reinforcers which include events such as praise, grades, money, and completion of a goal, have acquired reinforcing value through learning. Conditioned reinforcers are not automatically reinforcing. Stimuli or events which once were neutral in value may acquire reinforcing properties as a result of being paired with events that are already reinforcing (either primary or other conditioned reinforcers). By repeatedly presenting a neutral stimulus prior to or along with a reinforcing stimulus, the neutral stimulus becomes a reinforcer. For example, praise may not be reinforcing for some individuals. It is a neutral stimulus rather than a positive reinforcer. To establish praise as a reinforcer, it must be paired with an event that is reinforcing, such as food or money. When a behavior is performed, the individual is praised and reinforced with food. After several pairings of the food with praise, the praise alone serves as a reinforcer and can be used to increase the frequency of other responses. When praise is a neutral stimulus, it can be developed as a conditioned reinforcer by pairing it with another event which is a reinforcer (Miller & Drennen, 1970).

Some conditioned reinforcers are paired with more than one other primary or conditioned reinforcer. When a conditioned reinforcer is paired with many other reinforcers, it is referred to as a generalized conditioned reinforcer. Generalized conditioned reinforcers are extremely effective in altering behaviors because they have been paired with a variety of events rather than just one. Money and trading stamps are good examples of generalized conditioned reinforcers. They are conditioned reinforcers because their reinforcing value is acquired through learning. They are generalized reinforcers because a variety of reinforcing events contribute to their value. Additional examples of generalized conditioned reinforcers include attention, approval, and affection from others (Skinner, 1953). These are generalized reinforcers because their occurrence often is associated with a variety of other events which are themselves reinforcing. For example, attention from someone may be followed by physical contact, praise, smiles, affection, or delivery of tangible rewards such as food and other events.

In behavior modification programs, generalized reinforcers in the form of tokens are used frequently (Kazdin, 1977e). The tokens may consist of poker chips, coins, tickets, stars, points, or checkmarks. Tokens serve as generalized reinforcers because they can be exchanged for a variety of other events which are reinforcing. For example, in a psychiatric hospital tokens may be delivered to patients for attending group activities, grooming and bathing, and other behaviors. The tokens may be exchanged for snacks, cigarettes, and privileges such as watching television and attending social events. The potency of tokens derives from the reinforcers which "back up" their value. The events which tokens can purchase are referred to as *back-up reinforcers.* Generalized conditioned reinforcers, such as money or tokens, usually are more powerful than any single reinforcer because they can purchase a variety of back-up reinforcers. (Generalized conditioned reinforcers will be discussed at length in Chapter 6.)

In identifying positive reinforcers, it is important to keep two considerations in mind. First, an event (e.g., praise, candy, or pat on the back) may be a positive reinforcer for one person but not for another. Although some events have wide generality in serving as reinforcers (e.g., food or money), others may not (e.g., sour candy). Second, an event may be a reinforcer for one person under some circumstances or at some time, but not under other circumstances or at other times. These considerations require careful evaluation of what is reinforcing for a given individual. Because of cultural norms and common experiences of many people, some suggestions may be given as to events which probably serve as reinforcers. However, at any given time there is no guarantee in advance that a particular event will be reinforcing.

Reinforcing events referred to above include *stimuli* or specific events such as praise, smiles, food, or money that are presented after a response. However, reinforcers are not limited to stimuli presented to a client. Allowing an individual to engage in certain *responses* can be used as a reinforcer. Premack (1965) noted that behavior an individual performs with a relatively high frequency when given the opportunity to select among various responses can reinforce behaviors performed with a relatively low frequency. If the opportunity to perform a more probable response is made contingent upon performance of a less probable response, the frequency of the latter should increase. Hence, behaviors of a relatively higher probability in a person's repertory of behaviors are reinforcers of lower probability behaviors.

On the basis of laboratory research, the *Premack principle* has been formulated to reflect the following relationship: *of any pair of responses or activities in which an individual engages, the more frequent one will reinforce the less frequent one.* Stated more simply, a higher probability behavior can reinforce a lower probability behavior. To determine what behaviors are high or low frequency requires observing behavior that a person performs when given the opportunity to engage in behavior without restraints (e.g., what someone does when given free time at home, at school, on the weekends). The behavior observed to occur more frequently can be used to follow and reinforce a lower frequency behavior (e.g., studying, engaging in chores). For example, for many children, playing with friends is performed at a higher frequency than is practicing a musical instrument. If the higher frequency behavior (playing with friends) is made contingent upon the lower frequency behavior (playing the instrument), the lower probability will increase.

The Premack principle, as noted earlier, developed out of laboratory research showing that access to high probability behaviors can reinforce low probability behaviors. However, the theoretical basis of and laboratory evidence for the Premack principle have been critically evaluated (Danaher, 1974; Knapp, 1976). Difficulties in measuring the probability of a behavior and in demonstrating that pairing behaviors varying in probability is essential have made interpretation of the Premack principle ambiguous. Nevertheless, for applied work, the principle has been useful in expanding the range of reinforcers that can be used in treatment. Behaviors or activities that individuals appear to engage in during opportunities for free time or self-reported preferences about what clients like to do have been used to reinforce behavior in many applications. Of course, frequently performed behaviors or highly preferred activities may not necessarily serve as reinforcers. But a number of demonstrations attest to the utility of various activities as reinforcers (see Chapter 6).

An example of the use of the Premack principle was reported by Mitchell and Stoffelmayr (1973) who increased the activity of schizophrenic patients who were inactive on the ward. The patients frequently sat or paced on the ward. To increase activity, the investigators wished to develop work at a task (stripping coil from wires). The two behaviors of interest were inactivity or sitting (higher probability behavior) and work (lower probability behavior). To increase work, sitting was made contingent upon doing some work. The investigators set a criterion for completing work before the clients earned the opportunity to sit down. Gradually, the amount of work required to earn the opportunity to sit was increased. The results showed a marked increase in work behavior when it was followed with the sitting.

Numerous behaviors that an individual performs, such as engaging in certain activities, hobbies, or privileges, going on trips, being with friends, and other relatively frequent responses, can serve as reinforcers for other behaviors. The requirement of the Premack principle is that the target response to be altered is of a lower probability than the behavior which will reinforce that response. Of course, in everyday life, high probability behaviors often precede rather than follow low probability behaviors. For example, students may study (low probability behavior for many students) after going out with their friends (high probability behavior). Spouses may complete yard work (low probability behavior) after watching a football game (high probability behavior). In such cases, the low probability behavior is not likely to increase in frequency unless the sequence of behaviors is reversed. Performing the high probability behavior before performing the low probability behavior amounts to the noncontingent delivery of reinforcers.

Negative Reinforcement. *Negative reinforcement refers to an increase in the frequency of a response by removing an aversive event immediately after the response is performed.* Removal of an aversive event or negative reinforcer is contingent upon a response. An event is a *negative reinforcer* only if its removal after a response increases performance of that response (Skinner, 1953). Events which appear to be annoying, undesirable, or unpleasant are not necessarily negatively reinforcing. The qualifications made in the discussion of positive reinforcers hold for negative reinforcers as well. An undesirable event may serve as an aversive event for one individual but not for another. Also, an event may be a negative reinforcer for an individual at one time but not at another time. A negative reinforcer, just as a positive reinforcer, is defined solely by the effect it has on behavior.

It is important to note that reinforcement (positive or negative) *always* refers to an increase in behavior. Negative reinforcement requires an ongoing aversive event which can be removed or terminated after a specific response is performed. Examples of negative reinforcement are evident in everyday experience, such as putting on a coat while standing outside on a cold day. Putting on a coat (the behavior) usually removes an aversive state, namely, being cold. The probability of wearing a coat in cold weather is increased. Taking medicine to relieve a headache may be negatively reinforced by the termination of pain. Similarly, when putting the key into the ignition of a new car, a loud noise (aversive event) may sound. The noise can be terminated by putting on a seatbelt. Termination of the noise reinforces the response used to escape the noise. Strictly, whether negative reinforcement occurs in the above examples depends upon whether the behavior that terminates the undesirable state increases.

Interesting combinations of positive and negative reinforcement occur in social interaction and may foster socially undesirable behavior (Patterson & Reid, 1970). In social interactions, the response of one individual sometimes is negatively reinforced because it terminates an aversive behavior initiated by another individual. Yet, the aversive behavior of the other individual is positively reinforced. For example, parents may pick up a child who is whining. Whining is an aversive event for the parents which is terminated after they respond. Picking up the child is negatively reinforced by a cessation of whining. However, the child may be positively reinforced for whining since he or she receives parental attention contingent upon this behavior. As another example of positive and negative reinforcement in social interaction, someone who is the victim of an aggressive act (e.g., physical assault) may respond in a particular way (e.g., comply with the wishes of the aggressor) to terminate an aversive situation. Unfortunately, the act of compliance positively reinforces the aggressor. The probability of future aggression by the aggressor is increased. It should be evident from these examples that the principles of operant conditioning can explain how behavioral problems develop and are maintained as well as how they can be altered.

A frequently cited example of negative reinforcement was reported by Lovaas, Schaeffer, and Simmons (1965). These investigators developed social behaviors in a pair of autistic twins. A painful aversive stimulus (shock) was used because the children showed no improvement with conventional treatment methods. Moreover, the children were unresponsive to adults. Adults could not interact, express affection, or make requests effectively because the children either did not respond or actually resisted. A major goal with autistic children is to develop responsiveness to adults. Once the children are responsive, the relationship between the children and adults can serve as a basis of subsequent treatment and training. To begin the negative reinforcement procedure, the children were placed in a room which had an electrified floor. Electric shock could be given to individuals standing barefoot on the floor. Two adults stood at different sides of the room. One adult said, "Come here," and held out his hands. The shock (aversive stimulus) was turned on. As soon as the child moved toward an adult, the ongoing shock was terminated. Thus, movement toward an adult (the behavior) was negatively reinforced. This procedure dramatically increased the number of times the children responded to the instructions to come to the adults. A similar procedure was used to train the children to hug and kiss adults. A shock delivered to the buttocks was terminated when the children hugged or kissed the experimenter. Kissing and hugging were negatively reinforced because the aversive event was terminated when the responses were performed. These demonstrations of negative reinforcement are particularly impressive since many procedures often employed to alter the behavior of autistic children have little or no success (Lovaas et al., 1965).

Negative reinforcement requires some aversive event that is presented to the individual before he or she responds, such as shock, noise, isolation, and other events which can be removed or reduced immediately after a response. As with positive reinforcers, there are two types of negative reinforcers, primary and secondary. Intense stimuli, such as shock or loud noise, which impinge on sensory receptors of an organism serve as primary negative reinforcers. Their aversive properties are not learned. However, secondary or *conditioned aversive events* have become aversive by being paired with events which are already aversive. For example, disapproving facial expressions or saying the word "no" can serve as aversive events after being paired with events which are already aversive.

Negative reinforcement occurs whenever an individual *escapes* from an aversive event. Escape from aversive events is negatively reinforcing. However, *avoidance* of aversive events is negatively reinforcing, too. For example, one avoids eating rancid food, walking through an intersection with oncoming cars, and leaving the house without an umbrella on a rainy day. Avoidance occurs before the aversive event takes place (e.g., becoming sick from rancid food, being injured by a car, getting wet from rain). The avoidance response prevents the aversive event from occurring. How are avoidance behaviors maintained since no aversive events seem to have occurred?

Avoidance learning is an area where classical and operant conditioning are operative. Avoidance behavior is sometimes learned by pairing a neutral stimulus (conditioned stimulus) with an unconditioned aversive event (unconditioned stimulus). For example, a frown (conditioned stimulus) from a parent may precede corporal punishment (unconditioned stimulus) of the child. Corporal punishment may elicit crying and escape from the situation (unconditioned response). The child learns to *escape* from the situation when the adult frowns and thereby *avoids* corporal punishment. The sight of the frowning parent elicits crying and escape. Avoidance of unconditioned aversive events is actually escape from the conditioned aversive event. Thus, classical conditioning may initiate avoidance behavior. Operant conditioning is also involved in avoidance behavior. Behaviors which reduce or terminate an aversive event are negatively reinforced. The escape from the conditioned aversive event (e.g., frown) is negatively reinforced since it terminates the event. To reiterate, the conditioned aversive event elicits an escape response (classical conditioning) which is negatively reinforced (operant conditioning).

Operant conditioning is involved in yet another way in avoidance learning. A conditioned aversive event serves as a cue signaling that particular consequences will follow. The presence of the conditioned aversive stimulus signals that a certain response (escape) will be reinforced (Reynolds, 1968). A variety of cues control avoidance behavior in everyday life. Indeed, most avoidance behavior appears to be learned from verbal cues (warnings) by others rather than from direct experience with unconditioned aversive stimuli. For example, a sign saying, "Danger" or "Beware of Dog," signals that certain consequences (e.g., physical harm) are likely to occur if a particular response is performed (e.g., trespassing). The escape response made after reading the sign is not *elicited* in the sense discussed above with classical conditioning. The sign merely acts as a cue that consequences of a particular sort are likely to follow alternate courses of action. An individual does not have to experience physical harm to learn to avoid particular situations. In examples from everyday experience, avoidance behavior is under the control of antecedent stimuli (e.g., air raid sirens, screeching car brakes, threats, and traffic signals) which signal that a particular event is likely to follow.

The distinction between classical and operant conditioning is difficult to maintain. Traditionally, both types of conditioning have been considered to operate in avoidance learning. Yet, the processes by which avoidance behavior are developed, maintained, and eliminated are not completely understood (see Brush, 1971; Hineline, 1977).

■ PUNISHMENT

Punishment is the presentation of an aversive event or the removal of a positive event following a response which decreases the frequency of that response. This definition is somewhat different from the everyday use of the term. Punishment, as ordinarily defined, refers to a penalty imposed for performing a particular act. The technical definition includes an additional requirement, namely, that the frequency of the response is decreased (Azrin & Holz, 1966). Because of the negative connotations frequently associated with punishment, it is important to dispel some stereotypic notions that do not apply to the technical definition of punishment. Punishment does not necessarily entail pain or physical coercion.[2] In addition, punishment is not a means of retribution or payment for misbehaving. Sometimes punishment is employed in everyday life independently of its effects on subsequent behavior. For example, children are "taught a lesson" for misbehaving by undergoing a sacrifice of some kind. Similarly, criminals may receive penalties which do not necessarily decrease the frequency of their criminal acts. *Punishment in the technical sense is an empirical matter; it is defined solely by the effect on behavior.* Only if the frequency of a response is reduced can punishment be operative. Similarly, a punishing event is defined by its suppressive effect on the behavior which it follows. As is evident in later chapters, a variety of events which suppress behavior depart from ordinary practices which are termed punishment in everyday life.

There are two different types of punishment. In the first kind of punishment, an aversive event is *presented* after a response. Numerous examples of this pervade everyday life, such as being reprimanded or slapped after engaging in some behavior. Similarly, being burned after touching a hot stove involves the presentation of an aversive stimulus after a response. Of course, whether these examples in everyday life qualify as punishment depends, in part, upon whether there is a reduction in the responses.

A second type of punishment is the *removal* of a positive reinforcer after a response. Examples include losing privileges after staying out late, losing money for misbehaving, being isolated from others, and having one's driver's license revoked. In this form of punishment, some positive event is taken away after a response is performed. For example, in one report, loss of television time was used to train a child to dress herself each morning (Hall et al., 1972). The child spent a large amount of time dressing herself each morning. If the child spent over 30 minutes to dress herself after waking, she lost time from watching television that day. When the withdrawal of television privileges was contingent upon the response (taking over 30 minutes to dress), dressing time decreased considerably. From this example alone, it should be clear that punishment is not necessarily physically painful. However, in both types of punishment some consequence occurs which an individual is likely to label as undesirable.

Punishment and negative reinforcement often are confused even though they are very different. The key difference of course is that reinforcement, whether negative or positive, always refers to procedures that *increase* a response; punishment always refers to procedures that *decrease* a response. In negative reinforcement, an aversive event is *removed* after a response; in punishment an aversive consequence *follows* a response.

Figure 2–1 provides a simple way to help distinguish the operations involved in reinforcement and punishment. The figure depicts two operations that can occur after a response is performed. An event can be

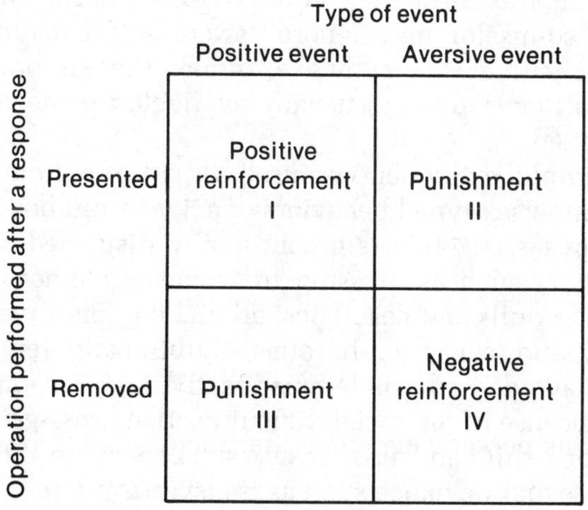

	Type of event	
	Positive event	Aversive event
Presented	Positive reinforcement I	Punishment II
Removed	Punishment III	Negative reinforcement IV

(Operation performed after a response)

FIGURE 2–1 Illustration of principles of operant conditioning based upon whether positive or aversive events are presented or removed after a response is performed.[3]

presented to or removed from the client after a response (left side of the figure). The figure also shows two types of events that may be presented or removed, namely, positive and aversive events. The four combinations forming the different cells depict the principles of positive reinforcement (Cell I), negative reinforcement (Cell IV) and two types of punishment (Cells II and III).

■ EXTINCTION

An important principle of operant conditioning is not represented in Figure 2–1. This principle does not involve presenting or withdrawing events in the usual sense. Rather, the principle refers to no longer following behavior with an event that was previously delivered.

Behaviors that are reinforced increase in frequency. However, a behavior which is no longer reinforced decreases in frequency. During extinction, a response which was previously reinforced is no longer reinforced. *Extinction refers to the cessation of reinforcement of a response.* Nonreinforcement of a response results in the eventual reduction or elimination of the behavior. It is important to keep this procedure distinct from punishment. In extinction, no consequence follows the response, that is, an event is not taken away nor is one presented. In punishment, some aversive event follows a response or some positive event is taken away. In everyday life, the usual use of extinction is in the form of ignoring a behavior that may have been reinforced previously with attention. A mother may ignore her child when the child whines. A physician may ignore the physical complaints of a hypochondriac. A teacher may ignore children who talk without raising their hands. A therapist or counselor may ignore certain self-defeating statements made by the client. In each of these examples, the reinforcer (e.g., attention, approval, or sympathy) usually available for the response is no longer presented.

As an example, extinction was used as part of a program to change several feminine sex-typed behaviors of a 5 year-old boy, named Kraig (Rekers & Lovaas, 1974). Kraig continually displayed several female typed behaviors such as dressing in women's clothes, playing with such objects as dolls and cosmetics, mimicking feminine gestures and mannerisms, and engaging in other traditionally female-typed activities. He avoided all male-typed activities. Treatment was implemented because of the social difficulties that cross-gender activities may create for a child and also because such behaviors often are precursors to later sexual deviance such as transvestism (cross dressing) and transsexualism (opposite sex-role identity). Treatment was conducted at the clinic and the child's home. At the clinic, the mother and child were placed in a room where the child had the opportunity to play with items traditionally regarded as feminine-typed activities (e.g., dolls, cosmetics, women's clothes) or as masculine-typed activities (e.g., cars, boats, guns). The mother was instructed to ignore any play with feminine-typed objects. The mother simply read a book she brought into the room. By withholding attention, the purpose was to *extinguish* play with feminine-typed objects. The mother also was instructed to reinforce play with masculine-typed objects. Whenever Kraig played with these objects, the mother provided attention, smiles, and praise. Thus, extinction was combined with positive reinforcement. The program was carried out at home where Kraig received token reinforcement for many gender-appropriate behaviors. Interestingly, the program led to dramatic changes showing an increase in masculine behaviors and a decrease in feminine behaviors. Treatment effects were maintained when Kraig was checked 26 months after treatment.[4]

In everyday life, extinction may contribute to behavior problems as well as ameliorate them. Often desirable behavior is accidentally extinguished. For example, parents sometimes ignore their children when they are playing quietly and provide abundant attention when the children are noisy. Essentially, quiet play may be extinguished while noisy play is positively reinforced. Merely altering parental attention so it follows appropriate play is often sufficient to develop appropriate behavior and to extinguish inappropriate behavior.

Cessation of attention is not the only example of extinction. For example, putting money into vending machines (a response) will cease if the reinforcer (e.g., cigarettes, food, or drink) is not forthcoming; turning on a radio will cease, if the radio no longer functions; and attempting to start a car will extinguish, if the car does not start. In each of these examples, the consequences which maintain the behavior are no longer forthcoming. The absence of reinforcing consequences reduces the behavior. Extinction can be used to reduce or eliminate behavior. However, the events which reinforce behavior must be identified so they can be prevented from occurring after the response.

■ SHAPING AND CHAINING

Frequently, the development of new behavior cannot be achieved by reinforcing the response when it occurs. In many cases, the response may never occur. The desired behavior may be so complex that the elements which make up the response are not in the repertoire of the individual. For example, developing the use of words requires, among other things, the use of sounds, syllables, and their combinations. *In shaping, the terminal behavior is achieved by reinforcing small steps or approximations toward the final response rather than reinforcing the final response itself.* Responses are reinforced which either resemble the final response or which include components of that response. By reinforcing *successive approximations* of the terminal response, the final response is achieved gradually. Responses which are increasingly similar to the final goal are reinforced and they increase, while those responses dissimilar to the final goal are not reinforced and they extinguish. Shaping, along with other procedures, is used to develop talking in children. Responses which approach the final goal (e.g., sounds and syllables) are reinforced. Responses which are emitted that do not approach the goal (e.g., screaming and whining) are extinguished along the way toward the final goal.

An obvious example of shaping is training animals to perform various "tricks." If the animal trainer waited until the tricks were performed (e.g., jumping through a burning hoop) to administer a reinforcer, it is unlikely that reinforcement would ever occur. However, by shaping the response, the trainer can readily achieve the terminal goal. First, food (positive reinforcer) might be delivered for running toward the trainer. As that response becomes stable, the trainer may reinforce running up to the trainer when he is holding the hoop. Other steps closer to the final goal would be reinforced in sequence, including walking through the hoop on the ground, jumping through the hoop when it is slightly off the ground, and then high off the ground, jumping through it when it is partially on fire and finally, jumping through it when the hoop is completely on fire. Eventually, the terminal response will be performed with a high frequency, whereas the responses or steps developed along the way are extinguished.

As an example, shaping was used to develop appropriate speech in a 15-year-old mentally retarded girl, named Alice, who was severely withdrawn (Jackson & Wallace, 1974). The girl's speech was almost completely inaudible. A reinforcement program was used to shape progressively louder speech while the girl read various words in experimental sessions with a trainer. A microphone that Alice wore was used to detect the volume of her speech. At the beginning of training, only slight increases in voice volume were required. When the desired volume was registered through the microphone, a token was automatically delivered. The tokens could be used for various items she desired such as a photo album and beauty aids. When Alice's voice consistently met the volume requirements to earn tokens, the criterion was increased slightly. Louder and louder speech was developed until her voice volume achieved the level of her peers.

Shaping requires reinforcing behaviors already in the repertoire of the individual which resemble the terminal response or approximate the goal. As the initial approximation is performed consistently, the criterion for reinforcement is altered slightly so that the response which is to be reinforced resembles the final goal more closely than the previous response. Through reinforcement of responses which approach the terminal goal and extinction of responses which do not, the terminal response is developed. In the above example, shaping was used to increase voice volume. Training began with the existing response and gradually increased volume over time. Reinforcing successive approximations is used in an identical fashion to develop new behaviors that have never been performed by the client such as feeding, walking, and dressing.

Most behaviors consist of a sequence of several responses. A sequence of responses is referred to as a *chain*. The component parts of a chain usually represent individual responses already in the repertoire of the individual. Yet the chain represents a combination of the individual responses ordered in a particular sequence. For example, one behavioral chain which illustrates the ordering of component responses is going to eat at a restaurant (Reynolds, 1968). Going out to eat may be initiated by a phone call from someone, hunger, or some other event. Having been initiated, several behaviors follow in a sequence, including leaving the house, entering the restaurant, being seated, looking at a menu, ordering a meal, and eating. Each response proceeds in a relatively fixed order until the chain is completed and the last response is reinforced (e.g., eating). Later responses in the chain (such as sitting at the table) are preceded by a series of responses (traveling in the car and so on). The order is fixed so that early responses must precede later ones. Interestingly, each response in the chain does not appear to be reinforced. Rather, only the last response (the response immediately preceding eating) is followed by the reinforcer (food). Because a reinforcer alters or maintains only the behavior that immediately precedes it, it is not obvious what maintains the entire chain of behaviors leading to the final response. However, there are many chains of responses that are maintained in everyday experience. For example, dieting, mastering a musical instrument, preparing for athletic competition, studying for an advanced degree, and writing a book all require a series of intermediate responses before the final reinforcing event is achieved. The major question is what maintains all of the intermediate responses that precede attaining the final goal? The answer requires explaining the factors that link the response components of a chain.

To begin with, it is important to note that an event which immediately precedes reinforcement becomes a signal for reinforcement. An event which signals that behavior will be reinforced is referred to as a *discriminative stimulus* (S^D). An S^D sets the *occasion* for behavior, that is, increases the probability that a previously reinforced behavior will occur. However, an S^D not only signals reinforcement but eventually becomes a reinforcer itself. The frequent pairing of an S^D and the reinforcer gives the S^D reinforcing properties of its own. This procedure was mentioned earlier in the discussion of conditioned reinforcement. The discriminative stimulus properties of events which precede reinforcement and the reinforcing properties of these events when they are frequently paired with reinforcers are important in explaining how chains of responses are maintained.

Consider the chain of responses involved in going out to eat, described above. (The chain could be divided into several smaller components than those listed above.) A phone call may have signaled the first response to go to a restaurant to eat. All of the behaviors in the chain of responses are performed ending in positive reinforcement (eating). The final response in the chain before reinforcement was ordering a meal. This response is directly reinforced with food. Recall that any event which precedes reinforcement becomes an S^D for reinforcement. In this chain of responses, the last response performed (ordering a meal) becomes an S^D for reinforcement, since the response signals that reinforcement will follow. Yet the constant pairing of an S^D with the reinforcer (food) eventually results in the S^D becoming a reinforcer as well as a discriminative stimulus. Hence, the response that preceded direct reinforcement has become an S^D for subsequent reinforcement and a reinforcer in its own right. The response serves as a reinforcer for the previous link in the chain of responses. The response (ordering food) becomes a reinforcer for the previous behavior (looking at a menu). Since looking at a menu now precedes reinforcement, it too becomes an S^D. As with other responses, the pairing of the S^D with reinforcement results in the S^D becoming a reinforcer. The process continues in a *backward* direction so that each response in the chain becomes an S^D and a reinforcer. (The very first response becomes an S^D but does not reinforce a prior response.) Each component response is both an S^D for the next response in the chain and serves as a reinforcer for the prior response in the chain. Although the sequence appears to be maintained by a single reinforcer at the end of the chain of responses (food in the above example), the links in the chain are assumed to take on conditioned reinforcement value. To accomplish this, building response chains requires training from the last response in the sequence which precedes direct reinforcement back to the first response. Since the last response in the sequence is paired immediately and directly with the reinforcer, it is most easily established as a conditioned reinforcer which can maintain other responses. Also the shorter the delay between a response and reinforcement, the greater the effect of reinforcement. The last response in the chain is immediately reinforced and is more likely to be performed frequently.

Shaping versus Chaining.   The differences between shaping and chaining and the conditions which dictate their use may be unclear. Generally, both shaping and chaining may be used to develop new behaviors. With each technique, discriminative stimuli (e.g., instructions, gestures) and direct reinforcement (e.g., praise) may be provided for the desired behavior. In some circumstances, shaping can be distinguished by focusing upon a series of steps that finally lead to the desired behavior. The steps themselves are only useful on the way to the final behavior. In contrast, chaining often is used to develop a sequence of separate behaviors. The final goal may be a sequence of several different responses (as in dressing). However, this difference between shaping and chaining is often a function of how the investigator views or explains behavior rather than an actual difference in the behaviors themselves.

Certainly, the major difference is that chaining proceeds in a backward direction beginning with the last response and building prior behaviors, whereas shaping works in a forward direction. Moreover, in shaping, the goal is to develop a terminal response. The behaviors along the way toward the goal usually are not evident when shaping is completed. In chaining, behaviors developed early in training are still evident when training is completed.

In spite of the differences in shaping and chaining, the relative utility of the procedures in applied settings has not been evaluated empirically. Sequences of behaviors (chains) can be developed by shaping and using cues and reinforcement for the performance of behaviors in a particular sequence. Thus, in many situations either chaining or shaping may be used. For example, toilet training of children consists of a series of responses which follow in sequence, including walking to a bathroom, lowering pants, positioning oneself in front of or on the toilet, and so on. Reinforcement for appropriate toileting following completion of the entire chain can be praise for proper elimination. Although chaining can be used to develop this sequence of responses, shaping also is effective (Azrin & Foxx, 1971; Mahoney, Van Wagenen, & Meyerson, 1971).

In light of current research, it is not clear when chaining or shaping should be selected. However, for some individuals cues normally used in shaping (e.g., instructions) may exert little influence on behavior so that the behaviors in a sequence of responses are not consistently performed. Chaining might be particularly useful in this situation because each behavior in the chain becomes a cue for the next response to be performed. Moreover, the conditioned reinforcement provided by each response in the chain facilitates performance of the correct order of responses. Shaping is particularly well suited to developing a single terminal behavior. However, it may work effectively in developing a chain of several responses, particularly when cues such as instructions are effective in initiating the early behaviors in the chain.

■ PROMPTING AND FADING

Developing behavior is facilitated by using cues, instructions, gestures, directions, examples, and models to initiate a response. *Events which help initiate a response are prompts.* Prompts precede a response. When the prompt results in the response, the response can be followed by reinforcement. When a prompt initiates behaviors that are reinforced, the prompt becomes an S^D for reinforcement. For example, if a parent tells a child to return from school early and the child is praised when he does this, the instruction (prompt) becomes an S^D. Instructions signal that reinforcement is likely when certain behaviors are performed. Eventually, instructions alone are likely to be followed by the behavior. As a general rule, when a prompt consistently precedes reinforcement of a response, the prompt becomes an S^D and can effectively control behavior.

Developing behavior can be facilitated in different ways, such as *guiding* the behavior physically (e.g., holding a child's arm to assist him in placing a spoon in his mouth); *instructing* the child to do something; *pointing* to the child to come inside the house; and *observing* another person (a model) perform a behavior (e.g., watching someone else play a game). Prompts play a major role in shaping and chaining. Developing a terminal response using reinforcement alone may be tedious and time consuming. By assisting the person in beginning the response, more rapid approximations to the final response can be made.

Mahoney et al. (1971) used a variety of prompts to train normal and retarded children to walk to the lavatory as a part of toileting skills. For example, toys were placed near the entrance to the lavatory to increase the likelihood of approach responses (visual prompt), the experimenter led the child by the hand to the lavatory (physical prompt), and instructions ("Let's go potty.") were used (verbal prompt) to initiate walking. An additional prompt consisted of an auditory signal (transmitted through an earphone in the child's ear) which sounded when the experimenter gave instructions, "Go potty." Pairing the auditory signal with instructions resulted in the signal alone initiating walking toward the lavatory.

The use of prompts increases the likelihood of the response. For example, walking to the lavatory was much more likely to occur when the experimenter actually guided the child than when the child was left to respond on his or her own. While a response is being shaped, prompts may be used frequently to facilitate performance of the terminal goal. As soon as a prompted response is performed, it can be reinforced. Further, the more frequently the response is reinforced, the more rapidly it will be learned. A final goal usually is to obtain the terminal response in the absence of prompts. Although prompts may be required early in training, they can be withdrawn gradually or faded as training progresses.

Fading refers to the gradual removal of a prompt. If a prompt is removed abruptly early in training, the response may no longer be performed. But if the response is performed consistently with a prompt, the prompt can be progressively reduced and finally omitted, thus faded. For example, in the toilet training project mentioned earlier (Mahoney et al., 1971), several prompts helped train walking to the lavatory. As the children began to perform the behavior with physical guidance and verbal prompts, the experimenter began to fade the prompts. Instead of holding the child's hand to guide walking, the experimenter walked in front of the child, further away from the child, and eventually behind the child, so the child led the way to the lavatory. Also, verbal prompts (instructions) were reduced. To achieve behavior without prompts requires fading and reinforcing the responses in the absence of prompts. It is not always necessary to remove all prompts. For example, it is important to train individuals to respond in the presence of certain prompts such as instructions which exert control over a variety of behaviors in everyday life.

■ DISCRIMINATION AND STIMULUS CONTROL

Operant behavior is influenced by the consequences which follow behavior. However, antecedent events also control behavior. Prompts, discussed earlier, represent a group of controlling events (e.g., instructions, physical guidance, models, and verbal cues) which precede and facilitate response performance. Yet, other antecedent stimuli come to exert control over behavior. In some situations (or in the presence of certain stimuli), a response may be reinforced, while in other situations (in the presence of other stimuli) the same response is not reinforced.

Differential reinforcement refers to reinforcing a response in the presence of one stimulus and not reinforcing the same response in the presence of another stimulus. When a response is consistently reinforced in the presence of a particular stimulus and consistently not reinforced in the presence of another stimulus, each stimulus signals the consequences which are likely to follow. The stimulus present when the response is reinforced signals that performance is likely to be reinforced. Conversely, the stimulus present during nonreinforcement signals that the response is not likely to be reinforced.

As mentioned earlier, a stimulus whose presence has been associated with reinforcement is referred to as an S^D. A stimulus whose presence has been associated with nonreinforcement is referred to as an S^Δ (S delta). The effect of differential reinforcement is that eventually the reinforced response is likely to occur in the presence of the S^D but unlikely to occur in the presence of the S^Δ. The probability of a response can be altered (increased or decreased) by presenting or removing the S^D (Skinner, 1953). The S^D occasions the previously reinforced response or increases the likelihood that the response is performed. When the individual responds differently in the presence of different stimuli, he or she has made a *discrimination*. When responses are differentially controlled by antecedent stimuli, behavior is considered to be under *stimulus control*.

Instances of stimulus control pervade everyday life. For example, the sound of a door bell signals that a certain behavior (opening the door) is likely to be reinforced (by seeing someone). Specifically, the sound of the bell frequently has been associated with the presence of visitors at the door (the reinforcer). The ring of the bell (S^D) increases the likelihood that the door will be opened. In the absence of the bell (S^Δ), the probability of opening the door for a visitor is very low. The ring of a door bell, telephone, alarm, and kitchen timer, all serve as discriminative stimuli and signal that certain responses are likely to be reinforced. Hence, the probability of the responses is increased. Stimulus control is also evident in the selection and consumption of food. For example, a ripe fruit (e.g., a red apple) is associated with a sweet taste, whereas a green apple (of the variety that is not ripe when green) is associated with a sour taste. The sweet taste of a ripe apple reinforces selection and consumption of a red apple. The color of the fruit is a stimulus which controls the future probability of eating certain fruit. In social interaction, stimulus control also is important. For example, a smile or wink from someone is likely to occasion a social response on our part (e.g., initiation of conversation). Whereas a smile serves as an S^D (signals that reinforcement is likely to follow our social response), a frown serves as an S^Δ (signals that reinforcement is not likely to follow a social response).

The notion of stimulus control is exceedingly important in behavior modification. In many behavior modification programs, the goal is to alter the relation between behavior and the stimulus conditions in which the behavior occurs. Some behavior problems stem from a failure of certain stimuli to control behavior although such control would be desirable. For example, children who do not follow instructions given by their parents illustrate a lack of stimulus control. The instructions do not exert influence over the children's behavior. The goal of a behavior modification program is to increase responsiveness to instructions. Other behavioral problems occur when certain behaviors *are* under control of antecedent stimuli when such control is undesirable. For example, the eating behavior of obese individuals often is controlled by the mere sight of food (among other stimuli), rather than hunger. Treatment of overeating focuses on eliminating the control that the sight of food has on eating. (Treatments based upon stimulus control will be discussed further in Chapter 10.)

Stimulus control is always operative in behavior modification programs. Programs are conducted in particular settings (e.g., the home) and are administered by particular individuals (e.g., parents). Insofar as certain client behaviors are reinforced or punished in the presence of certain environmental cues or of particular individuals and not in the presence of other stimuli, the behaviors will be under stimulus control. In the presence of those cues associated with the behavior modification program, the client will behave in a particular fashion. In the absence of those cues, behavior is likely to change because the contingencies in new situations are altered.

A familiar example of stimulus control that may arise in a behavior modification program pertains to the behavior of students when the teacher is in rather than out of the classroom. As most of us might recall from elementary school years, the amount of disruptive behavior often varied depending upon whether the teacher was in the room enforcing the rules of the classroom. Once the stimulus (teacher) associated with the reinforcing or punishing consequences was no longer present, behavior often deteriorated. Indeed, the stimulus control that individuals such as parents and teachers exert over behavior often creates a problem in behavior modification. The children may perform the responses in the presence of parents or teachers but not in their absence (e.g., Marholin & Steinman, 1977). Special contingency arrangements may be needed to ensure that the desired behaviors transfer to new people, situations, and places (see Chapter 11).

The control that different stimuli exert over behavior explains why behavior often is situation specific. Individuals may behave one way in a given situation or in the presence of a particular person and differently in another situation or in the presence of another person. Since different reinforcement contingencies operate in different circumstances, individuals can discriminate among those stimuli which are likely to be followed by reinforcement.

A dramatic example of discriminative responding and stimulus control was reported by Redd and Birnbrauer (1969). In this study, two adults working at different times provided retarded children with food (candy, ice cream, or sips of coke) and praise for performing a specified response (e.g., playing cooperatively with another child). When the first adult was with one child, reinforcement was administered for the cooperative response (contingent delivery of praise). When the second adult was present, the same child was reinforced independently of his actual behavior (noncontingent delivery of praise). Overall, each adult administered the same amount of the available reinforcers. In a short period, the adults exerted stimulus control over the behavior of the children. The presence of the adult who was associated with the contingent delivery of praise led to cooperative play, whereas the presence of the adult who was associated with the noncontingent delivery of praise did not. The children discriminated the different contingencies associated with the adults. Thus, adults can serve as discriminative stimuli for reinforcement. Children respond differentially to adults depending upon the behaviors that are differentially reinforced in each adult's presence.

People make discriminations across a variety of situations for most behaviors. For example, eating habits probably are slightly different depending upon whether one is at home or in a restaurant. Discriminations are made which are even more subtle. Eating behavior may be different depending upon whether one is in an "expensive" restaurant or in a road-side cafe. Individuals behave differently in the presence of their co-workers compared with their boss. Numerous other differences in behavior are evident because of differences in situations and the contingencies associated with them.

■ GENERALIZATION

The effect of reinforcement on behavior may extend beyond the conditions in which training has taken place or extend to other behaviors than the one(s) included in the program. The two ways in which the effects of the program may extend beyond the contingency are referred to as generalization.

Stimulus Generalization.   Behavior occurs in specific situations. A response which is repeatedly reinforced in the presence of a particular situation is likely to be repeated in that situation. However, situations and stimuli often share common properties. Control exerted by a given stimulus is shared by other stimuli which are similar or share common properties (Skinner, 1953). A behavior may be performed in new situations similar to the original situation in which reinforcement occurred. If a response reinforced in one situation or setting also increases in other settings (even though it is not reinforced in these other settings), this is referred to as stimulus generalization. *Stimulus generalization refers to the generalization or transfer of a response to situations other than those in which training takes place.* Generalization is the opposite of discrimination. When an individual discriminates in the performance of a response, this means that the response fails to generalize across situations. Alternatively, when a response generalizes across situations, the individual fails to discriminate in his or her performance of that response.

Figure 2–2 illustrates stimulus generalization. The term S_1 refers to the stimulus condition or situation in which the response is reinforced. R_1 refers to the behavior or response which is reinforced. The figure

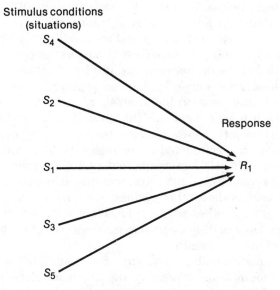

Stimulus conditions
(situations)

FIGURE 2–2 Stimulus generalization: A response (R_1) reinforced in one situation (S_1) generalizes to other situations (S_2, S_3, S_4, S_5) which are similar to the original situation.

shows that the trained response (R_1) is performed across a variety of stimuli or situations (S_2, S_3, S_4, S_5). The degree of stimulus generalization is a function of the similarity of new stimuli (or situations) to the stimulus under which the response was trained (Kimble, 1961). Of course, over a long period of time, a response may not generalize across situations because the individual discriminates that the response is reinforced in one situation but not in others.

Examples of stimulus generalization are frequent in everyday experience. For example, a child may say certain things in the presence of his family. Discussion of certain topics is reinforced (or not punished) among family members. However, the child may also discuss these same topics in the presence of company. Behavior of the child (talking about certain topics) has generalized across situations. Parents may show considerable embarrassment when children freely discuss "family secrets." Generalization also is readily apparent when a child responds to a teacher in a fashion similar to that of a parent (e.g., in the expression of affection). To the extent that parents and teachers are similar to a child, the stimulus control exerted by parents will be shared by the teacher.

An example of generalization across situations and stimulus conditions was reported in a program for a 21 year-old hospitalized schizophrenic patient (Fichter, Wallace, Liberman, & Davis, 1976). The patient was very withdrawn and spoke at an inaudible level when he did speak. Also, he spoke very briefly and engaged in inappropriate hand gestures such as tapping his face with his fingers, biting his fingers, and rocking with his hands between his thighs. Treatment consisted of prompting louder and longer speech and appropriate use of hands and arms (e.g., placing them on the armrests of a chair) while he socially interacted with a staff member. The prompting procedure was conducted in the hospital. However, after the patient was discharged, observations were also conducted in the residential care home where the patient lived and in a day-treatment center where he spent his days. The observations revealed that the improvements achieved in the hospital extended to each of these other settings, even though the prompts were never used in these other settings. Thus, behavior *generalized* to new staff members, new settings, and across new topics of conversation that were not included in training.

Stimulus generalization represents an exceedingly important issue in behavior modification. Invariably, training takes place in a restricted setting such as a classroom, home, hospital ward, and or institution. It is desirable that behaviors developed in these settings generalize or transfer to other settings and to the presence of other people.

Response Generalization. An additional type of generalization involves responses rather than stimulus conditions. Altering one response can inadvertently influence other responses. For example, if a person is praised for smiling, the frequency of laughing and talking might also increase. *The reinforcement of a response increases the probability of other responses which are similar* (Skinner, 1953). This is referred to as response generalization. To the extent that a nonreinforced response is similar to one that is reinforced, the similar response too is increased in probability. Figure 2–3 depicts response generalization, where S_1 refers to the stimulus condition in which training of a response takes place, and R_1 refers to the response which is reinforced. Although only one response is trained in the situation, a variety of other responses (R_2, R_3, R_4, R_5) which are similar may also be performed.

Altering one behavior often is associated with changes in other behaviors as well. For example, in one report, the inappropriate verbal behaviors (shouting, whining, using profanities, and complaining) were suppressed in a 10 year-old retarded boy (Jackson & Calhoun,

Responses

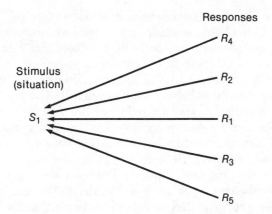

FIGURE 2–3 Response generalization: Reinforcement of one response (R_1) in a given situation
(S_1) may result in an increase of other responses (R_2,
R_3, R_4, R_5) which are similar to the reinforced response.

1977). Time out was used in which two minutes of isolation were given
for each verbal outburst. Interestingly, not only did verbal behavior
change but appropriate social behaviors such as joining in activities
and initiating conversation increased as well.

The notion of response generalization often is used to explain
changes in responses that are not included as the target response in a
given behavior modification program. Technically, response generalization may not be accurate as a term for two reasons. First, responses that
are not supposed to be focused upon may receive reinforcing consequences inadvertently. For example, a child who is praised for studying
in class may improve in reading even though reading may not be the
response that is supposed to be reinforced. Although one may speak of
this as generalization, it may reflect the direct operation of reinforcement and not be generalization at all. When a child is praised for paying
attention he or she may be reading on some of the occasions when
reinforcement is delivered. Thus, it is difficult to speak of response
generalization because the behavior was directly reinforced.

A second reason that response generalization may not accurately
account for the many changes that occur with treatment is slightly more
complex. Response generalization refers to changes in behaviors that are
similar to the target behavior. Yet, research has shown many examples
where change in one behavior has consistent effects on other behaviors
that appear to have no direct relation or resemblance to the target behavior. For example, in one study the excessive talking of a 7 year-old

boy was altered by withdrawing teacher attention (Sajwaj, Twardosz, & Burke, 1972). Other behaviors changed as well including an increase in conversation and cooperative play with his peers and a decrease in his use of "girl's" toys during free play. These behaviors have no clear relation to the target focus and could not be accounted for by changes in teacher attention to these behaviors. It is unclear why the other behaviors changed since only excessive verbalizations with the teacher were altered. Similarly other studies have shown that changing one behavior may result in changes in other behaviors that bear no obvious relation (Becker, Turner, & Sajwaj, 1978; Epstein et al., 1974).

The reasons that various responses change when treatment focuses on a particular behavior are unclear. Wahler (1975) has carefully observed children over extended periods in the home and at school and has found that individuals often have *clusters* of behaviors, that is, groups of specific behaviors which consistently go together. For example, for one child, behaviors such as engaging in self-stimulation, socially interacting with adults, and complying with adult instructions tended to go together. Treatment that focused on one of the behaviors that was part of a cluster altered other behaviors as well. In this case, the spread of treatment effects to different behaviors could not be explained by the similarity of the behaviors (see Wahler, Berland, & Coe, 1979).

In behavior modification, the concepts of stimulus and response generalization are usually used to denote that changes occur across various stimulus conditions (situations or settings) or across responses. In fact, rarely is there any evidence that the spread of treatment effects across stimulus or response dimensions is actually based upon the *similarity* of the stimulus or response conditions to those of training. Hence, technically the terms stimulus and response generalization are not used correctly. Yet, the technical difficulties in using the terms should not detract from the importance of the spread of treatment effects across stimulus conditions or behaviors during the course of treatment.

■ CONCLUSION

The principles outlined in this chapter provide the basis for the majority of operant conditioning programs in applied settings. The principles may seem overwhelming at first because of the many different terms that were introduced. Yet, the principles describe basic relationships between events and behavior and account for diverse treatment interventions. The complexity of the programs used in behavior modification cannot be conveyed by perusal of the principles. Each principle requires elaboration because of the several factors which determine its effective application. In later chapters, principles which have been widely employed in a variety of settings will receive detailed attention. Prior to discussing the techniques derived from the principles, it is important to consider some objections which are frequently voiced to using behavior modification principles.

■ NOTES

[1] Discussion of the principles introduces several new terms. To aid the reader, major terms and their definitions are included in italics. Also, a glossary at the end of the book provides a summary definition of major terms that arise in this chapter and throughout the text.

[2] As Skinner (1974) has noted, the word "pain" etymologically traces back to Latin and Greek. The Latin word from which it was derived refers to punishment which explains, in part, why the two notions are inextricably bound in language and thought.

[3] The figure provides a simple way to convey the major principles of operant conditioning. The simplicity of the figure has a price. In fact, a more technical discussion of the principles would quickly reveal inaccuracies in the figure. For example, the figure implies that a particular event which can negatively reinforce behavior also can be used to suppress (punish) some other response it follows. Although this usually is true, many exceptions exist. It is not necessarily the case that the same event which negatively reinforces a behavior when removed will suppress a behavior when it is presented, or vice versa (Azrin & Holz, 1966). Hence, in the present text, the term "aversive stimulus" or "aversive event" will be used to refer to any event that may be negatively reinforcing and/or punishing. In general, the principles of operant conditioning refer to more complex relationships than depicted here (see Morse & Kelleher, 1977). Interestingly, behavior modification programs tend to rely upon the simple versions of the principles discussed here.

[4] Altering sex-role behaviors raises many ethical issues about defining appropriate behaviors based upon traditional values, whether the child warranted treatment at all, and whether the long-term goals of heterosexual adjustment were appropriate or necessarily facilitated by treatment (see Nordyke, Baer, Etzel, & LeBlanc, 1977; Winkler, 1977). (Many value issues raised about the goals of treatment in general are discussed in Chapter 13.)

Misconceptions of Behavior Modification

The application of operant principles often is associated with misconceptions and objections about various techniques, how they are used, and their effects on behavior. People concerned about behavior change occasionally have discussed the misuse of behavioral techniques and adverse side effects that may result even when the techniques are used appropriately. As is often the case with objections and misconceptions, they embody threads of truth. However, it is important to identify those points where objections are valid and those where they are not. Several of the more common objections and misconceptions will be discussed, particularly those issues that stem from the use of positive reinforcers. Although objections pertaining to the use of aversive events will be discussed briefly, many issues regarding aversive stimuli are based upon ethical and legal considerations which are treated separately later in the book (Chapter 12).

■ REINFORCEMENT IS "BRIBERY"

A frequent concern with using reinforcers, especially tangible reinforcers such as candy, toys, and stars is that there is no "real" change in the person's behavior. The person is just being "bought" or "bribed" to perform a particular behavior. Actually, the definitions of "bribery" and "reinforcement" are slightly different. Bribery refers to the illicit use of rewards, gifts, or favors to pervert judgment or corrupt the conduct of someone. With bribery, reward is used to change behavior, but the behavior is corrupt, illegal, or immoral in some way. Although bribery and reinforcement both involve the delivery of favorable events, their *purposes* are different. With reinforcement, as typically employed, events are delivered for behaviors that are generally agreed upon to benefit the client, society, or both. Typically behaviors that are altered with reinforcement include social and academic skills, grooming behaviors, appropriate speech, or nonpsychotic behavior. These behaviors are rarely considered corrupt, illegal, or immoral. Thus, the *intent* of the individual who provides the incentive and the purpose for which the incentive is delivered dictate whether bribery or reinforcement is at issue. Reinforcement is clearly distinguished from bribery when the precise meaning of "bribery" is made explicit.

Bribery also is considered as a general way to influence others by giving them something; however, this general definition applies to reinforcement as well, so there is a broad similarity between bribery and reinforcement. Yet, when discussing reinforcement, it may be difficult to convey that bribery and reinforcement are similar only in that they can both influence behavior. The word "bribery" is so emotionally loaded that rarely can its superficial similarity to reinforcement be conveyed independently of the negative connotations.

Although reinforcement is *not* bribery, a related concern is that bribery may be learned by those individuals who are influenced by rewards. First, if reinforcement is used to alter the behavior of a child, this serves as a model for the child of how one person should go about influencing others. Perhaps, reinforcement may train bribery. Although there is little direct evidence, investigators have suggested that means of behavior control employed by parents may be adopted by their children. For example, parents who use punitive methods of discipline have children who are aggressive in their interactions with peers (Bandura & Walters, 1959). Thus, children may learn to use reinforcement and punishment in the way their parents do. Yet, teaching a child to influence others with reinforcers (e.g., smiles, approval, money, and others) is not inherently bad, but the child might use these techniques to entice others into performing dishonest acts, i.e., bribery.

A second and related objection is that individuals who are exposed to reinforcement will perform desirable behaviors only when a reward is offered. A person may withhold desirable behavior unless a reinforcer is given. Other individuals in the person's environment will be "manipulated" into providing the reinforcer. Manipulation of others can be inadvertently reinforced in an attempt to control behavior. For example, when a child has a tantrum, parents may try to control it with a variety of procedures (e.g., reprimands and physical control). If the tantrum does not end, a reinforcer may be offered to the child for "being nice." It is possible that the child may even have learned to say, "I will not stop unless you give me a reward."

When the child stops the tantrum (or even before that), he or she receives a reinforcer. Although the parents may have thought the cessation of the tantrum was reinforced, tantrums are likely to *increase*. A chain of responses culminating in termination of a full-blown tantrum was reinforced. From the child's standpoint, reinforcement in the future may depend upon having a tantrum. If a child deliberately engages in tantrums or makes "deals" to behave appropriately, these may be direct attempts to control others for his or her own advantage. If these manipulative responses successfully control parent behavior, they are likely to increase in the future. Increased manipulation does not necessarily result from the use of reinforcers, but only from their delivery after manipulative responses.

A dramatic instance of manipulation was reported by Meichenbaum, Bowers, and Ross (1968). These investigators implemented a program with a class of institutionalized adolescent females who were described as aggressive, manipulative, and uncontrollable. At one point in the program, the girls received money for appropriate behavior during afternoon classroom sessions. Although appropriate behavior improved in the afternoons, behavior became much worse in the mornings when no money was given. One girl reported, "If you don't pay us, we won't shape up [p. 349]." The girls were trying to manipulate the psychologists by offering appropriate behavior as a reward for the money! Of course, it might be undesirable if individuals consistently became manipulative after participating in a program and required reinforcers to perform desirable behaviors in new situations.

Although an instance of clients becoming manipulative to gain reinforcers is dramatic, evidence suggests that this is *not* widely found in behavior modification programs. For example, Eitzen (1975) evaluated the extent to which predelinquent youths became more manipulative and deceptive in their social interactions after participating in a reinforcement program. Although the youths had improved in many specific behaviors and such general characteristics as self-concept and achievement orientation, they did not change on a measure designed to assess their manipulative social behavior. Indeed, the delinquents were lower than their nondelinquent peers before treatment and continued to be lower in this regard after treatment.

Individuals who receive reinforcing consequences for their behavior rarely demand consequences for their behavior in other situations. In fact, in many programs individuals improve in other situations where no reinforcement is provided (e.g., Cooke & Apolloni, 1976; Hollandsworth, Glazeski, & Dressel, 1978; Kazdin, 1973b). Even when behavior fails to change in the situations in which reinforcement is not given, behavior typically does not become worse in those situations. Hence, the concern expressed in the objection does not appear to be well justified.

Many people object that extrinsic and tangible "rewards" are used in behavior modification. A frequent claim is that individuals should work for the intrinsic rewards associated with the activity rather than have to be "bribed." However, this claim fails to consider the pervasive use of extrinsic tangible reinforcers in everyday life. Few people would remain at their jobs if wages were not provided. In fact, sometimes when employees do not obtain high enough wages, they stop working and strike. Similarly, grades in school are used, in part, to provide incentives for academic performance. Although working and learning are implicitly regarded as worthwhile tasks in their own right, extrinsic reinforcers are used to enhance their performance. Other sources of tangible reinforcers for behavior include awards, prizes, medals, scholarships, pensions, advanced educational degrees, and trophies. Any objection levied against the use of extrinsic reinforcers in behavior modification programs applies as well to a variety of other consequences in everyday life. Extrinsic reinforcers are present everywhere. Any objection can only be based on the behaviors for which extrinsic reinforcers are used.

Reinforcers used to change behavior often are events which are ordinarily present in the situation (i.e., "naturally occurring" reinforcers). For example, praise, smiles, approving gestures or privileges are not extrinsic events introduced by a behavior modification program; they are ordinarily available. The major contribution of behavior modification in such programs is to ensure that consequences are delivered systematically and consistently so that they produce the desired results.

■ INDIVIDUALS BECOME "DEPENDENT" UPON
EXTRINSIC REINFORCERS

The notion of "bribes" has contributed to a related objection about the use of reinforcement. Implicitly bribes are considered to produce short-term changes in behavior. Perhaps behavior changes achieved with reinforcement would be transient as well. Behavior may become dependent upon the reinforcer and never performed without the promise of some consequence.

There are two ways in which "dependency" may be manifest: (1) clients may require special reinforcers (candy, extra privileges) in order to perform any desirable behavior, and (2) behaviors will not be maintained after reinforcers are withdrawn. The objection is that reinforcement leads to dependence upon reinforcers. If this means that extrinsic reinforcers will be required for the person to perform desirable behavior in any situation, the claim presently has no well established basis, as mentioned in the discussion of bribery. On the other hand, if this means that behavior change is limited to those situations or periods of time during which reinforcement is delivered, this is a different matter.

When reinforcement is no longer provided, the behavior usually extinguishes. In this sense, individuals do become dependent upon the delivery of reinforcers. Discontinuing reinforcement for appropriate behavior may be expected to result in a decrease of that behavior. Obviously, one might wonder why reinforcement or other techniques should be used at all if behavior which is no longer reinforced may extinguish. First, although reinforcement may need to be continued to maintain behavior, the form or type of reinforcement may change. For example, at the beginning of a program tangible reinforcers might be given but eventually praise, attention, and privileges can be substituted. Moreover, in the beginning of a program, a client may be dependent upon immediate reinforcement (e.g., candy for speaking), but eventually the reinforcement can be delayed considerably without loss of effectiveness. Finally, the frequency of reinforcement may be reduced by the end of a program. Thus, the type of reinforcement and various aspects regarding its delivery may change so that a person's behavior need not be reinforced each time by some extrinsic event. After behavior change has been achieved, the individual can be weaned systematically from the contingencies. Specific techniques can ensure that behavior is maintained once the contingencies are withdrawn. (The issue of response maintenance and the techniques useful in achieving long-term behavior change are considered in Chapter 11.)

The concern that behavior changes will not last beyond the program's duration is not always justified. When a program is terminated, extinction of the behavior does not always occur (e.g., Kazdin, 1973a; Paul & Lentz, 1978; Russo & Koegel, 1977). Changing an individual's behavior sometimes produces noticeable changes in how others in the person's environment respond to him. Even when extrinsic reinforcers are withdrawn, the reactions of others to the person whose behavior was changed may maintain the recently acquired behavior.

■ BEHAVIOR MODIFICATION IS "COERCIVE"

Another objection is that behavior modification is "coercive." The concern with "coercion" includes diverse but related issues, each of which has its own implications for designing treatment programs. The first and major objection pertaining to coercion is that *aversive means* may be used in behavior modification to compel or force individuals to perform various behaviors. The objection is to the means employed to modify behavior. Coercive techniques may include aversive methods in general, threats, and perhaps even physical abuse to overcome client resistance.

A second and related aspect of coercion is that an individual may be compelled to perform behavior *against his or her own volition*. A client may not agree to the goals of the program or personally select as desirable those behaviors which the program attempts to develop. This aspect of coercion emphasizes the *consent* of the client rather than merely the specific techniques that are used to alter behavior. Even if nonaversive techniques are used (e.g., positive reinforcement), the question is whether the client wishes to change at all and change along the lines specified by the program.

A third aspect of the coercion objection is that influencing behavior of other individuals, however benign, should be avoided. Exerting influence or "control" over the behavior of others may not necessarily rely on aversive means or be against the volition of the individual client. Rather, altering another person's behavior as a legitimate endeavor is objectionable to many individuals. Of course, behavior modification is inherently controlling and by design attempts to influence behavior, although it does not necessarily rely on aversive means or act against an individual's volition.

The different aspects which are included or implied in the objection that behavior modification is coercive are complex. The present discussion will focus on the issues pertaining to the use of force or aversive means to alter behavior and actions against the volition of the clients. Ethical and treatment considerations which arise by the use of aversive techniques and the ethics of behavior control in general, will be reserved for a separate discussion (Chapter 12).

The possibility always exists that even when the *goals* of the program seem beneficial to the client, the means used to achieve these goals may be harsh, unfair, and even cruel. An example of a program which relied on force and utilized unnecessarily harsh techniques was reported by Cotter (1967) who employed electric shock to alter the behavior of hospitalized psychiatric patients. One-hundred-thirty male patients were given a "choice" between receiving electric shock three times a week and working for their living in the hospital. Justification of the procedure was that escape from shock would serve as negative reinforcement for working. Individuals who worked would avoid shock. The procedure motivated most of the patients. However, it was then tried with a group of female patients with little success. Only 15 of 130 female patients were working by the end of 20 shock treatments. The procedures were made more severe for the females. Meals were made contingent upon working. The majority of patients missed three days of meals before finally giving in and working.

The program is objectionable for at least two reasons related to the issue of "coercion." First, extremely aversive means were employed. Second, the program goals certainly conflicted with the volition of the patients. Although some of the goals of the program may have been desirable (e.g., to increase activity and level of functioning of the patients), the means employed were cruel and against the patients' volition.[1]

Various precautions help ensure that a behavior modification program or any other treatment, for that matter, does not employ harsh means to force the performance of certain behaviors and infringe upon a client's rights. One source of protection is to require informed consent from the client or guardian of the client. Informed consent requires that the client be competent enough to understand the procedures, have knowledge of the risks and benefits of alternative forms of treatment available, and volunteer for the treatment without coercion (Friedman, 1975; Martin, 1975). Another source of protection consists of evaluation of intervention programs by various review committees before the programs are implemented. For example, in institutions, review committees evaluate whether treatment is appropriate to the problem, whether the client's rights are infringed upon, and whether any potential risks are outweighed by the likely benefits. (The sources of protection characteristic of treatment programs in general are highlighted in Chapter 12 on ethical and legal issues.)

Within behavior modification, additional sources of protection against coercion are available. For example, in many programs clients and those responsible for their treatment negotiate the contingencies. A *contingency contract* is used in which an actual written agreement or contract is drawn between the client and the parents, teachers, therapist, or others who are responsible for the program. The clients have a direct say regarding the nature of the program and the rewards and penalties for performance. If the program is coercive, the client can negotiate the conditions before it is implemented. There may be a clause in the contract which says that the contract can be changed at any time, if both parties agree. This ensures that any program can be altered as adjustments are needed or as inequities arise. (Contingency contracts are discussed in greater detail in Chapter 6.)

Another way of ensuring that the program is not coercive is to give clients control over deciding what some of the contingencies should be or letting them actually implement the contingencies. For example, in residential programs for delinquents (Phillips, Phillips, & Wolf, 1973) and for psychiatric patients (Greenberg, Scott, Pisa, & Friesen, 1975) residents have been able to select the reinforcing and punishing events or decide treatment goals for their peers.

Clients have input in their program in other ways. In some programs, clients administer consequences to themselves and select their individual goals (Wood & Flynn, 1978). In other programs, clients may elect peers who are responsible for administering consequences (Phillips, Phillips, Wolf, & Fixsen, 1973). When the clients or their peers take direct responsibility for the program, the likelihood of coercion is decreased. (Chapter 10 discusses many different self-control techniques where clients implement their own contingencies.)

Sometimes harsh and unfair methods may be viewed as necessary alternatives because individuals are not responding to less compelling procedures. Thus, force may be exerted to achieve effects that appear to be unobtainable with less severe techniques. Yet in behavior modification, a client's responsiveness to the program can be increased without relying on aversive techniques. The use of force and harsh methods can be avoided by making response requirements for positive reinforcement relatively lenient at the initial stages of a program so that it is extremely likely that the person will be able to perform them. If a client does not have the response well developed, it is unreasonable to devise a stringent contingency specifying that the response must be performed proficiently.

In many programs, the requirements for reinforcement are individualized so that the client only has to make some improvement rather than meet a rigidly specified criterion to earn reinforcers. As improvements are made, the criterion for reinforcement may be altered gradually. *A client's response to the contingencies is a function of how well the contingencies are devised.* If a client fails to respond, the criteria for reinforcement should be lowered until the behavior can be performed. Shaping and modeling can be useful in developing higher levels of performance. Thus, a second way that harsh or unfair treatment can be avoided is by initially making demands that can be met by the client. This can be determined by beginning with low performance demands and gradually increasing them as they are met. (Additional procedures to maximize responsiveness of a client to a program without relying on aversive techniques are discussed in Chapter 9.)

A third precaution against forcing clients to perform various behaviors against their volition or treating them unfairly and harshly is to allow them to leave the program when they wish. For example, Ayllon and Azrin (1968b) devised a program for psychiatric patients. A variety of reinforcers were available for performance of adaptive behaviors on the ward such as grooming, attending activities, and working on jobs. Clients were told explicitly that they could transfer to wards where there was no reward system. Other programs have allowed clients to leave the program when they wish or to earn their way off the contingencies.

A final procedure often employed to reduce aversive means is the reliance upon positive reinforcement rather than negative reinforcement or punishment. Presumably, programs exert less force if the individual is not deprived of essential reinforcers. Of course, it is possible to completely withhold powerful positive reinforcers (e.g., food) and dispense them for particular behaviors, as described in an example given earlier (Cotter, 1967). However, an obligation on the part of the program's designers is to provide incentives above and beyond essential everyday events which are normally granted and to which individuals are ethically and legally entitled. The distinction between enticing and forcing an individual can be difficult to make. Reliance upon positive reinforcement does eliminate aversive means to achieve behavior change but does not eliminate all aspects of "coercion," as defined earlier. With positive reinforcement, it is possible to seek treatment goals which are counter to a client's volition. Thus, reliance upon reinforcement does not completely ensure a "noncoercive" program.

The possibility of coercion in a behavior modification program should be recognized. However, in actual practice there are different ways in which the potential for unfair treatment, harsh methods, and forced compliance to arbitrary standards against the client's volition can be reduced. The many different ways in which clients are encouraged to participate in the development and execution of the contingencies help alleviate much of the threat of coercion.

■ NEGATIVE EFFECTS OF BEHAVIOR MODIFICATION ON OTHERS

Behavior modification programs often are implemented in group settings, such as institutions for psychiatric patients, retardates, delinquents, prisons, day-care centers, and classrooms. Frequently, programs are needed for only one or a few persons who are considered to warrant special attention because of behavior problems. The behaviors of other clients may be regarded as adequate without such a program. A concern that arises is that providing reinforcers to one or a few clients for behaving in a desirable fashion and not others who are already behaving appropriately may have deleterious effects on the latter. When the clients who already behave appropriately see that only the disruptive person earns rewards, will they too become disruptive to increase their opportunity for reinforcement?

An investigation by Christy (1975) attempted to test directly whether providing reinforcement to some children in a classroom situation resulted in negative reactions on the part of others who were excluded from the reinforcement contingency. Preschool children with mild behavior problems in two classrooms received attention and food (candy, raisins, or nuts) for sitting in their seats. The children who received these consequences stayed in their seats more often than before the program. Interestingly, some of the other children not included in the program also improved. A few children initially complained about not being included but these complaints quickly extinguished. The general findings from the Christy (1975) study suggest that implementing a program for selected individuals does not reduce the performance of others. Indeed, improvements were demonstrated even for those individuals not included in the program.

Aside from the above example, considerable evidence shows that when a program is implemented to improve the behavior of one person, the behaviors of others frequently improve as well, even though they are not included in the program (Kazdin, 1979c). Reinforcement programs in classroom settings (Aaron & Bostow, 1978), the home (Resick, Forehand, & McWhorter, 1976), sheltered workshops (Kazdin, 1973c), and day-care centers (Weisberg & Clements, 1977) have shown vicarious effects so that providing reinforcing consequences to one individual improves the behavior of others. (Vicarious reinforcement will be discussed in Chapter 6.)

Programs in group settings need not be limited to the performance of one individual. Often the reason that a few individuals come to mind when considering programs is that their behavioral "problems" may involve dramatic or intense behaviors such as psychotic verbalizations, tantrums, or fighting. However, in most settings, the behavior of *all* clients can be improved in some fashion. For example, the excellent well behaved elementary school student may profit from an incentive program to improve academic performance. Although one or a few individuals in a given setting may appear to require special programs, most or all of the individuals in the setting could profit from programs in which reinforcers were systematically delivered. The reinforced behaviors need not be the same for each individual even though the available reinforcers can be the same.

Even if behavior change only is necessary for one or a few individuals, the program can be structured to include the group. Programs can be devised so that the performance of one individual (or a few) earns extra reinforcers for the group as a whole including the individual person. The group members share in the reinforcing consequences which increase their involvement in the program. Programs in which one individual earns reinforcers for the group have been very effective for children in classrooms (Kazdin & Geesey, 1977), psychiatric patients (Olson & Greenberg, 1972), and delinquents (Phillips, 1968). When peers share in the reinforcing consequences, they frequently praise appropriate behavior because they earn reinforcers whenever the client does. The peer praise may contribute greatly to behavior change in the individual for whom the contingency was designed.

The major point is that even when a program seems to be required for one or a few individuals, others can be included. The main reason investigators plan individual programs to include the peer group is not necessarily to avoid negative effects on others but rather to provide peer reinforcement (e.g., praise) and group pressure to help the individual perform appropriately. If peers profit from an individual's performance, they are likely to increase praise for that individual and socialize more with him. These beneficial effects alone warrant using group programs to change the behavior of one individual.

■ BEHAVIOR MODIFICATION IS NOTHING NEW— EVERYONE DOES IT ALL OF THE TIME

When behavior modification is described, people often are impressed with the simplicity of the principles and their familiarity with the use of the techniques. The claim is made that the principles are not new, and the techniques have been and still are widely practiced. Indeed, in everyday life operant principles are used all of the time to deal with pets, children, spouses, roommates, students, parents, and others.

In many ways, the objection that behavior modification is not new is true. First, throughout history, rewarding and punishing consequences have been used to alter behavior long before the development of behavior modification! The examples that could be cited are endless. To mention a few, Greek and Roman gladiators in the first century AD received special prizes including wreaths, crowns, money, and property for their victories in the arena; ancient Chinese soldiers received colored feathers for bravery during battle; among American Indians of the Great Plains tribes, noteworthy deeds in combat or hunting earned the privilege of telling others of the experience in public (see Kazdin, 1978b).

Aside from isolated practices where rewards were given for socially valued behaviors, large-scale applications of reward systems were used long before the development of operant conditioning. For example, in England in the early 1800s, a reinforcement system was developed to provide rewards for appropriate classroom behavior. The system, developed by Joseph Lancaster, closely resembled sophisticated token economies in the classroom by using peers to deliver reinforcers, providing incentives for academic improvement, and utilizing group contingencies (Kazdin & Pulaski, 1977). Interestingly, the program was applied in schools among several countries throughout the world and in several areas within the United States. Historical examples of large reinforcement programs also could be cited for treatment of prisoners, psychiatric patients, and other populations (Kazdin, 1978b). Just this brief list here shows that the value of reward techniques has been long recognized.

Aside from historical precedents of behavior modification, behavioral techniques are not particularly novel or new in everyday life. Principles and techniques of behavior modification are deeply woven into the fabric of major social institutions and human existence in general as evidenced by child rearing, education, business, government and law, and religion (Skinner, 1953). In child rearing, parents rely on reinforcement in the form of privileges and praise, and punishment in the form of verbal reprimands and physical discipline to control behavior. In education, teachers increase the performance of academic skills in students by using grades and point systems. In business and industry, performance on the job is reinforced with bonuses, commissions, and promotions. These applications are deliberate attempts to alter behavior with positive reinforcement. Punishment also is widely practiced as evident in law enforcement. Sentences and penalties are invoked for a variety of behaviors that society wishes to suppress ranging from acts of violence to infractions of local traffic ordinances. The deliberate use of incentives is evident even in many religions where delayed (in some cases posthumous) positive or negative events are held to be contingent upon performance during one's life. Since reinforcement and punishment are embedded in major aspects of social living, it would be false to claim that the principles or their application are new.

The principles of operant conditioning suggest that behavior is always controlled even when these principles are not deliberately applied. Everyone reinforces, punishes, and extinguishes behaviors of others in everyday interaction even though no explicit attempts may be made to control behavior. In conversation with others we may smile, show interest, or agree with the person who is talking. These events are likely to increase the probability that the other person will converse with us. On the other hand, we may also look disinterested, disagree, or yawn which may punish the behavior of someone with whom we are conversing. Extinction often is used in a very deliberate fashion. Leaving the room or ignoring someone who is talking often is used to stop someone from saying something we do not wish to hear. "Nagging" is treated in this fashion. The point is that even without realizing it, everyone in contact with others is applying consequences for behavior and thereby modifying that behavior. When we provide consequences for a response (reinforcement or punishment) or ignore it altogether (extinction), we are modifying someone's behavior. So it would seem fair to claim that behavior modification is not new and everyone is using the techniques all of the time.

In a very important sense, however, the claim is untrue. Behavior modification is characterized by the *systematic* and *consistent* application of the principles of operant conditioning. If reinforcement is employed in a behavior modification program, the behavior it follows is carefully defined and the reinforcer is applied regularly, in a similar fashion each time, and with a particular goal in mind. Reinforcement, punishment, or extinction, as typically used in everyday life, are not carried out systematically.

The inconsistent application of behavior modification techniques can be easily seen in the home. Parents often try to use reinforcement and punishment to alter the behaviors of their children. For example, for cleaning one's room, a child may earn privileges such as going over to a friend's house. Yet, the definition of room cleaning may change from day to day so that sometimes the privilege is earned for thoroughly cleaning the room while at other times only a few tasks are required. Also, each parent may define room cleaning differently so the criteria are not consistently enforced. Similarly, the privilege that serves as a reinforcer may be given "free" (i.e., noncontingently) because an opportune occasion arises for the child to go out with peers. Noncontingent delivery of the reinforcer is not likely to improve room cleaning. In short, in a very loose sense behavioral techniques are applied in everyday life, but their effects probably are weak.

The difference between the haphazard and the systematic application of behavioral techniques has been demonstrated in many different programs. For example, when teachers use such techniques as prompting, shaping, and reinforcement and apply consequences consistently and contingently, child behavior markedly changes. When the techniques are applied, but less consistently or noncontingently, little and often no change occurs (Koegel, Russo, & Rincover, 1977; Redd, 1969). Hence, consistent application of consequences that might be used in everyday life has very different effects from the effects ordinarily achieved when the techniques are applied haphazardly.

Various characteristics of behavior modification differentiate it clearly from the accidental use of reinforcement and other principles in everyday life. First, the response to be changed in behavior modification is carefully defined so that observers agree as to what constitutes occurrences of the response. Second, data are collected to ascertain the frequency with which the behavior is performed. Observers who may be parents, teachers, attendants, therapists, or the clients themselves, record the behavior over a period of time to determine the extent of the problem. Third, when the program is implemented to alter behavior, data collection continues so that any behavior change will be evident. Finally, an attempt is made to determine whether the program and not some extraneous events caused the behavior change. The explicit use of behavioral techniques requires careful and precise evaluation of behavior change. This is rarely approximated when the principles of behavior modification are applied inadvertently in everyday life.

With regard to the notion that everyone does behavior modification all of the time, it should be clear that this is only partially true. The defining characteristics of behavior modification are methodical implementation of the principles and evaluation of the effects of the contingencies. Although people apply the principles in everyday life, in most cases they do not apply them systematically. The technological advances which have been made in the application of behavioral principles, discussed throughout remaining chapters, will clearly show the distinction between systematic and nonsystematic effects of the procedures.

■ GOALS OF BEHAVIOR MODIFICATION

In discussing objections to and misconceptions of behavior modification it is important to make goals of behavior-change programs explicit. Since the objections include some valid points, the reasons for undertaking behavior modification programs need to be clear.

In most settings where behavior modification is conducted, the goal is to make long-term changes in behavior of the clients. Achieving this goal may require an artificial arrangement of the situation on a temporary basis so that behavior is systematically changed. For example, an adult retardate working in a sheltered workshop may receive privileges and money for promptness in coming to work. In light of the objections discussed earlier, one might be concerned with the individual becoming dependent upon the reinforcers. Because the world outside a sheltered workshop will offer no special privileges for promptness, will the behavior be maintained? This concern is important but premature. The *initial* goal is to develop the behavior so it is performed consistently. After the behavior is well established, procedures need to be used to ensure its maintenance. At the early stage of a program, performance is likely to depend upon the delivery of reinforcement or punishment. If the adult retardate no longer received reinforcement for his or her behavior, promptness might quickly extinguish. Yet, the goals of behavior modification are to change behavior and to have the change maintained after the program is terminated, that is, remove dependence upon the contingencies that existed during the program. General long-range goals of behavior modification require sustained performance of socially appropriate behaviors.

For any individual participating in a therapeutic environment, a major objective is to maximize the reinforcement (praise, accomplishment, esteem from others, self-esteem, social interaction) and to minimize the punishment (stigma, social censure, self-depreciation, repeated failure) in one's life. To maximize reinforcement and minimize punishment in a social milieu requires that the individual perform social and personal skills and effectively control his or her environment. To achieve the latter may require temporary artificial programming of the situation to develop basic social and personal skills. Individuals in a therapeutic environment have not responded to the somewhat irregular contingencies operative in the "real world." If reinforcement were frequent enough for these individuals or delivered in a systematic fashion in ordinary social interaction, the use of behavior modification techniques might not be required. Where specific techniques are required, the interim goal is to develop specific target behaviors to enhance social and personal competence. However, the long-term goal is to provide the individual with the greatest opportunity possible for reinforcement in everyday life. An artificially programmed environment attempts to develop behavior so that it may be responsive to reinforcement and punishment contingencies which normally occur in the natural social environment.

The behavior modification program to which some individuals are exposed may not be temporary. For example, for clients whose behavioral deficits are so great as to require institutional care, it is not readily feasible to develop behavior to a point at which the reinforcement contingencies in the natural environment will control behavior. The alternatives for treatment consist of whether or not the environment in which such individuals live should be programmed to maximize the degree of behavior change, skill acquisition, and the amount of reinforcement available. In any case, in some settings behavior modification programs may constitute a semipermanent environment. Of course, it is the goal of such programs to increase skills in various areas (e.g., personal hygiene) so that gradually fewer behaviors need to be regulated by external control.

An ultimate goal of operant techniques, and indeed most treatment techniques, is to give an individual the means of controlling his or her own behavior. Control over behavior may be transferred from external agents to the individual. With many individuals, it is feasible to train them to analyze their own responses and to apply consequences to themselves for their own behavior. Self-control training is a goal of behavior modification. Of course, with several populations for whom behavior modification techniques are implemented (e.g., severely and profoundly retarded, autistic children, and psychiatric patients), it may not be feasible to achieve this goal. In cases where individuals can be trained to control their own behaviors, many objections to behavior modification subside. For example, there is less need to be concerned with the transience of behavior change if the individual has self-control skills. Presumably, the individual's behavior can achieve or sustain a certain level of performance at any time he or she chooses to arrange the environment in such a way as to increase or to decrease that behavior.

■ NOTE

[1] This program was conducted outside of the United States several years ago. Since the time of this program, legal restrictions on the nature of treatment programs for psychiatric patients and other populations have increased to protect individual rights (see Chapter 12).

How to Identify, Define, and Assess Behavior

P eople often assume that beginning a behavior modification program means selecting a behavioral technique and simply trying it out to alter a client's behavior. In fact, essential decisions need to be made and many practical matters need to be resolved before actually attempting to change behavior. These prior steps include identifying, defining, and assessing the target behavior. Assessing the target behavior is crucial for determining the effects of the program and the extent (or lack) of client improvement. The present chapter considers the requirements for assessing behavior and evaluating whether behavior change has occurred.

■ IDENTIFYING THE GOAL OF THE PROGRAM

Implementation of a behavior modification program requires a clear statement of the goal(s) of the program and a careful description of the target behavior. Although the goal of the program is to change some behavior, the change is not made by simply focusing on the behavior alone. It is important to specify the environmental conditions associated with the behavior and the conditions which will be used to achieve behavior change. Environmental conditions include those antecedent and consequent events which bear relation to and influence behavior.

Many behavioral problems stem from a failure of behavior to be performed in the presence of particular antecedent events. These behaviors are considered to reflect a lack of appropriate stimulus control. For example, a child may complete schoolwork when he or she should be looking at the board, reciting, or playing at recess. The teacher may constantly remind the child to put his or her materials away or pay attention. Yet the child's behavior is not controlled by these instructions (antecedent events). Training may focus on instructing the child to engage in some behavior and reinforcing compliance. Similarly, parents often cajole, coax, and command their children to engage in a variety of behaviors. Yet these verbalizations often have little influence on the behavior of their children. Thus, it is important to develop behaviors in the presence of certain antecedent events.

Other situations clearly involve consideration of antecedent conditions. For example, in developing talking in a mute psychiatric patient, it is important to reinforce verbalizations only in relation to specific conditions. A patient might be reinforced for talking to other individuals (antecedent stimuli) rather than to himself. Verbalization is only appropriate under a limited number of stimulus conditions. A program must associate verbalizations with reinforcement in these "appropriate" situations so that the situations provide a cue (S^D) for talking. From the above examples, it should be evident that development of behavioral objectives requires consideration of antecedent events. Under what circumstances or in the presence of what cues should the target behavior be performed? The program ultimately will focus upon developing specific behaviors in the presence of certain cues and not in the absence of these cues.

The goal for most clients is to develop behaviors in the presence of certain stimulus conditions. For some individuals, an initial goal is to train responsiveness to certain consequent events. These individuals normally do not respond to events which play a major role in social interaction, such as attention, physical contact, praise, or mild disapproval. Autistic children have been described as unresponsive to events that are reinforcing for most children (Ferster, 1961). Similarly, delinquents and conduct-problem children in the home are often unresponsive to praise (Wahler, 1972). In such cases, contingencies are devised to alter the value of stimuli such as physical contact or praise from an adult (Lovaas et al., 1965). In these programs neutral stimuli (e.g., statements of approval) are paired with events which are reinforcing (e.g., food and termination of an aversive event). Eventually, the previously neutral stimuli serve as positive reinforcers. Once the events are established as reinforcers, the program focuses on developing specific target behaviors. Thus, establishing effective consequences is usually a preliminary goal. Once achieved, other programs are begun. For example, once autistic children are trained to be responsive to adults (i.e.,

adults serve as reinforcers), various skills are trained, including language and interpersonal communication (Lovaas & Bucher, 1974).

The main goal of a program is to alter a particular target behavior. A
target behavior may not be performed at all or infrequently, or it is
performed too frequently and should be decreased or eliminated.
Again, the above statement applies to a particular stimulus condition
(e.g., home, classroom, certain times of the day, or presence of particular individuals). Nevertheless, the main question is what *behavior* is to
be changed in the stimulus conditions specified.

■ DEFINING THE TARGET BEHAVIOR

Identification of the target behavior may appear to be a relatively
simple task. In almost all settings there is general agreement among staff
members as to the behavioral "problems" of the clients, which individuals need to be changed, and the general goals to be achieved. The
general or global statements of behavior problems which are usually
provided are insufficient for actually beginning a program. For example, it is insufficient to select as the goal alteration of aggressiveness,
learning   deficits,   speech,   social   skills,   depression,   psychotic
symptoms, self-esteem, and similar notions. Traits, general summary
labels, and personality characteristics are too general to be of much use.
Moreover, definitions of the behaviors which make up these general
lables may be idiosyncratic across different staff members, parents, and
teachers. The target behaviors have to be defined explicitly so that they
can actually be observed, measured, and agreed upon by individuals
administering the program.

As a general rule, a response definition should meet three criteria:
objectivity, clarity, and completeness (Hawkins & Dobes, 1975). To be
objective, the definition should refer to observable characteristics of
behavior or environmental events. Definitions should not refer to inner
states of the individual such as aggressiveness or emotional disturbance. To be *clear*, the definition should be so unambiguous that it
could be read, repeated, and paraphrased by observers. Reading the
definition should provide a sufficient basis for beginning actual observations. To be *complete*, the boundary conditions of the definition must
be delineated so that the responses to be included and excluded are
enumerated.

Developing a definition that is complete often creates the greatest
problem because decision rules are needed to specify how behavior
should be scored. If the range of responses included in the definition is
not described carefully, observers have to infer whether the response
has occurred. For example, a simple greeting response such as waving

one's hand to greet someone may serve as the target behavior (Stokes, Baer, & Jackson, 1974). In most instances, when a person's hand is fully extended and moving back and forth, there would be no difficulty in agreeing that the person was waving. However, ambiguous instances may require judgments on the part of observers. A child might move his or her hand once (rather than back and forth) while the arm is not extended or the child may not move his or her arm at all but simply move all fingers on one hand up and down (in the way that infants often learn to say good-bye). These latter responses are instances of waving in everyday life because we can often see others reciprocate with similar greetings. For assessment purposes, the response definition must specify whether these and related variations of waving should be scored as waving.

Before developing a definition that is objective, clear, and complete, it may be useful to observe the client on an informal basis. Descriptive notes of what behaviors occur and which events are associated with their occurrence may be useful in generating specific response definitions. For example, if a psychiatric patient is labeled as being "withdrawn," it is essential to observe the patient's behavior on the ward and to isolate those specific behaviors that have led to the use of the label. The specific behaviors become the object of change rather than the global concept.

Behavior modification programs have reported clear behavioral definitions which were developed from global and imprecise terms. For example, the focus of treatment of one program was on aggressiveness of a 12-year-old institutionalized retarded girl (Repp & Deitz, 1974). The specific behaviors assessed included biting, hitting, scratching, and kicking others. In a program conducted in the home, the focus was upon bickering among the children (Christopherson, Arnold, Hill, & Quilitch, 1972). Bickering was defined as verbal arguments between any two or all three children that were louder than the normal speaking voice. Finally, one program focused on poor communication skills of a schizophrenic patient (Fichter et al., 1976). The conversational behaviors included speaking loud enough so another person could hear him (if about ten feet away) and speaking for a specified amount of time. These examples illustrate how clear behavioral definitions can be derived from general terms which may have diverse meanings to different individuals.

A useful preliminary exercise before embarking on a behavior modification program is to select various concepts and trait labels used in everyday language and to provide alternative behavioral definitions for each one. Although the definition of the target response may differ across behavior modification programs, even for two individual who are referred to as "aggressive," practice in specifying target behaviors is valuable.

■ ASSESSMENT

Target Behaviors.   When behavior has been defined in precise terms, assessment can begin. Assessment of behavior is essential for at least two reasons. First, assessment determines the extent to which the target behavior is performed. Assessment reflects the frequency of occurrence of behavior prior to the program. The rate of preprogram behavior is referred to as the *baseline* or *operant rate*. Second, assessment is required to reflect behavior change after the program is begun. Since the major purpose of the program is to alter behavior, behavior during the program must be compared with behavior during baseline. Careful assessment throughout the program is essential.

It may be tempting to rely upon human judgment rather than objective assessment to evaluate the extent to which behavior is performed or whether change has occurred with treatment. Yet, human judgment may greatly distort the actual rate of behavior. For example, some behaviors such as tantrums may be so intense that parents or teachers may recall them as occurring very often even when they may be relatively infrequent. In contrast, some children may have so many tantrums that parents have become accustomed to a high rate and perceive tantrums as being less frequent than they really are. Judgment also may be inadequate to evaluate whether behavior change has occurred. Human judgment sometimes does not correspond to the actual records of overt behavior. Indeed, parents, teachers, and institutional staff may judge behavior as improving when there is no change or even when behavior has become worse (Kazdin, 1973e; Loeber, 1971; Schnelle, 1974). Only careful assessment reveals the extent to which behavior is performed and the degree of behavior change that has been achieved.

Stimulus Events.   Recording the occurrence of the target behavior excludes a great deal of important information which may be useful in designing a behavior modification program. Various antecedent and consequent events are likely to be associated with the performance of the target behavior. In most applied settings, social stimuli or interactions with others constitute a major category of events which influences client behavior. For example, attendants, parents, and teachers may provide verbal statements (e.g., instructions or praise), gestures (e.g., physical contact, motions, or nonverbal directives), and expressions (e.g., smiles or frowns) which exert control over behavior. These stimuli may precede (e.g., instructions) or follow (e.g., praise) the behavior focused upon in a behavior change program.

In any given setting, it is useful to obtain descriptive notes to record the events which immediately precede or follow behavior (Bijou, Peterson, & Ault, 1968). Antecedent and consequent events associated with the target behavior may lead to hypotheses about which events control behavior and thereby can be used to alter behavior. These hypotheses can be tested directly by altering the events to determine their influence on behavior. For example, informal observation may indicate that the target behavior is performed at some particular time during the day, prior to a specific event, in the presence of some other person, and so on. These clues, if borne out by careful assessment, may provide insights about stimulus conditions which exert control over the target behavior.

Observing consequences which ordinarily follow behavior is exceedingly important. If an undesirable behavior is performed consistently, it is likely that some environmental event is maintaining it. Conversely, if a desirable behavior is not performed consistently, it may be that certain environmental events (i.e., positive reinforcers) fail to follow it. In a behavior modification program it is important to assess consequences that follow behavior. In the majority of programs, consequences which follow the target response are altered in some way. To ensure that the consequences are delivered in a particular fashion (e.g., contingently and with a high frequency), they must be assessed. If they are not assessed, there is no systematic way to determine whether the consequences were altered as intended.

Antecedent or consequent events can be assessed while the target response is being recorded. Investigators frequently record (and alter) events in the environment to demonstrate their influence on target behaviors. For example, altering the frequency of parent or teacher behavior (e.g., attention and praise, disapproval and reprimands) influences the behavior of children (e.g., Hardiman, Goetz, Reuter, & LeBlanc, 1975; Kazdin & Klock, 1973; Miller & Sloane, 1976). Antecedent or consequent events that exert control over target behaviors in clients often are the *behaviors* of the staff who supervise them. Hence, the behaviors of staff need to be assessed as well as the behaviors that are controlled or developed in the clients.

■ STRATEGIES OF ASSESSMENT

Assessment of overt behavior can be accomplished in different ways. In most behavior modification programs, behaviors are assessed on the basis of discrete response occurrences or the amount of time that the response occurs. However, several variations and different types of measures are available.

Frequency Measures. Frequency counts require simply tallying the number of times the behavior occurs in a given period of time. This measure is referred to as *response rate* (frequency of the response divided by time). Measures of response rate are particularly useful when the target response is *discrete* and when the response takes a *relatively constant amount of time* each time it is performed. A discrete response has a clearly delineated beginning and end so that separate instances of the response can be counted. The performance of the behavior should take a relatively constant amount of time so that the units which are counted are approximately equal. Ongoing behaviors, such as smiling, sitting in one's seat, lying down, and talking, are difficult to record simply by counting because each response may occur for different amounts of time. For example, if a person talks to a peer for 15 seconds and to another peer for 30 minutes, these might be counted as two instances of talking. However, a great deal of information is lost by simply counting instances of talking because they differ in duration. Similarly, in a classroom setting, recording the frequency of sitting in one's seat would be difficult because a student might be in his seat for 20 minutes and this would count as one response. Also a student may change positions drastically so that it is not readily apparent when sitting is ending and beginning, that is, it may not be discrete. On the other hand, the number of times a person performs a discrete behavior is amenable to frequency recording.

Frequency measures have been used for a variety of behaviors. For example, in a program for an autistic child, frequency measures were used to assess the number of times the child engaged in social responses such as saying "hello" or sharing a toy or object with someone and the number of self-stimulatory behaviors such as rocking or repetitive pulling of her clothing (Russo & Koegel, 1977). With hospitalized psychiatric patients, one program assessed the frequency that patients engaged in intolerable acts such as assaulting someone or setting fires and social behaviors such as initiating conversation or responding to someone else (Frederiksen, Jenkins, Foy, & Eisler, 1976). In an investigation designed to eliminate seizures among brain damage, retarded, and autistic children and adolescents, treatment was evaluated by simply counting the number of seizures each day (Zlutnick, Mayville, & Moffat, 1975). There are additional examples of discrete behaviors that can be easily assessed with frequency counts, including the number of cigarettes smoked, the number of times a person attends an activity or hits another person, number of objects thrown, number of vocabulary words used, number of errors in speech, and so on.

Frequency measures require merely noting instances in which behavior occurs. Usually there is an additional requirement that behavior be observed for a constant amount of time. Of course, if behavior is observed for 20 minutes on one day and 30 minutes on another day, the frequencies are not directly comparable. However, the rate of response each day can be achieved by dividing the frequency of responses by the number of minutes observed each day. This measure will yield frequency per minute or rate of response which is comparable for different durations of observation.

A frequency measure has several desirable features for use in applied settings. First, frequency of a response is relatively simple to score for individuals working in natural settings. Keeping a tally of behavior usually is all that is required. Moreover, counting devices are available, such as golf counters worn as a wristwatch to facilitate recording. Second, frequency measures readily reflect changes over time. The number of times a response occurs is sensitive to change resulting from alterations in contingencies. Since the principles of operant conditioning refer to changes in the frequency of a response, it is desirable to observe the response frequency or rate directly. Third, and related to the above, frequency expresses the *amount* of behavior performed, which usually is of concern to individuals in applied settings. In many cases, the goal of the program is to increase or decrease the number of times a certain behavior occurs. Frequency provides a direct measure of the amount of behavior.

Discrete Categorization. Often is is very useful to classify responses into discrete categories such as correct–incorrect, performed–not performed, or appropriate–inappropriate. In many ways, discrete categorization is like a frequency measure because it is used for behaviors that have a clear beginning and end and have a constant duration. Yet, there are at least two important differences. With a frequency measure, performances of a particular behavior are tallied. The focus is on a single response. Also, the number of times the behavior may occur is theoretically unlimited. For example, one child hitting another may be measured by frequency counts. How many times the behavior (hitting) may occur has no real limit. Discrete categorization is used to measure whether several different behaviors may have occurred or not. Also, there are only a limited number of opportunities to perform the response.

For example, discrete categorization might be used to measure how messy a college student's roommate is. To do this, a checklist can be devised that lists several different behaviors such as putting away one's shoes in the closet, removing underwear from the kitchen table, putting dishes in the sink, putting food away in the refrigerator, and so on. Each morning, the behaviors on the checklist could be *categorized* as performed or not performed. Each behavior is measured separately and is categorized as performed or not. The total number of behaviors or steps that have been performed correctly constitutes the measure.

Discrete categories have been used to assess behavior in many behavior modification programs. For example, Neef, Iwata, and Page (1978) trained mentally retarded and physically handicapped young adults to ride the bus in the community. Several different behaviors related to finding the bus, boarding it, and leaving the bus were included in a checklist and classified as performed correctly or incorrectly. The effect of training was evaluated on the number of steps performed correctly. In a very different focus, Komaki and Barnett (1977) improved the execution of plays by a football team of 9 and 10-year-old boys. Each play was broken down into separate steps that the players should perform. Whether each act was performed correctly or not was tallied. A reinforcement program increased the number of steps completed correctly. In a camp setting, the cabin-cleaning behaviors of emotionally disturbed boys was evaluated using discrete categorization (Peacock, Lyman, & Rickard, 1978). Tasks such as placing coats on hooks, making beds, having no objects on the bed, putting toothbrushing materials away, and other specific acts were categorized as completed or not to evaluate the effects of the program.

Discrete categorization is very easy to use because it requires listing a number of behaviors and checking off whether they were performed. The behaviors may consist of several different steps that all relate to completion of a task such as developing dressing or grooming behaviors in retarded children. Behavior can be evaluated by noting whether or how many steps are performed (e.g., removing a shirt from the drawer, putting one arm through, then the other arm, pulling it on down over one's head, and so on). On the other hand, the behaviors need not be related to each other so that performance of one may not necessarily have anything to do with performance of another one. For example, room-cleaning behaviors are not necessarily related in the sense that doing one correctly (making one's bed) may be unrelated to another (cleaning up dishes). Hence, discrete categorization is a very flexible method of observation which allows one to assess all sorts of behaviors independently of whether they are necessarily related to each other.

Number of Clients. Occasionally, the effectiveness of behavioral programs is evaluated on the basis of the number of clients who perform a response. This measure usually is used in group situations such as a classroom or psychiatric hospital where the purpose is to increase the overall performance of a particular behavior such as coming to an activity on time, completing homework, or speaking up in a group. Once the desired behavior is defined, observations consist of noting how many participants in the group have performed the response. As with frequency and categorization measures, the observations require classifying the response as having occurred or not. But, here the *individuals* are counted rather than the number of times an individual performs the response.

Several programs have evaluated the impact of treatment on the number of people who are affected. For example, in one program, mildly retarded women in a half-way house tended to be very inactive (Johnson & Bailey, 1977). A reinforcement program increased participation in various leisure activities (e.g., painting, playing games, working on puzzles, rugmaking) and was evaluated on the number of participants who performed these activities. Another program increased the extent that senior citizens participated in a community meal program that provided low-cost nutritious meals (Bunck & Iwata, 1978). The program was evaluated on the number of new participants from the community who sought out the meals. In a large institution for the retarded, a program was designed to increase the number of residents who were included in a toilet-training program that staff were supposed to implement (Greene, Willis, Levy, & Bailey, 1978). The program focused upon increasing the frequency that staff put the residents through the training procedure but was evaluated on the number of clients participating each day.

The number of individuals who perform a response is very useful when the explicit goal of the program is to increase performance in a large group of subjects. Developing behaviors in an institution and even in society at large is consistent with this overall goal. Increasing the number of people who exercise, give to charity, or seek treatment when early stages of serious diseases are apparent, and decreasing the number of people who smoke, overeat, and commit crimes all are important goals that behavioral interventions have addressed.

A problem with the measure in many treatment programs is that it does not provide information about the performance of particular individuals. The number of people who perform a response may be increased in an institution or society at large. However, performance of any particular individual may be sporadic or very low. One really does not know how a particular individual is affected. This information may or may not be important depending upon the goals of the program. Also, reinforcement and punishment contingencies are readily reflected on the frequency of an individual's response. The principles of operant conditioning are defined on the basis of response frequency. Using the number of individuals who engage in the behavior may be less sensitive to contingency changes. The principles do not operate directly on increasing or decreasing what many people do but upon altering the response frequency of a particular person. Of course, many programs already attest to improvements in increasing the number of individuals who perform a response. The point is mentioned here merely to note that such a measure may not be the most sensitive or reflect the greatest amount of change. Nevertheless, applied behavioral research focuses on many behaviors in everyday social life such as energy consumption, leisure activity, and so on. Hence, the number of people who perform a response is of increased interest.

Interval Recording. A frequent strategy of measuring behavior in an applied setting is based on units of time rather than discrete response units. Behavior is recorded during short periods of time for the total time that it is performed. The two methods of time-based measurement are interval recording and response duration.

With interval recording, behavior is observed for a *single block of time* such as 30 or 60 minutes once per day. A block of time is divided into a series of short intervals (e.g., each interval equaling 10 or 15 seconds). The behavior of the client is observed during each interval. The target behavior is scored as having occurred or not occurred during *each* interval. If a discrete behavior, such as hitting someone, occurs one or more times in a single interval, the response is scored as having occurred. Several response occurrences within an interval are not counted separately. If the behavior is ongoing with an unclear beginning or end, such as talking, playing, and sitting, or occurs for a long period of time, it is scored during each interval in which it is occurring.

Behavior modification programs in classroom settings frequently use interval recording to score whether students are paying attention, sitting in their seats, and working quietly. Behavior of an individual student may be observed for 10-second intervals over a 20-minute observational period. For each interval, an observer records whether the child is in his or her seat working quietly. If the child remains in his seat and works for a long period of time, many intervals will be scored for attentive behavior. If the child leaves his seat (without permission) or stops working, inattentive behavior will be scored. During some intervals, a child may be in his seat for half of the time and out of seat for the remaining time. Since the interval has to be scored for *either* attentive or inattentive behavior, a rule has to be devised how to score behavior in this instance. Often, getting out of the seat will be counted as inattentive behavior and will nullify the remaining period of attentive behavior within the interval.

Interval recording for a single block of time has been used in many programs beyond the classroom setting. For example, one program focused upon several inappropriate child behaviors (e.g., roughhousing, touching objects, playing with merchandise) that children performed while they accompanied their parents during shopping (Clark et al., 1977, Exp. 3). Observers followed the family in the store to record whether the inappropriate behaviors occurred during consecutive 15-second intervals. Interval assessment was also used in a program to develop conversational skills in delinquent girls (Minkin et al., 1976). Observations were made of whether appropriate conversational behaviors occurred (asking questions of another person and making comments that indicated understanding or agreement with what the other person said) during 10-second intervals while the youths conversed.

Interval scoring of behavior is facilitated by a scoring sheet where intervals are represented across time (see Figure 4–1). In Figure 4–1,

Intervals

1	2	3	4	5	6	7	8	9	10
+ 0	+ 0	+ 0	+ 0	+ 0	+ 0	+ 0	+ 0	+ 0	+ 0

Circle appropriate symbol in each interval
+ = behavior occurred during interval
0 = behavior did not occur during interval

FIGURE 4–1 Example of interval scoring sheet for one individual.

each number across the top denotes a time interval. During each interval a "+" or "0" is circled or checked to denote whether the behavior has occurred for the subject. The basic sheet can be expanded to include many individuals and intervals as shown in Figure 4–2. For example, each individual in a classroom or on a ward can be observed for a large number of intervals. The first subject would be observed for the first interval (e.g., 15 seconds). After behavior was recorded, the second

Intervals

	1	2	3	4	5	6	7	8	9	10
1	+ 0	+ 0	+ 0	+ 0	+ 0	+ 0	+ 0	+ 0	+ 0	+ 0
2	+ 0	+ 0	+ 0	+ 0	+ 0	+ 0	+ 0	+ 0	+ 0	+ 0
3	+ 0	+ 0	+ 0	+ 0	+ 0	+ 0	+ 0	+ 0	+ 0	+ 0
4	+ 0	+ 0	+ 0	+ 0	+ 0	+ 0	+ 0	+ 0	+ 0	+ 0
5	+ 0	+ 0	+ 0	+ 0	+ 0	+ 0	+ 0	+ 0	+ 0	+ 0
6	+ 0	+ 0	+ 0	+ 0	+ 0	+ 0	+ 0	+ 0	+ 0	+ 0
7	+ 0	+ 0	+ 0	+ 0	+ 0	+ 0	+ 0	+ 0	+ 0	+ 0
8	+ 0	+ 0	+ 0	+ 0	+ 0	+ 0	+ 0	+ 0	+ 0	+ 0
9	+ 0	+ 0	+ 0	+ 0	+ 0	+ 0	+ 0	+ 0	+ 0	+ 0
10	+ 0	+ 0	+ 0	+ 0	+ 0	+ 0	+ 0	+ 0	+ 0	+ 0

(Individuals)

FIGURE 4–2 Example of interval scoring sheet for many individuals.

subject would be observed. This would be continued until each subject has been observed for one interval (down the left column in Figure 4–2). The order would then be repeated until each subject was observed for another interval, and so on for remaining intervals. Often more than one behavior is scored in an interval so that the presence of several behaviors will be judged during each interval. To accomplish this, a data sheet may include many symbols in each interval block so various behaviors can be coded. A letter or symbol is checked or circled for different categories of behavior which occur during the interval.

In using an interval scoring method, an observer looks at the client during the interval. When one interval is over, the observer records whether the behavior occurred. If an observer is recording several behaviors in an interval, a few seconds may be needed to record all the behaviors that were observed in that interval. If the observer recorded a behavior as soon as it occurred (before the interval was over), he or she might miss other behaviors which occurred while the first behavior was being scored. Hence, many investigators use interval scoring procedures which allow time to record after each interval of observation. Intervals for observing behavior might be ten seconds, with five seconds after the interval for recording these observations. If a single behavior is scored in an interval, no time may be required for recording. Each interval might be ten seconds. As soon as a behavior occurred, it would be scored immediately. If behavior did not occur, a quick mark could indicate this at the end of the interval. Of course, it is desirable to use short recording times, when possible, because when behavior is being recorded, it is not being observed. Recording consumes time that might be used for observing behavior.

A variation of interval recording is referred to as *time-sampling*. This variation uses the interval method but the observations are conducted for brief periods at different times rather than in a single block of time. For example, with an interval method, a child might be observed for a 30-minute period. The period would be broken down into small intervals such as 10 seconds. With the time sampling method, the child might be observed for 10-second intervals but these intervals might be spread out over a full day instead of a single block of time.

As an illustration, psychiatric patients participating in a hospital reinforcement program were evaluated with time-sampling procedures (Paul & Lentz, 1977). Patients were observed each hour, at which point an observer looked at the patient for a two-second interval. At the end of the interval, the observer recorded the presence or absence of several behaviors related to the social interaction, activities, self-care, and other responses. The procedure was continued throughout the day sampling one interval at a time. The advantage of time sampling is that the observations represent performance over the entire day. Performance during one single time block (such as the morning) might not represent performance over the entire day.

There are significant features of interval recording which make it one of the most widely adopted strategies in applied settings. First, interval assessment is very flexible because virtually any behavior can be recorded. The presence or absence of a response during a time interval applies to any measurable response. Whether a response is discrete and does not vary in duration, is continuous, or sporadic, it can be classified as occurring or not occurring during any time period. Second, the observations resulting from interval recording can be easily converted into a percentage. The number of intervals during which the response is scored as occurring can be divided by the total number of intervals observed. This ratio multiplied by 100 yields a percentage of intervals that the response is performed. For example, if social responses are scored as occurring in 20 or 40 intervals that were observed, the percentage of intervals of social behavior is 50 percent (20/40 x 100). A percentage is easily communicated to others by noting that a certain behavior occurs a specific percentage of time (intervals). (Categorization measures also can provide a percentage of responses. For example, correct responses on an examination are readily converted into a percentage by forming a ratio of correct responses to total responses and multiplying by 100.) Whenever there is doubt as to what assessment strategy should be adopted, an interval approach is always applicable and can be readily employed. Yet, as discussed below, some practical considerations make interval recording more cumbersome than a simple frequency measure.

Duration.   Another time-based method of observation is *duration* or amount of time that the response is performed. This method is particularly useful for ongoing responses that are continuous rather than discrete acts or responses of extremely short duration. Programs that attempt to increase or decrease the length of time a response is performed might profit from a duration method.

Duration has been used in fewer studies than interval observations. As an example, one investigation trained two severely withdrawn children to engage in social interaction with other children (Whitman, Mercurio, & Caponigri, 1970). Interaction was measured by simply recording the amount of time that children were in contact with each other. Duration has been used for other responses such as the length of time that claustrophobic patient spent sitting voluntarily in a small room (Leitenberg, Agras, Thompson, & Wright, 1968), the time delinquent boys spent returning from school and errands (Phillips, 1968), and the time students spent working on assignments (Surratt, Ulrich, & Hawkins, 1969).

Another measure based upon duration is not how long the response is performed but rather how long it takes for the client to begin the response. The amount of time that elapses between a cue and the response is referred to as *latency*. Many programs have timed response latency to evaluate treatment. For example, in one report, an 8-year-old boy took extremely long to comply with classroom instructions which contributed to his academic difficulties (Fjellstedt & Sulzer-Azaroff, 1973). Reinforcing consequences were provided to decrease his response latencies when instructions were given. Compliance with instructions became much more rapid over the course of the program.

Assessment of response duration is a fairly simple matter requiring that one starts and stops a stopwatch or notes the time when the response begins and ends. However, the onset and termination of the response must be carefully defined. If these conditions have not been met, duration is extremely difficult to employ. For example, in recording the duration of a tantrum, a child may cry continuously for several minutes, whimper for short periods, stop all noise for a few seconds, and begin intense crying again. In recording duration, a decision is required to handle changes in the intensity of the behavior (e.g., crying to whimpering) and pauses (e.g., periods of silence) so they are consistently recorded as part of the response or as a different (e.g., nontantrum) response.

Use of response duration is generally restricted to situations where the length of time a behavior is performed is a major concern. In most behavior modification programs, the goal is to increase or decrease the frequency of a response rather than its duration. There are notable exceptions, of course. For example, it is desirable to increase the length of time that students study. However, because interval measures are so widely used and readily adaptable to virtually all responses, they are often selected as a measure over duration. The number or proportion of intervals in which study behavior occurs reflects changes in study time since interval recording is based on time.

Selection of an Assessment Strategy.   One of the above methods of assessment usually is used in behavioral programs. Occasionally, other measures might be used because they provide direct measures of behavior that are of obvious importance. For example, behavior modification programs for obesity or cigarette smoking have evaluated intervention effects by simply looking at client weight in pounds or the number of cigarettes smoked (Aragona, Cassady, & Drabman, 1975; Dericco, Brigham, & Garlington, 1977). In other programs, the specific behavior may lend itself to a measure unique to the investigation. For example, interventions designed to reduce energy consumption can monitor gas or electric meters or look at a car's odometer to record whether home or car use of energy has changed (Foxx & Hake, 1977; Palmer, Lloyd & Lloyd, 1977).

In most situations, the investigator needs to develop an assessment procedure based upon frequency, interval, or one of the other methods mentioned above. Some behaviors may lend themselves well to frequency counts or categorization because they are discrete, such as the number of profane words used or the number of toileting or eating responses; others to interval recording such as reading, working, or sitting; and still others to duration such as time spent studying, crying, or getting dressed. Target behaviors usually can be assessed in more than one way so there is no single strategy that must be adopted. For example, an investigator working in an institution for delinquents may wish to record aggressive behavior of a client. Hitting others (e.g., making physical contact with another individual with a closed fist) may be the response of interest. What assessment strategy should be used?

Aggressive behavior might be measured with a frequency count by having an observer record how many times the client hits others during a certain period each day. Each hit would count as one response. The behavior also could be observed using interval recording. A block of time such as 30 minutes could be set aside for observation. The 30 minutes could be divided into 10-second intervals. During each interval, the observer records whether any hitting occurs. A duration measure might be used. It might be difficult to time the duration of hitting because instances of hitting are too fast to start and stop a stopwatch unless there was a series of hits (as in a fight). An easier duration measure might be to record the amount of time from the beginning of each day until the first aggressive response. This is a latency measure and records the time without hitting. Presumably, if a program decreased aggressive behavior, the amount of time from the beginning of the day until the first aggressive response would increase.

Although many different measures can be used in a given program, the measure finally selected may be dictated by the purpose of the program. Different measures sometimes have slightly different goals. For example, consider two behavioral programs that focused upon increasing toothbrushing, a seemingly simple response could be assessed in many different ways. In one of the programs, the *number of individuals* who brushed their teeth in a boys summer camp was observed (Lattal, 1969). The boys knew how to brush their teeth, and an incentive system increased their performance of the response. In another program that increased toothbrushing, the clients were mentally retarded residents at a state hospital (Horner & Keilitz, 1975). The residents were unable to brush their teeth at the beginning of the program so the many behaviors involved in toothbrushing were developed. *Discrete categorization* was used to assess toothbrushing where each component step of the behavior (wetting the brush, removing the cap, applying the toothpaste, and so on) was scored as performed or not performed. The percent of steps correctly completed measured the effects of training. Although both of the above investigations assessed tooth-brushing, the different methods reflect slightly different goals, namely, getting children who can brush to do so or training the response in individual residents who did not know how to perform the response.

■ ISSUES AND PROBLEMS IN SAMPLING BEHAVIOR

The purpose of assessment is to provide a sample of the extent to which behavior is performed over the total period of time that behavior change is desired. Performance fluctuates over time on a given day and across days and weeks. It is important to determine the level of behavior without allowing the fluctuations to misrepresent the overall rate. If behavior were unvarying in its level over each hour and each day, any sample of that behavior (e.g., one hour) would be representative of behavior at all other times. For example, if behavior were performed once every 10 minutes of a client's waking hours, establishing the baseline rate of behavior would require one single 10-minute period. This assessment would accurately reflect performance. However, behavior is rarely performed at a consistent rate. (The only time there is virtually complete consistency is when the behavior is never performed and the rate is zero.) Thus, to obtain a representative sample, assessment must be carried out over an extended period of time.

Three decisions need to be made regarding the observations that are required. First, the number of times that data will be collected must be decided. When possible, it is desirable to observe behavior each day or during each session (e.g., in a classroom) that the target behavior may occur. The frequency of observation depends upon various factors including the variation of behavior over time, the availability of observers, and scheduling exigencies in the treatment setting. If the target behavior is very stable from one day to the next, daily assessment becomes less essential than if behavior fluctuates radically. Investigators have shown that observation of behavior every other day closely approximates the average rate obtained from daily observations (Bijou et al., 1969). As a general rule, behavior should be observed on as many occasions as possible. However, convenience and practical exigencies necessarily dictate the actual schedule. In many settings, there may not always be individuals who can devote time to recording behavior.

A second decision to be made prior to beginning assessment is the length of time set aside for a given observation period. As with the previous decision, demands of the setting (e.g., schedule of activities), observer availability, difficulty in recording behavior, and the frequency of the behavior determine this decision. However, the guiding general rule is that behavior should be observed for a period of time that will yield data representative of typical performance. The information should represent performance over the entire period of interest. For example, if it is desirable to alter behavior in the classroom, observational data should reflect performance over a relatively long period (e.g., one hour) rather than just a few minutes. For some behavioral problems or in some settings, the target behavior occurs for a specific period during the day. An observation period should be a period of time which provides a representative sample of performance. If a response has a low rate of occurrence, it might be possible simply to tally the behavior for an entire day. Observation of a low frequency behavior for a total of only five minutes per day may be too short to obtain a representative sample of behavior. Large periods of observation are not always required to reflect behavior change. For example, in studies in classroom settings, students may be observed for as little as 15 minutes each per observation period. However, it is unclear that performance during a short observation period represents performance over the entire school day.

A third decision related to the length of time behavior is observed is when the observations are conducted. Observations using frequency, interval, or duration methods can record behavior in a block of time in a single day or at different times throughout the day. The advantage of sampling behavior at various times over the entire day is that the observed behavior is more likely to be representative of behavior over different time periods.

Whether a sample of behavior represents behavior over the entire period of interest cannot be determined in advance. Assessment conducted at different times can be used to determine whether performance varies throughout the day. For practical reasons, often it is unfeasible to observe behavior over several periods throughout the day. In these instances, behavior might be observed for a single block of time during that period in which behavior change is most obviously required. An initial assessment over a few days at different times can determine those periods which in fact require the greatest attention. Subsequently, assessment can focus on those periods.

In addition to the above decisions, if interval assessment is used, the duration of the interval has to be decided. Although observations may be made for 30 minutes or one hour each day, the length of intervals within that period must be decided. If behavior occurs at a high rate or is an ongoing response, relatively short intervals might be used (e.g., 10 or 15 seconds). Longer intervals (such as 60 seconds) would exclude much of the responding because the interval is recorded for the presence or absence of only one response. If the behavior occurs 20 times during one 60-second interval, the interval is scored upon the occurrence of the first response. The behavior cannot be scored again until the next interval. However, a great deal of behavior has gone unrecorded. As a result of a behavior modification program, behavior may change from 20 to 10 times per 60-second interval. However, this change will not be reflected in the data because the interval will continue to be scored for the presence of the response. Thus, there are several points to consider which dictate the duration of intervals.

First, interval duration should be relatively short (e.g., 10 or 15 seconds) for discrete behaviors which occur frequently. Second, very short intervals (e.g., 5 or fewer seconds) sometimes are difficult to score reliably because observers have difficulty in synchronizing observations. The interval is so short that it is not clear in which interval the behavior was performed. Third, if behavior is continuous (e.g., reading or watching television), the length of the interval may not be as important as when behavior is discrete because shorter or longer intervals are not likely to exclude "instances" of behavior. Many studies have used 10-second intervals, whereas others have reported intervals of one or a few minutes. Since there are no fixed rules for interval length, a wide range of durations has been employed.

■ CONDUCTING OBSERVATIONS

Observations usually are completed by placing one or more observers in a position to see the client. Occasionally, the observer may be out of sight such as behind a one-way mirror in an observation booth that is adjacent to a classroom or hospital ward. Other times, the observations may be taken from videotapes so the observer is not present in the situation. Yet, in most studies, observers are in the situation such as the home, on the ward, or in the classroom where the client is present.

If the clients are aware of the observer's presence, the assessment procedure is said to be *obtrusive*. A potential problem with obtrusive assessment is that the client's behavior may be affected by knowing that observations are made. Assessment is *reactive* if the observer's presence alters the client's behavior.

A few investigations have evaluated whether the presence of observers affects the behavior of the clients, i.e., is reactive. In many cases, the presence of an observer has little or no effect on the behaviors that are observed (e.g., Nelson, Kapust, & Dorsey, 1978; Mercatoris & Craighead, 1974), although there are exceptions (White, 1977). As a precaution, many investigators place the observer into the situation on several occasions prior to actual assessment. For example, in a classroom situation an observer may conduct the observations for a week or two merely to have the children become accustomed to the procedures. The children become accustomed quickly and respond as they normally would if the observer were not present. This can be facilitated by minimizing any interaction between observers and the client. The observer may avoid eye contact, smiles, and conversation which might maintain the child's interest in the observer.

Another consideration for observing behavior pertains to the observers themselves. It is important not to provide observers with feedback about whether the intervention is having the intended effects. Telling observers that improvements in performance are expected and then providing them with praise when their data sheets reflect this expectation can lead to biased observations (O'Leary, Kent, & Kanowitz, 1975). Hence, observers should not be given feedback for their observations, at least feedback that tells them whether they provided the sort of information that the investigators want and expect. Of course, it is likely that observers will develop their own expectations when they see treatment implemented or detect the investigator's expectations. For example, when a reinforcement program is used with a hyperactive child, it is not difficult to conclude what everyone is expecting. Yet, even when observers expect behavior change, their observations may not reflect the expected change (Kent et al., 1974).

Another issue important in conducting observations pertains to the definitions of behaviors that observers use. In most programs, many different observers are used. When observers are first trained to record behavior, they may adhere to the same definition of behavior. Once observers master the definition, it is often assumed that they continue to apply the same definition and to record behavior accurately. However, evidence suggests that observers "drift" or gradually depart from the original definitions over time (Kent, Kanowitz, O'Leary, & Cheiken, 1977; Kent, O'Leary, Diament, & Dietz, 1974). For example, if observers record talking out in a class of students, the criterion for scoring the behavior may gradually change over time from the original definition. Whispers or brief vocalizations may be scored differently over time. The threshold for the observers to score the behavior may change.

To ensure that observers adhere to consistent definitions over time, many programs conduct periodic training of observers throughout a behavior modification program. Observers may meet as a group, rate behavior in the situation or from video tapes and receive feedback on the accuracy of the observations. The feedback conveys the extent to which observers correctly invoke the definitions for scoring behavior. Feedback about accuracy in applying the definitions helps reduce drift from the original behavioral codes (DeMaster, Reid, & Twentyman, 1977). (This feedback for accuracy in completing the observations is distinguished from the feedback mentioned earlier in which the investigator tells observers that the data are in line with what was expected.) Other recommendations have been provided for handling problems arising from reactive assessment, observer expectancies, and observer drift (Kazdin, 1977a, 1979b; Kent & Foster, 1977).

■ RELIABILITY OF ASSESSMENT

Need for Reliability. Independently of the assessment strategy used, it is important for individuals who observe the target behavior to agree on the occurrence of the response. Interobserver agreement, often referred to as *reliability* of assessment, is important for three major reasons. First, assessment is useful only when it can be achieved with some consistency. For example, if frequency counts differ greatly depending upon who is counting, it will be difficult to know what the client's actual performance is. The client may be scored as performing a response frequently on some days and infrequently on other days as a function of observers who score behavior rather than differences in actual client performance. Inconsistent measurement introduces variation in the data which adds to the variation stemming from "normal" fluctuations in client performance. If measurement variation is large, there may *appear* to be no systematic pattern to the behavior. If a behavior modification program were implemented, it might be difficult to determine whether behavior is changing because the data are highly variable as a function of inconsistent recording. Stable patterns of behavior are required to reflect behavior change. Hence, reliable recording is essential.

Even if there is a systematic pattern to behavior, there is a second reason for obtaining reliability. If a single observer is used to record the target behavior, any recorded change in behavior may result from a change in the observer's definition of the target behavior rather than in the actual behavior of the client. The observer might become lenient or stringent over time. For example, after a behavior modification program is introduced, the observer may perceive improvement in the target behavior even though no improvement actually occurs. If the program is withdrawn, the observer may expect behavior to become worse and reflect this expectation in inaccurate recording. Thus, an observer may unintentionally introduce systematic error which presents biased observation of behavior. Using several observers who vary in their familiarity with the program may help determine whether the definition of the target behavior changes as a function of a particular observer.

A final reason that agreement between observers is important is that it reflects whether the target behavior is well defined. If observers readily agree on the occurrence of the behavior, it will be easier for individuals carrying out the program (administering reinforcement or punishment) to agree on the occurrence of a response. If a response can be observed consistently, it is more likely to be reinforced or punished consistently.

Conducting Reliability Checks. Reliability checks need to be made before baseline data are gathered to ensure that the behavior is agreed upon. A few days of prebaseline observation usually are useful to finalize the rules for observing behavior and to handle instances in which it is not clear whether the target behavior has occurred. Once baseline begins, reliability checks need to be continued intermittently throughout the program to ensure that behavior is consistently observed. If checks are made only at the inception of the program, over time observers may become increasingly lax in their scoring. Hence, observations may become less reliable. In addition, systematic biases may influence observers so that they record improvement while a program is in effect, even though there is no actual change in the client's behavior. Also, idiosyncratic patterns of observing and interpreting behavior may change over time, so that there appears to be no systematic pattern in the client's behavior. Typically, reliability should be assessed intermittently (e.g., once a week or every three or four days) over the course of the project. When reliability is consistently high (near or at 100%), fewer checks would be required.

Reliability has to achieve an acceptable level prior to beginning baseline observations and to maintain this level throughout the project. Although no single criterion for acceptable agreement has been set, convention dictates agreement should be between 80 and 100 percent. Reliability lower than 80 percent suggests that a moderate amount of error occurs in recording. In many instances, low reliability signals that the response definition should be more carefully specified. Obtaining low reliability is no reason to be discouraged before a program is begun. It is a signal that additional work in specifying behavior is required. It is desirable to find this out early so the response definition can be clarified for those who administer the program as well as for those who observe behavior.

During the last several years, research has shown that how the reliability checks are conducted may influence the level of interobserver agreement. Hence, in addition to specifying the level of agreement, it is important to ensure that this is obtained under carefully conducted conditions. A major factor that may influence interobserver agreement is whether observers know that their agreement is being checked. When observers are aware that reliability is being assessed, they tend to show higher agreement than when they are led to believe their agreement is not under scrutiny (e.g., Kent et al., 1974, 1977). Also, knowledge that reliability is being assessed may even influence the behaviors that observers record. In some studies, observers have recorded less disruptive behavior when they were aware that their agreement was checked relative to when they were unaware (Reid, 1970; Romanczyk, Kent, Diament, & O'Leary, 1973).

It is important to make the conditions of assessment consistent on days that reliability is assessed and is not assessed. It may be useful to convey that all observations are being checked so that the data obtained on days with actual reliability assessment will not differ from non-checked days. Alternatively, it might be possible to conduct reliability checks without observers even knowing the checks were obtained. Observers could record the behavior of many different subjects. However, for some of the observation period, the observers may actually record data for the same subject.

In practice, it is difficult to conduct reliability checks without another observer knowing that a check is being made. Observers usually can tell they are observing the same individual at the same time, especially if something such as a child getting out of his or her seat in a classroom momentarily interferes with completing the observations. It might be easier to convey to observers that their observations are being checked all of the time and let them be aware of constant checking. Since observers tend to be more accurate when they believe their agreement is assessed, keeping them aware and informed of frequent reliability checks might be advantageous, even on days in which no checks are made (Reid, 1970; Taplin & Reid, 1973).

In general, reliability assessment should be structured so as to minimize the possibility of bias in judging how well observers agree with each other. First, observers should work independently without access to each other's scoring sheet. If observers communicate with each other or look at each other's sheet, their agreement may be inflated because they are influencing each other. Second, observers should be supervised during a reliability check. Supervision ensures that the observations are independent, particularly if observers are aware of the supervision. Third, observers should be unaware of the contingencies to alter client behavior and when these contingencies are implemented, if it is possible to hide this information. If all observers cannot be unaware, it may be useful to bring in an observer to check reliability who is unfamiliar with the program for the child and is less likely to present biased data. Finally, observers should not compute their own interobserver agreement. Observers left on their own to assess how well they are agreeing with each other tend to calculate higher reliability estimates than estimates calculated by an experimenter (Kent et al., 1974). If the above conditions can be met or closely approximated, the interpretation of interobserver agreement is likely to reflect the clarity of the behavioral codes and the extent to which observers agree in their behavioral definitions.

Estimating Reliability. Reliability provides an estimate of how consistently behavior is observed and scored. The procedures for estimating reliability differ somewhat depending upon the assessment method used. The procedures that estimate agreement for frequency and interval methods are described here because they can readily be adapted to the other assessment procedures.

Reliability of frequency measurement requires that two observers simultaneously, but independently, count the target response during the time set aside for observation. At the end of the observation period, the frequencies obtained by the observers are compared. The major interest is whether each observer records the target behavior with equal frequency. A percentage of agreement can be formed to measure the degree to which two observers agree in their final counts.

For any two observers, it is likely that they do not agree perfectly in their recorded frequency. That is, one observer will obtain a lower frequency count than the other. To determine the percentage of agreement, a fraction is formed from the frequency obtained by each observer. *Reliability is determined by dividing the smaller frequency by the larger frequency and multiplying by 100.* For example, in the home, parents may count the number of times a child spills food on the floor during a meal. During a reliability check, both parents independently count food spills. By the end of the meal, one parent has counted 20 instances of spilling, whereas the other parent has counted 18 instances. To form a percentage of agreement, the smaller number (18) is divided by the larger number (20) and multiplied by 100. Agreement for this observation period was 90 percent (18/20 × 100).

Interpretation of this percentage must be made cautiously. The figure indicates that observers agree on the total frequency of the behavior with a 10 percent (100 percent minus 90 percent) margin of error. It does not mean that the observers agree 90 percent of the time. Although one observer recorded 18 responses and the other recorded 20 responses, there is no way of knowing whether they recorded the *same* responses. For example, if both observers each recorded 18 responses, the percent of agreement would be 100 percent. Yet one observer may have seen 18 responses that were different from the 18 responses seen by the other observer. Although this is unlikely, it is possible that at least some of the responses recorded may not have been for the *same* behaviors. Thus, reliability reflects agreement on the total number of responses rather than agreement in any specific instance. A potential disadvantage in using a frequency measure is that when the behavior is not carefully defined, a high percentage of agreement for frequency data may still conceal a substantial amount of disagreement.

When response duration is used as the measure, calculation of reliability is similar to the above formula. Two observers independently record the duration of the behavior during an observation session.

Agreement is calculated by forming a fraction from the totals obtained by the observers. The smaller duration is divided by the larger duration and multiplied by 100. Similarly, when the measure is the number of clients who participate, agreement can be calculated by forming a fraction from the totals of the two observers (smaller number/larger number, multiplied by 100).

Calculation of reliability is different when an interval method of assessment is used. Reliability usually is computed on the basis of the proportion of intervals that two observers agree on the occurrence of a target response. An agreement is scored if both observers record the occurrence of behavior in the same interval. A disagreement is scored when one observer scores a behavior in an interval and the other does not. For example, a reliability check made between two observers independently recording aggressive behavior of a student in an elementary school classroom requires both observers to begin observing the child at the same time. Each observer records behaviors for several intervals. During each interval that the child is observed, the observer marks the occurrence or nonoccurrence of aggressive behavior. (If several different children are observed, the observers merely continue to look at different children in different intervals. Of course, both observers are always assessing the same child at the same time.) When the observers finish recording, reliability can be calculated.

Reliability is determined by dividing the number of intervals in which both observers mark the behavior as occurring (agreements) by the number of agreements plus the number of intervals in which one observer scored the behavior and the other did not (disagreements) and multiplying by 100. For example, if observers recorded behavior for 50 10-second intervals and both observers agreed on the occurrence of the behavior in 20 intervals and disagreed in 5 intervals, reliability would be $20/(20 + 5) \times 100$, or 80 percent.

Although observers recorded behavior for 50 intervals, all intervals were not used to calculate reliability. An interval is counted only if at least one observer recorded the *occurrence* of the target behavior. Excluding intervals in which neither observer records the target behavior is based on the following reasoning. If these intervals were counted, they would be considered as agreements since both observers "agree" that the response did not occur. Yet in observing behavior, many intervals may be marked without the occurrence of the target behavior. If these were included as agreements in the calculation of reliability, the reliability estimate would be inflated beyond the level obtained when occurrences alone were counted as agreements. In the above example, behavior was not scored as occurring by either observer in 25 intervals. By counting these as agreements, reliability would increase to 90 percent ($45/(45 + 5) \times 100 = 90$ percent) rather than 80 percent obtained originally. To avoid this increase in reliability, most investigators restrict agreements to response occurrence intervals.

The formula for estimating reliability for interval assessment can be used when discrete category rather than interval assessment is used. For example, if two observers record the occurrence or nonoccurrence of 10 room-cleaning behaviors, comparison of how each observer scored each behavior would yield agreements and disagreements that can be placed into the above formula. Reliability consists of the number of categories or behaviors that observers agreed upon divided by agreements plus disagreements and multiplied by 100.

The formula for estimating reliability for interval assessment given above is very commonly used. Yet, many investigators have questioned its adequacy. The main concern is whether agreement should be restricted to intervals where both observers record an occurrence of the behavior or also should include intervals where both say there is a nonoccurrence. In one sense, both types indicate that observers were in agreement for a particular interval. The issue is important because the estimate of reliability seems to depend upon the frequency of the client's behavior and whether occurrence and/or nonoccurrence agreements are included in the formula. If the client performs the target behavior relatively frequently or infrequently, observers are likely to have a high proportion of agreements on occurrences or nonoccurrences, respectively. Hence, the estimate of reliability may differ greatly depending upon what is counted as an agreement between observers. Several investigators have discussed the problem of deciding what should be counted as an agreement and have suggested additional formulae for possible ways of using both occurrence and nonoccurrence intervals (Harris & Lahey, 1978; Hawkins & Dotson, 1975; Hopkins & Hermann, 1977).

■ SUMMARY AND CONCLUSION

Prior to beginning a behavior modification program, the target behavior needs to be identified and carefully defined. The definition should ensure that few inferences need to be made by observers who assess behavior and others who ultimately will be responsible for providing consequences to alter behavior. Several different methods of assessment are available including frequency counts, discrete categorization, the number of clients who perform the response, interval assessment, and response duration.

Once the assessment strategy is selected, it is essential to evaluate the extent to which observers agree when scoring the response. Interobserver agreement or reliability of assessment is evaluated while observers record the response independently. The exact formula in which reliability is estimated varies depending upon the assessment method.

Also, the interpretation of reliability estimates depends upon the conditions under when reliability is conducted. Observers often slightly alter the definitions of behavior they invoke over the course of a program. Periodic training and constant reliability assessment help ensure that the observations reflect the client's actual performance. Assessment of the target behavior provides an important step that needs to be resolved adequately prior to actually implementing contingencies to alter client performance.

How to Evaluate a Behavior Modification Program

Assessment of behavior change is essential in behavior modification. Assessment may reveal that behavior has changed but it does not show what caused behavior change. Proponents of behavior modification are extremely interested in determining the cause of behavior change. Once the cause of behavior change is clear, our knowledge about the variables that control behavior is increased. Also, if treatment can be shown to be responsible for change, it can be applied to the same person in the future and to clients in other settings with increased confidence that behavior may change in the new applications as well.

In many cases, the person who conducts the program may only be interested in obtaining change in behavior rather than isolating the cause of the change. Determining the cause of behavior change may not be very important as long as the goal is achieved. Yet, for understanding behavior change, discovery of the cause is important. It is possible for behavior to change without the behavior modification program actually being responsible for that change.

For example, a program might be carried out in a home to reduce the frequency of fighting in two children. After a few weeks of recording fighting (baseline), a program is begun (e.g., praising the children for playing cooperatively). Assessment may reveal that behavior changed once praise was delivered for cooperative play. Was the delivery of praise responsible for behavior change? Alternative explanations of the change might be advanced. For example, there may have been changes at school which led to changes in the fighting at home. Further, one of the children may have been physically ill and irritable but improved at the same time the program began (or was healthy and became ill when the program began and had less opportunity to fight). Similarly, changes in behavior of the children's peers or parents (in addition to praising the child) may have contributed to behavior change. All of these explanations need to be ruled out to claim that praise was responsible for behavior change.

The cause of behavior change can be demonstrated in different ways. The person who designs the program must plan the situation so that the specific contribution of the program to behavior change can be demonstrated. The plan of the program which is used to demonstrate what accounted for behavior change is referred to as the *experimental design*. Different experimental designs can be used to show that the program, rather than extraneous events, altered behavior.[1]

■ REVERSAL OR ABAB DESIGN

The reversal design demonstrates the effect of the behavior modification program by alternating presentation and removal of the program over time. The purpose of the design is to demonstrate a *functional relationship* between the target behavior and the experimental condition (program). A functional relationship is demonstrated when alteration of the experimental condition or contingency results in a systematic change in behavior. Behavior is a function of the environmental events which produced change.

In a reversal design, behavior is assessed to obtain the baseline rate of performance prior to implementing specific contingencies. The baseline period or phase (referred to as the A phase) is continued until the rate of the response appears to be stable or until it is evident that the response does not improve over time. A stable rate of behavior during baseline serves as a basis for evaluating subsequent change. Baseline provides an estimate of what behavior would be in the future if the program were not introduced. After behavior stabilizes and follows a consistent pattern (several days are usually sufficient), the experimental phase is begun. During the experimental phase, the behavior modification procedure (e.g., reinforcement, punishment, extinction or some combination of procedures) is implemented. The experimental phase (referred to as the B phase) is continued until behavior reaches a stable level or diverges from the level predicted by the baseline rate.

Figure 5–1 provides a hypothetical example of observations of some desirable behavior plotted over several days. Although the behavior fluctuates during baseline, there is a reasonably stable pattern or a fairly narrow range within which the frequency occurs. During the experi-

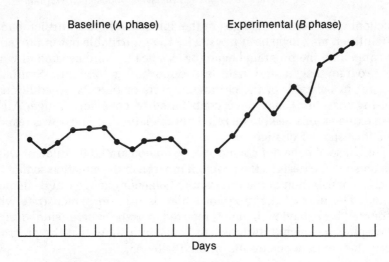

FIGURE 5-1   Hypothetical rate of some behavior plotted over baseline and experimental phases.

mental phase (e.g., reinforcement of the target behavior), there is an increase in performance. Up to this point in the program, the *change* in behavior is evident. However, the *cause* of the change is unclear. Since the change in behavior coincides with implementation of the program, it is likely that the program accounts for the change. However, one cannot be sure.

After behavior attains a stable level, the experimental condition is withdrawn and the baseline condition (A phase) is reinstated. During the baseline condition, of course, no program or intervention is used to control behavior. A return to baseline conditions is called a *reversal* phase because the experimental condition is withdrawn and behavior usually reverses (i.e., returns to or near the level of the original baseline). The purpose of the reversal phase is to determine whether performance would have remained unchanged (relative to baseline) had the program not been introduced. When behavior reverts to baseline, the experimental phase (B phase) is reinstated. Changes in A and B conditions from one phase to another are not made until performance during a given phase is stable or is clearly different from the previous phase.

The design is referred to as a reversal design because phases in the design are reversed to demonstrate the effect of the program. Alternatively, the design is referred to as the ABAB design because A and B phases are alternated. If performance changes in the experimental phase relative to baseline, reverts to baseline or near baseline levels during the second baseline phase, and again changes in the final experimental phase, this provides a clear demonstration of the experimental condition.

Examples of reversal designs are abundant. In one program (Kazdin & Klock, 1973), the effect of teacher praise on the behavior of retarded children was examined in a special education classroom. During baseline, students were observed for nine days to assess study behavior (paying attention to the teacher and working on assignments). Using an interval recording system, teacher approval (verbal and nonverbal) for student behavior and student attentiveness to classwork were observed each day. After baseline, the teacher was instructed to increase her use of nonverbal approval to the students by smiling, physically patting them on the back, and nodding approvingly for paying attention to her. When the teacher did this, study behavior increased. The use of nonverbal teacher approval to control student behavior was discontinued in a reversal phase to demonstrate that the program was responsible for behavior change. Finally, the experimental phase was reinstated and the teacher increased her use of nonverbal approval. The results for the group of 12 students as a whole are presented in Figure 5–2. The figure shows that performance during each reinforcement phase increased over baseline and reversal phases, respectively. This demonstrated that behavior improved only when nonverbal approval increased. By showing changes in behavior when the experimental condition is presented,

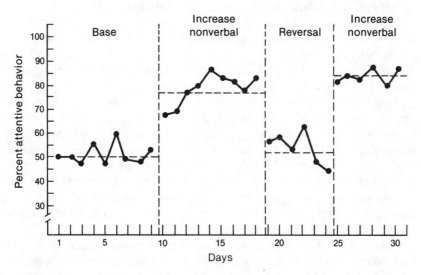

FIGURE 5–2 Mean daily rate of attentive behavior in the class.

Source: Kazdin, A. E. & Klock, J. The effect of nonverbal teacher approval on student attentive behavior. *Journal of Applied Behavior Analysis*, 1973, **6**, 643–54.

withdrawn, and re-presented, it is unlikely that other influences accounted for the results.

The reversal design requires that the experimental condition is presented and temporarily withdrawn at some point in time. There are variations of this basic design. Sometimes it is undesirable to begin with a baseline phase because some immediate intervention is urgently required. For example, if fighting among delinquents were frequent and intense in a given setting, it might be undesirable to begin with a baseline period because some immediate therapeutic intervention is needed. In other situations, it also might be reasonable to forego the initial baseline phase. For example, in some cases target behaviors such as social skills or talking have not been performed at all or their rates are exceedingly low (e.g., a mute psychiatric patient) so that baseline might not be the first phase of the program. In these instances where baseline is not employed initially, a BABA design might be used. This is the reversal design beginning with the experimental phase (B) followed by baseline or reversal (A) phases (cf. Kazdin & Polster, 1973).[2]

Reversal Phase. The requirement for the reversal design is that the contingency is altered during the reversal phase to determine whether behavior is controlled by the experimental intervention. Removing the contingency, thereby returning to baseline conditions, is frequently used to achieve a reversal. However, returning to baseline conditions is only one way to show a relationship between behavior and treatment. Alternative operations can be employed in the reversal phase (Goetz, Holmberg, & LeBlanc, 1975; Lindsay & Stoffelmayr, 1976).

One alternative during the reversal phase is *noncontingent delivery of the reinforcer.* Essentially, this refers to delivery of the consequences independently of behavior. This strategy is selected to show that it is not the event per se (e.g., praise) which results in behavior change but rather the relationship of the event to behavior. For example, Twardosz and Baer (1973) trained two severely retarded adolescent boys with limited speech to ask questions. The clients received praise and a token for asking questions in experimental sessions where speech was developed. After demonstrating behavior change, noncontingent reinforcement was given in which each subject received tokens and praise at the beginning of the session rather than after asking questions. The boys did not really have to perform the responses to earn the reinforcers. As expected, noncontingent reinforcement led to a reversal of behavior toward baseline levels of performance.

One way to administer noncontingent reinforcement, is to deliver the reinforcers whenever a certain amount of time passes. For example, reinforcers might be administered every 15 minutes in a classroom or on the ward no matter what the clients are doing. The procedure is noncontingent reinforcement because the consequences do not depend upon what anyone is doing. Noncontingent reinforcement administered in this fashion does not always achieve a clear reversal in behavior. The reason is that occasionally noncontingent reinforcement administered on the basis of time may accidentally follow the appropriate behavior once in a while. On some occasions the desired behaviors may be reinforced; on others, undesired behaviors may be reinforced. The effect of this might be to be a moderately effective program rather than a clear reversal of behavior back to baseline levels.

For example, Kazdin (1973e) provided noncontingent reinforcement to children in a fourth-grade classroom. The teacher administered tokens exchangeable for items such as toys and school supplies. Tokens were given at various intervals purely on the basis of a child's hair color (blonds versus brunnettes), gender (boys and girls), and initials (first name A–L or M–Z). Everyone received tokens but not every time the tokens were administered. For several students, attentiveness to the lesson increased even though the reinforcers were delivered noncontingently. Probably, tokens accidentally followed appropriate behavior and, hence, the program really was reinforcing the desired behavior on some occasions. Others have found that noncontingent delivery of reinforcers, if given periodically at different intervals, may lead to slight improvements in behavior (Lindsay & Stoffelmayr, 1976). Noncontingent reinforcement is more likely to show a reversal effect if it is delivered at the beginning of the session (e.g., class period) when no accidental association between performance and the reinforcer is made.

Another variation of the reversal phase is to continue contingent reinforcement. However, the contingency is altered so that the reinforcer is delivered for every behavior *except* the one that was reinforced during the experimental phase. The procedure for administering reinforcement for all behaviors except a specific response is called *differential reinforcement of other behavior* (or DRO schedule). During a reversal phase using a DRO schedule, all behaviors would be reinforced except the one that was reinforced during the experimental phase. For example, in the classroom setting, praise on a DRO schedule might be delivered whenever children were *not* studying. This strategy is selected to illustrate that the specific contingency is required for behavior change.

For example, Rowbury, Baer, and Baer (1976) provided behavior problem preschool children with praise and tokens that could be exchanged for play time. Reinforcers were given for *completing* various pre-academic tasks involving fitting puzzle pieces and matching forms. During a DRO phase, tokens were given for just sitting down or for starting the task rather than for completing the task. In short, behaviors other than completing the task were rewarded. Under the DRO schedule, each child completed fewer tasks than they had completed during the intervention.

The DRO schedule is different from the previous variation of the reversal phase in which reinforcement was delivered independently of behavior. During a DRO phase, reinforcement is contingent on behavior but on behaviors different from the one reinforced during the experimental phase. The reasons for using a DRO strategy in the reversal phase is to show the effect of the contingency rapidly. Behavior reverses more quickly when "other" behavior is reinforced directly than when noncontingent reinforcement is administered, even though both are suitable for use in reversal phases (Goetz et al., 1975). Whether a reversal phase employs a return to baseline, noncontingent presentation of the event, or a DRO schedule, the purpose is to show that altering the contingency changes behavior.

Problems and Considerations in Using a Reversal Design. A reversal design requires that behavior reverts to baseline or near baseline rates at some point to demonstrate that behavior change was caused by an alteration of the contingencies. Yet there are problems associated with this design related to the reversibility of behavior.

Sometimes when a program is withdrawn and a reversal phase is implemented, behavior does not return to the baseline rate of performance. When there is no reversal in behavior, it is not clear whether the experimental condition or some other event led to initial behavior change. For example, in one program (Kazdin, 1971), punishment was used to reduce incoherent statements made by a female retarded adult. In a psychiatric evaluation, the client was described as "prepsychotic" primarily because of talking to herself. The program, conducted in a sheltered workshop, began by obtaining baseline observations on the frequency of incoherent statements (statements made to herself). After baseline, a punishment procedure was invoked whereby a conditioned positive reinforcer (cards which purchased rewards, such as candy, toiletries, lounge privileges) was removed for each incoherent statement. The statements decreased dramatically. However, when baseline conditions were reinstated and positive reinforcers were no longer removed, behavior did not return to baseline levels. It remained at a very low rate. It appears reasonable to attribute the reduction of incoherent statements to the punishment procedure since incoherent statements had a long history. Strictly, however, it is not clear whether the punishment procedure *caused* the change because performance remained low even after the contingency was withdrawn.

In some programs removal of the experimental contingency has not resulted in a reversal of behavior. It is possible in these instances that factors (e.g., increased social contact with parents or teachers) other than contingencies programmed during the experimental phase were responsible for behavior change. The same factors might remain operative during a reversal phase and account for the failure of behavior to reverse. Because behavior does not always reverse when the experimental contingency is altered or withdrawn, the reversal design may not always demonstrate a causal relationship between behavior and environmental events even when contingency actually caused the initial change.

In some situations, a reversal design should not be used because behavior would not be expected to reverse in a reversal phase. Once certain behaviors are developed or altered, they may be maintained by favorable consequences which result directly from their performance. For example, if an "aggressive" child is praised by an attendant, improvement in behavior may lead to enduring changes in the child's environment. Peers in the child's environment may be more socially responsive because the previously aggressive child can play nicely with others. Even if there were a reversal phrase (removal of attendant praise), attention from the child's peers may maintain the desirable behavior. A reversal of behavior may be difficult to achieve in situations where the behavior is maintained by naturally occurring events in the environment which are not directly manipulated by the teacher, attendant, therapist, or investigator.

An extremely important practical consideration in using the reversal design is that even if it is possible to demonstrate a reversal of behavior, it may be undesirable. For example, autistic and retarded children sometimes severely injure themselves by banging their heads for extended periods of time. If a program decreased this behavior, it would be undesirable to show that headbanging would return in a reversal phase. Extensive physical damage to the child might result. Even when behavior is not dangerous, such as sitting on the floor in a hospital ward, daydreaming in class, or doing poorly on an academic assignment, it is usually undesirable to make behavior worse after gains have been made even if the reversal phase is short.

Finally, ethical issues obviously arise when implementing a reversal phase. A reversal phase essentially is designed to make the client's behavior worse in some way. Whether behavior should be made worse and when such a goal would be justified are difficult issues to resolve. In a given clinical situation, the consequences of making the client worse need to be weighed carefully for the client and for those in contact with the client. In fact, when reversal phases are used, they tend to be relatively brief—even for only one or a few days. Yet, the problems of reversing behavior may still arise. Fortunately, other designs are available to demonstrate the effects of the program without using a reversal of conditions.

■ MULTIPLE-BASELINE DESIGNS

Multiple-baseline designs do not rely on a reversal of conditions or phases to show the effect of the program. Rather, the effect of the contingency is demonstrated by showing that behavior change is associated with introduction of the contingency at different points in time. One of three types of multiple-baseline designs is usually used depending upon whether data are collected across behaviors, individuals, or across situations.

Multiple-Baseline across Behaviors. In this version of the design, baseline data are collected across *two* or *more behaviors* of a given individual or group of individuals. After each baseline has reached a stable rate, the experimental condition is implemented for only one of the behaviors while baseline conditions are continued for the other behavior(s). The initial behavior subjected to the experimental condition is expected to change while other behaviors remain at baseline levels. When rates are stable for all behaviors, the second behavior is included into the contingency. This procedure is continued until all behaviors for which baseline data were gathered are included into the contingency. Ideally, each behavior changes only as it is included into the experimental contingency and not before. Control of the specific experimental contingency is demonstrated when behavior change is associated in each case with the introduction of the contingency. No reversal is required to demonstrate what caused behavior change. The multiple-baseline design across behaviors is useful when an individual or group has a number of behaviors which are to be changed.

An example of this design was reported by Bornstein, Bellack, and Hersen (1977) who treated four elementary school children who were considered by their teachers to be excessively shy, passive, unassertive, and conforming. Training developed skills that would enable the children to communicate more effectively and in general to be more assertive. The children were deficient in specific behaviors such as making eye contact with others while speaking, speaking too softly, and not making requests. Individual behaviors were changed in a multiple-baseline design across behaviors for each child.

Baseline observations of behavior were obtained as a child behaved in a role-playing situation where he or she acted out various social situations with two other people. The child responded verbally to the other people in several everyday situations such as talking in class, playing in a game at school, borrowing objects from peers, and so on. After baseline, training was implemented to develop each of the specific behaviors. Training consisted of prompting the child to make a response in situations the child acted out, providing feedback about the response and how it might be improved, modeling of the response by the trainer, and continued practice to improve the response.

The results for Jane, an 8-year-old girl included in the program, are presented in Figure 5–3. The three behaviors that were trained included improving eye contact, increasing loudness of speech, and increasing

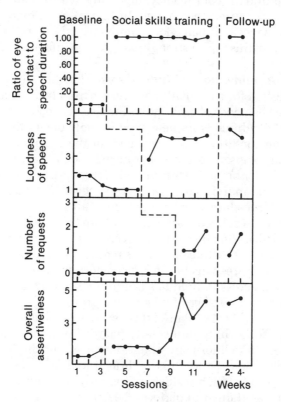

FIGURE 5–3 Sessions during baseline, social-skills training, and follow-up for Jane.

Source: Bornstein, M. R., Bellack, A. S., & Hersen, M. Social-skills training for unassertive children: A multiple-baseline analysis. *Journal of Applied Behavior Analysis,* 1977, **10,** 83–95.

the number of requests that the child made of other people. The last behavior graphed in the bottom of the figure was never focused upon directly but represented an overall rating of Jane's assertiveness. Presumably, if the other behaviors were changed, overall assertiveness ratings of the child would be expected to improve. Each behavior changed as it was included in training. Interestingly, the results were maintained when Jane was observed two and four weeks after treatment.

The requirements of the multiple-baseline design were clearly met in this report. If all three behaviors had changed when only the first one was included into the contingency, it would have been unclear whether the contingency caused the change. In that case, an extraneous event may have influenced all behaviors simultaneously. Yet, the specific effects obtained in this report strongly suggest the influence of training on each behavior.

Multiple-Baseline across Individuals. In this design, baseline data are collected for a *particular behavior across two or more individuals*. After the behavior of each individual has reached a stable rate, the experimental condition is implemented for only one of the individuals while baseline conditions are continued for the other(s). The behavior of the person exposed to the experimental condition should change while the behavior of the other individual(s) should not. When behavior stabilizes for all individuals, the contingency is extended to another person. This procedure is continued until all individuals for whom baseline data were collected are included into the contingency. As with other multiple-baseline designs, no reversal of the experimental condition (e.g., return to baseline or DRO) is required to demonstrate that the contingency was responsible for behavior change. The multiple-baseline design across individuals is useful when a given behavior is to be altered across a number of clients in a group.

Horner and Keilitz (1975) used this design to evaluate a program that developed toothbrushing in mentally retarded residents. Baseline data were gathered on toothbrushing behaviors (e.g., picking up the brush, wetting it, applying the toothpaste, brushing different surfaces of the teeth, and so on) for each resident. After only one day of baseline, the first resident was trained to perform the various behaviors required for toothbrushing. Training included instructions, physical guidance, praise and tokens (exchangeable for sugarless gum). Toothbrushing continued to be observed for each of the other residents who were not included in training. When the behavior of the first resident changed, training was extended to the second resident. Baseline data continued to be collected for the other residents. Eventually, training was provided to each of the other residents. As can be seen in Figure 5–4, toothbrushing skills improved only when training was provided. Events occurring in time other than training such as merely being given the opportunity to engage in toothbrushing or knowing that toothbrushing was desired by the staff do not explain why the changes occurred for each resident at the precise time that training was provided. The results strongly argue for the role of training as the crucial event to develop behavior.

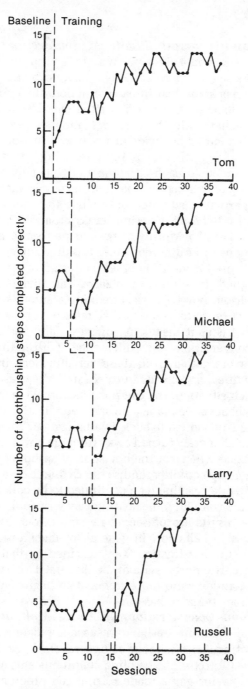

FIGURE 5–4 The number of toothbrushing steps performed correctly by the four subjects in the first group.

Source: Horner, R. D., & Keilitz, I. Training mentally retarded adolescents to brush their teeth. *Journal of Applied Behavior Analysis*, 1975, **8**, 301–9.

Multiple-Baseline across Situations, Settings, or Time. In this design, baseline data on a given behavior for an individual or group are collected *across two or more situations* (e.g., at home and at school). After behavior has stabilized in each situation, the experimental contingency is implemented in the first situation. The baseline phase is continued for behavior in the other situation(s). Eventually the contingency is extended to behavior in the next situation while baseline data continue to be gathered in the remaining situations. The contingency is extended to each situation until all situations have been included. The specific effect of the contingency is shown, if behavior changes in a particular situation only when the contingency is introduced. The multiple-baseline design across situations is useful when an individual or a group performs or fails to perform a behavior across different situations or at different times within a given situation.

Allen (1973) used a multiple-baseline design across situations in a program designed to eliminate bizarre verbalizations of a brain-damaged 8 year-old boy who was attending a summer camp. The boy engaged in bizarre verbalizations that referred to fictitious pets and characters. His frequent discussion of these fantasies interfered with appropriate conversation and interaction with adults and peers. Baseline data were gathered on these verbalizations in four different situations, activities, or settings in the camp. After baseline data were gathered in each situation, the camp counselors were instructed to ignore the boy whenever he made a bizarre verbalization or asked a question that previously had led to such a verbalization. To extinguish these responses, the staff merely turned away from the boy. However, the staff provided attention whenever the boy spoke appropriately such as discussing home, camp activities, and so on. Extinction was applied to the first situation, while baseline data continued to be collected during the other situations. Eventually, the contingency was applied to each of the situations. The results are presented in Figure 5–5. Extinction led to marked changes in behavior. In general, changes did not occur in a given situation until extinction was extended to that situation. The changes were particularly evident in the first two situations where bizarre verbalizations were more frequent to begin with and did not improve over the course of baseline.

Problems and Considerations in Using Multiple-Baseline Designs. Multiple-baseline designs are used for demonstrating the effects of the contingencies without using a reversal phase in the design. There is no need to return to baseline conditions and temporarily lose some of the behavior gains made during the program. Hence, these designs should be used when a reversal in behavior would be undesirable or unexpected. The designs require that there are either two or more behaviors, individuals, or situations which can be observed.

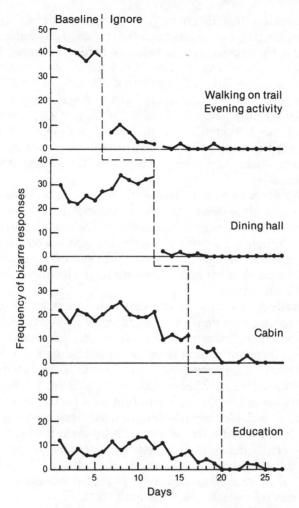

FIGURE 5-5 Bizarre verbalizations of a brain-damaged boy at summer camp. Baseline—before the intervention. Ignore—turning away from the boy for bizarre verbalizations and attending to appropriate verbalizations.

Source: Allen, G. J. Case study: Implementation of behavior modification techniques in summer camp settings. *Behavior Therapy*, 1973, **4**, 570–75.

There are possible problems with multiple-baseline designs which should be mentioned (Kazdin & Kopel, 1975). In the multiple-baseline design across behaviors, a clear demonstration of the effect of the contingency depends upon showing that behavior changes *only* when the contingency is introduced. If behavior changes before the contingency is introduced for that behavior (i.e., during baseline), it is unclear whether the contingency is responsible for change. If changing the first behavior also changes the second behavior before the second behavior is included into the contingency, the specific effect of the contingency on behavior is unclear. Studies report that altering one behavior of an individual sometimes results in changes in behaviors that are not included in the contingency (Jackson & Calhoun, 1977; Kazdin, 1973a; Maley, Feldman, & Ruskin, 1973; Marholin & Steinman, 1977). In situations where generalization across responses occurs, a multiple-baseline design across behaviors would not show the causal effect of the contingencies.

There are similar problems in the other multiple-baseline designs. In the multiple-baseline design across individuals, a clear demonstration of the effect of the contingency depends upon showing that behavior of different individuals changes only when the contingency is introduced. However, in some cases changes in the behavior of one individual may alter the behavior of other individuals for whom baseline conditions are in effect (Kazdin, 1979c).

In the multiple-baseline design across situations, a clear demonstration of the contingency depends upon changes in behavior only in those situations in which the contingency is in effect. However, in some cases alteration of behavior in one situation may change behavior in other situations even though the contingency is not introduced into these other situations (Hunt & Zimmerman, 1969; Kazdin, 1973e). In spite of the potential problems in demonstrating the specific effect of the contingency in a multiple-baseline design, these designs are usually quite useful in demonstrating the relationship between behavior and an experimental contingency. The problems appear to be exceptions. Yet, if it appears likely that altering one behavior (or behavior of one individual, or behavior in one situation) can produce generalized effects, a multiple-baseline design might be avoided.

An important consideration in using a multiple-baseline design is deciding the number of baselines that will be needed. While two baselines are a minimum, more usually are desirable. As a general rule, the more baselines across which the effect of the intervention is demonstrated, the more convincing the demonstration of a causal relationship. Whether an investigation provides a convincing demonstration across a given set of baselines depends upon such factors as the durations of the baselines, the presence of trends or excessive variability during baseline, the rapidity of behavior change after the intervention, and the magnitude of behavior change. Depending upon these factors, few or many baselines might be needed. Usually two or three baselines are enough if baseline data are stable and the intervention produces marked effects. Because it is difficult to predict the magnitude of behavior change and the stability of behavior within phases, it often is safer to choose a minimum of three baselines. Yet, reports vary widely in the number of baselines selected from a minimum of two up to nine different baselines (see Clark, Boyd, & Macrae, 1975).

■ CHANGING-CRITERION DESIGN

The effect of a contingency can be demonstrated without using a reversal or multiple-baseline design. A changing-criterion design demonstrates the effect of the contingency by showing that behavior matches a criterion which is set for reinforcement or punishment (Hartmann & Hall, 1976). As the criterion is repeatedly changed, behavior increases or decreases to match the criterion.

The design begins with a baseline period of observation. After baseline, the experimental contingency is introduced so that a certain level of performance is required to earn reinforcement. For example, the behavior may have to be performed a certain number of times per day to earn the reinforcer. When performance consistently meets or surpasses the criterion over a few days, the criterion is made more stringent. The criterion is repeatedly changed in a gradual fashion until the goal is achieved. The effect of the contingency is demonstrated if the behavior appears to match the criterion repeatedly as that criterion is changed. When behavior changes in response to alterations of the criterion, the demonstration suggests that the contingency, rather than extraneous influences, led to behavior change.

Dietz and Repp (1973) used a changing-criterion design to evaluate a program to decrease the rate that high school students engaged in social rather than academic discussions. During an academic lesson, students frequently changed subjects and inappropriately talked about other things than their work. Because the goal was to eliminate undesirable talking, students were rewarded for not engaging in inappropriate talking. Baseline observations recorded the daily rate of inappropriate verbalizations. When the program began, students received a reward for lowering their rate of inappropriate talking. Reinforcing a low rate of behavior is referred to as *differential reinforcement of low rates* (or DRL schedule). During the DRL phase, the investigators imposed different criteria for reinforcement. Over time, progressively fewer inappropriate verbalizations were allowed to earn the reinforcer. The reinforcer consisted of a free day (Friday) which the students could use as they wished if their inappropriate verbalizations had not exceeded the daily criterion on any of the previous days during that week. The four criteria were 5, 3, 2, and 0, each implemented for a week. If inappropriate verbalizations exceeded the criterion in effect for that day, depending upon which criterion was in effect, Friday would not be a free-activity

day. The results, presented in Figure 5–6, show that performance during the intervention phases always equalled or was below the criterion
(horizontal line). The last criterion was zero which meant that the reinforcer was earned only if inappropriate verbalizations did not occur
each day; and, no inappropriate verbalizations occurred. In the final

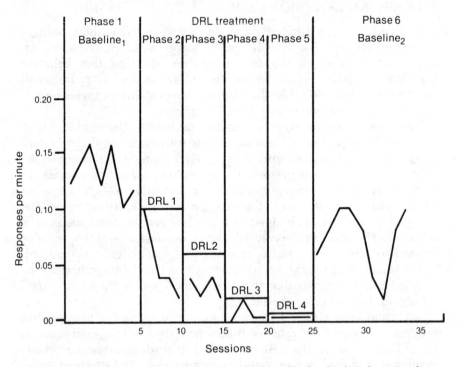

FIGURE 5–6 Inappropriate verbalizations of a class of high school students. Baseline$_1$—
before the intervention. Treatment—separate phases (PH) in which a decreasingly lower rate of
verbalizations was required to earn the reinforcer. The limit for the four phases was five or fewer
responses during the session, three or fewer, two or fewer, or zero responses, respectively.
Baseline$_2$—withdrawal of treatment.

Source: Dietz, S. M., & Repp, A. C. Decreasing classroom misbehavior through the use of DRL schedules of
reinforcement. *Journal of Applied Behavior Analysis,* 1973, **6,** 457–63.

phase, the original baseline was reinstated, thus making this an ABAB
design as well. This last phase is not essential to the changing-criterion
design. The original baseline and intervention phases with the different
criteria would have sufficed.

    *Problems and Considerations in Using a Changing-Criterion De-
sign.* The design is especially well suited to those responses that are
shaped gradually rather than acquired in one or a few trials. If performance shows a marked improvement or attainment of the final goal

when the criterion is not set at that level, the relationship between the intervention and behavior change is unclear. To show that alteration of the criterion accounts for changes in behavior, the behavior needs to occur relatively frequently so several changes can be made in the criterion before the terminal goal is achieved.

The changing-criterion design is less satisfactory than reversal and multiple-baseline designs in ruling out the influence of extraneous events that might account for behavior change. Even if behavior matches a criterion, behavior may be changing as a function of some other event in the person's life which led to a directional change (i.e., a decrease or increase) in behavior over time. A clear relationship is demonstrated only when performance matches the criterion very closely.

The design can be strengthened by making bidirectional changes in the criterion during the intervention phase. Rather than simply making the criterion increasingly more stringent, it can be made more stringent at some points and slightly less stringent at others. During the intervention phase, the criterion could be altered one or more times for brief periods to become more lenient. If behavior improves as the criterion is made more stringent and stops improving or decreases slightly as the criterion is made less stringent for a brief period, it is extremely unlikely that extraneous events could account for such bidirectional changes.

■ SIMULTANEOUS-TREATMENT DESIGN

The simultaneous-treatment design examines the effects of different interventions, each of which is implemented during the same phase. The design is especially useful when the investigator is interested in determining which among two or more experimental conditions is more or most effective (Kazdin & Hartmann, 1978).

The design begins with baseline observation of a response. After baseline, two or more interventions are implemented to alter the response. The different interventions are administered in the same phase but under varied stimulus conditions. For example, two interventions could be compared by implementing both of them on the same day but at different periods (morning and afternoon) and perhaps across different teachers who can administer the program (teacher or teacher aide). The different interventions are *balanced* across all conditions so that their effects can be separated from these conditions. That means that each intervention is given in the different periods (morning or afternoon) and is carried out by the different staff (teacher or aide). Each intervention is given daily but under different conditions (periods and staff) that vary each day. The intervention phase is continued under the varying conditions until the response stabilizes under the separate interventions. If the response stabilizes at different levels during the intervention phase, the interventions differ in effectiveness. Once the differential effectiveness is demonstrated, a phase may be implemented in which the more (or most) effective intervention is given under all possible conditions (e.g., each period and by each staff member).

Kazdin and Geesey (1977) used a simultaneous-treatment design to compare two different ways of earning reinforcers for two children in a special education classroom. Specifically, the investigation compared the effects of earning reinforcers for oneself versus earning reinforcers for oneself and for one's peers. For example, for one child named Max, observations of attentive behavior, the target behavior, were made at two different time periods. After baseline observations, the two different methods of earning reinforcers were implemented concurrently in the same phase. Both interventions were administered by the teacher who provided tokens to the child for appropriate classroom behavior. During the two time periods each day, the teacher administered tokens that could earn reinforcers for the child or for the child and his peers. The order of the different interventions varied each day. The cards in which the tokens (checks) were marked were separate for each intervention so the child could monitor his earnings. When a prespecified number of checks had been earned, Max selected a reinforcer from a list of events he had wanted (e.g., extra recess). This event was either given for him alone or for his peers depending upon the card that had achieved the required number of points. In the final phase, the more effective intervention was implemented during both daily time periods.

The results are presented in Figure 5–7. The upper portion shows the overall effect of the program plotted across both time periods combined. The bottom portion of the Figure is plotted according to the alternating time periods across which the interventions were balanced. The more effective intervention appeared to be the periods when Max earned reinforcers for the entire class rather than for himself alone. Hence, in the last phase, attentive behavior was reinforced with checks used to earn reinforcers for his peers during both time periods. During this last phase, performance during both time periods became high.

Problems and Considerations in Using the Simultaneous-Treatment Design.   The main feature of the design is that it permits comparison of different interventions concurrently implemented in a single treatment phase for a given client. The design addresses a very practical question of which among alternative treatments is the most effective for a particular client.

In practice, the design may be difficult to implement if more than two or three treatments are compared. As the number of treatments increase, it becomes increasingly difficult to ensure that each treatment is administered across each of the different conditions. For example, in

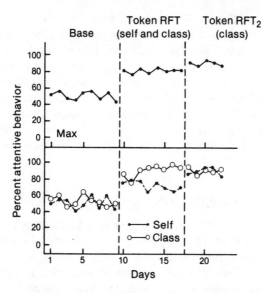

FIGURE 5–7 Attentive behavior of Max across experimental conditions. Baseline (base)—no experimental intervention. Token reinforcement (token rft)—implementation of the token program where tokens earned could purchase events for himself (self) or the entire class (class). Second phase of token reinforcement (token rft₂)—implementation of the class exchange intervention across both time periods. The upper panel presents the overall data collapsed across time periods and interventions. The lower panel presents the data according to the time periods across which the interventions were balanced, although the interventions were presented only in the last two phases.

Source: Kazdin, A. E., & Geesey, S. Simultaneous-treatment design comparisons of the effects of earning reinforcers for one's peers versus for oneself. *Behavior Therapy*, 1977, **8**, 682–93.

the above example, it would be difficult to balance three or four treatments so that they would be given an equal number of times during each of the two observation periods. Balancing the different treatments becomes especially difficult if the treatments are administered at different time periods and by different staff (e.g., Kazdin, 1977d). A large number of days are needed to ensure that each treatment is given under all of the combinations of the conditions of administration.

A few other restrictions of the design should be kept in mind (see Kazdin & Hartmann, 1978). For example, the design depends upon showing that a given behavior changes in response to changes in treatment on a given day. It is important that there is no carry-over effect from one intervention to another. For example, drug and behavioral treatments might not be easily compared in a simultaneous-treatment design because the influence of the drug might not be eliminated if the behavioral treatment were implemented later in the day. Also, the behavior selected for the simultaneous-treatment design must be able to change rapidly. The response must occur frequently enough during the observation periods to reflect change for each intervention and a differential amount of change across interventions, if the interventions have different effects.

■ CONTROL GROUP DESIGN

The control group design is another way to demonstrate the effect of an experimental contingency. There are a variety of control-group designs suitable for applied settings (e.g., Campbell & Stanley, 1963; Kazdin, 1980). The basic design requires at least two groups, one which receives the experimental program (the experimental group) and the other which does not (the control group). To determine whether the experimental contingency was effective, rates of the target behavior in the experimental and control groups are compared. For example, a reinforcement program might be conducted in one school classroom but not in another. Immediately before and after the program the behavior of all students in both classrooms is assessed. To determine whether the program is effective, the averages in performance for the groups are compared at the end of the program. If the group averages are different between the classes, it suggests that the program was responsible for the change. To be sure that any difference between the two groups is due to the program, the groups must be similar to begin with. The best procedure to control for systematic differences between groups before the program is implemented is to *randomly assign* clients to one of the two groups. If subjects are not randomly assigned to groups, the likelihood is greater that the groups may be different in their performance of the target behavior before the program is implemented and differentially change in the target behavior over time for some reason other than the effect of the program.

O'Brien and Azrin (1972) used a control-group design to evaluate the effects of a program to train mentally retarded adults to eat appropriately. The residents seldom used utensils, spilled food on themselves, and displayed grossly improper table manners such as stealing food from others and eating food previously spilled on the floor. The residents were randomly assigned to one of two groups that either received training or no training. Training consisted of individually meeting with a resident and providing praise for correct eating behaviors and reprimands (saying the word "no") and time out from reinforcement for inappropriate behavior. Also, instructions and manual guidance (physical prompts) were given to help the residents perform the desired responses. No-training residents, of course, did not receive the special training program to develop specific eating behaviors.

The program was evaluated by observing eating behavior of both groups of residents immediately before training (pretest) and after training (posttest) where each resident was observed while eating alone. A follow-up meal was observed two weeks later where residents ate in a group situation. The results of the program are presented in Figure 5–8. The results were evaluated with statistical tests that

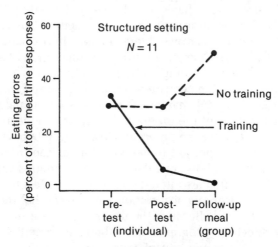

FIGURE 5–8   The percentage of mealtime responses performed improperly by institutionalized mental retardates.

Source: O'Brien, F., & Azrin, N. H. Developing proper mealtime behaviors of the institutionalized retarded. *Journal of Applied Behavior Analysis*, 1972, **5**, 389–99.

showed significantly greater improvement for the training group. The effects of the program also are clear from the figure which shows the much greater level of inappropriate eating response for the no-training group.

Problems and Considerations in Using a Control-Group Design.   The control-group design has not been employed extensively in behavior modification programs in applied settings. One reason is that usually it is not possible to assign subjects randomly to groups in settings such as schools and hospitals. Thus, there is no assurance that the differences obtained between groups after a program are not due to initial differences which the investigator was not able to control through random assignment. Yet, control-group designs are still worthwhile even when random assignment is not possible (Campbell & Stanley, 1963).

The major reason that the control-group design is not used is that it focuses on the behavior of groups rather than on the behavior of individuals. When the control-group study is done, the *average* frequency of behavior of individuals in the control group is compared with the average frequency of behavior of individuals in the experimental group. The focus on averages hides the behavior of individual clients. Thus, the average performance of a group may change although only a few individuals in the group may have actually been affected by the program. Behavior modification programs in applied settings usually are concerned with achieving relatively large changes in the behavior of individuals (Risley, 1970). Changes in group averages are not as important as ensuring the behavior change of the individual.

A final reason why the control-group design is used infrequently in applied settings is that behavior of groups is not usually measured continuously throughout the program. Behavior may be assessed prior to and immediately after the program. However, in behavior modification programs, it is important to assess behavior continuously so that the investigator knows how well the program is progressing while it is in effect. Programs often are altered after being in effect for only a short period of time. Continuous observation may reveal that the program is not working very well. Because the observations are made while the program is in effect, the program can be changed immediately. If behavior is assessed only at the end of the program, as it is usually in a control-group design, it is too late to change the program if it does not work.

The control-group design is used heavily in many areas of behavior modification research particularly to evaluate outpatient treatment for such problems as anxiety, obesity, marital discord, excessive alcohol consumption, and so on. However, evaluation of operant techniques has relied more heavily upon the intrasubject-replication designs highlighted here. Of course, the particular type of design selected depends upon many factors such as the purpose of treatment and the question of interest to the investigator rather than the type of techniques that are used.

For certain questions, a control group can provide valuable information that is difficult to obtain with single-case designs (Kazdin, 1980). For example, comparing the effectiveness of different experimental programs is readily accomplished by using different groups of subjects who receive the different treatments. Although the simultaneous-treatment design can compare treatments for the individual subject, large-scale demonstrations across many subjects and many treatments are restricted to control-group designs. In addition, when evaluating the effects of different treatments for different types of subjects (e.g., retarded versus autistic) control group designs are particularly useful. A large number of subjects may be needed to show a systematic and different pattern of results for different types of subjects.

■ EVALUATING CHANGE

In each of the intrasubject-replication designs, the degree of behavior change is reflected by comparing performance during baseline with performance during the experimental phase. A major issue is the degree of change needed to provide a convincing demonstration that behavior has improved. The decision that change has occurred is important in the execution of the design as well as in the evaluation of the overall effects of treatment. For example, in the reversal design, the experimental condition may be withdrawn, altered, or reinstated at different points based on evidence that behavior has changed or failed to change.

In many instances in intrasubject-replication research, behavior change is dramatic. Indeed, the purpose of the intervention usually is to obtain strong treatment effects. Usually, data are evaluated through visual inspection, that is, merely looking at the graphs to evaluate whether change was reliable (see Kazdin, 1976; Parsonson & Baer, 1978). Examination of a graph of the results sometimes reveals that performance during baseline does not overlap with performance during the experimental phase. During the program the data points may not approach the data points obtained during baseline. When there is no overlap of performance in baseline and intervention phases, there would be little disagreement that change has occurred.

When the effects are not strong enough to obtain nonoverlapping data across the separate phases, intervention effects may be evident by changes in trends over the different phases. For example, behavior may show a clear trend toward improvement during the intervention. The trend may stop or be reversed as treatment is withdrawn and begin again when treatment is reinstated.[3]

A major criterion for evaluating change is whether the effects of treatment are of *applied or clinical significance*. The effects produced by the intervention should be large enough to be of practical value (Risley, 1970). Also, individuals who are in constant contact with the patient, resident, or client who was in the program need to help evaluate whether an important change was obtained.

It is not enough to demonstrate that change occurred because the change may be too weak to be of any practical value. For example, an autistic child may hit himself in the head 100 times in an hour period. Treatment may reduce this to 50 times per hour. Even though change has been achieved, a much larger change is needed to eliminate behavior. Self-injurious behavior is maladaptive and potentially dangerous and needs to be eliminated.

Evaluating whether behavior change is of applied significance is referred to as *social validation* (Kazdin, 1977b; Wolf, 1978). Social validation consists of different methods to determine whether the amount of change is very important. One procedure that is used is to compare the level of the client's behavior after treatment with that of his or her peers or others who are considered to be functioning adequately in their environment. For example, Walker and Hops (1976) developed appropriate classroom behaviors such as working on assignments and following instructions in primary-grade students in a special education classroom. Prior to participating in a reinforcement program, the students were markedly lower in their appropriate behavior than were their nondisruptive peers. When the program was completed and the children were placed into regular classrooms, their appropriate behavior was up to the level of their nondisruptive peers. These results suggest that the changes in behavior were clinically important because the children were brought up to the level of peers who had not been identified as behavior problems. Several other programs have evaluated the extent of change achieved in treatment by comparing the level of behavior of the clients with people who are not considered to have problem behavior in the area focused upon in treatment. For example, eating habits of the retarded have been improved so that they are at the level of nonretarded individuals (O'Brien & Azrin, 1972). Similarly, social interaction of severely withdrawn children or inassertive adults has been brought to the level of their peers who are functioning adequately in these areas (e.g., McFall & Twentyman, 1973; O'Connor, 1969).

In general, applied operant programs seek treatment effects that clearly affect the level of the client's functioning in everyday situations. Showing that behavior brings the client to normative levels of functioning is an important step in demonstrating treatment effects. Occasionally, treatment not only affects how well the client does in everyday life but also how he or she is evaluated by others such as parents, teachers, and peers. Evaluations of others constitutes another source of information about whether treatment really has made a difference in everyday situations (see Chapter 13).

■ SUMMARY AND CONCLUSION

In this chapter, experimental designs were discussed that are used to evaluate the effects of intervention programs. Assessment of behavior can evaluate whether change has occurred when treatment is provided. Yet, experimental designs are needed in addition to assessment to determine whether the intervention was responsible for change. Different designs are available including the reversal or ABAB design, multiple-baseline designs, changing-criterion design, simultaneous-treatment design, and the control-group design. Although each design can demonstrate a relationship between the intervention and behavior change, selection of the design may be determined by demands of the clinical situation, the purposes of treatment, and various advantages and disadvantages of specific designs. Independently of the design selected, the purpose of treatment is to achieve marked changes in behavior. Evaluation of behavior change usually is made by visually inspecting the graphed results to assess whether treatment was consistently associated with marked changes or differences in trends across phases. The importance of change may be evaluated by comparing behavior of the client with others whose behaviors already appear to be at a satisfactory level of performance.

■ NOTES

[1] For a detailed discussion of various designs used to evaluate behavioral programs and the rationale underlying their use, other sources can be consulted (e.g., Baer, Wolf, & Risley, 1968; Hersen & Barlow, 1976; Kazdin, 1978a, 1978b).

[2] Many other versions of the ABAB design have been used (Hersen & Barlow, 1976). For example, several different treatments may be used such as in an $AB_1B_2B_3AB_3$ design. Different treatments may be needed if the first one used has not achieved strong enough effects or does not even work at all. Even when several different interventions are used, the demonstration is a reversal design if the basic requirement is met, namely, the effect of the intervention(s) is evaluated by implementing a phase which is intended to reverse behavior in the direction of the original baseline.

[3] Recently, several statistical techniques have been proposed for use to evaluate the effects of treatment in intrasubject-replication designs (e.g., Jones, Vaught, & Weinrott, 1977; Kazdin, 1976; Kratochwill, 1978). The use of statistical tests has been controversial. Some investigators have noted that developing a technology of behavior change means that very strong treatment effects should be sought. Visually inspecting the results which are graphed allows one to see only extremely clear treatment effects. In contrast, statistical analysis may identify intervention effects which are generally weak but meet a statistical criterion of significance. Independently of the alternative positions, visual inspection of intrasubject research still is the dominant method of data evaluation. However, use of statistical analyses has increased in recent years.

6

Positive Reinforcement

The problems of various populations in treatment, education, and rehabilitation settings often include behavioral deficits or lack of appropriate skills. For example, autistic and retarded children often lack a variety of personal, social, and intellectual skills. Problems of other individuals may include deficits but frequently are associated with disruptive and deviant behaviors as well. For example, adolescents identified as delinquents may perform deviant behaviors which have to be eliminated. However, elimination of the deviant behavior will not ensure that socially appropriate behavior will be performed. Socially appropriate behaviors need to be developed. For other individuals whose behavior is identified as problematic, there may be no deficit in behavior. Yet the conditions under which certain responses are performed may be different from those in which they should be performed in everyday life. For example, a "hyperactive" child may "know" how to sit down. However, this behavior rarely occurs in a classroom setting.

In the above cases, low frequency behaviors have to be increased, new behaviors have to be established, or behaviors have to be developed in new situations. Positive reinforcement is an appropriate technique to achieve these goals. Even in cases where the primary intent of the program is to eliminate an undesirable behavior, positive reinforcement plays a major role. Developing desirable and socially appropriate behavior can eliminate undesirable behaviors. By reinforcing socially appropriate behavior, the deviant responses frequently are replaced.

Positive reinforcement refers to an increase in the frequency of a response following the presentation of a positive reinforcer. Whether a particular event is a positive reinforcer is determined empirically. A reinforcer is defined by its effects on behavior. If response frequency increases when followed by the event, the event is a positive reinforcer. Defining a reinforcer by the effects on behavior appears to be circular. However, a reinforcer is not limited solely by its capacity to alter a particular behavior in a single situation. The reinforcer effective in altering one response in one situation may alter other responses in other situations as well. In addition, the Premack principle, discussed earlier, provides a way to assess whether an event is a reinforcer independently of the effects on behavior. Reinforcing consequences are those behaviors in a person's response repertoire that have a relatively high probability.

■ MAXIMIZING THE EFFECT OF POSITIVE REINFORCEMENT

The effectiveness of reinforcement depends upon several factors. These include the delay between performance of a response and the delivery of reinforcement, the magnitude and quality of the reinforcer, and the schedule of reinforcement.

Delay of Reinforcement.   Responses which occur in close proximity of reinforcement are learned better than responses remote from reinforcement (Kimble, 1961; Skinner, 1953). Thus, a reinforcer should be delivered immediately after the target response to maximize the effect of reinforcement. If reinforcement does not follow the response immediately, another response different from the target response may be performed in the intervening delay period. The intervening responses will be immediately reinforced whereas the target response will be reinforced after a delay period. The target response is less likely to change. For example, children are often praised (or punished) for a behavior long after the behavior is performed. If a child straightens his or her room, a parent would do well to provide praise immediately. If praise is postponed until the end of the day, a variety of intervening responses may occur (including, perhaps, messing up the room). Similarly, in a classroom setting, children are often told how "good" they are when they are on the verge of becoming disruptive or restless. The teacher may mention that the class was well behaved in the morning and she hopes they will remain well behaved. Although praise is delivered, it is delayed and will be minimally effective.

Immediate reinforcement is important in the early stages of a behavior modification program when the target response is developing. After a response is performed consistently, the amount of time between the response and reinforcement can be increased without a decrement in performance. For example, in classroom settings students sometimes receive points or candy daily while high rates of academic behavior develop. However, after behavior has stabilized, the reinforcers can be delivered every other day or at the end of several days without a deleterious effect on performance. If a program begins with delayed reinforcement, behavior might not change at all or not as rapidly as when reinforcement is immediate.

It is desirable to change from immediate to delayed reinforcement after a behavior is well developed so that behavior is not dependent upon immediate consequences. A great many consequences in everyday life follow long after behavior is performed. For example, accomplishments, wages, grades, and fame follow long after a series of responses is completed.

Magnitude or Amount of Reinforcement. The amount of reinforcement delivered for a response also determines the extent to which a response will be performed. The greater the amount of a reinforcer delivered for a response, the more frequent the response (Kimble, 1961). The amount can usually be specified in terms such as the quantity of food, the number of points, or the amount of money.

Although the magnitude of reinforcement is directly related to performance, there are limits to this relationship. An unlimited amount of reinforcement does not necessarily maintain a high rate of performance of the response. A reinforcer loses its effect when given in excessive amounts. This is referred to as *satiation*. Hence, the effect of magnitude of reinforcement is limited by the point at which the individual becomes satiated. Satiation is especially evident with primary reinforcers such as food, water, and sex. In a short time, each of these reinforcers in excessive amounts loses its reinforcing properties and may even become aversive. Of course, satiation of primary reinforcers is temporary because the events regain reinforcing value as deprivation increases. Secondary or conditioned reinforcers such as praise, attention, and tokens are also subject to satiation (Gewirtz & Baer, 1958; Winkler, 1971b). However, they are less susceptible to satiation than are primary reinforcers. Generalized conditioned reinforcers in particular, such as money, are virtually insatiable because they have been associated with a variety of other reinforcers. Satiation of generalized reinforcers is not likely to occur until the individual satiates on the other reinforcers with which they have been associated. The more reinforcers for which the generalized conditioned reinforcer such as money can be exchanged, the less likelihood that satiation will occur. It is no surprise that few people complain or cease to work because of too much money!

Satiation occasionally has been used to reduce the value of stimuli that appear to serve as reinforcers. In a frequently cited example, Ayllon (1963) treated a hospitalized psychiatric patient who hoarded towels in her room. The staff kept removing the towels that the patient had collected, a procedure which was not really effective in eliminating hoarding. Satiation was tried in which the staff kept bringing the patient towels in large numbers. In a matter of a few weeks the towels had accumulated to a very large number (625) and the staff no longer brought any more. The patient stopped hoarding towels and even removed those that had accumulated. Up to one year later, hoarding of towels no longer was a problem.

The effect of the amount of the reinforcer on behavior depends upon satiation and deprivation states of the individual with respect to that reinforcer. If the individual has unlimited access to the event (e.g., money), that event is not likely to be very effective as a reinforcer. The amount of a reinforcer needed to change behavior is not as great when the individual is partially deprived of the event. For example, individuals who are temporarily deprived of adult attention are more responsive to attention than are individuals who are not deprived of attention (Gewirtz & Baer, 1958). Of course, intentional deprivation of reinforcers in a behavior modification program is not essential for behavior change. In most everyday situations, people do not have unlimited access to events which are reinforcing (e.g., free time in a classroom situation or time with friends for children at home) and thereby normally undergo a mild form of deprivation. Thus, a variety of events are effective as reinforcers without introducing deprivation.

Quality or Type of Reinforcer.   The quality of a reinforcer is not usually specificable in physical terms as is the amount of the reinforcer (Kimble, 1961). Quality of a reinforcer is determined by the preference of the client. Reinforcers that are highly preferred lead to greater performance. Preference can be altered by taking a reinforcer such as food and changing its taste. For example, animals show greater performance when a food is sweet than when it is sour or neutral in taste (Hutt, 1954).

For a given client, it usually is not difficult to specify activities which are highly preferred. Behaviors engaged in frequently provide a helpful indication of highly preferred reinforcers. However, preference for a particular reinforcer depends upon satiation. At one point in time a reinforcer may be more effective in changing behavior than another because the client is satiated with one and deprived of another (Premack, 1965). However, as will be discussed below, certain reinforcers tend to result in higher performance than others. Hence, the type of reinforcer alone can determine the extent of behavior change.

Schedule of Reinforcement.   Schedule of reinforcement refers to the rule denoting how many responses or which specific responses will be reinforced. Reinforcers are always administered acccording to some schedule. In the simplest schedule a response is reinforced each time it occurs. This schedule is referred to as *continuous reinforcement*. For example, to train mentally retarded children to follow instructions, reinforcement can be given each time the child responds appropriately. On the other hand, reinforcement may be delivered after some of the responses rather than all of them. This is referred to as *intermittent reinforcement*.

There are important differences between continuous and intermittent reinforcement while the behaviors are reinforced and after reinforcement is withdrawn. A behavior developed with continuous reinforcement is performed at a higher rate during the acquisition or reinforcement phase than if it is developed with intermittent reinforcement. Thus, while a behavior is developing, a continuous or "generous" schedule of reinforcement should be used. However, the advantage of continuous reinforcement is compensated after the reinforcement ceases. In extinction, behaviors previously reinforced continuously diminish at a much more rapid rate than do behaviors previously reinforced intermittently.

The difference between responses developed with continuous and intermittent reinforcement is apparent in examples from everyday experience. One common response which is reinforced virtually every time is putting coins into a cigarette, candy, or soda machine and pressing the appropriate lever. The product almost always is delivered. (Technically this is not always continuous reinforcement because of mechanical failures. However, vending machines are designed to provide continuous reinforcement and will be used as an example of this schedule.) The response (depositing coins) follows a pattern identical to that of continuous reinforcement once reinforcement no longer occurs. As soon as the reinforcer (i.e., the product) is no longer delivered, extinction is almost immediate. Under these circumstances, few individuals repeatedly place more and more coins into that particular machine until there is some evidence that it has been repaired. Extinction of behaviors previously reinforced continuously (or almost continuously) is rapid.

A similar response, putting coins into a machine and pressing a lever, might be maintained by intermittent reinforcement as in the case of slot machines. Sometimes putting money into a slot machine is reinforced (with money) and many other times it is not. If money were no longer delivered (i.e., extinction), the response would continue to be performed at a high rate before extinguishing. It is difficult to discriminate when extinction begins on a highly intermittent schedule of reinforcement. The resistance of a response to extinction depends upon how intermittent or *thin* the reinforcement schedule is. If very few responses are reinforced, resistance to extinction is greater than if many responses are reinforced.

The advantage of continuous reinforcement is that performance occurs at a high level while behavior is reinforced. The advantage of intermittent reinforcement is that resistance to extinction is greater when reinforcement is discontinued. The advantages of both schedules can be obtained by developing behavior with continuous reinforcement until a high rate of behavior is well established. At that point, the schedule can be changed to intermittent reinforcement. The schedule can be made increasingly intermittent to ensure response maintenance.

Another advantage of intermittent reinforcement is its efficient use of available reinforcers. Intermittent reinforcement allows delivery of a few reinforcers for a large number of responses. In addition, by administering reinforcers only a few times, satiation is less likely to occur. For example, with intermittent food reinforcement the client is not likely to become full quickly and to become temporarily unresponsive to food. To sustain high levels of responding, it is important to avoid satiation by providing fewer reinforcers for an equivalent number of responses. A practical advantage in using intermittent reinforcement is that less time is required administering reinforcers than if continuous reinforcement is used.

Intermittent reinforcement can be scheduled many different ways (Ferster & Skinner, 1957), only a few of which will be considered here. Two simple types of reinforcement schedules can be distinguished. Reinforcement can be contingent upon the emission of a certain *number of responses*. This is referred to as a *ratio* schedule because the ratio of the total number of responses to the one which is reinforced is specified by the schedule. Alternatively, reinforcement can be given on the basis of the *amount of time* that passes before a response can be reinforced. This is referred to as an *interval* schedule. With a ratio schedule, the interval of time which passes for the subject to perform the response is irrelevant. The behavior of the subject controls the frequency of reinforcement. With interval schedules, the number of responses performed is irrelevant as long as one response is performed after the prescribed interval of time has elapsed. The frequency of reinforcement is partially determined by the clock.

In both ratio and interval schedules of reinforcement, the requirement for reinforcement can be *fixed* so that it is the same specified requirement each time. On the other hand, the requirement can be *variable* so that it is different from time to time. Four simple schedules of reinforcement will be discussed: fixed ratio (FR), variable ratio (VR), fixed interval (FI), and variable interval (VI).

A *fixed-ratio schedule* requires that an unvarying number of responses be performed before a response is reinforced. The number following "FR" specifies which response will be reinforced. For example, FR:1 specifies that only one response is required for the reinforcer to be delivered. (FR:1 is also called continuous reinforcement because every response is reinforced.) FR:10 denotes that every tenth response is reinforced.

Performance under fixed-ratio schedules differs to some extent depending upon whether the ratios are small or large. Characteristically there is a temporary pause in responding after reinforcement is delivered and then a rapid rise in response rate until the ratio is completed and reinforcement is delivered. The pause after responding is a function of the ratio with large ratios producing longer pauses. Once the responses resume, reinforcement is maximized by performing all of the responses as quickly as possible. Examples of an FR schedule include any instance in which the reinforcer is delivered for a certain number of responses. For example, factory workers who are paid according to how much they produce are reinforced on an FR schedule (commonly referred to as piecework). For every certain number of responses (product produced), the reinforcer (money) is earned. If there are several responses required for reinforcement, there may be a temporary pause (no production) immediately after reinforcement.

A *variable-ratio schedule* specifies that reinforcement occurs after a certain number of responses. However, that number *varies* unpredictably from occasion to occasion. On the average, a certain number of responses are performed before reinforcement is delivered. The number following "VR" specifies the average number of responses required for reinforcement. For example, VR:5 indicates that on the average 5 responses are performed before the reinforcer is delivered. On some occasions, the second response may be reinforced, whereas on other occasions the eighth response may be reinforced. A different number of responses may be required each time. However, across all occasions reinforcement is delivered on the average of the number specified (e.g., 5 in the VR:5 schedule). Of course, any number except 1 can be used in a VR schedule because that would be equivalent to reinforcing every response which is a continuous reinforcement or FR:1 schedule.

Performance under VR schedules is consistently high. The pauses which may be apparent with FR schedules can be virtually eliminated with a VR schedule, unless the average ratio is very long. Immediately after a response is reinforced, the subject begins to respond because the next reinforcer may follow only a few responses. Performance continues at a high rate until reinforcement is delivered and immediately resumes again. Behavior previously maintained under a VR schedule extinguishes more slowly than under a FR schedule, particularly if the variable schedule requires many responses for reinforcement. Performance is relatively persistent and consistent following a VR schedule. Thus, VR schedules are highly suited to forestalling extinction. Prior to withdrawing reinforcement, the ratio gradually can be made very *thin*.

To make a schedule thin is to increase the number of responses required for reinforcement. Resistance to extinction can be very great when reinforcement is administered on a relatively thin schedule.

Examples of VR schedules are abundant in everyday experience. The behavior of a fisherman is controlled, in part, by VR reinforcement. Each time a line is tossed into the water (response), a fish (reinforcer) is not caught. Rather, the response is reinforced only some of the time. Yet the variable nature of the schedule ensures that extinction will not take place rapidly. Slot machines, mentioned earlier, represent a dramatic application of VR schedules. Since any response can be reinforced, the person playing the machine usually performs at a consistently high rate. Performance is unlikely to extinguish for long periods of time.

A *fixed-interval schedule* requires that an interval of time (usually expressed in minutes) passes before the reinforcer is available. The first response which occurs after the interval passes is reinforced. In a fixed schedule, of course, the interval is unvarying. For example, an FI:1 schedule denotes that the first response after one minute passes is reinforced. An *interval schedule* requires that only one response be performed after the prescribed interval has elapsed. While this efficiency in responding rarely occurs, the characteristic of FI schedule responding is distinct. Following reinforcement there is usually a pronounced pause where no responses are performed. This does not interfere with receiving reinforcement since a response before the appropriate time elapses is never reinforced. Only if the pause is longer than the fixed interval will the subject postpone reinforcement. FI schedules lead to less consistent rates of responding than do FR schedules because non-responding immediately after reinforcement during an FI schedule does not postpone reinforcement as it does with an FR schedule.

An excellent example of an FI response pattern in everyday experience is looking to see whether one's mail has arrived. For most individuals, mail delivery is once a day with (fairly) fixed periods of time between deliveries. The response (looking for mail in the mail box) is reinforced (finding mail) daily. Immediately after reinforcement there is no longer a response. One does not resume looking for mail again until the interval is almost complete, the next day. At that point, looking for mail increases until reinforcement is obtained.

Behaviors that are controlled by time often follow the pattern of responding to interval schedules, even when it is difficult to identify the reinforcer at the end of the interval. For example, a study of the United States Congress showed that passing bills followed a characteristic pattern of FI responding (Weisberg & Waldrop, 1972). For both sessions of each Congress from 1947 to 1968, the number of bills passed was very low immediately after a session began. However, an increasing number of bills was passed as the session came to a close. Thus, a great number of responses was performed immediately before the interval ended. After the interval ended (one session) and a new interval began (second session), there was a pause in performance (few bills passed). Although the reinforcer at the end of the interval is unclear, the pattern of responding resembles fixed interval performance of laboratory animals working for food.

A *variable-interval schedule* specifies the *average length* of the intervals required for reinforcement. For example, a VI:10 schedule denotes that on the average, 10 minutes must pass before a response is reinforced. On any given occasion the interval may be more or less than 10 minutes. The reinforcer is delivered for the first response *after* the interval passes. Studying behavior of students follows a pattern characteristic of a VI schedule, if the instructor gives "pop quizzes." The interval between quizzes is unpredictable and varies from quiz to quiz. Studying tends to be relatively consistent under such a schedule.

Responding tends to be more rapid under VI than FI schedules. However, high rates of responding do not necessarily speed up reinforcement in an interval schedule as they do on a ratio schedule. Consequently, the rate of performance under interval schedules is usually lower. As with ratio schedules, extinction is prolonged with a thin variable schedule.

Schedules of reinforcement have important implications for behavior modification programs in applied settings. The implications will be particularly evident in the discussion of maintenance of behaviors (see Chapter 11). As mentioned earlier, in the beginning of a behavior change program, it is desirable to reinforce continuously. In practice, it is virtually impossible to survey behavior constantly to ensure that each performance of the target behavior is reinforced. However, a rich schedule can be used initially before changing to increasingly intermittent schedules. The type of intermittent schedule used needs to be determined by considering the characteristic response pattern of the schedule as well as practical exigencies. Although fixed schedules may be convenient to administer, characteristic performance includes pauses or lapses in performance of the reinforced behavior. For example, in an institutional setting, ward attendants may reinforce behavior on an FI schedule. At the end of the time periods (e.g., 30 minutes), staff may administer reinforcers to residents behaving "appropriately." However, it is very likely that performance of the residents will be high near the end of the interval with pauses immediately after reinforcement. Variable schedules can alleviate the inconsistency in resident performance.

To summarize the above discussion, the effect of reinforcement can be maximized by reinforcing the target behavior *immediately* with a potent *reinforcer* which is delivered on a *continuous* or near continuous (rich) *schedule* of reinforcement. The extent to which these conditions are met will determine the efficacy of the program. As behavior develops, reinforcement should be increasingly intermittent and increasingly delayed. By providing less reinforcement on a less immediate schedule, behavior can be maintained. In many cases, the ideal conditions for reinforcement delivery cannot be met. Also, potent reinforcers (e.g., food and money) sometimes are not available or are objected to on ethical grounds. Moreover, exigencies of the setting may interfere with immediate reinforcement. Finally, reinforcers differ in the ease with which they are administered. In spite of these difficulties, several reinforcement procedures are available. Usually the resources and demands of a particular setting are readily incorporated into a reinforcement program.

■ TYPES OF REINFORCERS

A major task in using reinforcement effectively is selecting powerful reinforcers. Reinforcers differ in their potency as well as the ease with which they are administered in a treatment or educational setting. Behavior modification programs employing different types of reinforcers will be discussed.

Food and Other Consumables.   Food qualifies as a primary reinforcer because its reinforcing value is unlearned. Of course, food preferences are learned which make some foods more reinforcing than others and some foods not reinforcing at all unless the individual has been deprived of all food. Because food is a primary reinforcer, it is very powerful. Studies have used food as a reinforcer, including entire meals, bits of cereal, candy, crackers, cookies, soft drinks, ice cream, and other foods.

There are other events which have been used which are nonfood consumables. For example, cigarettes and gum may be strong reinforcers for some individuals. However, since they are not primary reinforcers their appeal does not extend to as many individuals as does food. Although the reinforcing properties of nonfood consumables are learned, eventually the reinforcing power of these consumables resembles that of primary reinforcers. Deprivation may build up in a fashion analogous to that of food. In any case, when nonfood consumables are reinforcers, they tend to be very effective. Food and consumables will be discussed together because they share characteristic advantages and disadvantages.

Because food is a primary reinforcer and its effects should apply widely among different client populations, it has been used frequently, especially early in the development of reinforcement techniques in applied settings. For example, Hopkins (1968) used candy to increase the frequency of smiling of a retarded boy who constantly appeared sad and dejected. The author decided to increase the frequency of smiling during walks the child took in school. After obtaining the baseline rate of smiling, the child was given a piece of candy each time he smiled when he met another person during a walk. The number of smiles substantially increased. In later phases, candy reinforcement was withdrawn and social reinforcement (attention from others) was substituted. Eventually, no consequences were delivered and a high rate of smiling was maintained.

Whitman et al. (1970) used candy and praise to train social interaction between two severely retarded and withdrawn children. Reinforcers were delivered to the children for playing with each other (e.g., rolling a ball back and forth or coloring together). Social interaction increased and generalized to a situation in which reinforcement was not delivered. Moreover, although the children were reinforced for interacting only with each other, their interactions with other children also increased.

Kale et al. (1968) used cigarettes to reinforce social responses of psychotic patients. A cigarette was administered for greetings either made spontaneously or in response to greetings from staff. Over the training sessions, cigarettes were administered on an increasingly intermittent schedule so that fewer and fewer social responses were reinforced. Greeting responses remained at a high level even though reinforcement was eliminated.

Important Considerations in Using Food and Consumables. The effectiveness of food and other consumables depends heavily upon the deprivation state of the individual. The strength of food or another consumable as a reinforcer is maximized by depriving the individual. If the individual is not at least partially deprived, food may only serve as a weak reinforcer. As mentioned before, investigators sometimes use food reinforcement prior to mealtime or during mealtime itself. In addition, light meals may be given throughout the day so that slight deprivation is maintained and food will be reinforcing continuously (O'Brien, Bugle, & Azrin, 1972). Even if the individual is deprived of food before training, as training proceeds on a given day the reinforcing value of food may be reduced. The number of times food can be delivered and the quantity delivered after a response are limited because of the possibility of satiation. To forestall satiation, some investigators have delivered small portions of the consumable item such as a bit of food, a few pieces of popcorn, or half a cigarette. Nevertheless, food and consumables are still readily subject to satiation.

The effectiveness of food reinforcement depends upon the type of food used. Although food per se is a primary reinforcer, specific foods used in a given program may not be reinforcing for particular individuals. For example, although ice cream may reinforce most children, for many individuals the flavor is a relevant dimension which will determine the reinforcing properties. When a single food or consumable is relied upon, the possibility exists that the event will not be effective with a number of clients. Moreover, preferences within a given individual change from time to time so a single food or consumable item may have short-lived reinforcing properties.

There are potential problems in the administration of food reinforcers. The delivery and consumption of food after a response sometimes interrupt ongoing behavior. For example, if a special education classroom teacher distributed candy to her students while they were working attentively on an assignment, each individual might be distracted momentarily from the task. Although the purpose of reinforcement is to augment attentiveness to classwork, the consumption of the reinforcer may temporarily distract the students. Similar problems occur in the consumption of consumables such as cigarettes or gum.

Another feature related to administration of food and other consumables is that they may be difficult to dispense immediately because they are cumbersome. Although staff can carry pockets full of candy, other foods such as beverages and ice cream generally are not readily carried. Of course, the setting in which food is used dictates the ease with which a particular type of food can be administered. In the home, virtually any food can be administered. However, institutional life usually requires stringent guidelines and rigidly adhered to routines for food delivery.

A related problem is that food is not easily administered to several individuals in a group immediately after behavior is performed. Since the administration of food to several individuals takes some time (e.g., selecting the quantity of food, putting a spoon or fork into the person's mouth, or passing a piece to each individual), it is not particularly well suited to group situations where everyone receives reinforcers. Many programs using food have been conducted on an individual basis rather than in groups.

Ethical and legal considerations can restrict the use of food and consumable items. These reinforcers are most effective when clients are deprived. Yet, deprivation of food violates legal rights of clients and, hence, is not a viable treatment alternative in many programs. When used as a reinforcer, the client cannot be deprived of food he or she would normally receive. Thus, food and consumables are often given over and above the events normally available. Because the client normally has access to food, the extra food used as a reinforcer may be less potent than it would be if the client were deprived. In part because of the concern for ethical and legal rights of the client and the availability of alternative reinforcers, food and other consumables are not the most frequently used reinforcers in applied settings.

Despite the possible disadvantages of food and consumables, they are potent reinforcers. Food and consumables are particularly suited to those individuals who initially fail to respond to events such as approval. Indeed, food is useful in establishing the reinforcing properties of other events such as praise, feedback, attention, smiles, and physical contact. Programs using food and consumables invariably pair the delivery of the reinforcer with praise and other social events so that these latter events can be used to control behavior effectively.

Social Reinforcers. Social reinforcers such as verbal praise, attention, physical contact (including affectionate or approving touches, pats, and hand holding), and facial expressions (including smiles, eye contact, nods of approval, and winks) are conditioned reinforcers. Numerous studies have shown that attention from a parent, teacher, or attendant exerts considerable control over behavior. Praise has been used to increase cooperative behavior of obstreperous children both in the home and at school. Social reinforcement has been used extensively in classroom settings where praise is delivered for study behavior while disruptive or inattentive behaviors are ignored.

Kirby and Shields (1972) used praise to alter the behavior of a 13-year-old boy named Tom in a seventh-grade classroom. Tom was of average intelligence but was doing poorly on his class assignments, particularly arithmetic. Also, he rarely paid attention to the lesson and constantly had to be reminded to work. Praise was used to improve performance on arithmetic assignments. Each day in class, Tom was praised for correct answers on his arithmetic worksheet after he completed the assignment. At first, every couple of responses were praised but eventually, the number of correct problems required for praise was gradually increased. Praise consisted merely of saying "Good work," "Excellent job," and similar statements. The results of the praise contingency appear in Figure 6–1. The upper portion shows the improvements in the rate of correct answers per minute in the treatment phases of the ABAB design. The lower portion of the figure shows that Tom's attentive behavior also improved even though it was not focused upon directly. A number of other investigations have shown that reinforcing academic performance not only improves the specific behaviors focused upon but also increases classroom attentiveness and reduces disruptive behavior (e.g., Ayllon & Roberts, 1974; Marholin, Steinman, McInnis, & Heads, 1975).

In most classroom studies, teacher attention consists primarily of verbal praise supplemented with facial expressions and physical contact. However, as noted earlier, nonverbal teacher attention alone, con-

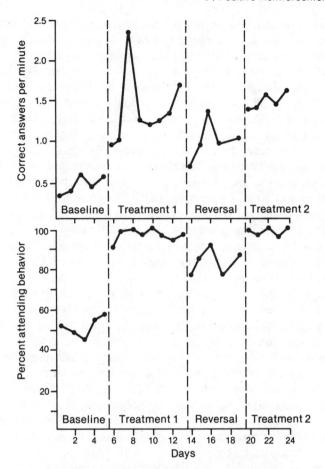

FIGURE 6–1 The number of correct arithmetic answers per minute and percent of times scored as attending behavior as a function of baseline and treatment conditions.

Source: Kirby, F. D., & Shields, F. Modification of arithmetic response rate and attending behavior in a seventh-grade student. *Journal of Applied Behavior Analysis*, 1972, **5**, 79–84.

sisting of smiles, physical contact, and approving nods contingent upon appropriate behavior, also improves classroom deportment (Kazdin & Klock, 1973).

Praise has been used in settings other than classrooms. In a psychiatric hospital (Milby, 1970), two psychotic patients received attention for socially interacting (talking, working, or playing with another patient). Social interaction increased when the nursing staff attended to patients, looked at them, or talked approvingly to them when the patients interacted.

In a study mentioned earlier (Hopkins, 1968), social reinforcement was used (following a phase using candy reinforcement) to maintain smiling of retarded boys. One of the boys wore a sign which said, "If I smile—talk to me. If I look sad—ignore me." Someone walking ahead of the child prompted others to read the sign and follow the instructions. The frequency of smiling increased. When the sign was altered ("If I smile—ignore me"), smiling decreased substantially. Thus, smiling was under control of social reinforcers.

Important Considerations in Using Social Reinforcers. Social consequences have a variety of advantages as reinforcers. First, they are easily administered by attendants, parents, and teachers. A verbal statement or smile can be given quickly. The complications of delivering food reinforcement are not present with praise and attention. Obviously, little preparation is involved before delivering praise. Providing praise takes little time so there is no delay in praising a number of individuals almost immediately. Indeed, praise can be delivered to a group as a whole as in a classroom.

A second consideration is that praise need not disrupt the behavior which is reinforced. A person can be praised or receive a pat on the back while engaging in appropriate behavior. Performance of the target behavior can continue. Third, praise is a generalized conditioned reinforcer because it has been paired with many reinforcing events. As mentioned earlier, conditioned reinforcers are less subject to satiation than are food and consumable items. Fourth, attention and praise are "naturally occurring" reinforcers employed in everyday life. Some reinforcers (such as food and consumables) do not normally follow desirable behavior such as paying attention in a classroom, interacting socially with others, talking rationally with peers, or working on a job. In contrast, social reinforcers such as attention from others often follow socially adaptive behaviors. Behaviors developed with social reinforcement in a treatment or training program may be more readily maintained outside of the setting than behaviors developed with other reinforcers. Social reinforcers in everyday life may continue to provide consequences for newly acquired behavior. In short, a desirable feature of using social reinforcement is that there is an increased likelihood that behaviors will be maintained outside of the specific training setting.

Before embarking on a program employing social reinforcement, it is important to keep a few considerations in mind. Praise, approval, and physical contact are not reinforcing for everyone. Because the reinforcement value of praise and attention has to be learned, one can expect to find individuals who do not respond to events which are normally socially reinforcing. Indeed, for some individuals praise may be aversive (Levin & Simmons, 1962). Because social events (praise, approval, and physical contact) are employed in everyday life, it is important to establish them as reinforcers by pairing them with events that are already reinforcers.

High-Probability Behaviors.   When persons are given the opportunity to engage in various behaviors, certain activities will be selected with a higher frequency than others. As mentioned in Chapter 2, the Premack principle denotes that activities that are selected with a relatively higher frequency often can serve as reinforcers for activities performed with a lower frequency. As a practical guide, allowing persons to engage in preferred activities and to earn various privileges can reinforce behavior. Laboratory research has attempted to determine higher frequency behaviors by observing performance or by depriving animals of certain sorts of activities, thereby making such activities more likely in the future. In clinical applications, higher probability behaviors often are inferred from expressed verbal preferences by the client or by seeing what the client does in his or her free time.

High probability behaviors have been used effectively in several applied programs. Reid, Schuh-Wear, and Brannon (1978) increased the attendance of staff to their jobs at an institution for the mentally retarded. A highly preferred reward, time off on the weekends, was used to reinforce low rates of absenteeism. Staff on the ward who showed high rates of attendance, according to criterion specified in advance, earned time off on the weekends. If the criterion was not met, staff reverted to their usual schedule with less time off. When time off was contingent upon improved attendance to work, absenteeism decreased.

Bateman (1975) increased the work performance of two institutionalized adult retardates. The clients were allowed to work on a more highly preferred task only after working on a less preferred task. Work on the less preferred task increased as a function of the contingency. Also, each client showed a reduction in time wasted (e.g., staring into space) during work.

Access to play has been used to reinforce accuracy of printing of kindergarten children (Salzberg, Wheeler, Devar, & Hopkins, 1971). When predetermined individualized levels of correct printing responses were achieved, the children could play. An interesting feature of this report is that each day, only some of the children were checked. The children who were checked were predetermined daily on a random basis. All nonchecked children automatically received access to play. Nevertheless, the quality of printing for *everyone* increased. Since a child never knew whether his or her performance was to be checked on a given day, the only way to guarantee receiving the reinforcer was to perform the target behavior each day.

In a program with hospitalized drug addicts (O'Brien, Raynes & Patch, 1971), patients earned the opportunity to engage in high probability behaviors (recreation, access to television and radio, pass privileges away from the hospital, and the opportunity to wear street clothes rather than institutional clothes in the hospital). To earn these privileges, patients were required to awaken and groom themselves on time, to attend meetings, and to carry out various routine behaviors on the ward. The percentage of patients who actively engaged in all of the low frequency target behaviors increased from 20% during baseline to 80% during the program.

Important Considerations in Using High Probability Behaviors. High probability behaviors offer distinct advantages as reinforcers. In most settings, activities and privileges are readily available. For example, in the home, access to television, peers, or the family automobile are likely to be high probability behaviors depending upon the age level of the person. At school, access to recess, free time, games, and entertaining reading materials may serve a similar function. In hospital and rehabilitation facilities, engaging in recreation, leaving the ward, access to desirable living quarters or personal possessions, and sitting with friends at meals can also be used. In short, activities and privileges which can be made contingent upon performance usually are available in any setting. Hence, extra reinforcers (e.g., candy or money) need not be introduced into the setting.

There are limitations in using high probability behaviors as reinforcing events. First, access to an activity cannot always immediately follow low probability behavior. For example, in a classroom setting, activities such as recess or games cannot readily be used to reinforce behavior immediately. Usually, activities and privileges have some scheduling limitations. Hence, in some cases there will be a delay of reinforcement. In cases where access to an activity is frequent, the routine of the setting is interrupted (e.g., Osborne, 1969). However, after performance of the lower probability behavior is established, access to the high probability activity can be delayed without loss of behavior gains.

A second consideration is that providing an activity is sometimes an all or none enterprise, so that it is either earned or not earned. This can limit the flexibility in administering the reinforcer. For example, in institutions for psychiatric patients or delinquents, access to overnight passes and trips to a nearby town are sometimes used as reinforcing activities. These activities cannot be parceled out so that "portions" of them are earned. They have to be given in their entirety or not given at all. If a client's behavior comes very near the performance criterion for reinforcement but does not quite meet the criterion, a decision has to be made whether to provide the reinforcer. A solution is to shape behavior by initially setting low criteria to earn the activity. Gradually the criteria for earning the reinforcer are increased. Another alternative is to incorporate many privileges and activities into the contingency system.

Different behaviors or varying degrees of a given behavior can be reinforced with different privileges.

A third consideration in using high probability behaviors as reinforcers is that relying on one or two activities as reinforcers runs the risk that some individuals may not find them reinforcing. Preferences for activities may be idiosyncratic so that different activities need to be available. Providing free time is desirable, if individuals can choose from a variety of activities.

A final consideration in using activities and privileges is that in many institutions, activities must be freely available to the clients. Activities which might be made contingent upon performance are delivered independently of the client's performance. The ideology of presenting activities and other potentially reinforcing events (e.g., meals and sleeping quarters) noncontingently was developed to ensure that individuals would not be deprived of basic human rights. Institutionalized clients are usually deprived of many amenities of living simply by virtue of their institutionalization. Withholding or depriving individuals of the already limited number of available reinforcers is viewed as unethical. (The issue of deprivation will be discussed in Chapter 12 along with other ethical considerations.) In any case, in some settings certain activities already given to the clients as part of the setting simply cannot be given contingently.

Informative Feedback.   Providing information about performance can serve as powerful reinforcement. Feedback is a conditioned reinforcer because it usually is associated with the delivery of other events that are reinforcing. Feedback is implicit in the delivery of any reinforcer because it indicates which responses are appropriate or desirable from the standpoint of those who provide reinforcement. Thus, when reinforcers such as food, praise, activities, or points are provided, a client receives feedback or knowledge of how well he or she is doing. Perhaps, feedback may include implicit social approval or disapproval. However, feedback can be employed independently of explicit approval or other reinforcers. Individuals can be informed of their behavior or of the extent to which their behavior has changed. Feedback refers to knowledge of results of one's performance without necessarily including additional events which may be reinforcing in their own right.

Feedback was used with a psychiatric patient who had a severe knife phobia (Leitenberg et al., 1968). She had obsessive thoughts about killing others when using a kitchen knife and became unable to look at or come into contact with sharp knives. The patient was told that practice in looking at the knife would help reduce her fear. The patient was told to look at a sharp knife displayed in a small compartment until she became uncomfortable. Feedback indicated how many seconds the patient kept the compartment open, thereby exposing herself to the knife.

140

Feedback steadily increased the time of self-exposure to the knife. Figure 6–2 shows an increase in seconds of looking at the knife. Adding praise (e.g., "That was great!") to the feedback (second phase) did not appear to augment the effect of feedback alone. Throughout the project, except for the reversal (fourth) phase, feedback continued to improve

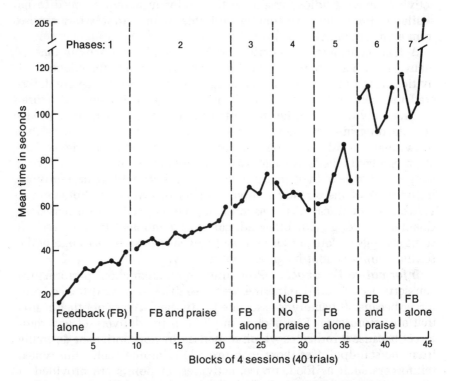

FIGURE 6–2 Time in which a knife was kept exposed by a phobic patient as a function of feedback, feedback plus praise, and no feedback or praise conditions.

Source: Leitenberg, H., Agras, W. S., Thompson, L. E., & Wright, D. E. Feedback in behavior modification: An experimental analysis in two phobic cases. *Journal of Applied Behavior Analysis*, 1968, **1**, 131–37.

performance. It is unclear whether praise during the sixth phase was responsible for behavior change. In any case, by the end of the study, the patient was able to use a knife to slice vegetables for use in the ward.

Van Houten, Hill, and Parsons (1975) used feedback in two fourth-grade classrooms to increase the length of compositions that children wrote in class. Children were given a certain period of time in which to write their compositions and received feedback on the number of words that were included in the compositions. Children counted their own word totals to receive immediate feedback and were instructed to see whether they could improve their totals in subsequent compositions. Feedback tended to improve the number of words written and student attentiveness in class. Immediate feedback on productivity of academic work has been used successfully to improve arithmetic, handwriting, and spelling as well (e.g., Fink & Carnine, 1975).

An interesting application of feedback was reported by Komaki and Barnett (1977) who improved the performance of boys who participated on a Pop Warner football team. The purpose was to improve execution of the plays by selected members of the team (backfield and center). A checklist of the behaviors (movements and actions) of the players was scored after each play to measure if each player did what he was supposed to. During a feedback phase, the boys came over to the coach after running the plays during scrimmage. The coach showed the checklist and pointed out what was done correctly and incorrectly. Feedback was introduced in a multiple-baseline design across various plays and improved the execution of each play.

An important area of research involving feedback is *biofeedback.* Biofeedback consists of providing information to people about various physiological processes such as blood pressure, heart rate, muscle tension, and brain waves. Immediate information is provided to help clients learn to control various bodily processes. Biofeedback represents an important area in its own right. Because it usually is used in individual treatment sessions rather than in applied settings, it will be discussed later in Chapter 10 rather than here.

Important Considerations in Using Feedback. Feedback has been widely employed with a variety of client populations and settings because of the ease with which it can be applied. Feedback can be readily employed when a performance criterion is explicit such as academic achievement or work productivity. In other situations, criteria can be set such as the number of cigarettes smoked, calories consumed, or irrational statements expressed by patients. Daily feedback can be presented to convey how well the client is doing in relation to the criterion. Evidence suggests that specifying a criterion for performance is essential (Locke, Cartledge, & Koeppel, 1968). Without such a criterion, at least an implicit one, the desired level of performance may be unclear. Feedback can be used without introducing other extrinsic reinforcers that are not ordinarily delivered as part of the routine in the setting. To those who view extrinsic reinforcers as undesirable in a given setting, feedback may provide an attractive alternative.

An extremely important consideration in using feedback is that its effects often are equivocal. Although feedback has been effective in many applications, it has been ineffective or only moderately effective in several other reports (e.g., Hall et al., 1972; Kazdin, 1973a; Salzberg et al., 1971; Van Houten et al., 1975). Feedback usually is not as effective alone as it is when combined with other reinforcers such as praise or tokens that can be used for other purchase tangible back-up reinforcers (e.g., Cossairt, Hall, & Hopkins, 1973; Drabman et al., 1973). Hence, feedback is not one of the more potent methods of altering behavior.

Programs based upon feedback often are relatively simple to implement compared with such other programs such as token economies, discussed below. Also, people who implement the program may be more favorably disposed to delivering feedback alone rather than providing extrinsic reinforcers. For these reasons, it may be useful to begin with a program based upon feedback, perhaps paired with praise, and then to resort to a more potent source of reinforcement and a more complex program if the desired goals have not been achieved.

Tokens. Tokens are conditioned reinforcers such as poker chips, coins, tickets, stars, points, or checkmarks. As discussed earlier, tokens are generalized reinforcers because they can be exchanged for a variety of reinforcing events referred to as back-up reinforcers. A reinforcement system based upon tokens is referred to as a token economy. In a token economy, tokens function the same way that money does in national economic systems. The tokens are earned and used to purchase back-up reinforcers including various goods and services. Back-up reinforcers usually include food, consumables, activities, and privileges. The rate of exchange of tokens for back-up reinforcers must be specified so that it is clear how many tokens are required to purchase various reinforcers. The target behavior or behaviors are made explicit, as in most programs, along with the number of tokens which are administered for their performance.

The tokens need to be established as conditioned reinforcers because they have no reinforcing properties in their own right. For some populations it is sufficient to explain that tokens can be exchanged for various goods. After the explanation, the tokens take on immediate value which is maintained by the actual exchange of tokens for other reinforcers. For individuals whose behavior is not controlled by instructions about the value of tokens, the tokens can be given noncontingently a few times. Immediately after they are delivered, they can be exchanged or traded for a back-up reinforcer. For example, a retarded child may be given a few poker chips immediately before entering a dining room. A few seconds after having the tokens, an attendant at the door can take the tokens. Thus, the tokens (poker chips) are followed by access to food. By pairing tokens with other back-up events, their value is achieved.

Token economies have been used extensively in special education, remedial, and "normal" classrooms (Kazdin, 1977e; O'Leary, 1978). For example, Breyer and Allen (1975) used a token economy to improve the behavior of 15 first-grade students whose academic and social behaviors were considered to be severe enough to interfere with their promotion into a regular second-grade classroom. The program was directed at eliminating disruptive behavior (e.g., hitting a peer) and improving appropriate on-task behavior (e.g., working on the assignment, responding appropriately to the teacher). After baseline observations, the program began by having the teacher praise appropriate behavior and ignore inappropriate behavior. Although praise improved student performance, additional gains were needed. Hence, token reinforcement was used in which children received points at various intervals depending upon how well they were working. The points were exchangeable for prizes ranging in value from $.05 to $1.50 at a "good study store" in class. The effects of the program are illustrated in Figure 6–3 that show rather clearly that the token system greatly improved on-task behavior.

Token economies in classroom settings have done more than merely improve general classroom behavior. Applications in elementary and secondary school settings have improved academic performance in reading, writing, composition, and arithmetic. Improvements in academic skills in the classroom also have been evident in performance on standardized achievement tests (e.g., Bushell, 1974; Kaufman & O'Leary, 1972).

Token economies have been used extensively in psychiatric settings (e.g., Ayllon & Azrin, 1968b; Kazdin, 1977e). A recent program reported by Paul and Lentz (1977) used token reinforcement with psychiatric patients. Patients received tokens (colored plastic strips) for such behaviors as attending activities on the ward, group meetings, and therapy sessions, and for grooming, making one's bed, showering, engaging in appropriate mealtime behaviors, and socially interacting. Tokens could be exchanged for a variety of back-up events such as purchase of cosmetics, candy, cigarettes, and clothing, renting chairs or bedside stands for one's room, ordering items from a mail order catalogue, using a piano, record player, radio, time in a lounge, watching television, the privilege of having a private room and sleeping late, and others. As patients improved in the ward they advanced to higher levels within the program where more reinforcers were available and higher expectations were made for performance. Patients could "buy" themselves off the system by doing well and carried a "credit card" which allowed them free access to all available reinforcers, as long as their performance was up to standards. The program was very successful in reducing and eliminating bizarre behaviors, improving social interaction and communication skills, and developing participation in activities. Moreover, the gains made in the hospital during treatment were reflected on a one and a half year follow-up after patients had been discharged and placed into the community. A large number of token

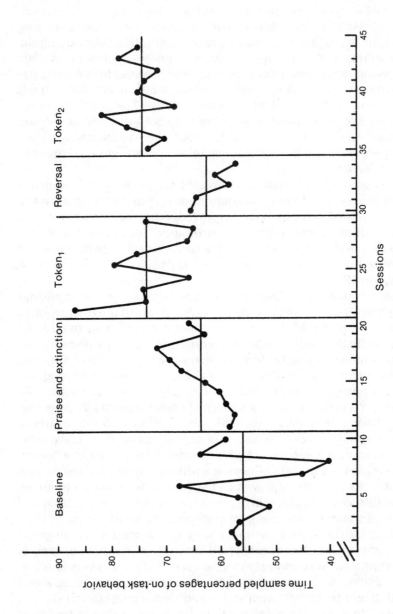

FIGURE 6–3 Percentage of on-task behavior during treatment phases.

Source: Breyer, N. L., & Allen, G. J. Effects of implementing a token economy on teacher attending behavior. *Journal of Applied Behavior Analysis*, 1975, **8**, 373–80.

economies with psychiatric patients have shown improvements in specific adaptive behaviors on the ward. Improvements on the ward often are associated with increased discharge rates from the hospital and decreased readmission rates later.

A well known program based upon a token economy has been used to rehabilitate predelinquent youths who have committed various offenses (e.g., thefts, fighting, school truancy, and academic failure) (Fixsen, Fixsen, Phillips, Phillips, & Wolf, 1976; Fixsen, Phillips, & Wolf, 1973; Phillips, 1968). The program was conducted at a home-style cottage setting, named Achievement Place, managed by two houseparents. Behaviors that earned points included watching the news, reading newspapers, keeping oneself neat and clean, performing chores around the house, receiving good grades at school, and others. However, points could be lost for poor grades, aggressive talk (making threats), disobeying rules, lying, stealing, being late, fighting, and other disruptive behaviors. Points could be used to purchase privileges such as staying up late, going downtown, watching TV, using tools, riding one's bicycle, and receiving an allowance. The token system has been shown to be effective in controlling a variety of behaviors in the facility and work at school. Interestingly, the boys participated actively in running the program by supervising each others' work, recording their own behavior, and developing and enforcing rules among their peers. Outcome evaluations of Achievement Place have suggested that youths participating in the program have fewer contacts with the police, are less likely to be reinstitutionalized within two years after treatment, and do better in school than delinquents placed on probation or in institutional settings (Fixsen et al., 1976; Kirigin, Wolf, Braukmann, Fixsen, & Phillips, 1979).

Token economies have been used as part of treatment for a number of medical problems such as ensuring that hypertensive patients monitor their blood pressure and increasing adherence to medication and exercise regimens. For example, a token system was used to help an 82-year-old man who had suffered a massive heart attack (Dapcich–Miura & Hovel, 1979). After leaving the hospital, he was instructed to increase his physical activity, gradually, to eat foods high in potassium (e.g., orange juice and bananas), and to take medication.[1] However, the patient rarely walked at all and neglected his diet and medication. A token reinforcement program was devised which provided poker chips for each time he walked around the block, drank orange juice, and took his medication. The program was conducted by his granddaughter with whom he lived. The poker chips could be saved and exchanged for selecting the dinner menu at home or for going out to dinner at a restaurant of his choice. The results, which appear in Figure 6–4, show that the token program was introduced for one behavior at a time in a

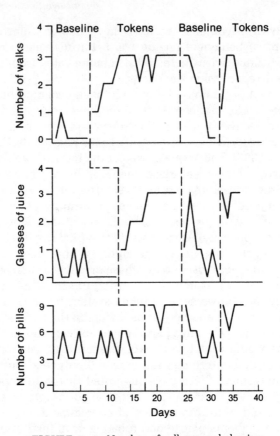

FIGURE 6–4 Number of adherence behaviors (walking, orange juice drinking, and pill taking) per day under baseline and token reinforcement conditions. The upper graph depicts the data for walking, the middle graph shows the number of glasses of orange juice consumed, and the third graph illustrates the number of pills taken.

Source: Dapcich-Miura, E., & Hovel, M. F. Contingency management of adherence to a complex medical regimen in an elderly heart patient. *Behavior Therapy,* 1979, **10**, 193–201.

multiple-baseline design. Improvements were obtained for each behavior as a function of token reinforcement. A temporary withdrawal of the program (second baseline) shows further how crucial the token system was in sustaining adherence to the medical regimen.

Token economies have been used with a variety of other populations than those illustrated here including the mentally retarded, prisoners, geriatric or nursing-home residents, alcoholics and drug addicts, and outpatient children and adults with a variety of problems (see Kazdin, 1977e). Similarly, the settings in which token economies have been applied include the home, schools, institutions and hospitals, day-care centers, nursing homes, and other places as well. Also, as evident in a later chapter, applications of reinforcement techniques to social problems such as energy conservation and littering have relied upon token economies to alter behavior in everyday life.

Important Considerations in Using Tokens. Tokens offer advantages over other reinforcers. First, tokens are potent reinforcers and can often maintain behavior at a higher level than other conditioned reinforcers such as praise, approval, and feedback. For example, praise alone often is very effective in altering behavior. However, even greater improvements in performance usually are evident when token reinforcement is used instead of or in conjunction with praise (e.g., Kazdin & Polster, 1973; Walker, Hops, & Fiegenbaum, 1976).

A second advantage of tokens is that they bridge the delay between the target response and back-up reinforcement. If a reinforcer (e.g., an activity) cannot be delivered immediately after desirable behavior, tokens can be delivered immediately and used to purchase a back-up reinforcer later. Third, since tokens are backed up by a variety of reinforcers, they are less subject to satiation than are other reinforcers. If a client is no longer interested in one or two back-up reinforcers, usually there are many other reinforcers which are of value. Similarly, if an individual is satiated from food, nonfood items can be purchased with tokens. Fourth, tokens can be easily administered without interrupting the target response. Since the reinforcer does not require consumption (e.g., food) or performance of behaviors which may be incompatible with the target response (e.g., participating in a special activity), the delivery of tokens does not usually disrupt behavior. Fifth, tokens permit administering a single reinforcer (tokens) to individuals who ordinarily have different reinforcer preferences. Individual preferences can be exercised in the exchange of back-up reinforcers. Hence, there is less concern with the reinforcers being of value to only a few individuals in the setting. Sixth, tokens permit parceling out other reinforcers (e.g., activities) which might have to be earned in an all-or-none fashion. The tokens can be earned toward the purchase of the back-up reinforcer. For example, in one report, a psychiatric patient could earn discharge from the hospital for accumulating a large sum of tokens (Linscheid, Malosky, & Zimmerman, 1974).

There are potential disadvantages in employing tokens. In some programs, back-up reinforcers are introduced which are extraneous to the setting. For example, in a classroom program tokens may be backed up with food. A potential problem is removing the token system after behavior gains have been made and transferring control of behavior to naturally occurring events such as privileges and activities. Food is not normally presented in a class and eventually needs to be eliminated. Of course, in a token economy, back-up reinforcers not normally available in the setting need not be introduced. Tokens can be used to purchase access to ordinary privileges, activities, and other events. Yet, introducing the tokens themselves may be disadvantageous. Tokens constitute a reinforcing event not available in most settings (excluding tokens such as money and grades). Because the delivery of tokens is clearly associated with reinforcement of desirable behavior, they may exert stimulus control over that behavior. Clients learn that the presence of tokens signals that desirable behavior is reinforced and the absence of tokens signals that desirable behavior is not likely to be reinforced. Once tokens are withdrawn, desirable behavior may decline. Specific procedures need to be implemented to withdraw the token program without a loss of behavior gains. In some settings, conditioned reinforcers normally available such as grades, money, and praise can be substituted for tokens. (Chapter 11 discusses techniques to maintain changes after a behavior modification program is withdrawn.)

A second possible disadvantage of tokens is that individuals in token economies may obtain tokens in unauthorized ways. For example, clients may steal tokens from each other. If tokens can be obtained without performing the target responses, their effect on behavior will decrease. To combat stealing, tokens can be individually coded so that they differ for each individual.

Types of Reinforcers: Summary. The variety of reinforcers reviewed above provides a great deal of flexibility in devising reinforcement programs. At the very minimum, praise, activities, and privileges can be used in virtually any setting. The use of consumables may be limited by restrictions of the setting. For example, food may be too difficult to administer in a large group. Although tokens usually are the most powerful positive reinforcer, they may not be required to change behavior in most settings. Praise, privileges, and feedback should be used prior to implementing a token economy. A token economy is somewhat more difficult to implement (e.g., delivering tokens plus back-up reinforcers, keeping track of token earnings) and introduces problems (e.g., stealing or hoarding tokens, and withdrawing tokens from the setting) that may not occur with other programs. Hence, tokens should be introduced only when more easily implemented programs have been ineffective.

The discussion of types of reinforcers should not imply that various reinforcers have to be used independently. If a program relies on a consumable item, that does not mean that other events such as praise or activities cannot be used as well. In fact, a program that incorporates a variety of reinforcers is likely to be more effective than one in which only a few reinforcers are used. Token programs are effective because a variety of reinforcers are available. More than one type of reinforcer should be used for an additional reason. Programs using activities, feedback, consumables, or tokens should pair these events with praise. One goal of any program is to increase a client's responsiveness to his or her social environment. Developing responsiveness to praise is an important step in this process. When the client functions in nonprogrammed settings, social reinforcers are likely to be a major source of positive consequences which control behavior.

■ CONTINGENCY CONTRACTS

Often reinforcement contingencies are designed in the form of behavioral contracts between individuals who wish behavior to change (e.g., parents, teachers, attendants) and those whose behavior is to be changed (students, children, patients). An actual contract is signed by both parties indicating that they agree to the terms. *The contract specifies the relationship between behaviors and their consequences.* Specifically, the contract specifies the reinforcers desired by the client and the behavior desired by the individual who wishes behavior change. Any of the reinforcers discussed above as well as idiosyncratic rewards may be used in the contract. When each participant signs the contract, the program is underway.

Ideally, contingency contracts contain five elements (Stuart, 1971). First, contracts should detail the privileges each party expects to gain from the contract. For example, parents may want a child to complete his or her work, attend school regularly, and so on. On the other hand, the child wants free time with friends, extra allowance, and other reinforcers. Second, the behaviors of the client must be readily observable. If parents or teachers cannot determine whether a responsibility has been met, they cannot grant a privilege. Thus, some behaviors may not readily be incorporated into the contract system. For example, parents often cannot easily monitor whether an adolescent visits certain friends so this would not be advisable to include in a contract. Third, the contract provides sanctions for a failure to meet the terms. The client is aware of the conditions for failing to meet the responsibility and what consequences will follow. The aversive consequences for not meeting the contract terms are systematic and planned in advance (i.e., agreed to by all parties) rather than arbitrary and after the fact. Fourth, a contract can provide a bonus clause which reinforces consistent compliance with the contract. Bonuses (extra privileges, activity, or extension of curfew limit) can be used to reinforce desirable performance over a prolonged period. Consistent performance often goes unrewarded in everyday life. Since individuals expect such performance, it often is neglected. For a client whose behavior is recently developed, it is crucial to provide reinforcement for consistent performance. Bonuses written into the contract serve this purpose. Fifth, a contract should provide a means of monitoring the rate of positive reinforcement given and received. The records kept inform each party when reinforcement is to occur and provide constant feedback. Moreover, the records may cue individuals to make favorable comments about desirable behavior as earning of the back-up reinforcer is about to occur (Stuart, 1971).

Contingency contracts need not be elaborate or complex. A sample contract is illustrated in Figure 6–5. This contract was used to alter the behavior of an 8-year-old second grade boy, named Andrew, who constantly fought at school (Bristol, 1976). The program involved both the teacher, parents, and Andrew. Each morning Andrew received a card with a smiling face on it. At morning, lunch, and the end of the day, the teacher signed his card if he had not engaged in fighting, as specified in the contract. The teacher's signatures served as points—each signature could be accumulated toward the purchase of a reward, as also specified in the contract. Parents provided praise, posted the cards in a conspicuous place, and gave extra rewards (staying up 15 minutes extra at bedtime) for the signatures he received. As shown in Figure 6–6, Andrew averaged about nine fights in the first week before the contingency contract. Fights were reduced during the contracting procedure. When the contract procedure was withdrawn, fights again returned. In the final phase, fights again were reduced and eliminated for the last three weeks of the program. A report obtained seven months after the program was terminated indicated that Andrew was doing well without any special assistance.

Another sample contingency contract is provided in Figure 6–7. This contract represents one of several that was used to alter the behavior of former psychiatric patients who moved from the hospital to foster home care. A foster home usually is a sheltered living environment for former patients which is managed by a married couple. The facility allows former patients to live in a relatively nondemanding situation while functioning in the community. Upper, Lochman, and Aveni (1977) used contracting to help foster parents (the couple who managed the facility) alter problematic behavior of the residents, who averaged about 58 years in age. Individual contracts were devised such as the one in Figure 6–7 for each resident. A variety of behaviors were altered such as refusing to eat meals, to go to one's job, to take medication, threatening assaults on others, frequently complaining or making irrational comments (e.g., suspiciousness, hearing voices, seeing strange objects), and other behaviors. Residents completed a questionnaire to identify various events (watching television, drinking beer in the home, going to dances, spending time with a foster parent, going to movies) that might

---

Date

Contract no.

Mrs. Harris will initial a smiley card for Andrew each time he does one of the following:

1. Comes into school, hangs up his wraps, and takes his seat without arguing or fighting with another child.
2. Eats his lunch and has his noon recess without arguing or fighting with another child.
3. Clears his desk, gets his wraps, and goes to the bus without arguing or fighting with another child.

When Andrew has received 15 signatures from Mrs. Harris and has had his cards signed by one of his parents, he may choose one of the following rewards:

> Read a story to someone.
> Be first in line for lunch.
> Pass out supplies.
> Get notes from the office.
> Bring a treat from home for the class.
> Go to the library for free reading.
> Choose a book for Mrs. Harris to read to the class.
> Choose a friend for a math game.
> Bring a carrot for Chopper and get a chance to hold him.
> Be a student helper in math for 30 minutes.

I, Andrew, agree to the terms of the above agreement,

I, the classroom teacher, agree to provide Andrew with the reinforcers specified above if Andrew keeps his part of the agreement. I also agree not to provide Andrew with any of the above reinforcers during the term of the contract if he does not earn the necessary signatures.

I, Andrew's parent, agree to sign each card that Andrew brings home, to post the cards where Andrew can see them, and to help Andrew keep track of the number of signatures he has earned. Andrew can earn 15 minutes of extra "stay up" time by bringing home 3 signatures.

WE UNDERSTAND THAT THIS IS NOT A LEGALLY BINDING CONTRACT, BUT RATHER A FIRM COMMITMENT OF GOOD WILL AMONG PARTIES WHO CARE ABOUT EACH OTHER.

FIGURE 6–5 Sample contingency contract.

Source: Bristol, M. M. Control of physical aggression through school- and home-based reinforcement. In J. D. Krumboltz & C. E. Thoresen (Eds.), Counseling methods. New York: Holt, Rinehart & Winston, 1976.

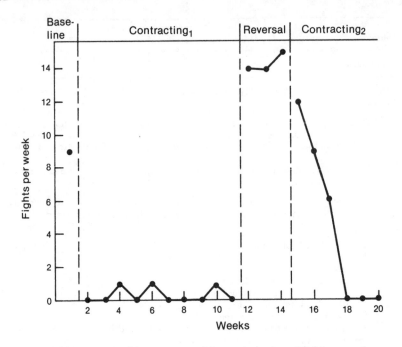

FIGURE 6–6 Weekly summary of the total number of fights occurring out of a possible maximum of fifteen.

Source: Bristol, M. M. Control of physical aggression through school- and home-based reinforcement. In J. D. Krumboltz & C. E. Thoresen (Eds.), *Counseling methods.* New York: Holt, Rinehart & Winston, 1976.

serve as positive reinforcers. Contingency contracting significantly reduced the frequency of problem behaviors. Former patients who had not received the contracting condition, tended to get worse over time.

Hall, Cooper, Burmaster, and Polk (1977) used contingency contracts with several drug addicts who attended a methadone maintenance clinic. Heroin addicts are encouraged to take methadone to reduce the dependency upon opiates that are obtained illegally and which may have a more severe withdrawal. Also, when addicts come to clinics for methadone, there is a better chance of introducing efforts for rehabilitation than with opiate habits maintained on the street. In the Hall et al. (1977) study, adult addicts individually drew up contracts to alter such behaviors as using drugs, not attending the clinic, and gaining weight. Reinforcers were provided on the basis of meeting specific goals in the contract and included special foods, bus tokens, lunches or dinners at restaurants, time off probation, and home delivery of methadone. The contracting procedure led to changes in the target behaviors. For example, for one addict who was still taking heroin,

Effective dates: From _____ 6/2/76 _____   to _____ 7/28/76 _____

We, the undersigned parties, agree to perform the following behaviors:

John agrees to:	Mr. & Mrs. Harris agree to:
1. Take his medication as prescribed.	1. Give John a package of cigarettes each morning after breakfast.
2. Attend his hospital work assignment daily (as an outpatient volunteer).	2. Give John $10 per week spending money (on Saturday morning).
3. Refrain from smoking cigarettes in his bedroom.	3. Stop nagging John about how much he smokes.
4. Before visiting his sister and brother-in-law, call and ask permission to visit.	4. Allow John to visit his sister's home once a month on a Sunday, from 2:00 p.m. to 8:30 p.m.

Bonus: If John follows clause 4 (above) for four weeks, he may move from his present room to a single room in the front of the house.

Penalty: If there are more than 10 infractions of the house rules against smoking in bedrooms, John will lose his smoking privileges entirely.

_____
(Foster home resident)

_____
(Foster parent)

_____
(Foster parent)

_____
(Behavioral counselor)

This contract will be reviewed one week from date of agreement.

FIGURE 6–7   Sample contingency contract.

Source: Upper, D., Lochman, J. E., & Aveni, C. A. Using contingency contracting to modify the problematic behaviors of foster home residents. *Behavior Modification*, 1977, **1**, 405–16.

samples of urine taken three times each week revealed less use of drugs during the contingency contracting period. Moreover, the reduction of heroin intake was maintained up to several months after treatment.

MacDonald, Gallimore, and MacDonald (1970) used contingency contracting to decrease truancy of high school students. Absenteeism was 70 percent for students participating in one of the projects. The high rate of absenteeism was altered by having individuals important in the life of the students (e.g., relatives, mother of a girl friend, pool hall proprietor) make deals with the students by contingently administering individualized reinforcers (e.g., access to family car, weekend privileges, time with a girl friend, and access to "fancy" clothing) for attending school. Attendance improved in a seven-week period. When the deals were discontinued and later reinstated, attendance decreased and improved, respectively, indicating that the contracts controlled absenteeism.

Contingency contracts have been used successfully to alter a variety of problems such as overeating, alcohol and drug abuse, cigarette smoking, problem behaviors of delinquents, disruptive behavior of elementary school children, studying in college students, and several others (Bristol & Sloane, 1974; Miller, 1972; Spring, Sipich, Trimble, & Goeckner, 1978; Stuart & Lott, 1972; White–Blackburn, Semb, & Semb, 1977). Various authors have described procedures for developing contracts that can be applied to a wide range of disorders and have illustrated additional applications (see DeRisi & Butz, 1975; Gelfand & Hartmann, 1975; Homme, Csanyi, Gonzales, & Rechs, 1969; Krumboltz & Thoresen, 1976).

Advantages in Using Contingency Contracts. There are distinct advantages in using contingency contracts. First, when clients are allowed to have some input into designing or implementing the program, their performance may be better than if the program is imposed upon them (cf. Lovitt & Curtiss, 1969). Hence, programs may generally be more effective, if a contract arrangement is made rather than if a program is imposed upon the client. Second, the contingencies specified in a contract are less likely to be aversive to the client. The client can negotiate the consequences and the requirements for reinforcement. If the system is minimally aversive, the client is less likely to attempt to escape from the contingencies or from those who administer them. Third, contingency contracts are usually flexible in that participants can renegotiate the terms to make revisions (Stuart & Lott, 1972). Reinforcers delivered for particular responses can be adjusted, response requirements can be increased, and so on. Thus, signing a contract does not necessarily fix the program. Indeed, as soon as there is dissatisfaction of one signee, the negotiations can begin. Fourth, the contract makes the contingencies explicit. The specification of the contingencies serves as rules or instructions for the client on how to behave and what consequences will follow behavior. Research has suggested that explicit instructions alone may not produce durable changes in performance but may increase the effectiveness of reinforcement (e.g., Ayllon & Azrin, 1964; Kazdin, 1973e; Resick, Forehand, & Peed, 1974). Fifth, the contract is particularly useful in structuring the relationship between persons who normally interact. For example, families of delinquents engage in a lower rate of positive social exchanges than do nondelinquent families. Delinquent families may inadequately reinforce socially appropriate behavior (Stuart, 1971). Contracts make explicit the requirements for delivering positive consequences and increase the likelihood that the consequences actually are provided. By putting the contingencies in writing, it is easier to monitor whether they are carried out in the desired fashion.

Contingency contracts have been used relatively frequently. However, research has not looked carefully at how contracts should be devised to make them maximally effective or acceptable to clients. The importance of a contingent relationship between behavior and consequences in the contract has been demonstrated but other characteristics such as the number of reinforcers and the use of bonuses have had unclear effects (e.g., Spring et al., 1978; Stuart & Lott, 1972). Although little work has been done to provide clear guidelines for how contracts should be constructed to achieve maximal effects, the use of contracts to structure reinforcement programs is to be strongly encouraged.

Contracts actively solicit client participation and agreement. Programs arranged on a contractual basis provide a voice for the client to state his or her own desires and to ensure that the program is fair. The active participation of the client may make the contingencies more acceptable to all parties participating in the program. The use of contingency contracts also is consistent with current ethical and legal guidelines that seek to ensure that the client is fully informed of the treatment program and gives consent to the procedures and goals (see Chapter 12).

■ REINFORCEMENT TECHNIQUES TO REDUCE UNDESIRABLE RESPONSES

Reinforcement is used to increase behavior, as shown in numerous illustrations of previous programs. In many situations in which behavior modification programs are used, the major goal of the program is to reduce undesirable behavior. Because reinforcement is discussed as a technique to increase behavior, people often believe that it is inappropriate to employ to decrease behavior. Hence, punishment and extinction, discussed in the following chapters, are employed because they decrease response frequency directly. However, undesirable target responses can be decreased or eliminated by reinforcement. Indeed, different reinforcement techniques are available to suppress behavior.

Reinforcement of Other Behavior.   One way to decrease the undesirable behavior is to provide reinforcement when the client engages in any behavior other than the target response. As discussed in the last chapter, differential reinforcement of other behavior (DRO) consists of providing the reinforcing consequences for all responses except for the behavior of interest. The effect of this schedule is to decrease the target behavior.

For example, Lowitz and Suib (1978) reduced the frequency that an 8-year-old girl sucked her thumb. The intervention was required in part because of the dental problems that resulted from the constant sucking. A DRO schedule was used in which the child received pennies during treatment sessions for each one-minute interval in which thumbsucking did not occur. Within five sessions, thumbsucking was virtually eliminated. The program was successfully extended to the home with a token system for nonthumbsucking. The behavior was eliminated and the effects were reported to be maintained up to one year of follow-up.

Rather than reinforce the nonoccurrence of the target response that is to be suppressed, reinforcement can be provided for behaviors that are directly incompatible with that response. By increasing the frequency of an incompatible behavior, the undesirable behavior is decreased. Usually, it is quite easy to select an incompatible response that can be reinforced. For example, if a child fights with siblings at home, reinforcement can be delivered for such behaviors as reading quietly, playing games cooperatively, and watching television without arguing. If an institutionalized patient has violent outbursts and tantrums, reinforcement can be delivered for talking and sitting quietly, and interacting with peers with a calm demeanor which are incompatible with the undesired responses.

The effects of reinforcing a behavior incompatible with the undesired response were demonstrated in a program by Nunes, Murphy, and Ruprecht (1977, Exp. 2) who treated a mentally retarded girl named Jane. Jane had a high rate of self-injurious behavior that included slapping her face, hitting her ears with her fists, and slamming her arms against the table when seated. The intervention was carried out in the classroom of a state hospital. To reduce self-injury, the reinforcer was provided when Jane used her hands to work on a puzzle rather than to hit herself. The reinforcer consisted of turning on a back massager while she was engaging in the desired behaviors and providing praise. If any self-injurious behavior occurred, the massager was turned off for 15 seconds. The effects of the program on self-injurious behavior are evident from Figure 6–8. Reinforcement of incompatible behavior systematically reduced self-injury, as shown in the ABAB design.

Reinforcement of incompatible behaviors has been used effectively in many programs. For example, the behaviors of hyperactive children in the classroom and at home have been altered using reinforcement techniques. Hyperactive behaviors have included disturbing others excessively, blurting out statements, being out of one's seat, destroying objects, speaking rapidly, running around the room, not complying with the requests of parents or teachers and in general very high levels of inappropriate activity. Rather than punish these behaviors, many programs have been designed to reinforce incompatible behaviors (Ayllon,

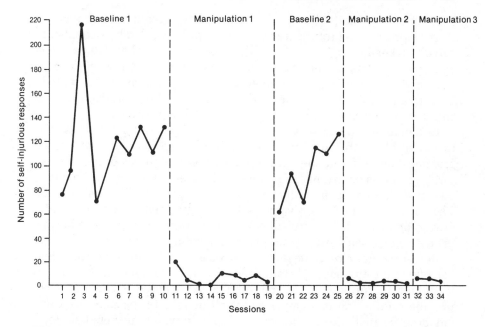

FIGURE 6–8 Number of self-injurious responses during each session exhibited by Jane across experimental conditions.

Source: Nunes, D. L., Murphy, R. J., & Ruprecht, M. L. Reducing self-injurious behavior of severely retarded individuals through withdrawal of reinforcement procedures. *Behavior Modification*, 1977, **1**, 499–516.

Layman, & Kandel, 1975; Shafto & Sulzbacher, 1977; Wulbert & Dries, 1977). Typically, programs provide tokens, praise, and consumable rewards (e.g., food) for such behaviors as correct responses on academic tasks, remaining in one's seat to work on specific tasks, and for more restrained and quiet types of activity. Such programs have shown a reduction in the hyperactive behaviors and increases in the performance of on-task and academic behaviors. Hence, even though a major impetus of the programs is to suppress behavior, reinforcement techniques can effectively accomplish the goal.

Reinforcement can be effective in suppressing behavior even when the reinforced response is not physically incompatible with the undesired target response. The frequency of a behavior may be decreased, if another behavior is reinforced because the reinforced behavior *displaces* the undesirable behavior in the individual's repertoire of responses. O'Brien and Azrin (1972b) used reinforcement to decrease screaming in a schizophrenic patient. Tokens were delivered to the patient for house-keeping tasks, grooming, and engaging in social behavior. As desirable behaviors increased, screaming decreased. Similarly, Hersen, Eisler, Alford, and Agras (1973) altered the behavior of three depressed neurotic patients in a hospital ward. The patients received tokens for engaging in a variety of behaviors related to personal hygiene and work on the ward. In a reversal design, ratings of depression of the patients decreased markedly as token earnings increased. Even though the contingencies did not focus on the depression per se, an increase in activity on the ward decreased depression.

In the above applications, the target behaviors were not necessarily incompatible with the behaviors that were suppressed. For example, grooming oneself and engaging in housekeeping chores do not necessarily preclude screaming. Yet, the development of adaptive behaviors had as a side effect the reduction of inappropriate behaviors as well. The development of adaptive behaviors through reinforcement should always be utilized in treatment even if the program is initiated for the primary purpose of suppressing an undesirable behavior.

Reinforcement of Low Response Rates. Reinforcement of other behavior than the one to be suppressed is not the only reinforcement technique to suppress undesirable behavior. Another technique is to provide reinforcing consequences for reductions in the undesired behavior or for increases in the period of time in which the behavior does not occur. These procedures are referred to as differential reinforcement of low rates of responding (DRL schedule) and can be used very effectively to suppress behavior (see Deitz, 1977).

In one variation of a DRL schedule, the client receives reinforcing consequences for showing a reduction in the frequency of the target behavior. For example, Deitz (1977, Exp. 2) decreased talking out of an educably retarded male adolescent who attended a special education class. After baseline observations of talking out, the teacher told the student that if he emitted three or less talk-outs during a 55-minute period, she would spend extra time working with him. The client would receive the reinforcing consequence only if he showed a low rate of disruptive behavior. This DRL contingency was evaluated in an ABAB design. The results, shown in Figure 6–9, illustrate that talking out decreased whenever the DRL contingency was in effect.

The DRL schedule can completely eliminate a behavior by making the requirements for reinforcement increasingly stringent. A client can be allowed a certain number of instances of the undesired behavior within a given time period to earn the reinforcer. However, this number may be decreased over time to earn the reinforcement in order to eliminate the behavior (Deitz & Repp, 1973). Alternatively, the client can receive reinforcing consequences for going longer and longer periods without performing the undesired behavior (Deitz, 1977, Exp. 1). In either of these variations, or others that have been studied, reinforcement for performance of a few or no instances of the response has

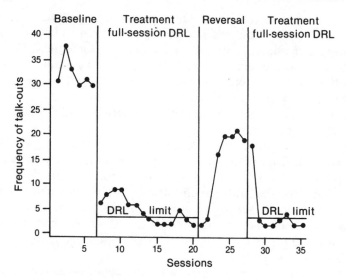

FIGURE 6–9   The frequency of talk-outs per 55-minute session of an educably retarded male. During treatment, if the client emitted three or less talk-outs per session, the teacher spent 15 minutes working with him.

Source: Deitz, S. M. An analysis of programming DRL schedules in educational settings. *Behaviour Research and Therapy*, 1977, **15**, 103–11.

effectively suppressed a variety of behaviors (Deitz, 1977; Deitz, Slack, Schwarzmueller, Wilander, Weatherly, & Hilliard, 1978).

Reinforcement techniques should be considered when developing programs designed to decrease behavior. The importance of using positive reinforcement will be especially clear in the discussion of punishment and extinction. Programs based upon both punishment and extinction usually can be greatly improved by incorporating positive reinforcement to develop appropriate behaviors.

■ SUMMARY AND CONCLUSION

The effectiveness of positive reinforcement in increasing behavior depends upon the delay of reinforcement, the magnitude or amount of reinforcement, the quality or type of reinforcer, and the schedule of reinforcement. To maximize performance, reinforcement should be delivered immediately after a response. Moreover, a highly preferred reinforcer should be used. During acquisition, continuous reinforcement should be used until the response is well established. Subsequently, intermittent reinforcement can be substituted to enhance resistance to extinction.

Different types of reinforcers have been used effectively in applied settings such as food and other consumables, praise and attention, high probability behaviors, feedback, and token reinforcement. Each reinforcer has its own advantages and limitations such as dependence upon deprivation and satiation states, ease of administration, and relative effectiveness. Token economies usually incorporate a variety of back-up reinforcers and overcome some of the limitations which accrue to the use of any single reinforcer.

Contingency contracting refers to a way of structuring a reinforcement program. Each participant in the program formally agrees to the terms of the contract. The reinforcers for performing the target behaviors and penalties for failing to perform the behaviors are made explicit and agreed upon in writing in advance of the program. The primary advantage of a contract arrangement is that the client has an opportunity to develop his or her own behavior change program and to ensure that the terms are not coercive.

Positive reinforcement represents the major basis for behavioral techniques in applied settings. Positive reinforcement programs are not only appropriate to increase behaviors but can be used to decrease or eliminate undesirable behaviors as well. To accomplish this later goal, differential reinforcement of other behaviors and differential reinforcement of low rates have been very effective. As other techniques are discussed throughout subsequent chapters, positive reinforcement will invariably continue to play a dominant role in behavior change.

■ NOTE

[1] A diet high in potassium was encouraged because the patient's medication probably included diuretics (medications that increase the flow of urine). With such medication, potassium often is lost from the body and has to be taken in extra quantities to maintain bodily functioning.

7

Punishment and Negative Reinforcement

Aversive events play a major role in everyday life. Indeed, aversive techniques are deeply enmeshed in many social institutions including government and law (e.g., fines and imprisonment), education (e.g., failing grades on exams, expulsion, and probation), religion (e.g., damnation), international relations (e.g., military coercion), and normal social intercourse (e.g., discrimination, disapproval, humiliation, and social stigma). Routine interactions of most individuals with both physical and social environments result in aversive events ranging from a burn on a hot stove to verbal abuse from an acquaintance.

In applied settings, aversive events are used in two ways, namely, punishment and negative reinforcement. As mentioned earlier, punishment refers to a decrease in response rate when the response is followed by an aversive consequence. Negative reinforcement refers to an increase in response rate when the response is contingently followed by termination of an aversive event. Aversive events require careful consideration for at least two reasons. First, to apply punishment effectively, many specific requirements must be met. The requirements are often difficult to meet in applied settings. Second, undesirable side effects sometimes result from using punishment. Although a punishment contingency may be effective, unintended side effects may create new problems. Nevertheless, punishment of an "undesirable" behavior can be used effectively, particularly if supplemented with positive reinforcement as part of the behavior change program.

■ PUNISHMENT

As discussed earlier, punishment in the technical sense refers solely to the empirical operation (presentation or removal of events) which reduces the frequency of a response. Punishment does not necessarily involve physical pain. Indeed, events which may be painful (e.g., a spanking) may not necessarily decrease the responses they are designed to punish and may not qualify as punishing events. Alternatively, a variety of procedures which serve as punishment do not entail physical discomfort and are not odious to the client. On rare occasions a punishing event which effectively suppresses behavior even may be evaluated favorably by the clients (Adams & Popelka, 1971). Punishment may take one of two forms, the presentation of aversive events or the removal of positive events after a response. Each of these types of punishment encompasses a variety of specific procedures.

After a response is performed, an aversive event such as spanking or a reprimand may be applied. There are two types of aversive events, primary and secondary or conditioned aversive stimuli. *Primary aversive stimuli* refer to those events which are inherently aversive. Stimuli such as electric shock, intense physical assault, bright lights, and loud noises are primary aversive stimuli. Their aversive properties are unlearned and are universal. *Secondary or conditioned aversive stimuli* acquire their aversive properties by being paired with events that are already aversive. For example, the word "no" serves as a conditioned aversive stimulus for many individuals. The word acquires its aversive value by being paired with events such as physical pain, loss of privileges, and so on. Conditioned aversive stimuli which typically control behavior include gestures, nods, frowns, and traffic tickets.

Stimuli may become aversive even if they are not paired with other specific aversive stimuli. When a stimulus is consistently associated with the absence of reinforcement, it too may become aversive. An event which signals that reinforcement will not be forthcoming was referred to earlier as a S^Δ and may serve as an aversive event (Azrin & Holz, 1966). The S^Δ serves as a signal that a period of nonreinforcement is in effect. For example, when a child breaks a valuable object, a parent may make a particular facial expression, become silent, and not respond to the child for a while. Nonresponsiveness of the parent denotes that the child will not be reinforced. During parental silence, virtually no behavior receives approval. The signal or cue (e.g., a facial expression) associated with nonreinforcement (silence) on the part of the parent becomes aversive in its own right.

Often punishment takes the form of withdrawing positive events rather than presenting aversive events after behavior. Familiar examples include the loss of privileges, money, or one's automobile license after behavior. Events that are positively valued and that may even have served as positive reinforcers are taken away as a form of penalty. Other forms of punishment are not easily categorized as presenting an aversive event or as taking away a positive event. Some punishment procedures require the client to engage in undesirable tasks after the behavior. The client may engage in chores or practice doing what he or she is supposed to do after occurrences of inappropriate behavior. Rather than presenting or withdrawing events, these forms of punishment require performance of specific activities.

In behavior modification, several forms of punishment have been developed based upon whether aversive events are presented, positive events are withdrawn, or work or effort on the part of the client is required after performance of a particular behavior. Some of the techniques used in behavior modification are familiar because they are commonly used in everyday life (e.g., reprimands). However, other techniques such as withdrawing reinforcing events for very brief periods or requiring clients to practice appropriate behavior are probably less familiar. Whether the techniques are familiar or not, it is important to examine the effectiveness of different techniques and the manner in which the techniques are most effectively administered.

■ TYPES OF PUNISHMENT

Verbal Statements

Verbal statements in the form of reprimands, warnings, disapproval, saying "no," and threats often are used in everyday interactions between teacher and student, parent and child, siblings, spouses, friends, and enemies. Verbal statements have been used to suppress behavior in applied research. For example, reprimands and disapproving statements occasionally have been applied in classroom settings to reduce playing during lessons, being out of one's seat, talking without permission, and other disruptive behaviors. Reprimands and disapproval in general have had inconsistent effects. In some cases, for example, disruptive student behavior has been suppressed relatively quickly by saying "no" after instances of disruptive behavior (Hall et al., 1971). In other cases, reprimands have served as a positive reinforcer rather than as a punisher. In one classroom, the teacher reprimanded the children by saying "sit down" when students were standing and out of their seats (Madsen et al., 1970). Interestingly, the reprimands increased the frequency of standing and, hence, served as a positive reinforcer for the behavior they were designed to suppress.

The manner in which the verbal statements are delivered may influence their effectiveness. Reprimands that are delivered quietly and privately to the student have been shown to suppress disruptive behavior, whereas loud reprimands that are shouted across the room often do not (O'Leary et al., 1970). Loud reprimands and disapproval may draw attention to and reinforce disruptive behavior. On the other hand, other studies have shown that loud reprimands by themselves or followed by disapproving looks suppress behavior (Doleys et al., 1976; Forehand, Roberts, Doley, Hobbs, & Resick, 1975; Moore & Bailey, 1973). Hence, the manner in which reprimands are delivered has not always influenced their effectiveness.

Threats also have been used to suppress behavior. When threats signal that some aversive consequence will follow, if a behavior is or is not performed, they become conditioned aversive events. Yet, most threats in everyday life are "idle," that is, are not backed by the threatened consequences. If threats are not backed by the consequences, they tend to lose their effectiveness. Hence, it is no surprise that threats by themselves without back-up consequences have not been very effective in behavior modification programs. For example, in a program with delinquents, threats were used to suppress aggressive statements (e.g., "I'll kill you.") (Phillips, 1968). Threats consisted of telling the boys that if they continued aggressive statements, they would lose points they earned in the token economy in the setting. The threats were not actually enforced. Although the first few threats appeared to reduce behavior, their effectiveness decreased over time. When the points were finally taken away, the aggressive statements were reduced. Other studies have shown that threats alone do not suppress behavior unless they are consistently followed by the threatened aversive consequences (Kazdin, 1971; Phillips, Phillips, Fixsen, & Wolf, 1971).

Considerations in Using Verbal Statements. Verbal reprimands and threats are easily administered and, hence, from a practical standpoint are readily available for use as a punishment technique. Perhaps one reason for using verbal punishment is that behavior eventually should be under control of verbal statements. In everyday life, it often is important to learn from statements rather than experiencing the undesirable consequences that otherwise would result. For example, it is important to teach individuals who are learning to drive that they are likely to be injured or to injure others if they back out of the driveway at 90 miles per hour. Profiting from hearing this warning will make life much easier than having to experience the untoward consequences themselves.

Another consideration in favor of verbal forms of punishment is that they cause no physical discomfort to the client. Receiving a reprimand may not be pleasant, but the unpleasantness is very different from that resulting from more extreme procedures such as electric shock. Because verbal reprimands are commonly practiced in everyday life and present no physical threat to the client, their use is less objectionable than other forms of punishment.

A major limitation of verbal statements as punishing events is their inconsistent effects; often they produce little or no change at all. For most behaviors brought to treatment, the weak or inconsistent effects of verbal reprimands are not sufficient to achieve therapeutic change. Another consideration is that people such as parents and teachers use reprimands relatively frequently. For example, observations of teachers throughout elementary and high school grades have shown a relatively high level of disapproval and low level of approval in the classroom (Thomas, Presland, Grant, Dilys, & Glynn, 1978; White, 1975). To improve teacher effectiveness, one might not want to increase the use of reprimands since they are already relatively frequent. Alternative behavior-change techniques such as positive reinforcement might be more appropriately implemented.

An important consideration is that reprimands and verbal admonitions in one form or another comprise a large part of naturally occurring events in everyday life. Hence, in treatment settings it may be desirable to train clients to respond to disapproval if they do not respond already. Verbal statements can be made to function as aversive events by pairing them with other events such as physical restraint, removal of positive events, and shock (e.g., Birnbrauer, 1968; Henriksen & Doughty, 1967). Here the purpose of the program is to develop responsiveness to naturally occurring events.

Electric Shock

Shock is another aversive event that can be presented after behavior. Shock has been used relatively infrequently. Applications typically have focused upon persons who engage in behaviors that are dangerous to themselves or to others and who have not responded to other procedures. Since shock is a primary aversive event, it is usually very effective and achieves its effects rapidly.

Linscheid and Cunningham (1977) used electric shock to eliminate chronic ruminative vomiting in a nine-month-old infant. Constant vomiting after meals had resulted in severe weight loss, malnutrition, and medical complications that were potentially fatal. When shock was applied, vomiting dropped from an average of over 100 instances per day to one instance after only three days of treatment. Follow-up evaluation nine months after the infant was released from the hospital revealed that ruminations no longer occurred and weight gain increased.

In an outpatient setting, Kushner (1968) used electric shock to suppress uncontrollable sneezing in a female high school student. The girl began to sneeze uncontrollably while hospitalized for treatment of a kidney infection. Before her discharge, the hospital corridors outside of her room were freshly painted. The onset of sneezing occurred at this time but continued long after discharge. Despite a variety of treatments including psychotherapy, hypnosis, trips to parts of the country with cleaner air, hospitalization, and medication, her sneezing continued. After six months, shock was applied. With shock (delivered to her finger tips) her sneezing was rapidly eliminated in a matter of only a few treatment sessions. A follow-up evaluation showed that uncontrollable sneezing no longer occurred up to 16 months after treatment.

In other applications, shock has been used to suppress such behaviors in children as self-injury (Lovaas & Simmons, 1969), playing with dangerous equipment (Bucher & King, 1971), and climbing dangerous places (Risley, 1968). With adults, usually in outpatient treatment, shock has been used to reduce or eliminate cigarette smoking, overeating, alcohol consumption, writer's cramp, stuttering, and various sexual responses such as transvestism and fetishism (e.g., Hallam & Rachman, 1976; Rachman & Teasdale, 1969). In adult outpatient treatment, shock is used very infrequently in part because alternative procedures of equal or greater effectiveness are readily available.

Considerations in Using Electric Shock. Shock has been very effective as an aversive consequence. In fact, it presents the most effective aversive event studied in laboratory research (Azrin & Holz, 1966). Shock has been especially useful in cases where behavior needs to be suppressed rapidly because of the danger it presents and where alternative procedures have not been effective. Because the procedure is painful, it is usually not resorted to unless alternative procedures have been unsuccessful. Indeed, in the examples provided above, shock was used only after several other procedures that had not suppressed behavior (e.g., chronic vomiting and uncontrollable sneezing). Given the range of effective alternative techniques, based upon both punishment and reinforcement, serious ethical objections might be raised if shock were considered as the first treatment to be applied.

Aside from ethical considerations, other limitations militate against the widespread use of shock in applied settings. To begin with, the administration of shock requires special equipment. Hence, shock has been generally restricted to laboratory or treatment settings where clients are seen individually and are closely supervised. In settings where individuals are treated in groups, it is not readily feasible to employ shock. In addition, the person using shock must be well trained so that accidents due to misuse of equipment do not occur and so that shock intensity is not necessarily severe. Because of ethical objections that most professionals and potential clients have over the use of shock, the availability of other procedures, and difficulties in administering shock

effectively, the procedure is only used rarely. Among alternative procedures to suppress behavior, shock usually is viewed as the most socially
unacceptable (Kazdin, 1979a). Hence, independently of its effectiveness, its use is very restricted to special cases where such extreme
procedures appear to be warranted.

Time Out from Reinforcement

Both the use of verbal reprimands and shock consist of *presenting* an
aversive event after a target behavior. Punishment often takes the form
of removing a positive event. One procedure for removing a positive
event is *time out from reinforcement* (or simply time out) *which refers
to the removal of all positive reinforcers for a certain period of time.*
During the time-out interval, the client does not have access to the
positive reinforcers that normally are available in the setting. For example, a resident in an institution may be isolated from others for 10
minutes. During the time period, the resident will not have access to
staff or peer interaction, activities, privileges, and other reinforcers usually available.

The crucial ingredient of time out is delineating a time period in
which reinforcement is unavailable. Ideally, during this time period *all*
sources of reinforcement are withdrawn. However, this ideal is not
always attained. For example, if a child is sent to his or her room as
punishment, removal from the existing sources of reinforcement qualifies as time out. However, all reinforcement may not be withheld since
the child might engage in any number of reinforcing activities such as
playing, listening to music, or sleeping. Even talking to oneself may
constitute a possible source of reinforcement that is not precluded during time out. Despite these technicalities, time out usually consists of
making reinforcing events unavailable to the client for a brief period of
time.

A variety of different time-out procedures have been used effectively
in treatment. In many variations, the client is physically isolated or
excluded in some way from the situation. The client may be sent to a
time-out room or booth, a special place that is partitioned off from
others. For example, Lahey, McNees, and McNees (1973) used time out
from reinforcement to suppress obscene verbalizations and facial
twitches in a 10-year-old boy. For instances of these behaviors, the boy
was placed in a small room adjacent to the classroom for 5 minutes.
Doleys et al. (1976) suppressed noncompliance with requests among
mentally retarded residents by requiring a child to sit in the corner of
the room for 40 seconds for instances of noncompliance. Similarly,
Bigelow, Liebson, and Griffiths (1974) suppressed alcohol consumption
among hospitalized chronic alcoholics. The patients were allowed ac-

cess to alcoholic beverages freely on the ward. During time out, patients were placed in a isolation booth for 10 to 15 minutes for drinking, a procedure that markedly reduced drinking.

Although many programs using time out have employed isolation (removal from the situation) as the time-out procedure, alternative procedures are available that still meet the definition of time out. With some variations, the client is not taken out of the situation. One time-out procedure that does not involve removing the individual from the situation was used to suppress disruptive behavior among toddlers (ranging in age from 1 to 3 years) who attended a day-care center (Porterfield, Herbert-Jackson, & Risley, 1976). Disruptive behaviors such as hitting or pushing peers, crying and fussing, engaging in tantrums, and breaking toys were punished with time-out procedures while children engaged in free-play activities. When disruptive behavior occurred, the child was told that the behavior was inappropriate and removed to the periphery of the activity of the other children. While away from the center of activity in the room, the child was allowed to observe the activities and other children. However, the child was not allowed to play with toys. After a brief period, usually less than one minute, the child was allowed to return to his or her activities in the center of the room. Partial removal of the children from their activities markedly decreased their disruptive behavior.

Other variations of time out have been used in which the client is not even partially removed from the situation. For example, Foxx and Shapiro (1978) evaluated time out as part of a reinforcement program for boys in a special education class for retarded children in a state institution. As part of the reinforcement system, children received praise and smiles for performing their work. Each child in class was given a ribbon to wear around his neck. The ribbon signified to the child and the teacher that the child could receive social and, occasionally, food reinforcers that were administered while the children worked. When any disruptive behavior was performed, a time-out procedure was used. Time out consisted of removing the child's ribbon for three minutes. Without the ribbon, the child could not receive any of the reinforcers normally delivered as part of the classroom. This time-out procedure effectively reduced disruptive classroom behavior.

Positive reinforcers have been made unavailable in other ways to accomplish time out from reinforcement. For example, Mansdorf (1977) applied time out to a mentally retarded adult who refused to comply with staff requests to take a shower. When the resident did not comply, she would simply sit in the day room and watch television, listen to music, or go back to bed. Time out was used for noncompliance by removing the opportunities for reinforcement for a brief period. If the resident did not comply, television or music was turned off, peers were asked to leave the day room, and the pillow and bedding were removed. Essentially, the reinforcers usually utilized by the resident were made temporarily unavailable. If she did comply, each of these reinforcing events was restored. The procedure was very effective in reducing the number of incidents of noncompliance, as shown in Figure 7–1. The effects were maintained six months after the program had been terminated.

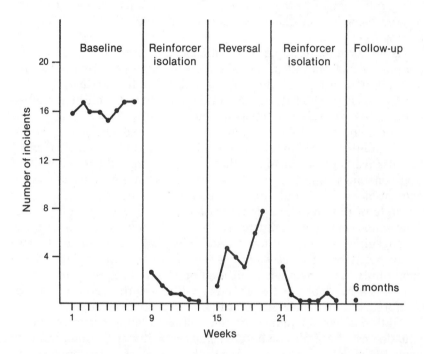

FIGURE 7–1 Number of noncompliant episodes per five day work week, for each experimental condition.

Source: Mansdorf, I. J. Reinforcer isolation: An alternative to subject isolation in time-out from positive reinforcement. *Journal of Behavior Therapy and Experimental Psychiatry*, 1977, **8**, 391–93.

Considerations in Using Time Out. Time out from reinforcement has been very effective in altering a number of behaviors including psychotic speech, toileting accidents, thumbsucking, and self-stimulatory and self-injurious behavior (see Hobbs & Forehand, 1977). Usually, short time-out durations such as several seconds or a few minutes are effective in suppressing behavior. Longer time-out periods do not necessarily enhance the effectiveness of the procedure (e.g., White, Nielson, & Johnson, 1972).

Obvious advantages of time out are that it can be relatively brief and that it does not involve pain. Additional advantages and disadvantages of time out depend upon the specific form it takes. Removing individuals from the situation in which deviant behavior occurs such as sending individuals to a time-out room, particularly for extended periods, has potential disadvantages. Removing individuals from the situation in which their performance is a problem reduces opportunities for positive reinforcement in the situation. Hence, the client cannot learn the desired behavior and the conditions under which these behaviors are appropriate.

As an extreme example of isolation in one program, a child who constantly misbehaved in the classroom (talked, remained out of his seat, threw objects) was immediately sent home in an attempt to alter these behaviors (Shier, 1969). With this procedure, the child missed 26 out of 83 days of school in about a 5-month period. This time spent out of the classroom was lost for training other desirable behaviors. Fortunately time out rarely involves extended time periods. Even so, a potential disadvantage of time out is that time away from the training situation consumes time that might be used for reinforcing behaviors incompatible with the undesirable response. The above case is not a good example of time out for another reason. Sending an individual home from school may not eliminate reinforcers but provide an opportunity for engaging in many reinforcing activities that are incompatible with study behavior such as watching television or roaming around the community. The effective application of time out requires removal of reinforcers available in the situation without introducing additional reinforcers to take their place during the time-out period.

Additional considerations are relevant in isolating persons from the situation as a form of time out. In some cases, it may be undesirable to leave the client alone isolated from others because of the opportunity that isolation provides for engaging in maladaptive behaviors. For example, Solnick, Rincover, and Peterson (1977) found that an autistic child engaged in self-stimulatory behaviors when isolated from others.

Isolation from others also may be undesirable for clients who are socially withdrawn. Removal from the social situation may further isolate clients who already have only minimal social skills. A main goal of treatment should be to develop prosocial behaviors in the presence of other individuals and not to foster any more isolation, whether physical or social, than might already result from the client's interpersonal deficits.

Many of the objections to time out are resolved with variations that do not remove the client from the situation. Leaving the client in the situation such as a classroom but setting aside brief time periods in which reinforcers are not available has many advantages. By allowing

the client to remain in the situation, he or she can continue to participate in the activities and perhaps even observe others receive desirable
consequences for appropriate behavior. Of course, it is possible that a
client's behavior is so disruptive that he or she has to be removed from
the situation so as not to disturb or interfere with the activities of others.
To handle this possible problem, some programs have allowed individuals to remain in the situation during time out unless their behavior is
very disruptive (LeBlanc, Busby, & Thomson, 1974; Porterfield et al.,
1976). Using social isolation to back up a less severe form of time out is
an excellent strategy because the client only will be removed from the
situation if necessary.

In general, time out provides an excellent alternative to many of
other forms of punishment used in everyday life such as reprimands
and corporal punishment. Very brief time out for several seconds or
only a few minutes has been effective. Time out has been especially
effective when many reinforcers are available in the setting so that time
out from these reinforcing events is especially aversive (Solnick et al.,
1977, Exp. 2). Occasionally, time out has not been effective for some
individuals and even has served as a positive reinforcer for others (Foxx
& Azrin, 1972; Plummer, Baer, & LeBlanc, 1977; Solnick et al., 1977,
Exp. 1). However, these findings are exceptions. The many variations of
time out that currently are available provide alternatives adaptable to
most clients and settings.

Response Cost

*Response cost refers to a loss of a positive reinforcer or to a penalty
involving some work or effort.* With response cost, there is no necessary
time period in which positive events are unavailable as is the case with
time out from reinforcement (Kazdin, 1972). Response cost requires a
penalty of some sort, usually in the form of fines. Examples of response
cost in everyday experience include fines for traffic violations, late fees
for filing income tax beyond the due date, and postage due for letters
with too little postage. Response cost is not always based upon losing
money. Penalties often are based upon requiring more effort or work as
in the case of a football team that is penalized 5 yards for delaying the
game. The penalty is a form of response cost because more effort is
required to achieve a score.

In applied settings, response cost usually takes the form of a fine. For
example, response cost was used as part of a contingency contract arrangement for an adult male alcoholic and his wife (Miller, 1972). The
husband drank excessively which served as a major source of marital
conflict. A contract was devised which specified that the husband could
have only one to three drinks a day (instead of the average of seven to

eight he consumed during baseline) and that these could be consumed only before dinner. Any other drinking would result in the husband paying $20 to the wife which she would spend as frivolously as possible, something which was very aversive to the husband. The wife agreed to refrain from negative verbal responses for her husband's drinking. She paid a $20 fine to the husband if she failed to carry this out. Drinking decreased quickly and stabilized at a rate within the contract agreement. The effects were maintained up to six months when last observed.

Clark et al. (1977) reported an effective response cost procedure implemented by parents to control child behavior during shopping trips. The purpose was to suppress such behaviors as touching the merchandise, roughhousing, and being away from the parent beyond a certain distance. The children were told they could spend 50¢ at the end of the parent's shopping in the store (e.g., dime or drug store). However, for each instance of inappropriate behavior, a cost of 5¢ would be subtracted. The results indicated that levying a fine markedly decreased inappropriate behavior in the stores, as assessed by observers who followed behind the families during baseline and experimental conditions.

Response cost often has been used as part of token economies where tokens are delivered for some behaviors and taken away for others. For example, in one program with psychiatric patients, fines were levied whenever patients violated a rule of the ward (Upper, 1973). Infractions included getting up late in the morning, undressing or exposing oneself, shouting, sleeping and several other behaviors. Violations dropped below baseline rates when a fine was subtracted from token earnings. Whether implemented alone or in conjunction with token economies, response cost has altered a wide variety of behaviors such as overeating, disruptive classroom behavior, speech disfluencies, psychotic speech, thumbsucking, toileting accidents, and others (see Kazdin, 1977e).

The effectiveness of response cost can be attested to by examining applications in everyday life. For example, several years ago, there was no charge for dialing directory assistance within the city and asking for information about a phone number. Charges have been initiated in most communities for dialing information. From the standpoint of telephone companies, providing directory assistance is expensive and, hence, is a service they would like to minimize or curtail. To this end, response cost has been used as a procedure in many communities in which a cost is levied on one's phone bill for dialing information within the community. Typically, one is allowed three directory assistance calls free before the cost (20¢ per call) is levied. The effect of this response-cost procedure was shown by McSweeny (1978) who gathered the data in one community before and after the cost was invoked. As evident in Figure 7–2, requests for directory assistance for local calls was greatly suppressed after the cost was invoked. However, requests for directory assistance for long distance calls, which were not fined, were not reduced.

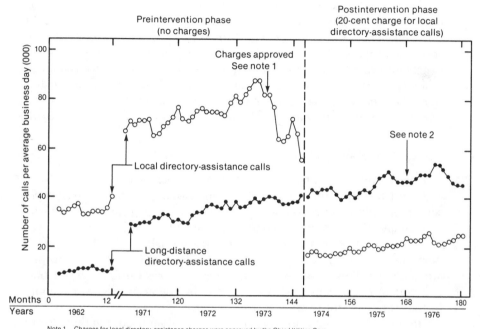

FIGURE 7–2   Number of local and long-distance directory-assistance calls placed per average business day before and after charges were introduced.

Source: McSweeny, A. J. Effects of response cost on the behavior of a million persons: Charging for directory assistance in Cincinnati. *Journal of Applied Behavior Analysis*, 1978, **11**, 47–51.

Considerations in Using Response Cost.   Response cost is a relatively easily implemented punishment procedure, particularly in the form of withdrawing points or tokens after behavior. One problem that may arise is that individual clients who lose many points may quickly become in debt so that they have no further points to be lost. Indeed, if a client has no points because of previous fines, how can further points be lost? The client must have points to lose them. Interestingly, clients can be given more points or tokens noncontingently (e.g., Hall et al., 1971) before losing them for inappropriate behavior. Even if clients lose all of their tokens, additional ones can be given to them and taken away one at a time (Kazdin, 1973a). Although this procedure seems to work, it may produce only temporary effects if the client learns that there is no reason to avoid losing points.

One clear benefit of the use of response cost in the form of fines is that the procedure provides the opportunity to deliver positive reinforcers for behavior. If tokens or points are to be withdrawn, they have to be delivered to the client. And, behavior change is likely to be more rapid if the tokens are delivered for behaviors that are incompatible with the responses that are to be suppressed. Hence, when using points or tokens, reinforcement and punishment in the form of response cost can be easily implemented as part of a single program. Research has suggested that token reinforcement and response cost combined are more effective than either procedure alone (Phillips et al., 1971; Walker et al., 1976).

Overcorrection

Another punishment technique that involves a penalty but usually is distinguished from the variations of response cost is referred to as *overcorrection*. With overcorrection, the penalty for engaging in an undesirable behavior is performing some other behaviors in the situation. Two components of overcorrection can be distinguished. The first component pertains to correcting the environmental effects of the inappropriate behavior. This is sometimes referred to as *restitution*. The second component consists of positively practicing the appropriate behaviors in the situation and is referred to as *positive practice*.

Both restitution and positive practice are often used together. As an illustration of these components, Foxx and Azrin (1972) used overcorrection with a 50-year old profoundly retarded female who had been hospitalized for 46 years. For several years, she had engaged in severely disruptive and aggressive behavior, especially throwing things. After baseline observations, overcorrection was implemented. When the client performed a disruptive behavior (e.g., overturning a bed), she was required to "correct" the physical effects of her behavior on the environment (i.e., turn the bed to its correct position and straighten the spread and pillows). In addition, she was required to rehearse the correct behavior by straightening all of the other beds on the ward. Thus, the client had to correct the immediate consequence of whatever inappropriate behavior she performed (restitution) and then to practice repeatedly the correct behavior throughout the ward (positive practice). After 11 weeks of training, the client no longer threw objects.

An interesting application of overcorrection was used to eliminate stealing among hospitalized retarded adults (Azrin & Wesolowski, 1974). The residents had a high rate of stealing from each other, especially food during meal and snack times when residents purchased items at a commissary (store) in the hospital. A staff member simply required the resident to return the food or the remaining portion if it had been partially consumed. With this procedure (called simple correction) stealing remained at a high rate. An overcorrection procedure was implemented which not only required the resident to return the food to the owner but also to purchase more of that food and give it to the victim. The results, illustrated in Figure 7–3, show that theft was eliminated among the 34 residents within a matter of a few days.

For many behaviors that are to be suppressed, it is not possible to have individuals "correct" the environmental consequences of their behavior. The behaviors may not have altered the environment. For

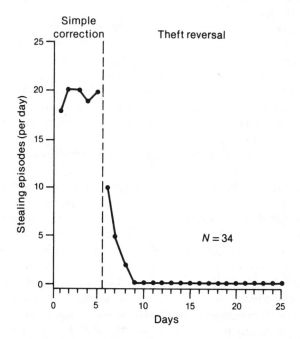

FIGURE 7–3 The number of stealing episodes committed each day by 34 adult retarded residents in an institution. During the five days of simple correction, the thief was required to return the stolen item. During the theft-reversal (overcorrection) procedure (subsequent to the vertical dashed line), the thief was required to give the victim an additional item identical to the one stolen, also returning the stolen item. The stealing episodes consisted of stealing food items from the other retarded residents during commissary periods.

Source: Azrin, N. H., & Wesolowski, M. D. Theft reversal: An overcorrection procedure for eliminating stealing by retarded persons. *Journal of Applied Behavior Analysis*, 1974, **7**, 577–81.

example, if a child whines, hits himself, rocks back and forth, or stutters, there are no clear consequences on the physical environment that could be corrected. For such behaviors, positive practice often is used alone. After the undesired behavior is performed, the client is required to positively practice the appropriate behavior. For example, in one study, two emotionally disturbed and retarded children frequently used toys inappropriately by putting them in their mouths or throwing them (Wells, Forehand, Hickey, & Green, 1977). For each occurrence of the behavior, a trainer came to the child, physically stopped the inappropriate response, and guided the child through 2½ minutes of appropriate play (positive practice) with toys. The trainer manually guided this positive practice play unless the child began the play by himself. The positive practice procedure markedly reduced inappropriate toy play.

Harris and Romanczyk (1976) used positive practice with a physically handicapped and retarded boy who frequently engaged in self-injurious behavior (head and chin banging). After instances of self-injury, the boy was required to move his head in up and down and left and right positions after each instance of self-injury. The different positions were guided by a trainer for 5 minutes. Essentially, the boy was required to practice movements incompatible with the self-injurious behaviors. Self-injury decreased from an average of about 32 instances per day to near zero several months after treatment had been terminated.

As a final example, positive practice was used by Azrin and Powers (1975) to control classroom behavior of six disruptive boys enrolled in a special summer class. Talking out and being out of one's seat were decreased by having the children who engaged in these behaviors remain in at recess. During this recess period, a child would practice appropriate classroom behavior by sitting in his seat, raising his hand, being recognized by the teacher, and asking permission to get up. This entire sequence was repeated for approximately 5 minutes, a procedure which markedly improved classroom performance. Loss of recess without engaging in positive practice did not achieve the marked changes associated with positive practice.

Considerations in Using Overcorrection. Overcorrection alone or in combination with other procedures has altered a variety of behaviors such as toileting accidents, aggressive acts, self-stimulatory behaviors, tantrums, nail biting, table manners, and others (see Axelrod, Bratner, & Meddock, 1978; Ollendick & Matson, 1978). Overcorrection procedures vary widely depending upon the specific behavior that is suppressed and the desired behavior developed in its place. The procedures are developed from the general principle of having individuals correct environmental consequences of their actions, where such consequences exist, and practicing the desired behavior repeatedly after each instance of the undesired behavior. The results of a few minutes of corrective training after the undesired behavior often has led to rapid and long-lasting therapeutic effects.

Certainly, the distinguishing feature of overcorrection, in relation to other punishment techniques, is that it focuses on the appropriate behavior that is incompatible with the undesired response. Most forms of punishment do not convey to the client the behaviors that are appropriate. The positive practice component of overcorrection is designed to train desirable behaviors and, hence, serves an educative function not included in other aversive techniques.

A few problems may arise in implementing overcorrection. To begin with, the client must be guided through the sequence of behaviors included in restitution and positive practice. Many clients can be instructed to go through the sequence and gently prompted with physical guidance. Some clients may need more guidance from staff to complete the sequence of behaviors. It is important to decide whether actual physical force would be needed for a resistant client. If so, an alternative procedure might be considered.

Another consideration in using overcorrection is that it often requires more staff supervision than alternative techniques. A staff member is needed to ensure that the client goes through the overcorrection sequence for the alotted time and to provide physical prompts if necessary. In some situations, it may not be feasible to provide one-to-one client supervision to conduct overcorrection. For example, in a classroom situation, overcorrection has been discontinued on occasion in part because of the difficulties in supervising overcorrection while managing the rest of the classroom activities (Kelly & Drabman, 1977). On the other hand, applications have shown that overcorrection can be delayed and conducted at recess time or during free-play periods in a classroom situation where direct supervision of the client need not detract from others in the room (Azrin & Powers, 1975; Barton & Osborne, 1978).

Overall, the rapid and dramatic effects of overcorrection have made this a viable treatment technique for a variety of problems. In many studies, overcorrection has achieved changes in behaviors where other techniques such as time out, reprimands, reinforcement of other behavior, and physical restraint have not proven effective. Although definitive statements about the relative effectiveness of alternative punishment techniques cannot be made at this time, overcorrection appears to be very effective in its own right.

Other Punishment Techniques

The procedures discussed above represent the most widely used punishment techniques, although other procedures have been used occasionally. For example, squirting lemon juice into a person's mouth has been used in a few treatment cases. In one application, lemon juice was used to suppress life-threatening vomiting in a six-month-old infant (Sajwaj, Libet, & Agras, 1974). When tongue movements that preceded vomiting occurred, lemon juice was squirted (using a syringe) into her mouth. The procedure markedly suppressed episodes of vomiting. At follow up several months after treatment, the infant continued to gain weight and vomiting did not recur. Similarly, in another report, squirting lemon juice from a plastic squirt bottle into the mouth of a severely retarded boy effectively eliminated public masturbation (Cook, Altman, Shaw, & Blaylock, 1978).

Another punishment technique that has been used in introducing the smell of aromatic ammonia (smelling salts) contingent upon undesirable behavior. For example, Altman, Haavik, and Cook (1978) used ammonia to suppress self-injurious behavior in two children. Severe hair pulling in a 4-year-old girl (who had made herself partially bald) and hand biting of a 3-year-old boy (who had tissue damage of his fingers) were suppressed by breaking a capsule of aromatic ammonia and placing it under the child's nose for a few seconds contingent upon the self-injurious behaviors.

Another form of punishment occasionally used has been to require individuals to engage in various chores that are aversive. For example, Fischer and Nehs (1978) altered the excessive swearing of an 11-year-old boy. The boy was told that each time he swore, he was required to wash windows in the residential facility for 10 minutes. The procedure, evaluated in an ABAB design, effectively suppressed swearing. Swearing remained at a low frequency two weeks after the program had been terminated.

Several other punishment procedures that have been used in a few applications could be cited including hair tugging, physically shaking the client, loudly shouting "no," and others. The rationale behind many of these techniques has been to develop procedures that provide minimal discomfort but can effectively suppress behavior. The use of lemon juice as an aversive event illustrates this rationale. Although the taste of lemon juice is obviously unattractive to most people, its use as an aversive event is probably much more socially acceptable than such other procedures as electric shock. Indeed, lemon juice has been used for severely dangerous behaviors, in one example above, where shock might have been a reasonable alternative.

In addition to more humane forms of punishment, new techniques often are developed that may be relatively easily implemented in natural settings. For example, it might be easier to require parents to use chores as an aversive event than it would be to have them supervise overcorrection. Both the availability of undesirable tasks in the natural environment and the skills required for implementing contingencies involving such activities may be slightly less than those involved in executing alternative procedures. Research on punishment in applied settings has several obligations. Not only should such research develop effective procedures, but the procedures should be humane, socially acceptable to clients, relatively easily implemented, and not readily subject to abuse. The development of alternative punishment procedures often has been based upon these multiple considerations.

■ SELECTING PROCEDURES TO SUPPRESS BEHAVIOR

Each of the above procedures has been shown to suppress behavior effectively. The precise procedure that should be selected in any instance may be determined by several considerations including severity of the behavior, the danger of the behavior to the client or to others, the ease of implementing the technique in a particular setting, and the training required of the person(s) who will administer the program. For example, verbal reprimands and response cost might be relatively easily administered and effective with many behaviors but require less time and supervision than would overcorrection. Overcorrection, if more difficult to implement, might be reserved for those cases where it was needed.

Aside from considerations related to the situation, client, and staff, the specific treatments themselves may be more or less objectionable. For example, severe punishment procedures such as electric shock are likely to be unacceptable to many people as viable treatment alternatives. Alternatives such as time out, response cost, or overcorrection are likely to be more acceptable and adhered to by clients and staff. Legal considerations also influence the punishment techniques that can be used. The courts have ruled on select punishment procedures and the conditions under which they can be used (see Chapter 12).

When aversive consequences are used to suppress behavior, special considerations might be given to the specific events that are used and the possible long-range consequences of using these events. For example, procedures commonly used in everyday life (but usually not in behavior modification) often require individuals to engage in tasks that probably should not be used as aversive events. For example, requiring children to stay in from recess or to remain after school, or to write "I shall not swear," 500 times on the board, or to see the principal when they are disruptive may defeat many of the goals inherent in school. Presumably, we do not want children to learn that staying in the classroom, writing sentences on the board, or visiting principals are aversive. An important goal is to develop positive attitudes and approach responses to these and similar events. To treat various activities or staff as aversive consequences may make school aversive. Indeed, the aversiveness of school seems to have been carefully programmed, even if unintentionally. Behavior modification programs occasionally have capitalized on the aversiveness of school by using escape from the classroom as a reinforcer for academic performance (Harris & Sherman, 1973).

At present, the long-term consequences of using particular aversive events on the subsequent evaluation of these events are not known. Hence, considerations about selection of the events need to be based upon information about the individual case and possible consequences that might result. In short, common sense rather than scientific evidence at this point is all that is available regarding many of the considerations that enter into selecting the specific punishing consequences.

■ MAXIMIZING THE EFFECTIVENESS OF PUNISHMENT

As with reinforcement, the efficacy of punishment depends upon several conditions. However, the conditions which contribute to the efficacy of punishment have been somewhat less well investigated than have the conditions which contribute to reinforcement. Although punishment has been evaluated extensively in the laboratory (Azrin & Holz, 1966; Hutchison, 1977), most of the work has evaluated the presentation of aversive events, particularly electric shock. Removal of positive events has been less well studied (cf. Coughlin, 1972; Kazdin, 1972; 1973f; Leitenberg, 1965). Nevertheless, general statements can be extrapolated from laboratory evidence regarding the conditions which should maximize the efficacy of punishment.

Intensity of Punishment. The greater the intensity of the aversive event, the greater the response suppression. Intense punishment with electric shock can result in complete and permanent suppression of a response (Azrin & Holz, 1966). Although this relationship has been established for electric shock, it may not apply to other aversive events in applied settings (e.g., reprimands).

The role of intensity of the aversive consequence is particularly unclear when the consequence is withdrawal of a positive reinforcer (Kazdin, 1973f). Even when a reinforcer is withdrawn for a short period of time (time out), which does not seem to be an "intense" aversive event, response suppression may be dramatic. Yet, under certain circumstances, the greater the duration of time out, up to several minutes, the more effective punishment tends to be (Burchard & Barrera, 1972; Hobbs, Forehand, & Murray, 1977; White et al., 1972). Similarly, for response cost (loss of tokens), larger costs tend to suppress behavior more than smaller ones do (Burchard & Barrera, 1972; Kazdin, 1971). However, these findings should *not* be considered as justification for long periods of time out or for large fines. For example, with time out extremely brief periods have been very effective in several studies— including periods ranging from 15 to 90 seconds (e.g., Barton, Guess, Garcia, & Baer, 1970; Porterfield et al., 1976; Solnick et al., 1977).

Manner of Introducing the Aversive Consequence. Another feature regarding punishment intensity is important to note. Punishment is more effective when the aversive consequence is introduced at full strength or maximum intensity than when its intensity is increased gradually (Azrin & Holz, 1966). Punishment which is not very intense (e.g., a mild threat) may make a temporary reduction of behavior, but there is an adaptation to it so it quickly loses its punishing properties (Kazdin, 1971; Phillips, 1968). Behavior recovers its prepunishment rate. More intense punishment will be required instead of the weak threat (e.g., a very firm threat). The individual will soon adapt to this latter event and it will lose its effectiveness. Eventually, a more severe form of punishment may be required (e.g., corporal punishment or isolation).

The effect of punishment can be enhanced by introducing the consequences at maximum intensity. Instead of beginning with a weak threat, and proceeding to a firm threat, corporal punishment, or isolation, it would be better if the final event were introduced initially rather than approached gradually. The notion of introducing aversive stimuli at maximum intensity for optimal effectiveness might justify severe punishment (e.g., imprisonment or torture) for minor offenses (e.g., traffic violations or being late for class or work). However, as discussed below, moderate or less intense forms of punishment can be very effective under certain circumstances.

Delay of Punishment. Punishment, as positive reinforcement, is more effective when it is delivered immediately after the target response than when it is delayed (Azrin & Holz, 1966; Kimble, 1961). If punishment of the undesirable response is delayed, it immediately follows some other behavior. The other behavior may be desirable. For example, a child may receive punishment at the end of the day from a parent for some behavior performed earlier that day. However, prior to punishment the child may have done some particularly desirable behavior such as cleaning up his or her room. The punishment would be quite delayed and its effect on the undesirable behavior would be weak. However, the desirable behavior is performed in close contiguity with punishment and may be suppressed. Independently of the specific response that occurs during the delay period, punishment is not likely to be associated with the response which is to be suppressed, if there is a delay.

Schedule of Punishment. Punishment is more effective when the punishing consequence occurs every time (continuous punishment) rather than once in a while (intermittent punishment). The greater the proportion of punished responses, the greater the response reduction. However, continuous punishment leads to greater recovery of the response when punishment is discontinued than does intermittent punishment (Azrin & Holz, 1966). For example, if time out is to be used in the home, it should be delivered every time the behavior occurs. Administering time out intermittently, rather than after each occurrence of the response, usually leads to less response suppression (Hobbs & Forehand, 1977). However, after a response has been suppressed, punishment can be delivered only intermittently to maintain low rates of the behavior (Calhoun & Lima, 1977; Clark, Rowbury, Baer, & Baer, 1973). At very high intensities of punishment (e.g., with electric shock), the relationship between punishment schedule and response suppression does *not* hold. There may be no recovery even when punishment was previously delivered on a continuous schedule.

Source of Reinforcement. If a punished response also is positively reinforced, punishment is less effective than if the response were not reinforced. That a punished behavior is performed at all suggests that some reinforcer is maintaining it, otherwise it would have extinguished. The effect of punishment can be enhanced by removing the source of reinforcement for the punished response (Azrin & Holz, 1966). For example, delinquents may frequently provide peer social reinforcement for committing deviant acts. Punishment of deviant acts is likely to be less effective when there is peer reinforcement for the acts than when there is no reinforcement.

When using punishment, reinforcement for the punished response should be eliminated if possible. In practice, it is sometimes difficult to identify the source of reinforcement maintaining a deviant behavior. However, in many instances it is evident that teachers and parents socially reinforce those behaviors they wish to suppress. In situations such as the classroom, peers probably reinforce inappropriate behaviors (e.g., "clowning," teasing). Punishing disruptive behavior would be expected to have less effect when peers provide reinforcement for the same behaviors than if such reinforcement were not delivered.

When reinforcement of the deviant behavior is removed, positive reinforcement should be provided for desirable behavior. If peer attention and recognition are delivered for inappropriate behavior, the situation should be arranged so that peer attention is still available but for appropriate behavior. The reinforcer is not withdrawn, it is only shifted so that it follows desirable rather than undesirable behavior.

Timing of Punishment in the Response Sequence. Punishment tends to be more effective the earlier it is delivered in the response chain (e.g. Aronfreed & Reber, 1965). An undesirable response is not a single behavior but a chain or sequence of behaviors which culminates in an act considered undesirable. For example, a child's "theft" of a cookie prior to dinner may consist of a series of behaviors such as walking into the kitchen, climbing onto a chair, reaching for the cookie jar, opening the jar, taking a cookie, and eating it. Punishment for going into the kitchen or climbing onto a chair will reduce stealing cookies to a greater extent than punishment after the cookie is taken and eaten.

The importance of the timing of punishment can be readily explained. If the response chain is completed, the terminal behavior is positively reinforced (e.g., cookie consumption). Punishment is then used to suppress a reinforced response. Moreover, reinforcement of the undesirable response is more immediate than the punishment, if the chain is completed. As mentioned above, punishment is more effective when the response to be suppressed is not reinforced than when it is reinforced. Hence, if a response is punished before it is reinforced, punishment should be more effective. Responses early in the chain of behavior may still be reinforced since behaviors in a chain reinforce prior behaviors in the sequence. Yet, the further back a behavior is in the chain from the terminal reinforcer, the less potent the reinforcement. Behaviors early in the sequence are further removed from behaviors later in the sequence and the terminal reinforcer so their conditioned reinforcing properties are less, and they are more readily suppressed when punishment is applied.

A potential problem in applying punishment to initial behaviors in a response sequence is that the behaviors at this point in the chain are also part of other response chains which constitute appropriate behavior. To continue the above example, punishment of cookie theft might be very effective, if delivered when the child enters the kitchen. However, entering the kitchen may be a part of other chains which are appropriate such as washing dishes, feeding a pet, or washing one's hands.

Reinforcement of Alternate Responses.   Punishment is most effective when the individual is reinforced for performing desirable or prosocial behaviors while being punished for an undesirable response (Azrin & Holz, 1966). When an alternate response is reinforced, the punished response is more likely to be suppressed (e.g., Kircher, Pear & Martin, 1971). *Aversive events of relatively weak intensity can effectively suppress behavior, if reinforcement is provided for an alternate response.* Thus, intense punishment is not always required or even necessarily desirable. Mildly aversive events (e.g., grimaces, statements of disapproval, or "no") may only temporarily suppress behavior. However, their suppressive effect will be enhanced by delivering reinforcement for another behavior.

Even aversive consequences which are not effective by themselves can be effective when combined with reinforcement for alternate forms of behavior (Azrin & Holz, 1966). As an example, in one program an attempt was made to train a profoundly retarded child to walk. Whenever the child crawled, he was restrained (held at the waist for five seconds) (O'Brien, Azrin, & Bugle, 1972). This procedure did not decrease crawling nor increase walking. The investigators added a positive aspect to the restraint procedure. Whenever the child crawled, he was restrained as before but then was aided in walking for a few seconds. By reinforcing an alternate response (continued movement in an upright position), crawling dramatically decreased and walking increased. Restraint alone subsequently was effective once walking had been established.

Most studies of punishment include reinforcement for desirable behavior. For example, O'Brien and Azrin (1972a) used verbal reprimands ("no!") and time out (removal of food for 30 seconds) to maintain previously trained mealtime behaviors of institutionalized retardates. However, reinforcement, in the form of verbal praise, also was provided for appropriate eating, as well as, of course, food reinforcement. Similarly, Porterfield et al. (1976) required toddlers to sit during the activities in a day-care center as a time-out procedure for disruptive behavior. Approval for appropriate behavior was also provided when the child was playing appropriately. Finally, Foxx and Martin (1975) used overcorrection to eliminate coprophagy (eating feces) and pica (eating trash). The procedures required several steps, some of which involved hygiene (toothbrushing or hand washing). Aside from applying overcorrection to instances of eating inappropriate materials, engaging in behaviors related to hygiene was reinforced with praise and food.

In some of the above studies, punishment alone might have been used to suppress the undesirable behavior. However, suppressing an undesirable behavior does not guarantee that a desirable behavior will take its place. *Punishment usually trains a person in what not to do rather than in what to do* (Thorndike, 1932). For example, suppression of food spilling during a meal does not necessarily result in desirable mealtime behavior (e.g., eating with utensils). Similarly, suppression of fighting in a delinquent does not guarantee that desirable social behavior will appear.

Overcorrection, as a punishment technique, has attempted to include practice of appropriate behavior as part of the procedure to help make punishment more educative than ordinarily is the case. However, the behaviors that are positively practiced in overcorrection are not always desirable prosocial responses. Rather, they often are behaviors that appear to be incompatible with the response that is to be suppressed. For example, Azrin, Gottlieb, Hughart, Wesolowski, and Rahn (1975) used overcorrection to eliminate self-injurious behavior in one psychotic and several retarded adults. The positive practice component of the procedure included engaging in fixed bodily postures (e.g., practice in holding hands away from the body in a sequence of exercises) that would compete with hitting oneself. These behaviors are not in their own right socially desirable. Separate reinforcement contingencies were included to develop appropriate social behaviors and participation in activities on the ward.

It is advisable to use positive reinforcement whenever punishment is employed, for three reasons. First, reinforcement for alternative responses increases the efficacy of punishment (Azrin & Holz, 1966). Second, reinforcement can develop appropriate behaviors to displace those inappropriate behaviors that are to be eliminated. Third, positive reinforcement combined with punishment may eliminate any undesirable side effects which might result from the use of punishment alone (see below). Punishment in the form of withdrawal of a positive event (time-out or some forms of response cost) can be readily combined with reinforcement. If a positive event is to be withdrawn, it has to be given to the client in advance. The positive reinforcer can be contingent upon a desirable response and its loss can be contingent upon an undesirable response. For example, in token economies with a variety of populations tokens are usually delivered for desirable behaviors and withdrawn for undesirable behaviors.

Possible Side Effects of Punishment

An argument against the use of punishment is that undesirable side effects may result. Even though the target behavior may be eliminated, other consequences resulting directly from punishment may be worse than the original behavior or at least be problematic in their own right. Laboratory research, usually with infrahuman subjects, provides evidence for a variety of undesirable side effects (Azrin & Holz, 1966; Hutchinson, 1977). These effects are important to consider because they occasionally arise in clinical situations where punishment is used.

Emotional Reactions. Undesirable emotional reactions may result from punishment. The emotional states may be temporarily disruptive to the individual. For example, when a child receives a spanking, crying, anger, and other similar emotional states will probably occur. These states are not essential ingredients of punishment but undesirable concomitant effects. They are undesirable, in part, because they may interfere with new learning. The child may be temporarily unresponsive to his social environment until he is no longer upset. An additional consideration is that undesirable emotional states may be frequently paired with cues in the punishment situation. Eventually the cues themselves (e.g., a given individual such as a parent or teacher or a situation such as the home) may elicit similar emotional reactions in the absence of punishment.

Escape and Avoidance. One side effect of punishment is that it can lead to escape from or avoidance of the punishment situation. If a situation is aversive, an individual can terminate the aversive condition by escaping. Successful escape from a situation associated with punishment is negatively reinforced because it terminates an aversive condition. Even if the punishing event is only mildly aversive and too weak to be very effective in suppressing behavior, it may result in escape behavior (Azrin & Holz, 1966). Hence, the use of aversive stimuli fosters escape and reinforcement of escape behaviors. For example, reliance upon punishment in the home may result in attempts to avoid or escape from the home.

Stimuli associated with the aversive situation may also lead to escape. Recall that any event associated with an aversive event becomes aversive in its own right. If one person is constantly punishing someone else, the punishing agent will take on properties of a conditioned aversive stimulus. The individual who is punished will attempt to escape from or avoid the punishing agent because of these aversive stimulus properties. This side effect is undesirable because if individuals (e.g., children) escape or avoid punishing agents (e.g., parents and teachers), the agents will be unable to provide reinforcement to train desirable responses. Perhaps, the most pervasive example of escape and avoidance behavior is evident in the responses and attitudes that the police evoke from the public. For most people, the police are associated with punishment more than anything else. It is no surprise that for many individuals the police become a conditioned aversive stimulus to be avoided or escaped whenever possible.

Aggression. In laboratory work, punishment sometimes results in one organism attacking another or attacking the source of punishment (Hutchinson, 1977). These phenomena have not been demonstrated with the wide range of punishing events used in applied settings but only with painful stimuli. Yet in using punishment of any kind there is the possibility that the punished individual will aggress toward the punishing agent. By attacking the agent, the source of punishment may be temporarily removed. Hence, the individual's aggression toward the punishing agent is *negatively reinforced* by terminating an aversive event. For example, protesters may be reinforced for attacking police because attacking police may temporarily reduce aversive events (e.g., tear gas or physical assault). Of course, the same contingencies operate to control aggressive behavior of police.

Modeled Punishment. The punishing agent *models* or provides an example of certain behaviors, namely, the use of aversive behavior control techniques, which may be learned by the individual who is punished. If a parent uses physical punishment with a child, the likelihood of the child engaging in physically aggressive behaviors is increased. Aggressive behavior patterns can be readily learned from adult models (Bandura, 1965). Moreover, children appear to use behavioral control techniques in interactions with their peers that are similar to those techniques used by their parents to control them (Hoffman, 1960). In addition, children respond to their own behavior on the basis of the consequences they see others provide themselves (Bandura, Grusec, & Menlove, 1967). Children of punitive parents may learn to criticize and punish themselves through modeling. Certainly, a degree of caution is required in using aversive techniques, particularly physical punishment, because of the modeling influences which may result.

Perpetuation of Punishment.   Another undesirable side effect of punishment is that agents who use punishment are reinforced for punishing. Punishment usually results in rapid reduction of the target response (Azrin & Holz, 1966). If a parent shouts at a child, the child's behavior usually is altered immediately. The parent's behavior (shout) is *negatively reinforced* (termination of some undesirable child behavior). Since reinforcement is a powerful technique, particularly if it is immediate, the parent is likely to increase in the frequency of delivering punishment. Even though the child's behavior may not be altered for very long, the obvious failure of punishment is delayed, whereas the short-term effect is immediate. Hence, the parent is likely to rely increasingly on punishment and runs the risk of encountering the side effects discussed above.

■ EVIDENCE FOR SIDE EFFECTS IN APPLIED SETTINGS

The evidence for side effects of punishment in humans is relatively sparse. Not all of the problems demonstrated in the laboratory have been systematically studied in behavior modification programs using punishment. Nevertheless, a few studies have reported results that closely resemble the side effects demonstrated in laboratory research.

In one program, mentally retarded children received verbal reprimands for noncompliance with requests (Doleys et al., 1976). Some of the children showed brief periods of crying, soiling and wetting their pants. Similarly, other reports using overcorrection, response cost, time out, and shock, occasionally have noted that the clients have increased in crying, tantrums, and emotional outbursts, and were generally upset (Azrin & Wesolowski, 1975; Doleys & Arnold, 1975; Meichenbaum et al., 1968; Matson & Ollendick, 1977; Tate & Baroff, 1966). These reports suggest *emotional side effects* may be associated with punishment.

A few studies have demonstrated that *escape and avoidance* may be associated with punishment. In one program, hospitalized delinquent soldiers lost tokens for not attending meetings on the ward (Boren & Colman, 1970). This response cost contingency *increased* absenteeism (i.e., avoiding the situation). In another project in which individuals were to shock themselves for cigarette smoking, 50 percent of the clients dropped out of the project (Powell & Azrin, 1968). Many clients said they wanted to stop smoking but not at the expense of experiencing shock. Hence, they avoided participation.

An unfortunate consequence of punishment might be to avoid agents who administer aversive consequences. Very few experiments have looked carefully at the avoidance reactions toward punishing agents that punishment may foster. Two experiments exposed children to adults who administered different consequences during play activities (Morris & Redd, 1975; Redd, Morris, & Martin, 1975). Subsequently, to assess their preferences, children were asked to choose with whom they wished to interact. Adults who had been associated with the delivery of punishment (reprimands) were generally not selected for further interaction, whereas those associated with positive reinforcement (praise) were the most frequently selected for further interaction. This research suggests a clear preference for agents on the basis of whether they administer reinforcing or punishing consequences. Agents who primarily administer punishment are not sought out when clients are given the opportunity for additional interaction. If these findings extend to education and child-rearing, the avoidance of children of their teachers or parents might be fostered in part by the types of consequences that are administered.

Aggression also has been found as an occasional side effect of punishment. Applications of overcorrection, reprimands, and brief slaps to the hand have effectively suppressed the behaviors included in treatment (Foxx & Azrin, 1972; Mayhew & Harris, 1978). However, increases in attacks on the trainer (e.g., hitting, pinching, throwing things) have been reported early in training. Similarly, Knight and McKenzie (1974) decreased thumbsucking in three children by reading to each child (positive reinforcement) when the behavior was *not* performed. As soon as thumbsucking occurred, reading was stopped (withdrawal of the reinforcer). One of the children hit the experimenter when the reinforcer was withdrawn. Occasionally, the aggression associated with punishment has been self-inflicted. For example, applications of overcorrection have been associated with increases in self-injurious behavior in some clients (Azrin et al., 1975; Rollings, Baumeister, & Baumeister, 1977).

The negative side effects obtained in using punishment programs appear to be exceptions rather than the rule. And, when undesirable side effects appear, they usually are temporary and subside over the course of treatment. In spite of the reports of side effects cited above, studies occasionally have attempted to assess undesirable effects without finding them (Kaufman & O'Leary, 1972; Kazdin, 1972). Moreover, studies have often reported *desirable* side effects associated with punishment.

For example, Jackson and Calhoun (1977) used time out to punish disruptive behavior of a 10-year-old child in a classroom. Appropriate social behavior such as initiating conversations with peers and joining in activities increased even though these were not specifically focused upon. Similarly, Becker et al. (1978) found that reductions achieved in vomiting using lemon juice were associated with a decrease in episodes of crying and increases in verbal behaviors. Foxx and Azrin (1972) found that after overcorrection successfully suppressed aggression in one retarded adult, social interaction and participation in activities increased. Several other studies have found that use of punishment techniques such as overcorrection, shock, time out, and others are associated with decreases in such behaviors as aggressiveness, whining and fussing and increases in participation in activities, attentiveness to others and smiling (Doleys et al., 1976; Foxx & Azrin, 1972; Lovaas & Simmons, 1969; Risley, 1968).

It is clear that undesirable side effects are not necessary concomitants of the use of punishment procedures. Perhaps, a major reason that undesirable side effects have been less apparent in the research with humans in applied settings is that reinforcement for alternate responses is usually used in conjunction with punishment. If some behavior is reinforced, even though others are punished, it is less likely that the situation and punishing agent will be as aversive as would be the case if punishment were administered in the absence of reinforcement. Hence, less escape and avoidance on the part of the client would be evident. In addition, if a punishing agent also delivers reinforcement, the negative effects of modeling may be alleviated. Another reason that undesirable side effects have not been widely found is that mild forms of punishment are usually used in applied settings. Mild forms of punishment are effective in suppressing behavior when reinforcement is delivered for other behaviors. Of course, when mild intensities of punishment are used it is likely that fewer undesirable side effects would result. Emotional disruption and aggressive behavior are less likely to result from mild forms of punishment than from intense forms resulting from painful stimuli.

■ CHARACTERISTICS OF THE PUNISHMENT PROCESS

Immediacy of Effects.   A reduction in response rate following punishment usually occurs immediately. Using punishment for prolonged periods may result in further suppression. However, if there is no immediate effect, it probably is not advantageous to continue the aversive contingency. It is difficult to specify precisely how immediate the effect of punishment should be to justify being continued. Laboratory work has shown that some response suppression occurs as soon as the punishing stimulus is delivered a few times (Azrin & Holz, 1966). Yet, several factors determine the immediacy of punishment effects. The most important factor is intensity of the aversive event, with greater intensities associated with more immediate response suppression. Other conditions for maximizing the efficacy of punishment, described earlier, presumably also contribute to the immediacy of response suppression.

In applied settings, the rapidity of punishment effects has been especially evident with shock. In a matter of only a few sessions or even only one application of shock, behaviors are reduced and sometimes completely eliminated. The rapid and dramatic effects of shock were illustrated in a report with a 14-year-old boy who had a chronic cough (Creer, Chai, & Hoffman, 1977). The cough did not respond to medical treatment nor attempts to remove attention for coughing and to provide praise for periods of not coughing. The cough was so disruptive and distracting to others that the child was expelled from school until his cough could be controlled. After further medical tests proved negative, a punishment procedure was used. Baseline observations revealed that the boy coughed 22 times in a one-hour period. Treatment began by applying a mild electric shock (to the forearm) for coughing. Application of only one shock after the first cough eliminated the behavior. The boy immediately returned to school and did not suffer episodes of coughing up to 2½ years after treatment.

Immediate effects also occur with less intense forms of punishment. Applications of time out, verbal reprimands, overcorrection, lemon juice, and other procedures have shown that reductions in behavior occur after one or a few days of punishment (e.g., Bornstein, Hamilton, & Quevillon, 1977; Marholin & Townsend, 1978; Wilson et al., 1979). Although exceptions to these studies can be found, the general pattern is a reduction in behavior relatively soon after treatment is applied. This does not mean that the behavior will be eliminated or suppressed in only a few days. Yet, the beneficial effects of punishment, when they occur, should be evident very soon after the punishment contingency is begun.

The immediacy of punishment effects is important to keep in mind when applying punishment. The effects of punishment should be monitored closely to ensure that improvements are evident in client behavior within a relatively brief period (e.g., a few days). If signs of progress are not evident to justify continuation of the program, perhaps alternative procedures should be attempted.

Specificity of Effects. Punishment often leads to effects that are specific to the situation in which the response is punished. Investigators have frequently noted that punishing a response in one setting or during one time period does not carry over to other settings or to other times. For example, punishment effects achieved in special training sessions in a small room off the ward in an institution may not be evident after the sessions in the same room (Marholin & Townsend, 1978) or on the ward after the client leaves the session (Rollings et al., 1977). As might be expected, behaviors suppressed in a treatment setting often do not extend to the client's home, unless punishment is implemented in the new setting (Risley, 1968).

The specificity of punishment effects has been evident in other ways. Occasionally, only the precise response that is punished will be suppressed. For example, Bucher and King (1972) suppressed a child's touching and playing with electrical appliances by shocking the child's arm when he approached appliances. When the situation was changed and the appliances were varied, the undesirable responses were still performed. When these responses in the new situations were shocked, they rapidly diminished. In general, it may be necessary to extend the punishment contingency to more than one situation if response suppression across settings is desired. Usually, when punishment is extended in this fashion, responses are suppressed with increasing rapidity in the new situation.

The effect of punishment may be restricted to the presence of the person who previously administered it. For example, verbal warnings and reprimands sometimes are effective when administered only by persons previously associated with more severe punishment (Birnbrauer, 1968). The specificity of punishment effects was shown in one report that examined the influence of the proximity of the trainer on response suppression (Marholin & Townsend, 1978). Outside of the training sessions, the proximity of the trainer to the adult retardate on the ward was related to the frequency of self-stimulatory behaviors in the client. Self-stimulatory behaviors, which had been punished with overcorrection, were less frequent when the trainer was relatively close to the client than when he was further away. Response suppression may occur only in the presence of the trainer who administers punishment and not in the presence of nonpunishing adults. However, when punishment is administered by more than one trainer, responses may be suppressed across several other people who have not administered punishment to the client (Lovaas & Simmons, 1969). Thus, the specificity of punishment effects can be overcome.

Recovery after Punishment Withdrawal. The effects of punishment often are quite rapid so that the frequency of a behavior is reduced in a short time. However, the effect of punishment may not last so that when the punishment contingency is withdrawn, behavior recovers or returns to its baseline rate. Recovery is likely to occur when punishment has not completely suppressed the response while the contingency was in effect (Azrin & Holz, 1966) and reinforcement has not been used to develop an alternate response. As mentioned earlier, whether punishment is highly effective in suppressing behavior depends upon a variety of factors. For example, use of electric shock to suppress self-destructive behavior can completely eliminate that behavior with a few shocks. Moreover, the suppression is complete and the response does not recover even though the contingency is withdrawn.

Since shock typically is not used to suppress behavior in applied settings, factors other than intensity of the aversive event must be considered to ensure response suppression and little or no recovery. Ordinarily mild forms of punishment will result in recovery after the punishment contingency is withdrawn. Indeed, even when punishment is in effect the individual may adapt to mild punishment so it loses its suppressive effects. For example, threats lose their suppressive effects the more frequently they are used (Phillips, 1968; Phillips et al., 1971). To maximize response suppression with punishment and to minimize recovery, reinforcement can be provided for behaviors incompatible with the punished response. When the punishment contingency is removed, the reinforced response will be of a higher relative frequency than the punished response. The reinforced response will have replaced the previously punished response and can be maintained with continued reinforcement.

■ WHEN AND HOW TO USE PUNISHMENT

In light of the above discussion, punishment is a procedure to be used cautiously because of the possible undesirable effects as well as ethical considerations that arise in using aversive procedures. As a general rule other procedures should be employed in advance of punishment. An initial question that should be asked is whether punishment is needed at all. *The fact that a goal may be to suppress behavior, does not necessarily mean that the program should be based upon punishment.* Response suppression can be achieved with variations of positive reinforcement techniques. As noted in an earlier chapter, many reinforcement programs have been designed with the goal of eliminating or reducing undesirable responses. To achieve this goal, reinforcement of incompatible responses or differential reinforcement of low rates can be used. Both techniques provide clients with positively reinforcing consequences for appropriate behavior or for at least not engaging in the undesired behaviors.

Even though reinforcement techniques present viable alternatives to punishment, several situations are likely to arise in which punishment will be useful, required, and even essential. First, punishment is essential when the inappropriate behavior may be physically dangerous to oneself or others. Some immediate intervention is required to suppress responses before the relatively delayed effects of reinforcement and extinction might operate.

Second, punishment is useful when reinforcement of a behavior incompatible with the disruptive behavior cannot be easily administered. For example, if a "hyperactive" student is literally out of his seat all of the time, it will be impossible to reinforce in-seat behavior. Punishment (along with shaping) may be helpful in initially obtaining the desirable response. Eventually, of course, punishment can be faded with increasing reliance upon shaping with positive reinforcement and extinction.

Third, punishment is useful in temporarily suppressing a behavior while another behavior is reinforced. This latter use may be the most common application of punishment in applied settings. However, it should be remembered that mild forms of punishment (e.g., quiet reprimands, brief time-out durations, and small penalties or costs) usually are sufficient to suppress behavior as long as reinforcement for alternate responses is provided. Indeed, mild punishment can sometimes enhance the effect of reinforcement.

In one program, reinforcement was used to control the behavior of an extremely stubborn and disobedient child in the home (Wahler et al., 1965). Differential reinforcement was used whereby the mother praised cooperative behavior and ignored a failure to comply with requests. However, cooperative behavior had only increased slightly, so punishment was added. Whenever the boy was uncooperative, he was isolated in his room for five minutes. During the reinforcement-punishment program, cooperative behavior increased dramatically. This example suggests that punishment can augment the effect of reinforcement. In some reports the combination of punishment and reinforcement is more effective than either procedure used alone (Phillips et al., 1971; Walker, Mattson, & Buckley, 1971). Yet in many cases, positive reinforcement combined with extinction will be effective without the addition of punishment.

It should be clear that the best use of punishment in applied settings is as an *ancillary* technique to accompany positive reinforcement. Usually, punishment will only suppress undesirable responses but not train desirable behaviors. Reinforcement is essential to develop appropriate behaviors which replace the suppressed behaviors.

■ NEGATIVE REINFORCEMENT

A behavior is increased or strengthened through negative reinforcement when it results in escape from or avoidance of an aversive event. Escape occurs when a response terminates or eliminates the aversive event. In an escape situation the individual comes in contact with the aversive event and the appropriate behavior eliminates the event. Many behaviors in everyday life are maintained by negative reinforcement through escape. For example, leaving the house to escape from an argument with one's roommate or spouse, turning off an alarm to escape from a loud noise, screaming to quiet noisy neighbors, and taking medicine to alleviate pain all represent escape.

Avoidance behavior allows the individual to prevent or indefinitely postpone contact with the aversive event. As mentioned in Chapter 2, avoidance learning may develop after an individual learns to escape an aversive event. Through classical conditioning, a previously neutral event acquires the capacity to elicit escape behavior. The escape behavior is automatically reinforced by terminating the conditioned aversive event. Thus, avoidance involves classical and operant conditioning. Avoidance refers to escape from a conditioned aversive event.

Most avoidance behavior is acquired without direct experience with the aversive event. Verbal cues from other individuals instruct us that certain things are to be avoided. The cues are discriminative stimuli indicating certain untoward consequences may follow, if we behave in a particular way. Examples of avoidance based on verbal cues are present in everyday experience. For example, one can avoid personal harm by responding to a threat of an impending flood. Avoidance of the flood is escape from or elimination of the threat. When a threat portends an aversive event if certain behaviors are (or are not) performed, avoidance conditioning is operative. Behavior which reduces the threat is strengthened through negative reinforcement. Other examples of negative reinforcement through avoidance include parking one's car in a particular place to avoid a traffic fine, wearing a coat to avoid a chill, drinking alcohol sparingly to avoid a driving mishap, and leaving a sinking ship to avoid drowning.

Negative reinforcement, in the form of escape from an aversive event, has not been widely used in applied settings for various reasons. First, when the treatment goal is to increase behavior, positive reinforcement is usually employed. By selecting positive instead of negative reinforcement, one can avoid all of the potentially undesirable features of aversive consequences outlined above. Negative reinforcement need only be employed when positive reinforcement and shaping have proved inadequate or when there is a paucity of positive events that serve as reinforcers. Second, negative reinforcement requires an ongoing aversive event which can be terminated when the desired target response occurs. This means that aversive events must be delivered frequently before reinforcement can occur. The extensive use of aversive events may be even more likely to result in undesirable side effects than if the aversive event were applied less frequently in the form of punishment. Third, the termination of the aversive state must be carefully controlled so that the appropriate response is reinforced. Usually this requires carefully monitoring behavior, often with certain apparatus. For the above reasons, it is no surprise that negative reinforcement has been restricted to relatively few settings.

Yet, negative reinforcement has been used in some cases to alter behaviors not readily amenable to change with other techniques. Negative reinforcement has been used to develop behaviors in schizophrenic children using shock as the aversive event (Lovaas et al., 1965). Shock removal negatively reinforced social behaviors such as approaching or hugging and kissing adults. Termination of the shock after these behaviors increased their probability.

Electric shock was used to increase a retarded child's use of toys (Whaley & Tough, 1970). The use of toys was important since it permitted the child to do something with his hands other than severely beating his head. Touching the toys was incompatible with head pounding. A toy truck was placed in front of the child. A buzzer and shock were presented to the child to provide an ongoing aversive event. The experimenter guided the boy's hand to the truck which resulted in cessation of the shock. Soon the boy avoided the shock by holding onto the toy truck. Additional toys were substituted and the buzzer alone, which had been previously paired with shock, served as the aversive stimulus. When the toy was released, the buzzer sounded. The buzzer was terminated when the toy was held. The child eventually used several toys and did not resume self-inflicted headbanging.

Negative reinforcement was used to increase conversation among psychiatric patients during their group therapy sessions (Heckel, Wiggins, & Salzberg, 1962). After the group had been silent for more than one minute, a loud noise sounded through a speaker hidden in the air conditioning vent of the room. The noise continued until one patient broke the silence. Hence, the desired response (talking) terminated the aversive event (noise). Patient conversation increased dramatically using this negative reinforcement contingency.

A particularly interesting example of negative reinforcement was reported by Fichter et al. (1976) who used "nagging" as an aversive event to alter behavior of a socially withdrawn psychiatric patient. The purpose of treatment was to increase the volume and duration of the patient's speech because he spoke inaudibly and only for very brief periods. Also, the patient used his hands in a ritualistic and self-stimulatory fashion by repetitively tapping or biting his fingers. Nagging consisted of constantly reminding the patient to speak louder or for longer periods during conversations he had with the staff. If the patient did not comply within a brief period (3 seconds), the prompt was repeated. If the desired behavior occurred, the request to perform the behavior was not given. From the patient's standpoint, the appropriate behavior (e.g., louder and longer speech) avoided further nagging. Positive reinforcement was not provided; rather, avoidance of the aversive event was the basis for changing behavior. The results demonstrated that each of the behaviors that staff nagged the client to perform increased with this avoidance contingency.

This study is especially interesting because of the experimental evaluation of "nagging," a technique that people are familiar with if they have ever been a child or parent. However, on the basis of this single application, it would not be appropriate to conclude that nagging would be effective in a variety of circumstances. Nagging (perhaps like a threat) may lose its effectiveness over time if there are no additional contingencies for failing to perform the response. Nagging could readily lose its aversive properties if not followed by other events. Also, clients might simply avoid the people who nag in the way that children often avoid their nagging parents.

In many cases, negative reinforcement is combined with punishment to alter behavior. If aversive stimuli are to be employed, it is probably desirable to use negative reinforcement rather than punishment alone. Negative reinforcement can increase adaptive behavior and thereby increase the efficacy of punishment. For example, Hobbs and Forehand (1975) compared two variations of time out to decrease the frequency that children failed to comply with their mothers' requests. When a child did not comply, time out was used. The mother simply left the room and removed the toys that the child was playing with. This procedure is punishment, as discussed earlier. For half of the children, time out was terminated at the end of a brief period. For others, time out (aversive event) was terminated only after they were not disruptive for 15 seconds. For this latter group, the aversive event (time out) was terminated by appropriate behavior. Hence, appropriate behavior was negatively reinforced. The results showed that negative reinforcement plus time out was more effective than time out alone in decreasing noncompliance and disruptive behavior.

Winkler (1971a) used negative reinforcement to control behavior of institutionalized psychiatric and retarded patients. The aversive event was time out from reinforcement during which tokens could not be earned for any behavior for a period of time on the ward (one day). Time out was imposed for not performing routine ward behaviors (e.g., making the bed). A patient could terminate time out any time by performing the desired response. Removal of the aversive state after a response exemplifies negative reinforcement.

Television distortion was used as an aversive event to control work behavior of a retarded adult (Greene & Hoats, 1969). Whenever work dropped below a certain rate, the TV picture he was viewing became grossly distorted (punishment). To remove the distortion, he had to increase his speed to the appropriate rate. Weekly work rates increased under the punishment and negative reinforcement contingency.

An interesting use of punishment and avoidance was employed in a sheltered workshop for multiply handicapped retarded clients (Zimmerman, Overpeck, Eisenberg, & Garlick, 1969). Clients worked on a piece-work assembly job. To increase performance, a client was told that if he failed to complete a certain number of work units per day, he had to work at a table isolated from others. Hence, punishment was delivered for a slow work rate. The client could avoid isolation by producing work rates above an individually-determined criterion. Avoidance of the anticipated aversive event could be achieved by performing the desired response (working at a relatively high rate). Interestingly, the procedure dramatically increased work. When the avoidance contingency was withdrawn, high rates of work behavior were maintained.

Negative reinforcement has been effectively combined with positive reinforcement. For example, Ayllon and Michael (1959) described a psychiatric patient who had to be spoon-fed at each meal. The patient liked to have clean clothes so the investigators developed an aversive contingency in which her clothes were soiled whenever she was spoon-fed. While the nurse fed her, she periodically spilled food on the patient. The patient could avoid this by feeding herself, which she quickly did. As soon as the patient began to feed herself, the nurse positively reinforced her by attending to and talking with her.

Negative reinforcement has occasionally been applied as part of therapy techniques to alter such behaviors as excessive alcohol consumption, overeating, and sexual deviance including transvestism and fetishism (Hallam & Rachman, 1976). For example, one form of treatment for alcoholics that involves punishment and negative reinforcement requires the client to ingest a drug disulfiram (Antabuse). If the client drinks alcohol within a 24-hour period following ingestion of the drug, intense nausea results. Nausea can be *avoided* by not consuming alcohol. Of course, the person also can avoid the aversive contingency altogether by failing to take the drug.

■ EVALUATION OF NEGATIVE REINFORCEMENT

A major restriction in using negative reinforcement is the risk of undesirable side effects. From the standpoint of designing a behavior modification program, aversive stimuli should be avoided or minimized. When they are used, emphasis should be placed upon positive reinforcement for desirable behavior. In many applications of negative reinforcement, strong aversive stimuli are required because other procedures have failed or because the response (e.g., sexual deviance) is strongly reinforced. In such instances, aversive stimuli including punishment and/or negative reinforcement constitute a last resort.

■ SUMMARY AND CONCLUSION

A variety of aversive events are available for suppressing (punishment) or increasing behavior (negative reinforcement). Punishment consists of presenting aversive events such as shock or verbal reprimands and disapproval or removing positive events through time out from reinforcement and response cost. Punishment needs to be used carefully to ensure that the procedure will be maximally effective. The most important element when punishment is used is to provide positive reinforcement for behaviors incompatible with the punished response. By reinforcing an alternate response, even mild forms of punishment can change behavior dramatically.

Use of punishment can lead to side effects which may be undesirable, such as emotional reactions, escape from the situation or from the person who administers punishment, aggression, the use of punishment by the individual who is punished, and overreliance upon aversive control procedures. These undesirable side effects have not been widely demonstrated in applied settings. Indeed, in some instances positive side effects result from suppressing deviant behavior. Nevertheless, at the present time, the possibility of adverse side effects makes extensive reliance upon aversive procedures somewhat hazardous. Additionally, punishment effects may be very specific both in the responses that are altered and the situations in which behavior change occurs. Negative reinforcement is not widely used as a behavior change technique in most applied settings. This is due, in part, to reliance upon positive reinforcement to increase behavior whenever possible. Nevertheless, negative reinforcement has been used successfully, particularly in those instances where positive reinforcement has not been effective or has been difficult to administer.

8

Extinction

Extinction refers to withholding reinforcement from a previously reinforced response. A response undergoing extinction eventually decreases in frequency until it returns to its pre-reinforcement level or is eliminated. Numerous examples of extinction are evident in everyday life. For example, trying to start a defective automobile extinguishes after several unsuccessful attempts; warmly greeting an acquaintance each day decreases, if he or she repeatedly does not reciprocate; and raising one's hand in class will cease, if it is never followed by teacher attention. In each case, the behavior decreases because the reinforcing consequence no longer occurs.

Extinction in applied settings usually is used for behaviors which have been *positively* reinforced. In fact, each of the above examples refers to behaviors maintained by positive reinforcement. However, extinction can also be used with responses maintained by negative reinforcement. Extinction of responses developed or maintained through negative reinforcement is somewhat different from extinction of responses maintained with positive reinforcement.

■ EXTINCTION OF NEGATIVELY REINFORCED RESPONSES

As discussed earlier, many behaviors are performed to avoid anticipated aversive consequences and hence are maintained by negative reinforcement. For example, a student may study for exams to avoid poor grades. Similarly, some people spend money judiciously to avoid a lack of funds at the end of the month. Many behaviors are maintained by their success in avoiding the occurrence of anticipated undesirable consequences.

Laboratory research has shown that avoidance behaviors are highly resistant to extinction. In classic experiments, Solomon, Kamin, and Wynne (1953) trained dogs to avoid brief electric shocks by responding to a buzzer which preceded the shock. A dog could avoid the shock by jumping over a barrier in the middle of the compartment when the buzzer sounded. The avoidance training procedure was repeated in each side of the compartment. At the beginning of training, the animal was shocked and escaped over the barrier. In a short time, the dog repeatedly jumped back and forth over the barrier in response to the buzzer. Although the shock eventually was completely withdrawn from the situation, the avoidance responses did not extinguish. The dog never remained in the situation long enough to find out that extinction (removal of shock) began.

Anxiety is presumed to play a role in the development and maintenance of avoidance responses. A previously neutral stimulus elicits anxiety and escape through the process of classical conditioning, described earlier. Cues associated with the unconditioned aversive event can elicit the anxiety and escape response. In the case of avoidance in animals, anxiety or fear increases when the buzzer sounds because the buzzer preceded shock. Escape from the buzzer reduces fear. Thus, anxiety reduction, by termination of the unconditioned aversive event, negatively reinforces escape. Although the unconditioned aversive event (shock) no longer occurs, successful escape from the anxiety-arousing conditioned aversive event maintains avoidance behavior.

Fear and anxiety in human behavior often have been conceptualized on the basis of avoidance conditioning studied in laboratory research. With humans it is not clear how most fears develop, as it is in animal research where specific fear reactions are induced. However, like laboratory-induced fear, human avoidance behavior is highly resistant to extinction. Fearful persons rarely place themselves in the fear-provoking situation. If they did, escape and avoidance behaviors might extinguish, as described below. Anxiety can be reduced by remaining in the provoking situation to allow the conditioned anxiety to extinguish. Most people do not gain the benefit of extinction because they either do not enter into the situation they fear or only remain in the situation for a brief period. Avoidance of or escape from the situation still will be reinforced by anxiety reduction.

Several techniques have been effective in extinguishing avoidance responses (see Leitenberg, 1976; Marks, 1978). One of the more widely practiced techniques is *systematic desensitization* which has been derived from a classical conditioning framework (Wolpe, 1958). As mentioned earlier, desensitization alters the valence of the conditioned stimuli so they no longer elicit anxiety. Anxiety-eliciting conditioned stimuli are paired with nonanxiety states of the client. To achieve a nonanxiety state, the client usually is trained to relax very deeply. The relaxation eventually is paired with actually being in the anxiety-provoking situation or imagining that one is in these situations. For example, in the more commonly used variation, the client imagines approaching situations that are only mildly provoking while he or she is deeply relaxed. As treatment progresses and the person has successfully associated relaxation with these scenes, increasingly more arousing scenes are imagined. Eventually, the client can imagine these latter scenes without anxiety. The previously anxiety-provoking stimuli no longer elicit anxiety. The changes made in the client's anxiety responses are not restricted to images or thoughts about the situation but extend to the actual situations themselves.

Another technique often used to extinguish avoidance reactions is *flooding*. Flooding nicely illustrates the rationale for extinguishing anxiety responses because it involves exposing the client to the anxiety-eliciting stimuli for prolonged periods. As in desensitization, flooding can be conducted in imagination or in the actual situations themselves. The procedure consists of exposing the client to the fear-provoking stimuli directly. For example, a client who is afraid of heights might imagine being in very high places. When the client first imagines the situation, intense anxiety is produced. However, as he or she continues to imagine the situation for a prolonged period (several minutes or even an hour or more) anxiety decreases. Repeated presentation of the same situation is likely to evoke much less anxiety. As the situation is repeated and others are presented, anxiety is completely eliminated. The conditioned stimuli have lost their capacity to evoke anxiety.

Operant techniques also have been used to extinguish avoidance responses. For example, contingent feedback and praise were used in one report to eliminate anxiety of a 56-year-old female psychiatric patient (Leitenberg, Agras, Allen, Butz, & Edwards, 1975). The patient had a fear of knives and other pointed objects and avoided situations (e.g., kitchens, gift shops) in which she thought she might have contact with sharp objects. Treatment consisted of exposing the woman to a knife for various periods of time and providing feedback and praise. The knife was placed in a box that had a sliding door so the woman could expose or conceal the knife. She was allowed to close the door whenever she wanted but encouraged to increase the amount of time she could tolerate looking at it without becoming anxious. Feedback consisted of conveying how many seconds she had been able to look at the knife. Praise was added to provide approval for looking at the knife for extended periods. Eventually, the client was able to look at the knife without discomfort.

Systematic desensitization, flooding, and reinforcement, as described above, have been successfully used in many reports to overcome anxiety. Each technique exposes the individual to the situation that is usually avoided and prevents or minimizes the need for an avoidance response. Avoidance behavior extinguishes because no untoward consequences actually occur in the situation, and contact with the feared stimuli is actually encouraged. Extinction of avoidance responses may occur inadvertently in the context of counseling or psychotherapy. In therapy, clients frequently express feelings and thoughts that elicit anxiety and guilt in themselves. These feelings and thoughts may be avoided at the beginning of therapy precisely because of the anxiety they evoke. Therapists typically respond in a permissive and nonpunitive fashion so that maladaptive emotional responses extinguish. As therapy progresses, self-reported as well as physiological arousal associated with anxiety-provoking topics, such as sex, may decrease over time (e.g., Dittes, 1957).

Behavior modification techniques to extinguish negatively reinforced behaviors such as avoidance reactions are not widely employed by parents, teachers, attendants and others in applied settings. Although these procedures often can be conducted by nonprofessionals, usually treatment is administered by a professional in an outpatient setting. Treatment may be supplemented by assistance from the client's relatives or others with whom he or she interacts. The major focus of extinction in applied settings is the elimination of behaviors maintained by positive reinforcement. Hence, the remaining discussion of extinction will focus on behaviors maintained by positive reinforcement.

■ EXTINCTION OF POSITIVELY REINFORCED RESPONSES

Initial Considerations in Using Extinction

Extinction of positively reinforced behaviors is almost always used in a behavior modification program. For example, in a reinforcement program, when a target response is reinforced, implicitly, nontarget responses which are no longer reinforced are undergoing extinction. Although extinction is an ingredient in most programs, it may be used as the major technique to decrease undesirable behavior. When relied upon as the major technique, various factors determine whether it will be effective.

Schedule of Reinforcement. The efficacy of extinction and the speed with which response reduction is achieved depends upon the schedule of reinforcement which previously maintained the response. As mentioned in the discussion of reinforcement, a response reinforced every time (continuous reinforcement) rapidly extinguishes once the reinforcer is withheld. In contrast, a response reinforced once in a while (intermittent reinforcement) extinguishes less rapidly when the reinforcer is withheld. The more intermittent the schedule (or less frequent the reinforcement), the greater the resistance of the response to extinction.

The relationship of reinforcement schedules and extinction creates a major problem for programs relying primarily on extinction because most behaviors are maintained by intermittent reinforcement. For example, incoherent verbalizations in psychiatric patients often are attended to but sometimes are ignored. Decreasing the frequency of these behaviors may be difficult because of the intermittent schedule on which they have been maintained. If all the sources of reinforcement were removed from a behavior previously maintained by intermittent reinforcement, the behavior would eventually decrease and perhaps be eliminated. Intermittent reinforcement *delays* the extinction process. Yet, the delay may be unfortunate. While the long extinction process is underway, it is possible that the response will be *accidentally reinforced*. The possibility of accidental reinforcement during extinction is always a problem and is only exacerbated with a long extinction period.

An example of accidental reinforcement was reported in a program designed to eliminate a child's bedtime tantrum behavior (Williams, 1959). The child's parents were instructed to no longer provide attention for this behavior. Extinction proceeded uneventfully until tantrums were nearly eliminated within a few days. However, one night the child fussed when put to bed by his aunt. The aunt provided a great deal of attention to the tantrum by staying with the child until he went to sleep. The tantrums had to be extinguished a second time. After tantrums were eliminated the second time, they did not occur in the following two years.

Other Variables Affecting Extinction. The effects of reinforcement schedules on extinction have been more thoroughly studied than the influence of other variables. Yet, general statements can be extrapolated from laboratory research on variables which contribute to resistance to extinction (Kimble, 1961; Reynolds, 1968). First, the amount or magnitude of reinforcement used to develop the response affects extinction. The greater the amount of a particular reinforcer given for a response, the greater the resistance of the response to extinction. Similarly, the longer the period of time that the response has been reinforced, the greater the resistance to extinction. Finally, the greater the number of times that extinction has been used in the past to reduce the behavior, the more rapid extinction will be. The individual learns to discriminate periods of reinforcement and extinction more rapidly. If a strong or powerful reinforcer is maintaining a response, and if the response has been sustained over a long period, it is likely to be more resistant to extinction than if weak reinforcers were used and reinforcers were delivered over a short period of time. Of course, these effects act in concert with the schedule of reinforcement in influencing extinction.

Identifying the Reinforcer Maintaining Behavior. Extinction requires that the reinforcer(s) maintaining behavior be identified and withheld when the response is performed. While this appears simple enough, in practice it may be difficult to isolate the reinforcer. For example, an "emotionally disturbed" child may behave aggressively with peers. Various reinforcers might maintain aggressive behavior, such as the control aggressive behavior exerts over peers, a submissive response of the victim, admiration from friends, or special attention from a teacher or parent. It is difficult to identify which potential reinforcer or combination of reinforcers is maintaining behavior. Extinction may be attempted by removing teacher and parent attention without decreasing aggressive behavior because other reinforcers are operative. For example, in a classroom program, an attempt was made to extinguish disruptive behavior by withdrawing teacher attention (Madsen et al., 1968). However, disruptive behavior increased. Apparently, reinforcement resulting from peer attention or from disruptive acts themselves maintained inappropriate behavior.

The only method for determining which reinforcer is maintaining behavior is empirical observation. By repeatedly observing events which consistently follow the target response, the consequence which appears responsible for maintaining behavior can be examined. The consequence is removed while data on the frequency of the response are continuously gathered. It is useful to record the frequency of the consequence (e.g., teacher or parent attention) to ensure that the consequence is consistently withheld. If the response declines and the consequence is consistently withheld, the consequence served as a positive reinforcer and maintained behavior. This can be evaluated carefully by employing a reversal or multiple-baseline design, as outlined earlier.

In many instances, the reinforcer maintaining behavior may be difficult to identify because it follows behavior very infrequently. For example, in a psychiatric hospital disruptive patient behavior may be maintained by attention from a psychiatrist or psychologist. However, the psychiatrist or psychologist may have little interaction with the patient. Yet, the interaction may follow particularly bizarre patient behavior. The interaction may be so infrequent that it is assumed not to be responsible for maintaining bizarre behavior. Identification of the reinforcer maintaining behavior is likely to be delayed. If the reinforcer is not quickly identified, there can be considerable delay in beginning the extinction process. For this reason, it is desirable to supplement extinction with other procedures (e.g., reinforcement for appropriate behavior), as will be elaborated below.

Controlling the Source of Reinforcement. Once the reinforcer maintaining an undesirable behavior has been identified, a major problem may be withholding it after behavior. As mentioned earlier, extinction requires very careful control over reinforcers. Any accidental reinforcement may rapidly reinstate the inappropriate behavior and prolong the extinction process.

An example of the problem in controlling reinforcement delivery was reported by Ayllon and Michael (1959). These investigators used extinction to decrease delusional talk of a hospitalized psychotic patient. The patient consistently talked about her illegitimate child and the men she claimed were always pursuing her. Her psychotic talk had persisted for at least three years. Typically, nurses responded to the delusional talk by listening to understand and get at the "root" of the problem. When extinction was implemented, the nurses did not attend to the psychotic talk and provided attention for sensible talk. At three different times during the extinction phase, delusional talk was accidentally reinforced. Once a social worker attended to psychotic talk. On two other occasions, when another employee and volunteers visited the ward, the extinction procedure again was sacrificed. Although extinction decreased behavior, the accidental reinforcement appeared to account for temporary increases.

Reinforcement is particularly difficult to control when it is delivered by peers. Peers often provide reinforcing consequences for each other's behavior without parents, teachers, or staff members even knowing about it. For example, "clowning" in a classroom or stealing among delinquents in the community may be reinforced by peers. Constant surveillance would be required to ensure that no peer reinforcement occurred. From a practical standpoint, constant surveillance usually is not possible in applied settings or the community.

One alternative is to enlist peers so that they ignore (extinguish) the deviant behavior of a particular individual. For example, in one classroom program (Pierce, 1971), a 12-year-old girl engaged in bizarre behaviors including frenzied hand flapping, aimless running, "crazy" talk referring to fictitious events, and paralysis. The teacher instructed the girl's classmates that the student had trouble with her imagination and needed their help. They were told that her "acting crazy" would probably continue, if people paid attention to her. The classmates were instructed to ignore bizarre behavior and to reinforce appropriate behavior. The girl was reported to have changed considerably although the program was not rigorously evaluated.

Peers can be reinforced for systematically ignoring certain behaviors. By providing a strong peer incentive for extinguishing a response, it is likely that there will be little or no accidental reinforcement. For example, students in one elementary classroom received candy if they ignored a peer who had severe tantrums which consisted of profane screaming and throwing objects (Carlson, Arnold, Becker, & Madsen, 1968). By reinforcing peer behavior, these authors decreased the likelihood of any uncontrolled reinforcement.

It is virtually impossible to control reinforcement for some behaviors. For example, criminal acts such as theft are reinforced intermittently. It is not readily feasible to design society so that reinforcers are never provided for theft. All objects for which thefts are committed cannot be locked up. So theft is likely to be reinforced once in a while and maintained. Extinction alone is exceedingly unlikely to control theft and other crimes where the source of reinforcement cannot be controlled.

■ CHARACTERISTICS OF THE EXTINCTION PROCESS

Gradual Reduction in Behavior.   Although extinction effectively decreases and often eliminates behavior, *the process of extinction is usually gradual.* Unlike the effects of punishment, described in the last chapter, extinction typically does not show an immediate response reduction. Rather, several unreinforced responses are performed prior to demonstrating an effect.

When the undesirable behaviors are dangerous or severely disruptive, the delayed effects of extinction can be deleterious either to the individual himself or to others. For example, self-destructive behavior of retarded and autistic children often is severe enough to render serious self-inflicted physical damage. Ignoring the behavior may reduce its frequency. Yet the physical damage rendered in the process may be unfortunate. One child who engaged in self-inflicted headbanging had multiple scars over his head and face from the injuries (Lovaas & Simmons, 1969). During extinction, the child was taken out of physical restraints and placed in a small room with no adults who could reinforce (attend to) the destructive behavior. The child's behavior, observed through a one-way mirror, eventually extinguished in ten sessions over a total of 15 hours. However, from the beginning of extinction until the response finally decreased to zero, the child had hit himself almost 9,000 times. Thus, a great deal of self-inflicted injury occurred during the course of extinction. Although extinction can reduce behavior, dangerous behavior requires an intervention with more rapid results than extinction usually provides.

Extinction Burst.   At the beginning of extinction, the frequency of the response may increase compared to what it was while the response was reinforced. The response may be performed several times in rapid succession. The increase in responding at the beginning of extinction is referred to as a "burst" of responses. Numerous examples of a burst of responses at the beginning of extinction pervade everyday experience. For example, turning on a radio is usually followed by some sound (e.g., music or news). If the radio no longer works so that no reinforcement (sound) occurs, eventually attempts to turn the radio on will extinguish. However, before this occurs, the response may temporarily increase in frequency (several on-off turns) and intensity or vigor. These responses will eventually cease, if the radio does not work.

A burst of responses at the beginning of extinction occasionally has been reported in behavior modification programs. For example, Neisworth and Moore (1972) used extinction to reduce the frequent asthmatic attacks of a 7-year-old boy. The child's prolonged wheezing, coughing, gasping, and similar responses were usually associated with excessive verbal as well as physical attention at bed time. During extinction, the child was put to bed and asthmatic attacks were ignored. When asthmatic attacks were of a shorter duration than on the previous night, the child was rewarded in the morning with lunch money so he could purchase his lunch at school, rather than take his lunch. The results of the program are plotted in Figure 8–1. Of special note is the first phase of extinction (treatment conditions). At the beginning of extinction, the asthmatic attacks lasted longer than during baseline. A similar burst of responses was evident the second time extinction was begun. Eventually, the asthmatic attacks were eliminated but not before temporarily becoming worse.

In another example, extinction was used to decrease the tantrums of a 4½-year-old boy in a Head Start classroom (Allen, Turner, & Everett, 1970). The boy's outbursts and aggressive attacks on others disrupted the entire class. Baseline observations revealed an average duration of five minutes for each tantrum. After baseline, the teacher agreed to ignore each tantrum no matter how severe it was. The first tantrum during extinction was much more severe than previous tantrums and lasted 27 minutes. While this tantrum was occurring, the teacher anticipated that it might last a long time so she took the other children out to the playground. This prevented accidental peer reinforcement of tantrum behavior. On the second day of extinction the one tantrum that occurred lasted about 15 minutes and on the third day there was one mild tantrum of 4 minutes. From that point on no further tantrums occurred. Thus, extinction eliminated behavior but not until behavior became worse for a short time.

When extinction is used as a treatment strategy, it is important to prepare those persons who will ignore the behavior for a possible burst of

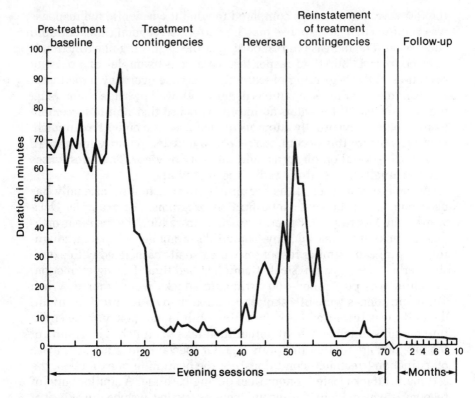

FIGURE 8–1 Duration of bedtime asthmatic responding as a function of contingency changes.

Source: Neisworth, J. T., & Moore, F. Operant treatment of asthmatic responding with the parent as therapist. *Behavior Therapy*, 1972, **3**, 95–99.

responses so that obstreperous behavior will not be reinforced when it becomes worse. In the above report (Allen et al., 1970), the investigators prepared the teacher for the increase in response intensity. However, in another classroom project, the teacher who ignored disruptive classroom behavior was unprepared for the consequences. At the beginning of the extinction phase, the class reportedly became worse and she was very upset (Madsen et al., 1968).

A burst of responses is especially serious with behaviors that may threaten the client's physical well being. For example, Wright, Brown, and Andrews (1978) treated a 9-month-old girl who constantly engaged in ruminative vomiting (regurgitating food after eating, as well as between meals). The girl weighed only eight pounds (normal weight would be about 20 pounds) because she received little nourishment from her meals. Because of the excessive attention from the staff that the girl received from ruminative vomiting, an extinction contingency was implemented. Staff was instructed to leave the child's presence immediately when vomiting began. When she was not vomiting, the staff engaged in normal interaction such as holding and looking at her and so on. At the beginning of extinction, there was a burst of vomiting responses. This may be especially unfortunate because it means even greater food deprivation than she normally experienced during baseline. By vomiting more of her food, less of her meal would be digested. Fortunately, the burst lasted only two days and was followed by a decrease in vomiting and an increase in weight. The benefits of treatment were evident over a year later when follow-up data were obtained.

With other physically dangerous behaviors, a burst of responses may even be more risky to the client. For example, Lovaas and Simmons (1969) noted that self-injurious behavior in children initially increased at the beginning of extinction over their dangerously high rate. For one child, the burst of self-destructive responses at the beginning of extinction led to considerable bleeding and physical discomfort. The investigators decided against the use of extinction for another child who already had physical damage from self-destructive behaviors over concern with further damage.

With behaviors that are not physically dangerous, a burst of responses may still be undesirable. It may be exceedingly difficult for someone to tolerate the undesirable behavior as it intensifies at the beginning of extinction (Patterson & Reid, 1970). Thus, during a burst of responses, the likelihood that reinforcement will occur is increased. For example, a tantrum may become worse when parents systematically ignore the behavior. When the tantrum is worse, the parents may give in to the child and provide attention and comfort. Parental reinforcement will increase the probability of intense tantrums because reinforcement is provided when the behavior is worse than usual. To the parents, of course, extinction may appear to be failing because behavior has become worse. However, the effect of extinction is merely beginning. It is likely that reinforcement during a burst of responses is a basis for behaviors such as protracted whining and excessive demands for attention often seen in children. It should be noted that an initial burst of responses does not always occur. However, when the burst occurs, the possibility of reinforcement adds to the risk in relying on extinction in the absence of other procedures.

Spontaneous Recovery.   After extinction has progressed, the response may temporarily reappear even though it has not been reinforced. *The temporary recurrence of a nonreinforced response during extinction is referred to as spontaneous recovery* (Kimble, 1961). When the response recovers during extinction, its strength ordinarily will be less than it was prior to extinction. For example, if a child's tantrum is ignored, the frequency of tantrums probably will decrease over time, possibly, after an initial burst of responses. However, there may be a tantrum that occurs after extinction has progressed for some time. The tantrum is likely to be of a lower intensity or magnitude than the original tantrums during baseline.

As with extinction burst, a major concern with spontaneous recovery is that the response will be reinforced. Spontaneous recovery occurs after several responses have not been reinforced. If reinforcement is provided, it follows a long series of nonreinforced responses. This is tantamount to a highly intermittent reinforcement schedule which may further increase resistance to extinction. If extinction continues and no accidental reinforcement occurs, the frequency and intensity of the spontaneously recovered response decreases. It is important to realize that extinction may include the spontaneous recurrence of the response. A recurrence is less likely to be interpreted as the inefficacy of the procedure but rather a characteristic of the extinction process.

Possible Side Effects. Another characteristic of extinction is that the cessation of reinforcement may result in "emotional responses" such as agitation, frustration, feelings of failure, or rage (Lawson, 1965; Skinner, 1953). In addition, aggressive behavior is sometimes produced when reinforcement is discontinued (see Rilling, 1977). Apparently, the transition from positive reinforcement to extinction is aversive.

Examples of emotional reactions in response to extinction abound in everyday experience. For example, after individuals place money into a malfunctioning vending machine (i.e., reinforcement no longer delivered), exhortations of frustration and aggressive attacks on the machine are common events. For individuals who have experienced repeated reinforcement of certain responses, the cessation of reinforcement may be experienced as failure. For example, when an athlete performs poorly he or she may swear, express feelings of failure, and throw something to the ground in disgust. The notion of being a "poor loser" denotes that emotional behavior occurs when a person's responses are not reinforced in a contest, that is, the person loses.

The emotional effects of extinction have not been widely studied in applied settings. Nevertheless, extrapolation from laboratory evidence suggests that the emotional effects may only be temporary and diminish as the response decreases. However, if the response is performed for a long period during extinction, emotional responses may also continue for some time (Hutchinson, Azrin, & Hunt, 1968).

Adverse side effects of extinction occasionally have been reported in behavioral programs. For example, to eliminate effeminate behavior of a boy with a gender-identity problem, Rekers and Lovaas (1974) instructed the boy's mother to ignore him whenever he engaged in "feminine" play (with girls' toys). When the mother failed to provide attention for the child's play behavior, he cried excessively and engaged in aggressive behavior toward her. In fact, the session had to be stopped to reassure the mother than she was doing what she was supposed to and that extinction should be continued.

In applications of extinction, adverse side effects might be expected. Any situation in which reinforcement is no longer provided may become aversive. An aversive situation can result in escape and avoidance and reduce the opportunity for providing the client with positive reinforcement for desirable behavior. To avoid this, reinforcement should be delivered for an alternate response from the one to be eliminated. Thus, there is no net loss in reinforcement for the client. Rather, the reinforcement is provided for a new behavior.

■ APPLICATIONS OF EXTINCTION

Extinction has been successfully applied to diverse problems. In one of the first reports of this technique, extinction was used to reduce the frequency that a psychiatric patient visited the nurses' office (Ayllon & Michael, 1959). The visits, which had been going on for two years, interfered with the nurses' work. The nurses usually paid attention to the patient when she visited and frequently pushed her back into the ward. After baseline observations, the nurses were instructed not to provide attention to the patient when she visited. Extinction decreased visits from 16 times a day during baseline to 2 per day at the end of seven weeks.

In another report, extinction was used with a patient in a psychiatric ward who had a 10-year history of vomiting after meals (Alford, Blanchard, & Buckley, 1972). Drug therapy had not suppressed vomiting. To begin the extinction program, the patient ate in the presence of two staff members. Vomiting was frequent when staff members attended to her and engaged in conversation after vomiting. As soon as staff members failed to attend to her when she vomited (e.g., left the room), vomiting ceased. To ensure that treatment effects would be maintained, other patients on the ward were told to ignore her when she vomited or even spoke of feeling nauseous. Since the patient failed to vomit, the program was terminated. A follow-up interview with the patient and her parents revealed that she only vomited once in the seven months after discharge.

Extinction usually is used in conjunction with other procedures, especially reinforcement. For example, in a preschool classroom, extinction and reinforcement were used to alter the aggressive behavior of a 3½-year-old boy, named Cain, who would choke, push, bite, hit, kick, and poke his peers (Pinkston, Reese, LeBlanc, & Baer, 1973). The teacher usually reprimanded the boy which seemed to have little effect. An extinction program was initiated whereby the teacher ignored aggressive behavior. Of course, a problem with ignoring this behavior is that several other children who were the victims of aggression might be seriously injured. To avoid this, the teacher immediately interrupted the aggressive activity by attending to the victim and helping the victim begin another activity away from Cain. While doing this, she ignored Cain. Thus, Cain did not receive attention from the teacher nor submission and adverse reactions from the victim, which also might help reinforce aggressive behavior.

Concurrently with the extinction program, the teacher provided attention to Cain whenever he initiated appropriate (nonaggressive interaction) with his peers. The effects of the extinction and reinforcement program appear in Figure 8–2. Extinction reduced aggressive behavior, as shown in an ABAB design (upper portion of the figure). Eventually, the aggressiveness remained low one month after the program (last data point) even though no special procedures remained in effect. The effects of extinction of aggressive behavior probably were helped by the reinforcement program (lower portion of the figure) which increased appropriate peer interaction.

Extinction and reinforcement were combined to control a 15-year-old handicapped, retarded boy in a junior high classroom (Hall, Fox, Willard, Goldsmith, Emerson, Owen, Davis, & Porcia, 1971). The boy argued constantly with his teacher. After a baseline period of several days, the teacher simply ignored and walked away from the boy when he began to argue. Praise was delivered when he worked on his assignment without arguing. The combination of extinction and reinforcement markedly reduced the number of arguments from seven per day during baseline to less than one per day a few days after the contingency was in effect. Six weeks after the experiment had terminated, the teacher reported that arguments were no longer a problem.

Extinction was combined with reinforcement to reduce the delusional speech that four psychiatric patients engaged in (Liberman, Teigen, Patterson, & Baker, 1973). The delusional speech included comments about being persecuted, poisoned by the staff, being injected with monkey blood, being James Bond or an agent of the FBI, insisting that they were someone else, and so on. In daily individual interviews with the staff, extinction was used by having the staff simply leave the room (no longer pay attention) when delusional speech began. Each patient could also earn reinforcement which involved an evening chat with a therapist. During the chat, the patient and therapist chatted in a comfortable room while snacks were served. However, the amount of time earned toward the evening chat depended upon how much rational (nondelusional) conversation the patient engaged in on inter-

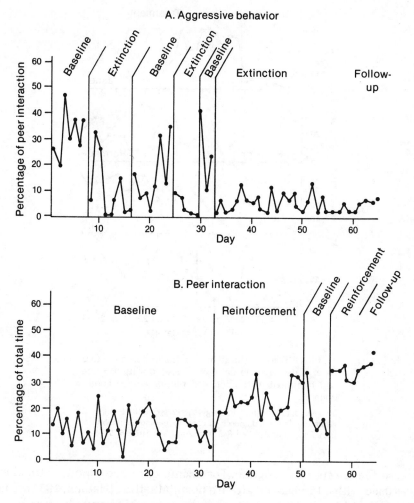

FIGURE 8-2 Subject's daily aggressive behaviors as a percentage of all peer interaction observed (top), and his daily peer interaction as a percentage of time observed (bottom).

Source: Pinkston, E. M., Reese, N. M., LeBlanc, J. M., & Baer, D. M. Independent control of a pre-school child's aggression and peer interaction by contingent teacher attention. *Journal of Applied Behavior Analysis*, 1973, **6**, 115–24.

views earlier that day. The effects of extinguishing irrational speech and rewarding rational speech can be seen in Figure 8–3. In a multiple-baseline design across four different patients, the effects of treatment appear clear. Rational speech increased when the program was introduced.

Extinction occasionally has been combined with punishment to in-

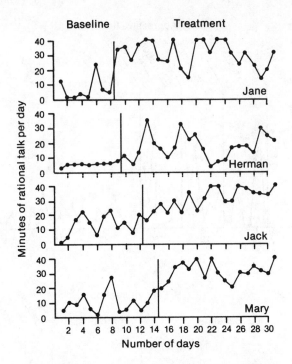

FIGURE 8–3 Duration of rational speech before onset of delusions in daily interviews during baseline and treatment (extinction and reinforcement) conditions.

Source: Liberman, R. P., Teigen, J., Patterson, R., & Baker, V. Reducing delusional speech in chronic, paranoid schizophrenics. *Journal of Applied Behavior Analysis*, 1973, **6**, 57–64.

crease the effects of a program. For example, in one report, extinction was used with a 15-year-old girl in a hospital setting (Hallam, 1974). The girl engaged in compulsive rituals such as washing and cleaning, and rubbing her face. Her main compulsive behavior was repetitively asking questions about her physical appearance. Extinction was used by having staff ignore the question rather than respond with an answer. The staff simply looked away and said nothing when the girl asked one of the repetitive questions. After one week of the procedure, the question decreased substantially. However, to make even more rapid progress, a response cost contingency was introduced. The girl was told that she would lose one minute of her free social time in the evening during which she could watch television and interact with others, for each repetitive question asked during the day. The program virtually eliminated these questions. A check on the behavior 5 months and then 14 months later after she had been discharged showed that the repetitive questions had been eliminated.

Many other reports have shown the successful application of extinction alone or in conjunction with other procedures, particularly reinforcement. Hypochondriacal complaints (Ayllon & Haughton, 1964), vomiting (Wolf, Birnbrauer, Williams, & Lawler, 1965), persistent obsessive comments (Silverman, 1977), self-injurious scratching (Allen & Harris, 1966), and excessive conversation in the classroom (Sajwaj et al., 1972) illustrate the range of problems treated with extinction and reinforcement. The above applications are particularly noteworthy because they reveal that several behaviors considered to be maladaptive are maintained by their social consequences.

■ WHEN AND HOW TO USE EXTINCTION

Extinction as a behavior change procedure is useful in those situations when the reinforcer which maintains behavior can be readily identified and controlled. In some situations, it is plausible that only one or a few reinforcers maintain behavior. For example, parents may attend to a child's tantrum before the child goes to bed. The reinforcers for tantrums may include attention and food, if a snack is given to placate the child. In this example, the reinforcers maintaining behavior probably are limited to attention and food. Each can readily be withdrawn to test this notion. Of course, if there are other relatives in the house (e.g., siblings and grandparents) who can inadvertently provide reinforcement, identifying and controlling available reinforcers are more difficult. Another consideration in using extinction is whether the burst which may occur will be harmful to the client himself or to others or tolerable to the agents responsible for the client. If the above conditions for extinction can be satisfied, extinction may eliminate the target behavior so that it is unnecessary to employ other procedures (e.g., punishment).

Extinction is enhanced tremendously when combined with positive reinforcement for behavior which is incompatible with the response to be extinguished. There are many reasons to combine reinforcement with extinction. First, the problems of executing extinction effectively are mitigated. Identifying and controlling reinforcement which maintains the undesirable response are not as essential, if other reinforcers are provided to develop desirable behavior. Second, the potentially undesirable side effects of extinction and the problematic characteristics of the course of extinction are less likely to occur, if reinforcement is provided for alternate responses. By providing reinforcement, the side effects which result from reinforcer loss should not appear. In addition, a burst of responses and spontaneous recovery may not occur, if the reinforced response replaces the extinguished response. Third, extinction may effectively decrease behavior but it does not ensure that a desirable behavior will replace the behavior that has been eliminated.

However, reinforcement can effectively strengthen behavior. If certain undesirable behaviors are extinguished and desirable behaviors are not simultaneously reinforced, extinction may not be very effective. When extinction is terminated, the undesirable behavior is likely to return because no alternate responses have been developed and no alternate means of obtaining reinforcement have been provided. Thus, the recommendations made for using punishment apply to extinction. *When extinction or punishment is used, reinforcement should be delivered to develop a behavior to replace the response to be eliminated.*

■ SUMMARY AND CONCLUSION

Extinction often is an effective procedure to eliminate behavior. The effectiveness of withholding reinforcement for a response depends primarily upon the schedule of reinforcement on which the response has been maintained. Behavior maintained with highly intermittent reinforcement is particularly resistant to extinction. In practice, extinction can be difficult to implement because the source of reinforcement maintaining behavior cannot always be readily identified and controlled. Several features of extinction warrant consideration.

First, for behaviors which are dangerous (e.g., self-destructive) or highly disruptive (e.g., shouting and screaming), extinction is not recommended. Since the decrease in behavior is usually *gradual* during extinction, a large number of responses may be performed before the undesirable behavior is eliminated. If an immediate intervention is required, extinction may be too slow to effect change. A second consideration is that responses may increase at the beginning of extinction. During this burst of responses, behavior may be reinforced inadvertently. If behavior is reinforced when it becomes worse, increasingly deviant behavior may result. Third, extinguished behavior sometimes recovers spontaneously even though responses are not reinforced. Again, a potential problem is that inadvertent reinforcement will reinstate the behavior when spontaneous recovery occurs. Fourth, extinction may be accompanied by undesirable emotional side effects such as anger or frustration. These states are not necessarily inherent in response reduction but are side effects which are likely to occur when alternate means of reinforcement are not provided.

While extinction can decrease or eliminate behaviors, it cannot develop new prosocial behaviors to replace those responses which have been extinguished. The most effective use of extinction is in combination with positive reinforcement for behaviors which are incompatible with or which will replace the undesirable behavior. This latter use of extinction is included in most behavior modification programs.

Staff Training and Technique Variations to Enhance Client Performance

Implementing modification programs may appear to be relatively easy. However, marked changes in behavior usually are achieved only after careful planning and implementation. The present chapter considers a number of issues relevant for developing and implementing effective programs. The first issue pertains to those individuals, such as parents, teachers, hospital staff, relatives, and others, who are responsible for altering the behavior of clients in most applied settings. Effective implementation of behavior-change programs requires that the contingencies be implemented systematically and consistently. Ensuring that behavior-change agents correctly implement the contingencies raises several obstacles that need to be resolved.

Even when programs are carefully implemented, clients may not respond to the contingencies or may not respond very well. Several procedures can be incorporated into a program to improve client behavior. These techniques involve prompting behavior to increase its frequency, increasing client utilization of reinforcing events, involving the peer group into the contingencies, and other procedures. Many special contingency arrangements are available to supplement other procedures addressed in previous chapters. These arrangements not only enhance client performance when a program may otherwise be faltering but provide useful practical advantages for developing programs in general.

■ TRAINING BEHAVIOR-CHANGE AGENTS

Effective reinforcement, punishment, and extinction techniques depend very heavily upon the precise manner in which the procedures are implemented. Hence, a major determinant of program effectiveness is how well those who carry out the procedures are trained. As noted earlier, a distinguishing characteristic of behavior modification relative to other attempts at behavior change in everyday life is the systematic manner in which behavioral programs are implemented. If a program is to be effective, the contingencies need to be applied to the client in a precise fashion. For example, investigations have shown that when a person receives reinforcing consequences contingently on some occasions and noncontingently on other occasions, behavior is not dramatically altered. In contrast, when the consequences are consistently contingent, behavior changes markedly (Koegel et al., 1977; Redd, 1969). Thus, the degree to which the contingencies are administered systematically determines the efficacy of the program. Before a program can be implemented to alter the behavior of a given client, attention has to be given to those agents who will administer the program.

In many cases, it is obvious that the behavior of the person who desires change in a given client needs to be modified. For example, parents often seek consultation to alter the behavior of their children. Frequently, behavior problems in the home are inadvertently maintained by the parents themselves. Parents may contribute to disobedient behavior of their children by providing extra attention to the children when they are obstinate, and by "letting well enough alone" (ignoring the children) when they are cooperative (cf. Wahler, 1972). Similarly, psychiatric aides frequently attend to bizarre behaviors of patients on the ward. When a patient is particularly bizarre, the attendants may give "tender loving care." Although the sympathetic behavior on the part of the staff is well intended, it may reinforce the bizarre behaviors. When attendants are trained to ignore bizarre behavior and reinforce appropriate behavior, patients behave more appropriately on the ward (Ayllon & Michael, 1959). Teachers also can inadvertently reinforce undesirable behavior. Children may repeatedly shout out loud in class without raising their hands. While the teacher may want the children to raise their hands, she often attends to the students who shout, allowing the child who raises his or her hand to go unnoticed. In this way, shouting is frequently reinforced while raising one's hand is extinguished (McNamara, 1971).

The purpose of these examples is not to oversimplify how deviant behavior may develop or be maintained. Rather, the purpose is to illustrate that a client's behavior is performed in a social environment and that many contingencies adhered to by others can contribute to undesirable behavior.

The problems with the contingencies as they normally occur in the natural environment have been documented in a variety of settings. These results point to the need to intervene to change teachers, parents, institutional staff and others. For example, White (1975) reported observations of in-class approval and disapproval of 104 classroom teachers spanning grades 1 through 12. Interestingly, high rates of teacher approval were evident in the first two grades but rates consistently declined over subsequent grades. After the second grade, teacher disapproval was consistently more frequent than was approval. Subsequent research showed similar results in several seventh-grade classrooms (Thomas et al., 1978). The results of such data are somewhat discouraging because of the very marked effects that high rates of contingent social approval can achieve in classrooms and because of the disadvantages of relying upon punishment as a primary behavior change technique.

The problems in administering contingencies that exist in everyday life are not restricted to teachers. Prison staff have been shown to display very little positive behavior to inmates and to attend equally to appropriate and inappropriate behavior (Sanson-Fisher & Jenkins, 1978). Similarly, attendants in facilities for psychiatric patients, the mentally retarded and delinquents, have been reported to attend indiscriminately to appropriate and inappropriate behaviors (Buehler, Patterson, & Furniss, 1966; Gelfand, Gelfand, & Dobson, 1967; Warren & Mondy, 1971).

The manner in which contingencies are normally administered in everyday life are somewhat discouraging. Attention and social approval of behavior change agents have been shown in many programs to achieve dramatic changes in behavior among several different populations. Yet, the manner in which attention and approval are usually administered outside of the context of a behavioral program may sustain inappropriate behaviors among clients in settings that are designed to educate, treat, and rehabilitate. Hence, even if behavior modification programs were not to be implemented in a large scale, there would be a strong need to train staff, teachers, parents, and aides in more productive patterns of interacting with those for whom they are responsible.

Procedures to Train Staff and Other Behavior-Change Agents

A major task in establishing an effective behavior-modification program is training agents to administer the contingencies correctly. Behavior-change agents, are referred to here collectively as "staff" of the program, and include hospital attendants, aides, teachers, parents, spouses, peers and others who in a particular program may be responsible for administering the contingencies. Those individuals in charge of the program must be trained very carefully. A major question arises, namely, what is the best way to alter the behaviors of people who serve as behavior-change agents?

Before mentioning the specific training techniques, it is important to keep in mind that developing behaviors of staff or behavior-change agents requires knowledge of the principles of behavior change. The principles that have been discussed in the context of altering client behavior apply to all of us even though our behavior may not be identified as problematic. Thus, to change staff behavior, many of the principles and techniques used to alter client behavior often are employed.

Essentially, altering the behavior of individuals in contact with the client requires a behavior modification program in its own right. Initially, the target behaviors that need to be changed in the individuals who serve as the behavior modifiers have to be identified. In a general sense, of course, these individuals have to use the principles of learning effectively, as outlined earlier. Yet, "using the principles" is not a specific target behavior and must be defined more carefully. The specific behaviors to be learned by the behavior modifiers will vary as a function of the clients they supervise. For example, in training teachers, a goal might be to have them provide reinforcement (e.g., praise) to children for achieving high rates of correct responses on academic assignments and studying, and to ignore disruptive behavior. In training parents, the goals might be to ignore (extinguish) excessive talking in a verbose child, but to praise (reinforce) talking in a sibling who appears extremely reticent. Of course, the goal in training behavior modifiers is to develop competence in simultaneously managing a number of contingencies beyond those included in a specific program to alter a single target behavior. However, training usually begins by changing only one or a few behaviors of the behavior modifier.

Many approaches have been used to train parents, teachers, and attendants to implement behavior modification programs. The techniques and their effects resemble many of those discussed in previous chapters. However, the applications differ slightly and hence warrant brief comment.

Instructional Methods. Most programs attempting to alter staff behavior rely upon instructional methods such as classroom lectures, discussions, workshops, and inservice training, and course work. For example, workshops may be conducted for teachers or parents who are interested in a particular set of childhood problems. At the workshop, client behavior problems and techniques to alter them are discussed. A well trained consultant is likely to present and explain the procedures.

Several studies have shown instructional methods to produce transient effects or no change in staff behavior at all (e.g., Katz, Johnson, & Gelfand, 1972; Pommer & Streedbeck, 1974). Merely informing people about behavior modification techniques does not usually influence their use of the techniques. Even if staff are given constant verbal or written reminders to use behavior change techniques they have learned, their behavior does not change reliably (Katz et al., 1972; Quilitch, 1975). Instructional methods apparently are most suited to develop knowledge about behavior modification, but this knowledge does not translate into how the staff member actually performs in everyday interactions with the client (Gardner, 1972; Nay, 1975).

Instructional methods have been effective when they are supplemented with practice in using the techniques. Practice consists of having individuals alternately take the role of the staff member or client and praise appropriate behavior, shape a particular response, provide prompts, and so on. When actual practice is included in training, people's behaviors actually change in relation to the clients (Gardner, 1972; Nay, 1975). Because merely instructing people in the principles of behavior modification has not proven especially effective in altering their behavior, many investigators have employed other techniques.

Modeling and Role-Playing. With modeling, staff members observe someone else perform the target behaviors that are to be developed. Although modeling has been used relatively infrequently as the sole basis of training staff, it has been effective in the few available reports. For example, Ringer (1973) used modeling in a fourth-grade classroom. The experimenter (model) administered verbal and token reinforcement to improve student classroom behavior and to reduce inappropriate behavior such as getting out of one's seat, fighting, and so on. The investigator circulated in the classroom and administered praise and tokens. The teacher observed the experimenter and gradually was given greater responsibility for administering the program. Eventually the experimenter was completely out of the classroom and the teacher conducted the program entirely. After working with the experimenter and seeing how to administer the program, the teacher was able to maintain relatively low rates of inappropriate behavior.

In another program, Gladstone and Spencer (1977) used modeling to train the staff at an institution for the retarded. The purpose of training was to increase staff use of praise as the staff trained residents in toothbrushing. During training, the experimenter modeled the desired behaviors while conducting training with a client. After several modeling sessions, staff use of praise increased. Interestingly, staff carried over their use of praise in training another behavior in the clients. Also, increased rates of praise were maintained up to two weeks after training.

Role-playing has been used as a training technique by allowing individuals to rehearse the behaviors that are going to be used in administering the reinforcement program. Role-playing usually includes modeling to demonstrate the desired behaviors in simulated situations. For example, Jones and Eimers (1975) trained elementary school teachers after school by modeling diverse behaviors (e.g., use of praise, disapproval, instructions and time out) and having the teachers practice the modeled skills. Participants in the sessions alternated the role of the teacher and a "good" or "bad" student. Prompts, feedback, and praise by the experimenter were provided as well. Training was associated with marked reductions of inappropriate student behaviors in the teacher's original classrooms.

Feedback.   Feedback as a method of staff training consists of providing individuals with verbal, written, or graphically displayed information about their behavior. For example, Parsonson, Baer, and Baer (1974) trained two aides in a kindergarten program for institutionalized mentally retarded children. Training was conducted in a large playroom where the children engaged in various activities involving music, exercise, play, and pre-academic tasks. The purpose of training was to develop the use of social reinforcement of the two aides. Feedback consisted of periodically handing the aides slips of paper that told them the proportion of times that they attended to appropriate and inappropriate child behavior. When feedback was used, the two teachers increased their attention to appropriate child behavior. Two weeks after training was terminated, staff behavior was still up to the level achieved during the feedback sessions.

Gelfand, Elton, and Harman (1972) used daily videotaped feedback to staff in a day-care facility for disturbed, brain-injured, and retarded children. As staff viewed taped replays of their individual interactions with a child, experimenters praised appropriate staff behavior (e.g., administering consequences to the children contingently), ignored inappropriate behavior (e.g., providing disapproval), and gave instructions. Staff delivery of contingent consequences increased.

Feedback often consists of publicly displaying what staff are doing in the situation. For example, Greene et al. (1978) wished to increase the participation of retarded residents in a toilet training program in the institution. Staff were reminded to place residents on the toilet and to engage in the training procedures. Reminders did not lead to very high performance. A feedback system was then implemented in which each staff member's name was posted along with a graph that kept track of client participation in the toilet training activities. Staff greatly increased the frequency that they placed clients through the training activities when the feedback posting system was in effect.

Several other studies have shown that feedback enhances staff performance (see Kazdin & Moyer, 1976). As with programs for client behavior, one of the problems with feedback for staff training that it often produces little or no effect (e.g., Breyer & Allen, 1975; Cossairt et al., 1973; Rule, 1972). Thus, interventions with more consistent effects have often been sought.

Social Reinforcement. Praise, approval, and attention have been used successfully to alter staff behavior. For example, Cossairt et al. (1973) evaluated the effects of comments by a consultant on the behavior of teachers. The experimenter met individually with two teachers after class to provide feedback and praise for teacher performance. Teachers were told how often the students paid attention and the amount of praise given. Feedback for teacher behavior did not produce clear changes in teacher or student behavior. Praise was introduced in which the experimenter made positive comments about appropriate teacher performance. Praise plus feedback markedly increased both teachers' use of praise in their classrooms. Moreover, students showed dramatic improvements in their attentive behavior.

Approval was used to increase the frequency that staff members interacted with adolescents and adults on a ward of profoundly retarded residents in a state institution (Montegar, Reid, Madsen, & Ewell, 1977). Staff received in-service training, role-playing, and demonstrations of how to interact with the residents. After training, the supervisor of the staff circulated through the unit and provided verbal approval for staff who were engaged in physical contact, verbalizations, and plays with the residents or were providing instructions or reinforcement. Supervisor reinforcement of staff greatly increased staff interaction with the residents.

An especially interesting use of social consequences to alter staff behavior relied upon the clients as behavior-change agents. Graubard and his associates have trained special education students who were considered to have behavior problems to alter behaviors of their teachers (Graubard, Rosenberg, & Miller, 1974; Gray, Graubard, & Rosenberg, 1974). Students with ages ranging from 12 to 15 years, received instruction and practice in behavior modification skills with the use of videotapes and role-playing exercises. To increase positive teacher–student contacts, students were taught to reinforce appropriate and to extinguish or mildly punish inappropriate teacher behavior. Students reinforced teacher responses by smiling, making eye contact, sitting up straight, and making comments such as "I work so much better when you praise me." To discourage negative teacher contacts, students made statements such as, "It's hard for me to do good work when you're cross with me." The effect of student social consequences on teacher behavior was evaluated in an ABA design. As evident from Figure 9–1, positive teacher comments increased and negative comments decreased during the intervention by the students. Hence, the students proved to be excellent behavior-change agents.

Similarly, Polirstok and Greer (1977) trained a behavior problem

224

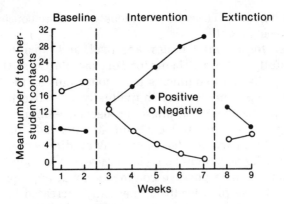

FIGURE 9–1 Mean number of positive and negative teacher-student contacts during baseline, intervention, and extinction phases.

Source: Graubard, P. S., Rosenberg, H., & Miller, M. B. Student applications of behavior modification to teachers and environments or ecological approaches to social deviance. In R. Ulrich, T. Stachnik, & J. Mabry (Eds.), *Control of human behavior*, Vol. 3. Glenview, Ill.: Scott, Foresman, & Co., 1974.

junior high-school girl to alter the behaviors of four teachers she had daily through the course of her school day. The student role-played and practiced administering social reinforcement for teacher behavior in counseling sessions outside of the class. When the intervention began, the student provided social reinforcement (statements such as "I appreciate that", "cool", and smiles) for instances of teacher approval. The student effectively increased teacher approval and decreased teacher disapproval in this fashion. Interestingly, both the student and the teachers appeared to view each other more favorably as a result of this program. Other programs have used clients to alter behavior of staff. For example, Seymour and Stokes (1976) trained institutionalized delinquent girls to solicit reinforcement from the staff. When the girls' work appeared to be good and when staff were nearby, the girls called the staff member's attention to their work. The comments included such statements as "Am I working well?", and "Look how much work I've done." The prompting procedure increased both the frequency of staff praise and the amount of work the girls completed.

Special Privileges. Occasionally various privileges or activities have been used as reinforcers to develop appropriate staff behavior. For example, in one program conducted in an institutional setting for the retarded, staff could earn weekends off for increased interaction with the residents (Iwata, Bailey, Brown, Foshee, & Alpern, 1976). Target behaviors focused upon with the staff included socially interacting with the resident, engaging in physical contact, playing a game with or reading to residents, providing instructions, or taking the residents out of bed, and cleaning soiled clothing. Staff who met prespecified criteria for performing these behaviors had their names written on a slip of paper and placed into a jar for a lottery drawing. One name was drawn to determine who would receive the days off from work for the following week. The procedure increased the frequency that staff carried out activities with the residents. An especially interesting feature of this program was the use of a lottery system. For practical reasons, all staff could not be given time off if they met the behavioral criteria. The lottery provided a way to deliver a desirable reinforcer to only one person a week and yet to maintain behavior of all of the staff.

Reid et al. (1978) also used a special privilege to alter staff behavior in an institutional setting for the retarded. Time off on weekends was used to reinforce low absenteeism among staff. When time off on the weekend was contingent upon a good attendance record, attendance increased. This example illustrates the utility of privileges within the setting as reinforcing events for staff, but the specific behaviors focused upon do not include skills in implementing behavior modification programs for the residents.

Token Reinforcement. Tangible conditioned reinforcers have been used effectively to alter staff behavior in many different programs. For example, Pomerleau, Bobrove, and Smith (1973) used cash awards ($10, $20, or $30) for staff in a psychiatric hospital. These awards were delivered for improvements shown by specific patients to which the staff members had been assigned. If a patient showed the greatest improvement in ratings of appearance, verbal behavior, and adaptation to the ward routine, the staff member earned a cash award. The program led to marked improvements in patient behavior whereas noncontingent delivery of cash and feedback to staff did not.

Hollander and Plutchik (1972; Hollander, Plutchik, & Horner, 1973) used a token reinforcement system as part of a training program to develop behaviors in hospital staff. Instructions, role-playing, and discussions were also used in training. However, to develop behaviors on the ward with the psychiatric patients, a nationally known brand of trading stamps redeemable at a stamp-redemption center were delivered for completing assigned tasks with the patients. The effects of the stamp contingency on the behavior of the staff are shown in Figure 9–2 which reveals a marked improvement in performance.

In a classroom setting, McNamara (1971) provided points to teachers for attending to appropriate child behavior. Points were exchangeable for cans of beer. In some cases, extra beer was given for especially good teacher behavior (i.e., no instances of attention to inappropriate student

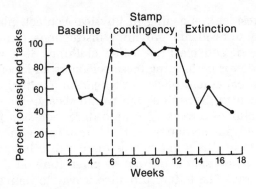

FIGURE 9–2 Percent of assigned tasks completed by attendants during baseline, stamp contingency, and extinction phases.

Source: Hollander, M. A., & Plutchik, R. A reinforcement program for psychiatric attendants. *Journal of Behavior Therapy and Experimental Psychiatry*, 1972, **3**, 297–300.

behavior). The contingent delivery of points effectively altered teacher behavior, particularly when the bonus contingency (extra beer) was in effect.

Several other forms of token reinforcement programs have been developed to alter staff behavior. The effect of tokens on staff behavior is no surprise. Token reinforcement has been extremely effective in altering client behavior, as discussed in an earlier chapter. Programs have shown that both staff and client behavior changes when tokens are delivered to staff for particular behaviors related to implementing contingencies.

Examples of token reinforcement mentioned above include programs where staff behaviors are directly reinforced with tokens. Occasionally, implementing token economies for clients rather than staff has been found to alter staff behavior inadvertently. Apparently when staff implement a token program for their clients, they change in a variety of behaviors aside from merely delivering tokens. For example, staff who administered a token program for psychiatric patients showed more praise, smiles, and approval for appropriate patient behavior than did staff on another ward without such a program (Trudel, Boisvert, Maruca, Laroux, 1974). Similarly, teachers who administer a token economy in their classrooms increase in their use of approval and overall contact with the students and decrease in their use of disapproval (Breyer & Allen, 1975; Chadwick & Day, 1971; Mandelker, Brigham, & Bushell, 1970). In general, implementing a token economy for clients occasionally has beneficial side effects in altering a variety of staff behaviors.

Important Considerations in Training Behavior-Change Agents

Often various techniques mentioned above are combined into a larger training program to have the greatest amount of impact on staff performance. Thus, training may begin with instructions, feedback, modeling, and role-playing but rely upon social and token reinforcement as well to develop high levels of performance (e.g., Fo & O'Donnell, 1974; Gladstone & Sherman, 1975; Koegel, Russo, & Rincover, 1975). An effective technology exists for developing behaviors in staff in most settings either by individual techniques or combinations of several techniques.

One reason for combining techniques is to provide a broad range of skills in staff so that they can readily apply the principles of behavior change to different clients, behaviors, and settings. Occasionally, training programs have shown that only those specific behaviors that are trained in staff are likely to be changed and related behaviors that might be desirable (e.g., decreasing the use of disapproval) may not change unless they are focused upon (e.g., Speidel & Tharp, 1978). Also, training people to implement a behavioral program in one situation or setting may not carry over to other situations. For example, parents may not carry out the contingencies in a variety of settings in which their child's behavior needs to be altered (Miller & Sloane, 1976). Finally, if training focuses merely upon having parents or teachers alter a particular behavior, the behavior-change agents may not extend their skills to other client behaviors (e.g., Koegel, Glahn, & Nieminen, 1978). In general, behavior-change agents may learn very specific skills and not apply behavioral techniques beyond the areas focused upon in training. Hence, combining several different training techniques and applying the techniques to diverse situations, behaviors, and clients help build skills that can be extended broadly to client problems as they arise.

A major issue is not changing staff behavior but ensuring that the changes last. As a general rule, staff-training programs have shown that as soon as training is terminated or extrinsic consequences for attendant and teacher behavior are withdrawn, behavior reverts to pretraining levels (e.g., Katz et al., 1972; Kazdin, 1974a; Pomerleau et al., 1973), although there are exceptions (e.g., Cossairt et al., 1973; Parsonson et al., 1974; Speidel & Tharp, 1978). Thus, it may be necessary to maintain staff performance by implementing a reinforcement system for staff that is part of the usual requirements of the setting. However, often practical difficulties militate against implementing a program. For example, ensuring that teachers praise their students would require carefully observing teacher behavior, monitoring student performance, and providing contingent reinforcement. Practical problems alone make even a simple reinforcement program difficult to implement on a very large scale.

At present, additional work is needed to develop staff-training programs that can be readily implemented and maintained so that lasting changes in staff performance are achieved. Many programs that might be implemented for clients depend heavily upon training staff to do them and ensuring that staff can continue the programs when they are not closely monitored. Programs have occasionally reported that staff do not implement the contingencies or do not implement them very well when they are not closely supervised. For example, Bassett and Blanchard (1977) reported that prison staff who conducted a token economy in a prison deviated from the contingencies when the director of the program was absent. Specifically, when the program director was away, staff greatly increased the frequency that they administered punishment (fines) and increased the magnitude of the punishment. Staff tended to be inconsistent in administering the contingencies and did not follow the program that inmates had expected. The program became so aversive during the supervisor's absence that many inmates quit the program.

Programs reported in the treatment of child behaviors in the home occasionally have noted the difficulty in continuing the contingencies without direct supervision. For example, Becker et al. (1978) greatly reduced ruminative vomiting of an infant girl enrolled in a day-care center for emotionally disturbed children. The program's effects were not maintained in the home 11 months after treatment apparently because of the inconsistent application of the contingencies on the part of the parents.

In general, staff training represents a major issue for effective program implementation. Not only is it important to develop techniques that can readily alter behavior but also to devise them in such a way that they can be readily implemented. Additional work is needed to ensure that those responsible for the care of clients can readily carry out the techniques to achieve the desired changes.

■ ENHANCING CLIENT PERFORMANCE

Although behavioral programs have been very effective, on occasion a few individuals do not respond to the contingencies or respond only minimally (Kazdin, 1973d). There are several procedures which can be incorporated into a program to enhance performance. Specifically, procedures will be discussed which help clients initiate responses so that reinforcement can be delivered and increase the client's utilization of potential reinforcers in the setting.

Response Priming. In some programs the client does not perform the target behavior so reinforcement cannot be delivered. In the case of behavior deficits where new skills are required, shaping procedures can be employed. The terminal behavior is approached by reinforcing successive approximations, as discussed earlier. In many instances, the client can perform the response but simply does not. In these cases, the response can be primed.

Response priming refers to any procedure which initiates early steps in a sequence of responses. Prompts, such as instructions, serve a response-priming function because they initiate performance. However, response priming encompasses more than the use of prompts. As mentioned earlier, any act can be broken down into a sequence or chain of responses. The chain of responses is maintained by reinforcement which results from completing the sequence. The influence of the terminal reinforcer on earlier responses in the chain is much weaker than is its influence on responses later in the chain (Reynolds, 1968). For responses early in the sequence of behaviors, the final reinforcer is delayed, whereas for responses late in the sequence the reinforcer is immediate. For example, assume a person wishes his or her date would go to a distant restaurant to eat. The chain of responses includes all those behaviors leading up to and including eating in the restaurant. Food reinforcement along with any other reinforcing events in the restaurant may be too weak to provide an incentive for the responses early in the response chain. However, the likelihood of completing the chain is increased, if behaviors in close proximity of the final reinforcer are performed. If the individual would drive near the distant restaurant or walk inside, this would increase the likelihood of performing the final response (eating). The probability of eating at the restaurant would be increased because the strength of a response increases, the closer one is to the reinforcer.

The notion of response priming suggests that performance of a given behavioral sequence can be facilitated by encouraging or requiring the client to engage in the initial components of the sequence. By engaging in responses which are early in the sequence, the probability of performing the final behaviors in the sequence is increased.

Response priming has been used to initiate responses that otherwise have an exceedingly low frequency. For example, McClannahan and Risley (1975) used a priming procedure to increase the frequency that residents of a nursing home engaged in various activities in the facility. Several of the residents were physically disabled and confined to wheel chairs or beds, some were retarded, and most had medical disorders (e.g., cardiovascular diseases). Typically, residents remained in their rooms, did not engage in many activities, sat around the facility, and avoided social interaction. Activities were increased by making equipment and recreational materials available (e.g., puzzles and games) in the lounge. As a resident entered the lounge, he or she was given some materials, even if the materials were not requested. An activity leader demonstrated how to use the materials and provided assistance until the resident began working on them. The priming procedure led to very marked increases in the percentage of residents participating in activities. The effects were not just due to making the equipment available. In a phase in which the equipment was available but clients were not prompted to work on the activities, the materials were infrequently utilized. This procedure illustrates the use of response priming because clients were encouraged to engage in the initial steps of the response, namely, to take the materials and to begin work with them. Once the behavior was begun, it continued.

Response priming was used to increase the duration and frequency that three hospitalized patients visited with their relatives (O'Brien & Azrin, 1973). Normally, relatives of the patients could visit the psychiatric ward or request that the patients visit them at home for any length of time. This procedure resulted in virtually no visiting by the relatives. A response priming procedure was used in which relatives were invited to visit the hospital, and told in a letter that if a visit was inconvenient, the hospital would bring the patient to them for a short time. Patients were driven to their relatives weekly and stayed for a very short time. In fact, every 15 minutes during a visit a staff member who accompanied the patient said, "We should return to the hospital, now." The staff member and patient left unless the family objected to this statement. The priming procedure (transporting patients to their relatives) dramatically increased visits. During this phase, visits averaged over two hours per week for the three patients compared with less than an average of one minute per week during the normal visiting procedure. The relatives did not simply maintain the visit for the minimum 15-minute period. Even though the patients could have left at this time, the visits continued. Once visiting was primed, it continued for longer periods. A reversal of conditions demonstrated that without the priming procedure, the visits decreased. After the priming procedure was reinstated, relatives for all three patients expressed a desire for the patients to be discharged and to live with them. In two of the three cases this was successfully accomplished.

Response priming has been used to improve a variety of behaviors that occur at low rates. Priming has increased the attendance of clients to a mental-health center by providing prompts reminding them of their appointments by telephone (Turner & Vernon, 1976), has increased the frequency that chronic psychiatric patients made suggestions for managing the ward by requiring patients to attend meetings where such suggestions were solicited (O'Brien, Azrin, & Henson, 1969), and has decreased the frequency of littering by providing antilitter messages (prompts) on cups from which people drank (Geller, 1973).

The priming procedures achieve their effects by making the initial responses easier or more likely. In programs where the target responses are performed infrequently even though they are in the repertoire of the clients, a priming procedure can be used. Even where the responses are not in the clients' repertoire of responses, the priming procedure can initiate early response components and facilitate shaping.

Reinforcer Sampling.   Reinforcer sampling is a special case of response priming but warrants discussion in its own right. The responses primed are those involving utilization of a potentially reinforcing event. Utilization of a reinforcer can be viewed as a sequence of responses. If the initial responses in the sequence can be primed, the likelihood of completing the sequence is increased. To initiate the sequence, a client can engage in the initial part of or briefly *sample* the reinforcing event.

In reinforcement programs, it is very important that the clients utilize the available reinforcers when they are made available. The more frequently the reinforcers are used, the more the clients will engage in the appropriate target behavior required to obtain them. Yet, for many individuals, there may be few events which serve as reinforcers. There may be several potentially reinforcing events in the setting, but the clients may not engage in them. An event might be reinforcing, if the clients were familiar with it. Of course, even after familiarity with the event, it still may not serve as a reinforcer. However, the probability is increased that the event will be reinforcing after familiarity has been established. For other individuals, a given event may be reinforcing although it is not utilized frequently. The reason the event is not utilized frequently is unclear. It is not a matter of unfamiliarity because the event may be engaged in sporadically. Moreover, the event may appear to be enjoyable to the clients. The reinforcer may not be as potent as other reinforcers which are utilized more frequently.

Reinforcer sampling has been used relatively infrequently despite the rather consistent evidence attesting to its effectiveness. In one of the first reports of the procedure several years ago, Ayllon and Azrin (1968a) used reinforcer sampling to increase the frequency that psychiatric patients engaged in various activities on the ward. The activities were included in a large list of back-up reinforcers which could be purchased with tokens. Patients were told twice daily that they could go for a walk on the hospital grounds. Payment of tokens was required to engage in the walk. After a few days of baseline, the reinforcer sampling procedure was implemented. Not only were walks announced, but all patients were required to assemble outside of the ward for a few minutes before deciding whether they would purchase the walk. Many cues associated with walking such as outdoor sights, sounds, and fresh air would be present before the patient decided to go back in the ward or go for a walk. While outside, patients were asked whether they wished to go for a walk. Those who decided not to go for a walk returned to the ward. The reinforcer sampling procedure increased the utilization of walks. For individuals who had or had not engaged in walks during baseline, the number of times walks were purchased increased. During a reversal phase, when the sampling procedure was discontinued, the frequency of walks decreased. However, some patients still continued to engage in a higher rate of walks than during baseline.

Reinforcer sampling was also used to increase attendance of patients at religious services in the hospital (Ayllon & Azrin, 1968b). Although many patients paid tokens to attend services without a sampling procedure, attendance increased markedly when all the patients were required to see five minutes of the service. Those who never attended the services before the sampling procedure, as well as those who were familiar with the services, increased in attendance. Similar results were found by using reinforcer sampling to augment the utilization of recreational and social events.

Sobell, Schaefer, Sobell, and Kremer (1970) used reinforcer sampling to increase eating of meals by psychiatric patients. Three sampling procedures were used. Patients either watched others eat, sampled one teaspoon of each type of food, or were given a free meal. All three procedures increased attendance at meals. Thus, even if an individual is given more than a small sample of the reinforcer, utilization of the reinforcer may be increased.

Importantly, the sampling procedure appears to initiate performance for those individuals who previously did not engage in the event. For these individuals, reinforcer sampling provides familiarity of the reinforcer which subsequently augments its use. However, reinforcer sampling provides more than familiarity. Individuals who are already quite familiar with the reinforcer and have utilized it on previous occasions are also affected by reinforcer sampling. After reinforcer sampling is terminated, participation in the event does not necessarily return to baseline levels. Clients may continue to utilize the reinforcer to a greater extent than they did during the baseline period. Thus, the effects of the sampling procedure are maintained (Ayllon & Azrin, 1968a, b).

In any situation in which it is possible to provide a small sample of the reinforcer, the sampling procedure should enhance performance. In utilizing reinforcer sampling, it usually is important to provide only a small sample of the event to avoid satiation. If an individual samples a large portion of the event such as food or an activity, there may be little incentive to earn and utilize the entire event. In fact, Sobell et al. (1970) found that giving an entire free meal instead of a sample of a meal temporarily *decreased* purchasing meals with tokens.

In applied settings, the effect of a reinforcement program may be relatively weak, in part, because the events selected by the staff as reinforcers are not utilized by the clients. Hence, the "reinforcers" provide little incentive to engage in the target behaviors. If the activity which is designed to serve as a reinforcer can be made more "valuable" to the client, the likelihood of engaging in the target behaviors to earn that activity is increased.

Vicarious Processes. Performance of a client can be altered by observing the consequences which follow the behavior of other individuals. Laboratory evidence has shown that individuals who observe others (models) receive reinforcing consequences for engaging in certain behaviors are more likely to engage in those behaviors. In contrast, individuals who observe models receive punishing consequences for engaging in certain behaviors are less likely to engage in those behaviors (Bandura, 1971; Rachman, 1972). These two processes are referred to as vicarious reinforcement and vicarious punishment, respectively.

Vicarious reinforcement has received the greater attention of the two processes and has been studied in classrooms, rehabilitation settings, and the home (see Kazdin, 1979c). Investigations have shown that the behavior of one person can be altered by providing reinforcing consequences to others. For example, in a class for behaviorally handicapped children, Strain, Shores, and Kerr (1976) found that administering praise for social interaction to three children led to increases in social interaction among other children who did not receive teacher praise. Also, Resick et al. (1976) found that praising one child for compliance with parental instructions and time out for noncompliance controlled the behavior of an uncooperative boy in his home. Interestingly, some behaviors of the boy's brother also improved although these were not directly praised or punished.

Most of the studies on vicarious reinforcement in applied settings has been in the classroom where several demonstrations have shown that providing praise to one child leads to improvements in that child as well as in his peers (see Kazdin, 1979c). The usual interpretation of vicarious reinforcement is that the children who do not receive direct reinforcement change in their behavior because they observe the behavior that the target subject performs. However, copying a model (the child who receives the consequences) may not always be responsible for vicarious reinforcement. For example, in a class of retarded children, praise was delivered to one child for paying attention. An adjacent individual who was not directly praised also increased in attentiveness. However, when the reinforced student was praised for not paying attention, the adjacent individual *increased* in attentiveness to the lesson (Kazdin, 1973b, 1977f). Thus, whether one student was praised for attentive or inattentive behavior, the adjacent individual improved in attentiveness. A possible explanation is that whenever praise is delivered in a classroom, it is a cue to perform appropriate behaviors. Praise to one child is often a signal (S^D) that other children will be praised if they are behaving appropriately. Hence, children hearing praise may improve their behavior to increase the likelihood that they, too, will be reinforced.

Although vicarious reinforcement has been demonstrated in several studies, the effects occasionally have been weak or inconsistent among different subjects. For example, vicarious reinforcement effects may diminish over time (Christy, 1975). Also, many subjects do not respond to the consequences others receive (Budd & Stokes, 1977). Some studies have suggested that how reinforcement is administered to the target subject may influence whether others show vicarious effects. For example, delivering reinforcement in a conspicuous fashion and providing individuals with many opportunities to observe others receive reinforcing consequences tend to enhance vicarious reinforcement effects (Kazdin, Silverman, & Sittler, 1975; Strain et al., 1976).

Vicarious punishment has received little attention in applied programs. Naturalistic studies of teacher behavior in the classroom have shown that when one student is punished, others may show reduced disruptive behavior as well (Kounin, 1970). Experimental research has corroborated this effect. Wilson, Robertson, Herlong, and Haynes (1979) evaluated the vicarious effects of time out from reinforcement in a kindergarten class. One boy with a high rate of aggressive behavior (e.g., tripping, kicking, and throwing things at others) was placed in time out for instances of these behaviors. Time out consisted of sitting in a booth in class for 5 minutes where he could not see his peers. When time out was used, the target child and his classmates showed a decrease in aggressive acts even though his classmates never experienced time out directly for their aggressive behaviors.

In general, client performance may be improved by providing reinforcing and/or punishing consequences to others who are engaging in the target behavior. Of course, vicarious reinforcement and punishment are not substitutes for providing direct consequences to the client. However, vicarious events can serve to prompt behavior by signaling that certain behaviors may be reinforced. Once the behaviors are performed after this prompt, they can be reinforced directly.

■ PEER INVOLVEMENT IN BEHAVIORAL PROGRAMS

In most applications of behavior modification, a behavior-change agent administers the contingencies to the client to develop particular behaviors. Programs can be designed to take advantage of peers with whom the client interacts. For many clients, peers can serve as a powerful source of reinforcement.

Another reason for considering peers as behavior-change agents is the fact that they often observe client behavior under more circumstances than do staff members. For example, a teacher is responsible for several students and may not easily monitor each student's behavior very closely. Many problem behaviors may occur when the teacher turns his or her back or is attending to a particular student while a deviant child's behavior may go unnoticed. In contrast, peers may see the behavior often and perhaps are in a better position to provide contingent consequences.

Finally, clients may perform the behavior in the presence of only those individuals (parents, teachers, staff) who administer the contingencies. Behavior is more likely to come under stimulus control if staff administer the contingencies in a relatively restricted range of situations. If peers administer the contingencies, client behavior may be performed more readily across a variety of situations. In behavior-modification programs, peers have been incorporated into the contingencies by using group-based consequences or by direct peer administration of the contingencies. Each of these methods includes a variety of techniques that can facilitate implementation of a behavior modification program.

Group-Based Programs

In most programs discussed throughout previous chapters, reinforcing and punishing consequences were applied to particular clients. Even when programs are conducted with groups of individuals such as a class of students or ward of patients, consequences typically are provided to individual clients based upon their own performance. Although most programs are individualized in this sense, it is possible and often desirable to administer the program in such a way that the peer group is involved in the contingencies. Programs utilizing the peer group can be implemented in several ways (see Kazdin, 1977e; Litow & Pumroy, 1975). Three major methods of using the group discussed here include group consequences, team competition, and consequence sharing.

Group Contingencies. Group contingencies refer to programs in which the criterion for reinforcement is based upon performance of the *group as a whole.* The group must perform in a particular way in order for the reinforcing consequences to be delivered. For example, Switzer, Deal, and Bailey (1977) used a group contingency to reduce stealing in three second-grade classrooms. Students in the classes frequently stole things from each other (e.g., money, pens, toys) as well as from the teacher. The investigators assessed the frequency of theft by placing various items around the room each day such as money, magic markers, gum, and other items. Prior to initiating the group contingency, the teachers lectured the students by telling them the virtues of honesty and how they should be "good boys and girls." When the group contingency was implemented in a later phase, the teacher told the students that if nothing was missing from the classroom, the class as a whole could have 10 extra minutes of free time. This is a group contingency because the consequences were provided on the basis of how the class as a group responded. The group contingency was introduced to the classes in a multiple-baseline design. As shown in Figure 9–3, the number of items stolen was not affected by the lecture emphasizing honesty. On the other hand, whenever the group contingency was introduced into one of the classrooms, marked reductions in theft were obtained.

Marholin and Gray (1976) used a group contingency to reduce the shortage of cash in the register of a family-style restaurant. Cash register receipts were carefully monitored. At the end of the day, the cash in the register was lower than the amount automatically recorded on an internal record of the register. After a baseline period of recording the shortages, a group-response cost contingency was devised. For any cash shortage equal or greater than one percent of the day's total cash receipts, the money shortage was subtracted from the salary of all persons who worked in the register that day. The total cash shortage was simply divided by the number of individuals who worked on the register. This procedure greatly reduced cash shortages. The results were accomplished by monitoring the performance of all cashiers as a group and assessing a fine on the basis of the group's performance.

Group contingencies can be combined with other types of contingencies. For example, Greenberg, Scott, Pisa, and Friesen (1975) placed psychiatric patients into small decision-making groups. The purpose of the groups was to develop treatment plans for the individual patients that would lead to eventual discharge from the hospital. The groups were to make recommendations in the form of written proposals. Staff provided tokens to members of the group based upon the adequacy of the proposal that the group produced. This group contingency was included in a larger token program in which patients received tokens for self-care, social, and work behaviors.

Team-Based Contingencies. The team-based contingencies repre-

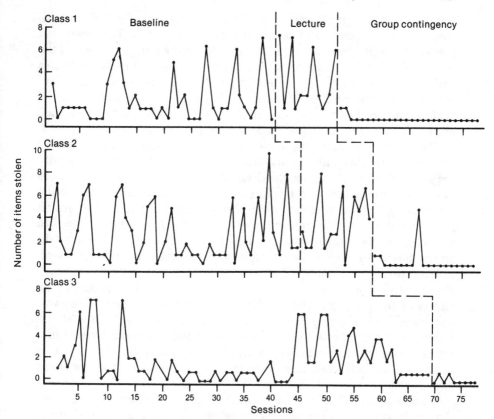

FIGURE 9–3 The number of items stolen per day in each of the three second-grade classrooms.

Source: From Switzer, E. B., Deal, T. E., & Bailey, J. S. The reduction of stealing in second graders using a group contingency. *Journal of Applied Behavior Analysis*, 1977, **10**, 267–72.

sents a special type of group contingencies but are worthy of separate treatment because of their effectiveness. *In a team-based contingency, a group is divided up into two or more subgroups (or teams). Each subgroup functions on a separate group contingency.* As with group contingencies discussed above, an individual client can still earn or lose for the group, and the collective behavior of the group determines what consequences the individual receives. However, the subgroups compete against each other. The consequences are delivered to the subgroup or team with better performance.

For example, Maloney and Hopkins (1973) evaluated the effect of a team contingency on the writing skills of elementary-school students attending a remedial summer-school session. Students were on one of two teams. Students received points for writing behaviors that would improve their compositions such as increasing the use of different adjectives, action verbs, and novel sentence beginnings. The team that earned the higher number of points (by adding the points for each of the individual members on a team) was allowed to go to recess 5 minutes early and received a small piece of candy. To ensure that excellent performance was reinforced, both teams could win on a given day if performance met a prespecified high criterion. The team contingency markedly increased the specific writing skills focused upon.

The above program may have been effective independently of the division of the class into teams because group contingencies generally are very effective. However, the division of a group into teams appears to enhance the effects of a reinforcement program over and above the use of the group contingency alone. For example, Harris and Sherman (1973) used a team contingency to control disruptive behaviors in fifth and sixth-grade elementary school classrooms. Teams received marks on the board for inappropriate classroom behavior (being out of seat, talking, throwing objects). The team with fewer marks won and was allowed to leave school early at the end of the day. Interestingly, the effects of the program when a class was divided into two teams was compared with a group contingency in which the class was a single group. Disruptive behavior was lower when the class was divided into teams. Thus, the contribution of the team competition seemed to be important, even though each variation of the group contingency was effective.

Consequence Sharing. Another type of contingency that involves the group consists of consequence sharing. *With consequence sharing, the client's peer group is involved because they share in the reinforcing consequences earned by the client.* The group members do not earn the reinforcers for their own behavior but profit when the target client performs certain behaviors.

Consequence sharing is particularly useful in situations where there may only be a need to focus on the behavior of one or a few clients. A reinforcement system can be developed for that client but the consequences that the client earns can be provided to the client as well as his or her peers. When peers share in the consequences, they become involved with the program indirectly and can support and contribute to the client's improvement.

Kazdin and Geesey (1977) evaluated the effect of consequence sharing on the behavior of two retarded elementary-school children in a special-education classroom. Tokens were provided for working on academic tasks and paying attention to the lesson. When a predetermined number of tokens had been earned, each child earned a reinforcer selected from a list of reinforcers (e.g., extra recess) developed in advance of the program. As might be expected, contingent token reinforcement improved appropriate classroom performance. However, the token program was markedly more effective when the reinforcers earned by the children were given to everyone in class (consequence sharing) rather than when the children earned them for themselves.

Feingold and Migler (1972) used consequence sharing to improve the behavior of a 50-year-old psychiatric patient diagnosed as schizophrenic and brain damaged. The patient participated in a token economy which did not have much impact on her behavior. The patient engaged in little social interaction, infrequently completed her work, did not keep well groomed, and showed inappropriate verbal behavior. To increase her responsiveness to the program, a consequence-sharing contingency was developed in which two other patients on the ward received the same number of tokens earned by the target patient. (The other patients were on separate contingencies for their own behaviors as well.) In an ABA design, the responsiveness of the target patient to the contingencies was evaluated when she was in the usual program where she only earned tokens for herself and when she earned for herself plus her peers. As shown in Figure 9–4, the number of tokens she earned and

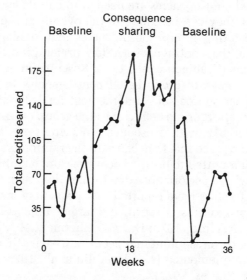

FIGURE 9–4 Token earnings during baseline, consequence sharing, and return to baseline phases. During baseline, the patient actually earned tokens for herself. During the consequence sharing phase, she also earned tokens for her peers as well as for herself.

Source: From Feingold, L., & Migler, B. The use of experimental dependency relationships as a motivating procedure on a token economy ward. In R. D. Rubin, H. Fensterheim, J. D. Henderson, & L. P. Ullmann (Eds.), *Advances in behavior therapy*. New York: Academic Press, 1972.

hence the extent of her appropriate job and self-care behaviors greatly increased during the consequence sharing contingency.

Other programs encompassing the mentally retarded, and "emotionally disturbed," and "normal" children have demonstrated the effectiveness of consequence sharing in altering behavior of selected target clients (e.g., Kubany, Weiss, & Sloggett, 1971; Rosenbaum et al., 1975; Wolf, Hanley, King, Lachowicz, & Giles, 1970).

Considerations in Using Group-Based Programs

Group-based contingencies have several advantages. To begin with, group contingencies provide an extremely convenient way to implement a program. The clients are considered as a group and reinforcing and punishing consequences are more easily administered than when each person is focused upon individually. Indeed, in many settings in which behavior modification programs are implemented, too few staff are available to conduct individual programs. Hence group contingencies often can be implemented more readily than individual programs. If individualized contingencies are needed to handle special behaviors of a few clients, they can be added to the overall group program. The ease of administering group contingencies may explain why people who implement the contingencies often prefer group over individualized programs (Drabman et al., 1974; Rosenbaum et al., 1975).

Another advantage of group-based contingencies is that they help bring to bear peer sources of reinforcement for behavior. Peers often actively support appropriate behavior so the group or team can earn the reinforcers. Similarly, with consequence sharing peers may encourage appropriate behavior so that they can earn the reinforcers. Occasionally, peers have been reported to bring to bear pressure on other group members of clients whose performance determines their own reinforcers. For example, investigators have reported that peers may make threatening verbalizations or gestures or reprimand target subjects for not earning the reinforcers (Axelrod, 1973; Harris & Sherman, 1973). On the other hand, other reports have found that peers help each other when a group contingency is implemented (e.g., Hamblin et al., 1974; McCarty, Griffin, Apolloni, & Shores, 1977).

The interactions resulting from group-based contingencies may depend upon the manner in which the program is implemented. Aversive peer interactions may be more likely to result if available reinforcers in the setting are lost if the group does not meet the criterion for performance. Yet, reinforcers normally available in the setting should not depend upon group performance because individuals who are doing well may lose events they would usually receive even if their performance is up to standard. Group consequences should include special events over and above what individuals normally would receive so that reinforcers are not lost because someone else in the group or the target subject did not perform adequately.

Peer-Administered Contingencies

The use of group-based contingencies illustrates an indirect way in which peers are involved in the program. The contingency arrangements discussed above structure the situation in such a way as to increase peer investment in appropriate behavior. Hence, peers support the target behavior and supplement the influence of the direct contingencies. A more direct way to involve peers into the program is to have them administer reinforcing and punishing consequences (McGee, Kauffman, & Nussen, 1977). In peer-administered contingencies, the peers serve as the behavior-change agents and provide direct consequences to the target subject(s).

Peers have been used in a variety of programs with considerable success. For example, Strain, Shores, and Timm (1977) utilized peers to alter the social withdrawal of boys in a preschool classroom. Two boys, 3 and 4 years old, who were especially social were instructed to help others to play with them. Through role-playing, these boys were trained to initiate play and praised for their social interaction. After training the boys tried to increase social interaction among other children who were socially withdrawn. The teacher in charge of the class did not prompt or reinforce social behavior so the entire program was in the hands of the peers. Peers were very effective in increasing the social interaction of the withdrawn children. The withdrawn children not only increased their interaction with the peers who served as behavior-change agents but also with each other.

Peers have been used in the Achievement Place program for predelinquents (Phillips, 1968; Phillips, Phillips, Wolf, & Fixsen, 1973). One of the boys served as a manager of his peers and delivered or fined tokens to develop room-cleaning behavior among his peers. The boy who served as a manager either purchased this privilege with tokens or was elected by his peers. Once the manager was determined, he was responsible for ensuring that the room-cleaning behaviors were completed. The manager assigned the jobs and provided tokens or fines for the performance of the tasks. When the room was checked by the teaching parents in the facility, the manager earned or lost tokens based upon how well the task had been completed. The peer-manager system of administering consequences was very effective in obtaining high rates of room-cleaning and was even more effective than contingencies administered by the teaching parents (Phillips et al., 1973).

At the same facility for predelinquents, peers were involved in administering the program in yet another way (Fixsen, Phillips, & Wolf, 1973). A self-government system was devised in which the boys could determine whether one of their peers was guilty of violating a rule or misbehaving (e.g., borrowing personal belongings from others without permission, excessive teasing) and what consequences should be delivered. At nightly "family conferences" the rule violation would be discussed and one's peers would decide whether the alleged violator was guilty and what penalties should be applied.

In addition to peers, siblings have been used to alter behavior. For example, Doleys and Slapion (1975) used a punishment procedure to alter the verbal behavior of a 15-year-old mildly retarded adolescent. The boy frequently repeated short verbal utterances. The focus of the program was to suppress these utterances. The boy's program was conducted by his 19-year-old sister. The boy was given 10 points a day at dinner time if he had not engaged in these repetitive verbal utterances. Each time he repeated himself, he would lose a point. When the point earnings accumulated to a large number, he could purchase a game of his choice. The effects of the program are shown in Figure 9–5. When the token reinforcement and response cost program was introduced, repetitions were low and virtually absent. Two weeks after the program was terminated, verbal repetitions remained relatively low.

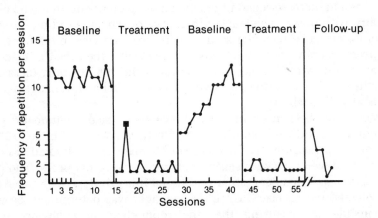

FIGURE 9–5 The frequency of repetitions during each of the recording periods in the study. The particular phase of the study in effect when each data point was collected is indicated along the top of the graph. The data point enclosed in a square indicates the frequency of repetitions recorded on the date the subject had an epileptic seizure.

Source: Doleys, D. M., & Slapion, M. J. The reduction of verbal repetitions by response cost controlled by a sibling. *Journal of Behavior Therapy and Experimental Psychiatry*, 1975, **6**, 61–63.

Considerations in Using Peer-Administered Contingencies

Several advantages have been reported to result from peer administration of the contingencies. First, having the opportunity to work with one's peers often is a positive reinforcer for clients. For example, Robertson, DeReus, and Drabman (1976) found that second-grade students decreased their disruptive behavior to earn the opportunity to work with a peer tutor (from the fifth grade) on reading tasks. When opportunities to work with a peer tutor were contingent upon classroom performance, marked changes in student behavior were obtained. A second, and related advantage of peer-administered contingencies is that the opportunity to serve as a peer behavior-change agent itself can be a reinforcer. Peers often work and pay (in tokens) for the opportunity to participate in the training of another client. For example, in a token economy with predelinquents, Phillips et al. (1973) found that youths would bid for the privilege of serving as a manager in the program. The privilege was periodically auctioned to the highest bidder, i.e., the person who offered the highest number of tokens to purchase the privilege.

A third advantage of peer-administered contingencies is their ancillary side effects. Occasionally, peer-administered contingencies have been shown to improve the social interaction among clients. For example, peers who administer reinforcing consequences may increase in their social contact with the clients (Abrams, Hines, Pollack, Ross, Stubbs, & Polyot, 1974). Also, peers are evaluated more favorably by clients if they are associated with reinforcing consequences (Sanders & Glynn, 1977). Thus, utilizing peers as behavior-change agents can improve aspects of the relationships among peers and target clients. Other side effects have been associated with peer-administered contingencies. For example, Dineen, Clark, and Risley (1977) found that elementary school children who tutored their peers also showed gains in academic areas in which they tutored. Thus, peer administration of the program can be beneficial for the target clients as well as those who administer the contingencies.

A fourth advantage is that peer-administration of the contingencies occasionally facilitates maintenance and transfer of the behavior. Programs conducted by peers in the classroom and institutional settings have reported that behaviors may be maintained even when the peer-administered contingencies are not in effect (e.g., Johnston & Johnston, 1972; Stokes & Baer, 1976). Also with predelinquent youths, behaviors developed by peer therapists have been maintained and have transferred to new settings after the program is terminated (Bailey et al., 1971). When peers administer the contingencies, they may continue to exert stimulus control over the client. The client maintains the behavior in the presence of the peers.

Finally, the use of peers as behavior-change agents has obvious practical advantages. By utilizing peers, clients receive more individualized attention and training than can be provided by the staff in the setting. Peers provide an important resource to administer programs that might not otherwise be conducted because of the paucity of staff members in classrooms, institutions, and other settings.

■ SUMMARY AND CONCLUSION

Implementing an effective behavior modification program usually requires that those individuals who administer the contingencies are well trained. Only when the contingencies are implemented systematically and consistently can the marked changes illustrated throughout previous chapters be expected. Several techniques have been used to train parents, teachers, aides, and other behavior-change agents to conduct behavior modification programs. The techniques have included instructional methods, modeling and role-playing, feedback, social reinforcement, special privileges, and token reinforcement. Reinforcement procedures have been particularly effective in altering staff behavior. Maintaining high levels of appropriate staff behavior and ensuring that the behaviors extend to a variety of clients and settings raise problems for training behavior-change agents.

In many behavior modification programs, a small number of clients may not respond to the contingencies or respond minimally. Several techniques can be implemented to enhance performance. Response priming, reinforcement sampling, and vicarious reinforcement and punishment have been effective in altering behavior and can be incorporated into most existing programs. Special contingency arrangements, which can enhance performance as well as provide many practical advantages, rely in various ways on the client's peer group. Several techniques are available using group-based reinforcement or peer-administered contingencies. These techniques provide resources to help administer contingencies in situations where staff might not be able to conduct all of the programs.

Self-Control

$\mathbf{T}$he principles of behavior modification describe lawful relations between various environmental conditions and behavior. These lawful relations and the techniques derived from them hold independently of who actually uses them. The techniques discussed previously represent instances in which one individual (the agent) manages the contingencies to alter the behavior of someone else (the client). Yet, the techniques can be applied by the client to control his or her own behavior. The present chapter will focus on self-control or the application of behavioral principles to modify one's own behavior.

In virtually every behavior modification program, external agents administer the reinforcing or punishing consequences. There are potential disadvantages in relying entirely on staff-administered contingencies. First, teachers, parents, and other agents usually miss a great deal of behavior when applying reinforcement. Monitoring several clients in a group situation makes it virtually impossible to notice, not to mention reinforce, all instances of a target response. Second, agents who administer the contingencies may become a cue for performance of the target behavior because of their association with reinforcement and punishment. Behavior may be performed only in the presence of those who administer reinforcers. Third, and related to the above, behaviors may not be performed as readily in situations in which external agents are not administering reinforcement because the client can easily discriminate different contingencies across situations. Fourth, individuals sometimes perform better when they are allowed to contribute to the planning of the program or choose the behaviors they are to perform rather than having the contingencies imposed upon them. Thus, performance may be enhanced by allowing the client some control over his or her own behavior.

Aside from the possible limitations of externally-administered contingencies, there are other reasons for interest in self-control. Several problems for which people seek therapy are not readily accessible to the therapist. For example, overeating, deviant sexual behavior, obsessive thoughts, phobic responses, and marital discord are not easily observable to the therapist. Of course, there are problems which therapists can readily observe such as tics, "free-floating" anxiety, and stuttering which are likely to be present both in the therapy session as well as extratherapy settings.

There is one area where only the client has access to the problem. Many problems for which individuals seek therapy entail *covert* or *private events* which include thoughts, images, fantasies, hallucinations, and dreams which are not "observable" by anyone other than the individual to whom they occur. As noted earlier, it has been suggested that covert events can be viewed as covert operant responses (referred to as *coverants*) (Homme, 1965). As overt operant responses, covert responses can be altered by varying the consequences which follow them. Since the client is the only one who can identify the occurrence of the coverant, he or she is in the best position to provide contingent consequences. Thus, for therapeutic problems involving private events, only the client can manage the contingencies.

Whether the behavior to be changed is overt or covert, behavior change in the situation in which the problem is occurring is the goal of therapeutic intervention. The therapist may ask the client to collect data on the extent of the target behavior, such as the number of cigarettes smoked, number of hours studied, or number of obsessive thoughts. After a clear rate of behavior has emerged, procedures are implemented in the client's everyday life to control performance outside of the therapy setting. Frequently individuals in the client's environment can serve this function and alter behavior (Copeland & Hall, 1976; Graziano, 1977). However, the person in the best position to monitor behavior and provide consequences is the client himself. The client consults with the therapist for directions on precisely how this is done. The function of the therapist is to teach the client to alter the environment and serve as his or her own therapist. Therapy is instigated by the therapist but ultimately conducted entirely by the client. Thus, to change behavior in the actual setting in which it is problematic, self-control techniques are helpful.

There is one additional reason for interest in self-control. The goal of behavior modification is to train an individual to control his or her own behavior and achieve self-selected goals. To require continuous control over a client by an external agent is not an end in itself. Whenever possible, external control is a means to achieve self-control. Self-control and external control can be viewed as opposite ends on a *continuum* rather than as discrete procedures. Behavior modification programs vary in the degree to which the client has control over the contingencies and the administration of reinforcing or punishing consequences. Programs discussed in this chapter attempt to maximize the control the individual has over the training procedure. Of course, external control in some form is essential to initiate the program. Therapists train clients to exert self-control by providing recommendations, strong advice, systematic praise, and feedback, all of which are external influences on client behavior. Hopefully, after training is completed, the person can apply techniques to himself or herself to alter new behaviors across different situations. When this final stage is complete, self-control has been achieved.

■ SELF-CONTROL IN EVERYDAY LIFE

People exert control over their own behavior in everyday actions such as selecting a course of action, abstaining from particular excesses, adhering to various rituals to sustain or recover health, and acting in ways which appear to violate self-interest. Yet, people control their own behavior using techniques which resemble those they would use to control the behaviors of others, namely, by altering the antecedent and consequent conditions (Skinner, 1953).

Skinner has noted that individuals control their own behavior in everyday life with a variety of techniques. First, an individual uses *physical restraint* such as clasping one's mouth to stifle a laugh, covering one's eyes to avoid seeing something, and clasping one's hands to avoid nailbiting. With this technique, the individual physically places restrictions on himself to achieve a particular end. Second, *changing the stimulus conditions* or cues which occasion the response is used to control behavior. For example, an individual usually selects a place to relax where there are few cues associated with work. Also, one lists appointments or important dates on a calendar so that these stimuli will increase the probability of engaging in certain behaviors at a later date. The cues (relaxing environs or written reminders) increase the likelihood that certain behaviors are performed. Third, *depriving or satiating* oneself can be used as a self-control technique. A person may deprive himself or herself of lunch in anticipation of a special dinner or prior to participation in an athletic event. Fourth, *emotional reactions* can be altered. A person can prevent an emotional reaction such as laughing by eliciting an incompatible response such as biting one's tongue. Pleasant or unpleasant feelings can be reinstated by conjuring up emotive memories and images. Fifth, people use *aversive events* in the environment to control behavior. For example, setting an alarm clock ensures that an aversive event (noise) will be presented. An individual may also make threatening statements to himself or herself such as, "If I don't do this, I will be late." Sixth, *drugs, alcohol, and stimulants* may be ingested specifically for self-control purposes. Alcohol may be consumed to alter one's mood or alleviate anxiety. Coffee may be consumed to increase alertness during studying or driving. Seven, *self-reinforcing and self-punishing operations* are employed to control behaviors. A person may derogate himself after failing to achieve a goal or verbally praise himself after accomplishing a feat. Finally, *doing something else* is a technique commonly used to control one's own behavior. An individual can engage in behaviors other than the one which leads to aversive consequences. For example, one can alter topics in the middle of the conversation to avoid an argument or whistle a happy tune whenever one feels afraid. Similarly, one can count sheep to avoid anxiety-provoking thoughts prior to going to sleep.

The above techniques used in everyday life allow the individual to control his or her own behavior. Most of the techniques operate by having the individual perform one behavior (a *controlling* response) which alters the probability of another behavior (a *controlled* response). Thus, a person may chew gum (controlling response) to reduce the likelihood of smoking cigarettes (controlled response). On the other hand, a person may wear a blindfold (controlling response) in a well lighted room to increase the likelihood of sleeping (controlled response). In self-control training, the client is taught not only how to control a particular response, but also a technique which may be applied to new situations and behaviors as the client deems necessary.

■ DEFINITION OF SELF-CONTROL

As a general definition, *self-control usually refers to those behaviors a person deliberately undertakes to achieve self-selected outcomes.* The individual must choose goals and implement the procedures to achieve these goals. External pressures may be brought to bear such as influences or coercion by parents, peers, or spouse to control certain behaviors. However, to qualify as self-control, the individual must commit himself or herself to that goal and apply the procedures (Goldfried & Merbaum, 1973; Thoresen & Mahoney, 1974).

Debates have frequently emerged in defining self-control (e.g., Bandura, 1976; Catania, 1975; Rachlin, 1978). Whether an individual ever can "really" control his or her own behavior can easily be argued. When a person appears to be the source of control over a particular act, it is possible to explain behavior on the basis of events in one's past that perhaps have determined the person's current decision. Hence, the perennial debate about free will and determinism is easily entered into when discussing self-control. However, in behavior modification, an attempt has been made to consider self-control as a matter of degree rather than an all or none phenomenon (Kanfer, 1977; Thoresen & Mahoney, 1974).

"Self-control" has been used to refer to situations in which the individual actively implements specific procedures to control his or her own behavior. The extent to which a person can be involved in his or her own treatment is a matter of degree. The person can be a complete *object* of the treatment procedure that others administer (external control), or the person can completely design and implement treatment for himself or herself (self-control). And, the person or external agents of change may be involved in varying degrees so that self-control and external control both operate. Self-control procedures in behavior modification refer primarily to techniques where the client plays an active part and occasionally the sole part in administering treatment.

The notion of self-control usually is used to refer to regulating behaviors that have conflicting consequences, that is, both positive reinforcement and punishment (Kanfer & Phillips, 1970). Reinforcing consequences that follow behavior may be immediate while the punishing consequences are delayed. Behaviors in this category include excessive consumption of food, cigarettes, alcohol, and drugs. For example, excessive eating results in immediate positive reinforcement derived from the food. However, aversive consequences that follow overeating such as physical discomfort, obesity, and social ostracism attendant upon being overweight are delayed. Alternatively, aversive or potentially aversive consequences that follow behavior may be immediate and the reinforcing consequences, if present at all, may be delayed. Behaviors in this category include heroic, altruistic, and charitable acts.

Acts of self-control often appear to forego immediate rewards for future rewards. Thus, a student may forego the opportunity to attend a new disco club on a Friday night as an apparent act of self-control. The immediate reward (entertainment) may be sacrificed for the prospect of future rewards (doing well in courses that will increase the chances of getting into graduate school). Similarly, people often undergo moderate discomfort in the present to avoid potentially greater discomfort in the future. For example, going to the dentist for cleanings, check-ups, and occasional fillings may be uncomfortable in the present. Yet, such acts reduce the chance of much greater discomfort in the distant future when serious dental problems may warrant treatment.

In the context of treatment, self-control procedures have been applied primarily to behaviors that appear to have immediate positively reinforcing consequences and delayed aversive consequences. A person performs a response that counteracts or appears to counteract the effects one would expect from external reinforcers. Thus, refusing a rich dessert after a meal appears to run counter to the normal contingencies. Of course, self-control often is invoked when simplistic accounts of behavior are proposed. Behaviors normally may be controlled by a variety of positive and aversive consequences both in the present, past, and future (anticipated consequences). Simply refusing dessert may result from all sorts of influences that are not immediately apparent (pain from eating too much, previous experiences of nausea when overeating, allergic reactions to ingredients in the dessert, anticipation of not being able to get into one's clothes). In applications of self-control, the issue is not whether the individual or other events account for certain sorts of responses. Rather, the focus is on helping the individual bring to bear influences to achieve ends he or she would like to attain.

■ DEVELOPMENT OF SELF-CONTROL

Self-control is assumed to be a behavior learned in much the same way as other behaviors. Individuals learn to control their own behavior according to the principles of learning, discussed earlier. As any other behavior, self-control may be specific to particular situations or somewhat general across many situations. For example, an athlete may adhere to a rigorous self-planned training regimen. Yet, the same individual may evince little or no "control" in other areas such as completing academic assignments. Alternatively, some athletes adhere both to rigorous athletic and academic schedules and perform well in both areas.

In early development, a child's behavior is controlled by external agents such as parents and teachers who set standards and provide consequences for performance. The standards vary for different behaviors. Some parents set high standards for musical or academic achievement but not for mechanical or social skills, or household chores. Indeed, standards may vary for different sex siblings within the same home. Positive reinforcement is provided when the child achieves the standard, whereas punishment (or lack of reward) is provided for performance below the standard. As training continues, achieving a particular standard may take on reinforcing consequences because achievement in the past was paired with external reinforcement. Conversely, the failure to achieve a standard may become aversive by being paired with punishment or lack of reward. Thus, attainment or lack of attainment of an externally or self-imposed standard may contain its own reward or punishment. Through early training, the process of standard setting and providing consequences for achievement eventually becomes independent of external consequences.

The above interpretation of how self-reinforcement and punishment patterns of behavior develop has received some support (Bandura, 1971). Laboratory research has shown that patterns of standard setting and self-reinforcement can be transmitted in ways consistent with that interpretation. For example, a person can learn to evaluate his or her own performance based upon how others evaluate that performance. Individuals who are rewarded generously by others are more generous in rewarding themselves (Kanfer & Marston, 1963). Thus, one administers reinforcers to oneself consistent with the way others have provided reinforcement.

Modeling also is extremely important in transmitting self-control patterns. For example, children adopt standards of reinforcement they observe in a model. If a child is exposed to a model who sets high or low standards for self-reinforcement, the child adopts similar standards for himself (see Bandura, 1971b; Karoly, 1977). Individuals exposed to models who have had low achievement standards tend to reward themselves highly for relatively mediocre performance. The self-rewarding and self-critical statements made by a model are transmitted to and made by observers (Bandura & Kupers, 1964; Liebert & Allen, 1967).

Self-held standards and self-administered consequences for achievement also are regulated by others in everyday interaction. For example, self-reinforcement for achieving consensually low standards of performance is not looked upon favorably. Students rarely flaunt a "D" grade-point average in part because consensually the standard is low. Thus, standards of performance in self-reinforcing patterns are conveyed both through modeling, direct reinforcement, and social control (Bandura, 1971b; Meichenbaum, 1979).

■ TECHNIQUES OF SELF-CONTROL

Self-control patterns can be developed through behavior-modification techniques to achieve specific therapeutic ends. Several major techniques can be identified to train people to control their own behavior. The techniques, each of which may include several variations, consist of stimulus control, self-observation, self-reinforcement and self-punishment, self-instruction, alternate response training, imagery-based procedures, biofeedback, and self-help manuals. Although other techniques are available, they are less commonly employed than those listed here. Detailed accounts of other techniques can be obtained from additional sources (Karoly, 1977; Mahoney & Arnkoff, 1978; Stuart, 1977).

Stimulus Control. Specific behaviors are performed in the presence of specific stimuli. Eventually, the stimuli regularly associated with a behavior serve as cues and increase the probability that the behavior is performed. Three related types of behavioral problems result from maladaptive stimulus control. First, some behaviors are under the control of stimuli the client wishes to change. For example, cigarette smoking may be under the control of many stimuli, such as getting up in the morning, drinking coffee, talking with friends, studying, and being alone. Smoking is cued by a variety of situations because it has been associated with these situations. The therapeutic goal is to eliminate the control that these stimuli exert over smoking. Second, some behaviors are not controlled by a narrow range of stimuli when such control would be desirable. For example, students who have difficulty studying often have no particular setting, time, or cues associated with studying. Studying is not consistently performed in the presence of any particular stimuli. The therapeutic goal is to develop stimulus control over study behavior. Third, some behaviors are under control of inappropriate stimuli. Sexual deviance such as exhibitionism and fetishism are included in this category. In these behaviors, sexual responses are controlled by stimuli which deviate from appropriate stimuli as determined by social standards.

A person who is aware of how certain stimuli control behavior can structure his or her environment to maximize the likelihood that the desired behavior occurs. For example, avoiding a bakery is one example of using stimulus control as a self-control technique. When going by the window of a bakery, a person may not be able to "control himself" from entering and purchasing pastries. However, not walking by the bakery or crossing the street right before approaching the bakery can remove the sight of the tempting stimuli (pastries) in the window so they cannot exert their influence. Self-control can be attained in the actual tempting situation by gradually approximating the original controlling stimulus in mild doses. The individual tempted by the bakery window can pass the window when the bakery is closed, walk by the bakery quickly when it is crowded, walk by while looking away, and stopping by the window after eating a large meal. By not entering the bakery in the presence of increasingly tempting cues, the bakery may no longer exert its influence over behavior.

Use of stimulus control ordinarily requires that a therapist initially consult with the client to explain the manner in which stimulus control operates and to help the client identify events that control or fail to control his or her behavior. Actual treatment may consist of helping the client begin to perform behavior under a narrow or new set of stimuli to develop stimulus control or to perform new behaviors under familiar stimuli to eliminate existing sources of control. For example, early applications of stimulus control in behavioral research instructed clients who failed to study or who ate excessively to perform the behaviors only under certain stimulus conditions (e.g., studying in a special place and at a certain time of the day or eating only at the table with a full place setting) (Fox, 1962; Goldiamond, 1965). Such procedures were designed to bring behavior under control of specific stimuli to help increase studying when the students were in certain situations or decrease eating when clients were not in specific situations that ordinarily were associated with eating.

Stimulus control has been used as the basis for treatment of many clinical problems. For example, VanDeventer and Laws (1978) altered the sexual attraction that two adult males had toward male children (pedophilia). Each client had repeated sexual experiences with children and adolescents and were not attracted to adult females. The problem might be conceptualized as one of stimulus control where a socially inappropriate stimuli (children) evoked sexual arousal whereas socially appropriate stimuli (women) did not. To increase sexual arousal toward women, the clients were instructed to masturbate in treatment sessions (administered individually for each client) while verbalizing a fantasy involving sexual relations with women. Clients were instructed that masturbation outside of the laboratory should also be associated with verbalizations of relations with women. The purpose of this intervention, of course, was to associate sexual arousal with women.

To evaluate treatment, sexual arousal was measured directly by penile blood volume (penile circumference) as clients viewed slides of male children or female adults. Prior to treatment, the clients showed high arousal toward males and little arousal toward females. For one of the clients, this pattern was reversed with treatment. Also, on self-report measures, the client viewed women more favorably than he did children. Follow-up data available up to two months after treatment showed that sexual arousal for children was low or absent and relatively high for women. The other client did not show the effects of treatment; sexual arousal to both male and female stimuli decreased.

Insomnia has been treated using stimulus control procedures. For whatever reason insomnia develops, it follows a familiar pattern. A person may be tired before retiring. As soon as the person goes to bed, he or she may begin to worry about the day's activities before going to sleep. The stimuli that are usually associated with sleeping (bed, darkness, and a specific time and place) become associated with behaviors incompatible with sleeping. For example, one adult insomniac went to bed about midnight, but was unable to fall asleep until approximately 3 A.M. or 4 A.M. (Bootzin, 1972). Before sleeping, he worried about several mundane problems and finally turned on the television. He fell asleep while the television was still going. Treatment attempted to bring sleep under control of the stimuli associated with going to bed. The client was told to go to bed when he felt sleepy but not to read or watch television. If unable to sleep, he was to go into another room and stay up as long as he liked. When he again felt sleepy, he was to return to the bedroom. If he still could not sleep, he was to repeat the procedure continuously. For the first few days of treatment, the client got up four or five times each night before going to sleep. Yet after two weeks, he no longer got up at all. When he went to bed, he stayed there and fell asleep. The client reported sleeping much better as well as getting much more sleep each night. During a follow-up period conducted up to two months after treatment began, the client got up during the night less than once a week. Thus, the treatment appeared to work very well. Interestingly, the therapist who directed this case never had any contact with the client. The client's wife was responsible for explaining the procedure and reporting the results. Subsequent experiments have shown that stimulus control is an effective treatment for insomnia and is superior to alternative techniques such as relaxation training (see Bootzin & Nicassio, 1978).

Although stimulus control requires the therapist to explain the principles, techniques, and recommended applications, the clients themselves apply the procedures in their daily lives. Ideally, the clients can extend the use of stimulus-control techniques beyond the original area that served as the impetus for seeking treatment.

Self-Observation. Control over behavior can be enhanced by observation of one's own behavior. As mentioned earlier, individuals adhere to certain standards of performance for various tasks and activities. When behavior departs from one's own standard or from a consensually held standard, a person may attempt to control his or her behavior (Kanfer, 1977; Karoly, 1977). For example, individuals who feel they are overweight, whether or not they are by medical standards, try to regulate their eating by carefully watching what they eat.

Most people are not entirely aware of the extent to which they engage in various behaviors. Habitual behaviors are automatic. People rarely observe their own behavior in a systematic fashion. However, when people are provided with the opportunity to observe their own behavior carefully, dramatic changes often occur. Careful observation of a response provides feedback to the individual, which can be compared with the standard the individual believes is appropriate. If behavior clearly departs from a cultural or self-imposed standard, self-corrective procedures begin to be employed until an acceptable level of behavior is met (Kanfer & Phillips, 1970). Thus, self-observation is effective insofar as it initiates other action on the part of the individual. The act of observation itself may be reinforcing or punishing (Homme, 1965). For example, for an individual who wishes to stop smoking, each time he or she records having smoked a cigarette may serve as mild punishment. On the other hand, for the individual who records hours of study behavior, each hour tallied may provide reinforcement. Although it is not entirely clear why self-observation is effective, it has been widely applied as a therapy technique (Kazdin, 1974b; Nelson, 1977).

The use of self-observation was illustrated in a program with a 25-year-old house wife who complained of obsessive thoughts about cancer of the breast and stomach (Frederikson, 1975). She was very upset about these frequent thoughts which appeared to have become worse over a 6-year period prior to treatment. Of course, thoughts are not immediately observable to others since they are private events. The client was instructed to monitor the frequency of the obsessive thoughts while at home. Keeping a daily tally of the thoughts was apparently associated with a rapid reduction in their frequency from a high of 13 per day to about 2 per day. The client was instructed to monitor her thoughts in a more detailed fashion by recording the time of the thought, what she was doing at that time, the specific content of each thought, and so on. When this more detailed assessment procedure began, thoughts decreased further. The thoughts did not recur up to 4 months after treatment.

Self-observation was used effectively to train two mothers to use behavior modification to control behavior of their "hyperactive" children at home (Herbert & Baer, 1972). Observers in each home recorded behavior of both the mother and child. The mothers attended to a variety of undesirable behaviors which probably contributed to the high frequency of breaking things, pounding on or marking furniture, stealing food, screaming, shouting, making threats, and hitting others, among other disruptive behaviors. The mothers were told to observe the number of times they attended to appropriate behavior of their children and record their own behavior on a wrist counter that each mother wore. When the mothers observed their own behavior, their attention to appropriate child behavior increased. In addition, the children engaged in greater appropriate behavior. At the end of the program, one mother continued to monitor her behavior once in a while, whereas another mother stopped monitoring altogether. However, both mothers continued to attend to appropriate child behavior which remained at a high level.

An interesting application of self-recording was reported by McKenzie and Rushall (1974) who increased the frequency that members of a swimming team attended practice. The team, consisting of boys and girls from 9 to 16 years old, practiced eight times per week. After baseline observations, the swimmers were instructed to record daily attendance on a publicly displayed board. Each swimmer simply placed a check in the place on the board when he or she arrived each day.

Self-recording of attendance on a publicly displayed board reduced absenteeism. Also, extensions of the procedures decreased the number of people who arrived for practice late or left early.

Investigations have shown that self-recording behavior can influence smoking, overeating, tics, studying, nailbiting, and several other behaviors (Kazdin, 1974b; Nelson, 1977). However, the effectiveness of self-observation has been inconsistent. A number of studies have shown that self-observation does not alter behavior; others have shown that when behaviors do change, the effects are transient. Consequently, self-observation is infrequently used as a technique in its own right. It usually is combined with other techniques such as self-reinforcement and self-punishment. Indeed, to apply consequences to one's own behavior, one needs to know when and how frequently the behavior is occurring.

Self-Reinforcement and Self-Punishment. Providing reinforcing and punishing consequences to oneself have been used rather extensively as self-control techniques (Jones, Nelson, & Kazdin, 1977). Clients are trained to administer consequences to themselves contingent upon behavior instead of receiving consequences from an external agent. Self-reinforcement has received more attention than self-punishment.

The major requirement of self-reinforcement is that the individual is free to reward him or herself at *any time* whether or not a particular response is performed (Skinner, 1953). If an external agent influences or partially controls the delivery of the reinforcers, the client's ability to control the contingency is reduced. The person who administers reinforcers to himself or herself must not be constrained to perform a response or to deliver or withhold consequences. An additional requirement to qualify as reinforcement is that the behavior which is followed by a self-administered consequence must increase in frequency. Similarly, a behavior followed by self-administered aversive events must decrease to qualify as punishment.

In most applications of self-reinforcement, two different procedures are used. First, the client can determine the response requirements needed for a given amount of reinforcement. The client controls when to deliver reinforcement and the amount to be delivered. When the individual determines the criteria for reinforcement, this is referred to as *self-determined reinforcement* (Glynn, 1970). Second, the client can dispense reinforcement for achieving a particular criterion, which may or may not be self-determined. When the client administers reinforcers to himself or herself, this is referred to as *self-administered reinforcement*. Who administers the reinforcers (oneself or someone else) may not be crucial. The crucial element is determining *when* to deliver reinforcement and for *what* behaviors. However, if a person is not permitted to self-administer reinforcers, there may be external agents who influence the self-reinforcement process. Thus, self-reinforcement is probably best achieved when the client self-determines and self-administers the reinforcers. Self-reinforcement usually requires the client to observe and record his or her own behavior to determine whether it has met a criterion. Thus, self-observation is an ingredient included in the procedure.

Self-reinforcement has been used in several behavioral programs conducted in classroom settings (Rosenbaum & Drabman, in press). As an example, Ballard and Glynn (1975) used self-reinforcement to improve the story writing of elementary school children. Students self-recorded the number of different sentences, different descriptive words, and different action words on a special sheet. Self-recording did not alter these behaviors. However, self-reinforcement was added in which children were told to administer one point to themselves for increases in each of the different sentences they had written. The points were exchangeable for such activities as free time, access to games, art materials and books, and public display of one's story. The number of sentences increased markedly with self-reinforcement. An extension of the self-reinforcement contingency to the other writing behaviors also showed increases. Interestingly, the quality and interest value of the stories were rated as better during the self-reinforcement phases than during baseline by two university faculty in English who were unaware of the program.

Self-reinforcement often has been used in outpatient treatment. Bellack (1976) evaluated the relative effects of self-observation alone and self-observation plus self-reinforcement in treating obesity. All subjects observed their daily food intake. Self-reinforcement subjects were instructed to give themselves a letter grade (A through F) depending upon how well their eating was consistent with the overall daily caloric goals and how well they followed recommendations of the program. After seven weeks of treatment, self-reinforcement subjects lost significantly more weight than did self-observation subjects. These effects were maintained at a follow-up assessment up to several weeks after treatment.

Self-punishment has been used relatively infrequently in behavior-modification programs. Early applications in the field included self-punishment as part of outpatient treatment to control overeating (Ferster, Nurnberger, & Levitt, 1962; Harris, 1969). Clients were instructed to compose a list of the consequences of eating that they found to be especially aversive. Consequences such as being rejected socially, overhearing verbal references of other people to obesity, incurring physical diseases, and having problems in attracting a mate were some of the reasons listed and served as the aversive consequences of eating.

These aversive consequences were used to suppress undesirable kinds of eating by applying them immediately before eating. For example, when an individual sits down to eat a rich dessert, he or she can vividly imagine or recite the aversive consequences of overeating. The aversive consequences which are normally delayed and, hence, not very effective in controlling immediate behavior can be brought close to the actual act of eating. In this way self-punishment can be used to suppress behaviors leading to overeating. For the treatment of obesity, self-punishment usually is only one ingredient of a larger self-management treatment. Other procedures such as stimulus control, nutritional training, and reinforcement for weight loss are also included.

Wilson, Leaf, and Nathan (1975) reported the use of self-punishment with hospitalized alcoholics. Patients had access to alcoholic beverages on the ward. Electric shock was used to suppress the amount of alcohol that patients consumed. Some patients were encouraged to self-administer shocks for drinking. When these patients drank, the staff either brought the patients to the room where the shock apparatus was connected or simply asked them whether they wanted to go to the room where shock was delivered. In either case, the patients administered the shock to themselves. The results indicated that self-administered shock was effective in suppressing alcohol consumption. As might be expected, when patients were not required to go to the room to administer shock, instances of drinking were not consistently shocked. Some of the patients drank without subsequently administering shock to themselves or administering far fewer shocks than expected given the amount of drinking.

Some programs have combined self-reinforcement and self-punishment contingencies. For example, Mahoney, Moura, and Wade (1973) evaluated different self-control techniques for weight loss. Self-reward clients initially deposited money with the experimenter and at each weigh-in over the course of treatment and could reward themselves by taking back some of the money. Self-punishment subjects fined themselves money (response cost) that they initially deposited, when they did not lose weight. Another group received both the self-reward and self-punishment treatment combined and could gain or lose money. After four weeks of treatment, only the self-reward group showed a greater reduction in weight relative to a self-observation control group. The combination of self-reward and self-punishment was not more effective than self-reward alone. Interestingly, weight loss in the program was maintained four months after treatment.

Self-reinforcement and self-punishment techniques have been applied to a wide range of problems including craving drugs, engaging in deviant sexual behavior, cigarette smoking, dating skills, and so on. In many applications, clients do not administer an overt consequence such as money or points. Rather, clients may *imagine* various events or consequences. Imagery-based procedures are addressed in a separate section below because they encompass a variety of techniques in addition to reinforcement and punishment.

Self-Instruction and Self-Statements. The things that people say to themselves have been considered important in controlling their own behavior (e.g., Luria, 1961; Skinner, 1953). Indeed, psychotherapy often focuses on self-defeating verbalizations clients may make to themselves which contribute to maladaptive and irrational behavior (Beck, 1976; Ellis, 1970). The influence that one's own speech has on behavior has been suggested to result from childhood learning.

Developmental psychologists have proposed that the speech of external agents (e.g., parents) controls and directs behavior in early childhood. The child eventually develops a self-directed verbal repertoire which derives from the speech of these external agents. For example, children self-administer verbal praise and criticism which they observe in the behavior of adult models (Bandura & Kupers, 1964; Liebert & Allen, 1967). Similarly, children verbally administer self-instructional statements to guide their actions. While the instructions of others continue to influence behavior throughout life, the self-instructional statements also exert control. Self-instructional statements, while usually private or covert, are sometimes evident in everyday life when an individual "thinks out loud" and describes a particular course of action he believes he should pursue. For example, in preparation for asking an employer for a raise, an individual may tell himself what he would say when the situation arises. Indeed, the self-verbalizations may be used while the individual performs the actual conversation.

Self-instruction training has been used directly to develop self-control. The individual is trained to control his or her behavior by making suggestions and specific comments which guide behavior in a fashion similar to being instructed by someone else. Investigations have shown that children use or can be trained to make statements to themselves which guide their behavior.

In an early investigation, self-instruction was applied to impulsive and hyperactive children (Meichenbaum & Goodman, 1971). The children tended to make errors that resulted from performing tasks quickly without deliberation. To train methodical work habits, the experimenter modeled careful performance on tasks such as coloring figures, copying lines, and solving problems. As the experimenter performed the tasks, he talked out loud to himself. The verbalizations modeled by the experimenter included: (1) questions about the nature of the task, (2) answers to these questions by mentally rehearsing and planning his actions, (3) self-instructions in the form of self-guidance, and (4) self-reinforcement. Essentially, the experimenter modeled "thinking out loud." Then the impulsive children were trained to do the task while instructing themselves out loud just as the experimenter had done. Eventually they were trained to do the task while whispering the instructions and then saying them covertly (privately) without lip movements or sounds. Training in self-instruction resulted in a reduction of "impulsive" errors. Children who met with the experimenter and practiced the tasks but did not receive self-instruction training failed to improve.

Bornstein and Quevillon (1976) demonstrated the effects of self-instruction training with three Head Start children who were highly disruptive in the classroom. After baseline observations of in-class behavior, each child was trained to engage in self-instructions. Training was conducted for two hours outside of the classroom where the children worked on tasks (e.g., copying figures, solving problems). For each task, an experimenter modeled the type of question the child should ask (e.g., "what does the teacher want me to do?"), directions (e.g., "I'm supposed to copy that picture."), and self-praise (e.g., "I really did that one well.") In general, the instructions were designed to convey how to complete work successfully over a variety of tasks. The children were instructed to administer instructions to themselves, first aloud, then in a whisper, and finally without sound (covertly). Self-instruction training improved classroom performance. As shown in Figure 10–1, self-instruction training was administered in a multiple-baseline design across each of the children and was associated with marked increases in on-task behavior. Moreover, these effects were maintained several weeks after treatment was initiated.

Many applications of self-instruction training have been conducted with adults. For example, Holroyd, Andrasic, and Westbrook (1977) used a self-statement procedure to treat headaches. Adults reporting a history of headaches (average of 6 years) were trained to identify thoughts about events or situations that precipitated stress. Clients practiced reappraising stressful events with self-statements (e.g., "What am I thinking to induce my distress.") and to emit self-instructions that helped cope with the situation (e.g., "Calm down, concentrate on the present," "Imagine myself for a moment carefree, at the beach."). Clients were encouraged to implement their coping skills at the first sign of a headache. Treatment resulted in reported reductions in headaches. The self-instruction subjects showed greater reductions than did other subjects who received biofeedback or no treatment. The effects were maintained up to a 15-week follow-up assessment.

Meyers, Mercatoris, and Sirota (1976) used self-instruction training with a hospitalized schizophrenic patient. The patient frequently engaged in irrational speech by introducing irrelevant components into conversation, repeating questions others asked of him, and giving in-

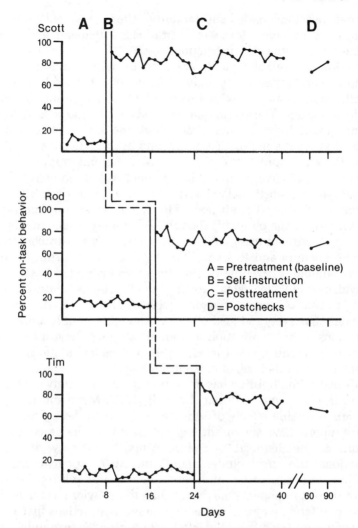

FIGURE 10–1 Daily percent on-task behaviors for Scott, Rod, and Tim across experimental conditions.

Source: Bornstein, P. H., & Quevillon, R. P. The effects of a self-instructional package on overactive preschool boys. *Journal of Applied Behavior Analysis,* 1976, **9,** 179–88.

correct answers to questions when the answers were seemingly obvious. The patient was trained to engage in several self-instructions (e.g., "Don't repeat an answer," "Pay attention to what others say," "People think it's crazy to ramble on."). The patient heard the therapist verbalize these and other statements and eventually said them to himself.

Irrational speech decreased substantially. After the patient's discharge, he continued to have a low rate of irrational statements and reported continued use of the self-instructions.

Occasionally, self-statements are used to help individuals control undesirable and repetitive thoughts. The client is trained to stop his or her bothersome thoughts, with a technique that is appropriately called *thought stopping*. The technique proceeds similar to self-instruction training in which the therapist first models the desired statement, then the client states the instruction aloud, and eventually covertly. For example, Hackman and McLean (1975) used thought stopping to treat obsessive–compulsive clients. When a client had an obsessive thought or imagined a ritualistic behavior, the therapist hit the desk with a ruler and shouted, "Stop!" The purpose of hitting the ruler and shouting stop was to interrupt the obsessive thought. After a few trials, the therapist said "Stop!" without using the ruler. The client was instructed to carry out the procedure and to shout "Stop!" aloud to interrupt his or her obsessive thoughts. Eventually, the client was instructed to say "Stop" in a whisper and then later subvocally. The clients could effectively interrupt their obsessive thoughts without the aid of the therapist. Treatment effectively reduced obsessive thoughts in only a matter of a few sessions. Other applications of thought stopping have attested to its efficacy (e.g., Lombardo & Turner, 1979), but the technique is less well researched than other self-statement methods.

Self-instruction training has been used to alter a variety of behaviors both with adults and children (Kendall, 1977; Meichenbaum, 1977). Although favorable effects of self-instruction have been found, occasionally reports have shown little or no effect with the procedure (e.g., Margolis & Shemberg, 1976; Robin, Armel, & O'Leary, 1975). Self-instructional training includes many different components including modeling, self-instruction, and experimenter and self-reinforcement. Each of these components may contribute to behavior change and contribute in different ways. Even the precise self-instructions that are used may account for the differential effects of training. For example, Kanfer, Karoly, and Newman (1975) compared different types of self-instruction in helping young children handle fear of the dark. Children trained to make self-statements reflecting competence ("I can take care of myself in the dark") were better able to remain in the dark than children instructed to make other kinds of statements that reevaluated the situation (e.g., "The dark is a fun place to be.") or tried to distract themselves with other types of statements (e.g., "Mary had a little lamb."). The type of statements that adults make when coping with anxiety also has been important in treatment outcome (Meichenbaum, 1971).

Alternate Response Training. Another self-control technique is training a person to engage in responses that interfere with or replace the response which is to be controlled or eliminated. Essentially, the individual is trained to replace one response with another. Of course, to accomplish this, the client must have an alternate response in which to engage. For example, people can think of pleasant thoughts to control worrying, relax to control tension, or whistle a happy tune whenever they feel afraid.

The most common focus of alternate response training is to control anxiety. Relaxation has been widely used as a response which is incompatible with and, therefore, an alternative to anxiety. Typically, a client is trained by a therapist to relax deeply. Many different methods to achieve relaxation are available. In behavior therapy, usually a client is trained to tense and relax individual muscle groups (Jacobson, 1938). Alternately tensing and relaxing helps the person discriminate different levels of muscle relaxation. Other procedures have been used such as having the individual make suggestions to himself or herself (i.e., self-instructions) of feeling warmth and heaviness in the muscles to help relaxation (Schultz & Luthe, 1959). Various forms of meditation also can be used to develop relaxation skills.

Once relaxation is taught, it can be used as a self-control technique. The person can relax in situations to overcome anxiety. Individuals have been reported to apply relaxation to themselves effectively for such problems as anxiety in interactions with the opposite sex, fears associated with natural childbirth, public speaking, interviews, and many other problems (e.g., Goldfried, 1977).

Relaxation training has been used effectively to reduce hypertension (elevated blood pressure). Beiman, Graham, and Ciminero (1978) trained two adult males with hypertension to relax deeply. The clients were instructed to practice relaxation at home and to apply relaxation when they felt tense or anxious or felt pressures of time or anger with others. Blood pressure readings were taken in the client's everyday life and in sessions with the therapist. As shown in Figure 10–2, the effects of relaxation reduced both systolic and dialostic blood pressure demonstrated in a multiple-baseline design. Follow-up assessment one and two months later revealed that treatment effects were maintained. The blood pressure of both clients fell within the range of normal blood pressure readings (represented by the dashed horizontal lines in the figure).

Relaxation was used to help an 11-year-old girl control insomnia (Weil & Goldfried, 1973). The girl spent approximately two hours awake each night trying to go to sleep. She ruminated about the previous day's activities and was sensitive to external noises which interferred with sleep. She was also upset whenever her parents left for the evening and remained awake until they returned. Focusing on the in-

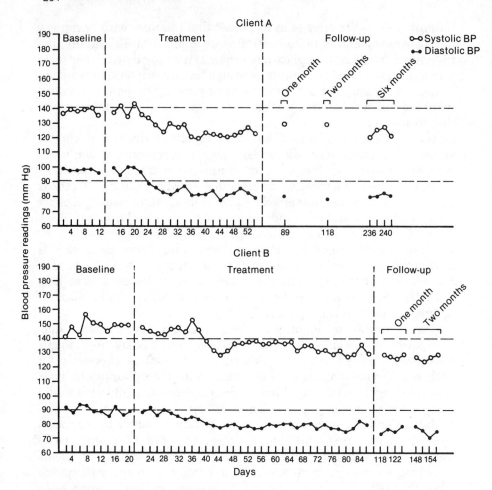

FIGURE 10–2 Mean blood pressure readings averaged over two-day periods.

Source: Beiman, I., Graham, L. E., & Ciminero, A. R. Self-control progressive relaxation training as an alternative nonpharmacological treatment for essential hypertension: Therapeutic effects in the natural environment. *Behavior Research and Therapy*, 1978, **16**, 371–75.

somnia, a therapist visited one night while the girl was going to sleep and gave her relaxation instructions. The therapist told her to tense and relax her muscles and gradually become more and more relaxed. The girl eventually went to sleep within one hour rather than the usual two hours. A 30-minute tape with relaxation instructions was given to her. She used it for a few weeks before going to bed each night. Tapes of a shorter duration were eventually substituted until the final one which was only five minutes long. After a total of five weeks of treatment, the tape was withdrawn. The girl was told to concentrate on self-relaxation when she went to bed. She reported going to sleep immediately. Going to sleep was not a problem when checked six months after treatment. Initially, the therapist provided a technique to help the child. Yet, the child eventually applied the procedures to herself.

Other responses than engaging in relaxation have been effective in altering behavior. For example, Watson, Tharp, and Krisberg (1972) used alternate response training to decrease persistant scratching in a 21-year-old woman. The woman had suffered from itchy rashes on her legs, arms, and hands since the age of four. The woman was instructed to stroke or pat herself everytime she felt like scratching. As the frequency of these alternate responses increased, scratching decreased and was eliminated after approximately two weeks of treatment. During 1½ years after treatment, scratching had returned twice but was eliminated with the self-application of behavioral treatment.

Imagery-Based Procedures. A number of self-control procedures have been based upon having clients imagine various events to alter their own behavior. Depending upon the manner in which this is accomplished, the techniques may include self-reinforcement, self-punishment, modeling, alternate response training, and others. However, the use of imagery makes the techniques unique and worthy of separate treatment here.

One procedure based upon imagery is referred to as *covert sensitization* (Cautela, 1967). The technique consists of having the client imagine himself or herself engaging in an undesirable behavior (e.g., overeating or excessive alcohol consumption). When this image is vivid, the client imagines an aversive consequence associated with the behavior (e.g., feeling nauseous). The purpose of treatment is to build up an aversion toward stimuli which previously served as a source of attraction. The technique is referred to as *covert* because the procedure is conducted in imagination. The client does not have to engage in the behavior but only imagine behaviors associated with particular consequences. The effects of treatment, however, carry over to actual behavior.

Hayes, Brownell, and Barlow (1978) used covert sensitization to alter sexual deviation of an adult male who was in a psychiatric facility because of his multiple sexual deviations. The client's history included attempted rape, multiple fantasies involving sadistic sexual acts (e.g., forced sexual acts with bound women, use of pins and whips during intercourse) as well as exhibitionism. He had been arrested both for attempted rape and for exhibitionism.

Treatment consisted of having the client imagine aversive consequences associated with situations in which exhibitionistic and sadistic acts were performed. For example, a typical exhibitionistic scene with aversive consequences was:

> "I call her over to the car. She doesn't see what I'm doing. I say 'Can you please help me with this?' She looks down and sees my dick. It's hard and she's really shocked. Her face looks all kinds of distorted. I quick drive away. As I drive away I see her look back. I think 'Oh, shit, she's seen my licence plate!' I begin to worry that she might call the police . . . I get home and I'm still worried. My wife keeps saying 'What's wrong?' . . . As we all sit down to dinner I hear a knock on the door. I go open it and there are four pigs. They come charging in and throw me up against the wall and say 'You're under arrest for indecent exposure!' My wife starts to cry and says 'This is it! This is the last straw!'"*

After several days of treatment, similar scenes were developed to associate imagined aversive consequences with sadistic acts. Over the course of treatment, sexual arousal was directly measured by the degree of client's erection (penile blood volume) as the client viewed slides of exhibitionistic, sadistic, and heterosexual scenes. For example, heterosexual slides displayed pictures of nude females, sadistic slides displayed nude females tied or chained down in a number of provocative positions. Also, the client reported his degree of arousal to cards describing various sexual situations.

The effects of covert sensitization were evaluated in a multiple-baseline design since the procedure was introduced at different points in time for scenes related to exhibitionism and sadism. As shown in Figure 10–3, both physiological arousal and self-reported attraction to deviant sexual stimuli decreased as a function of treatment. On the other hand, arousal to heterosexual stimuli was never focused upon and did not change. Moreover, these effects were maintained up to eight weeks after treatment.

Another imagery-based procedure is referred to as *covert modeling* (Cautela, 1976) and consists of imagining a person other than oneself engaging in various behaviors that the client would like to develop. Modeling is a behavior-therapy technique in its own right that is conducted by having clients observe another person (e.g., the therapist) who engages in behaviors the clients would like to develop (e.g., approach a feared situation, engage in social interaction). By observing a model engage in a variety of behaviors, the clients improve as well. Modeling has been effective in altering a variety of problems related to anxiety and interpersonal skills (Rosenthal & Bandura, 1978).

---

* Hayes, S. C., Brownell, K. D., & Barlow, D. H. The use of self-administered covert sensitization in the treatment of exhibitionism and sadism. *Behavior Therapy*, 1978, **9**, 286.

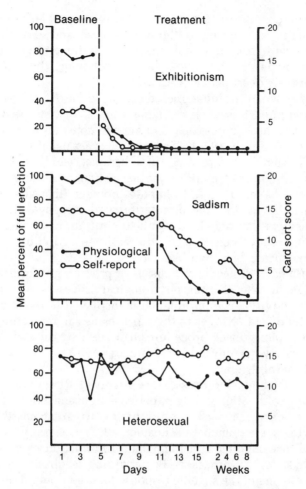

FIGURE 10–3 Percentage of full erection and self-reported arousal to exhibitionistic, sadistic, and heterosexual stimuli during baseline, treatment, and follow-up phases. Card-sort data are daily averages in the baseline and treatment phases and weekly averages in the follow-up phase.

Source: Hayes, S. C., Brownell, K. D., & Barlow, D. H. The use of self-administered covert sensitization in the treatment of exhibitionism and sadism. *Behavior Therapy*, 1978, **9**, 283–89.

In covert modeling, clients *imagine* rather than observe models. For example, covert modeling has been used in outpatient treatment to train shy adults to act more assertively in a variety of social situations (Kazdin, 1978a). In treatment, clients imagine situations in which a person similar to themselves behaves assertively in situations such as returning merchandise at a store, asking an apartment landlord to make needed repairs, responding to high-pressure salespersons, speaking to one's employer to ask for a raise, and so on. By imagining situations in which the model performs the desired behavior, the clients show changes in their overt behavior as well.

Imagery-based techniques include many different procedures that have been applied to several problems such as anxiety, sexual deviation, inassertiveness, obsessions, and alcohol consumption, to mention a few (Kazdin & Smith, 1979). The techniques are usually conducted in treatment sessions in the presence of a therapist. However, they can be viewed as self-control techniques because clients can imagine various scenes in their everyday life to handle problems that arise long after contact with the therapist has been terminated. By rehearsing in imagination behaviors that may be difficult to perform, or by imagining rewarding or aversive consequences to facilitate or inhibit a response, clients can control their own behavior.

Biofeedback. Biofeedback consists of providing information to individuals about their ongoing physiological processes (e.g., heart rate, brain-wave activity). The information is displayed to the client so that moment-to-moment changes in these processes can be monitored. Several different biofeedback procedures can be distinguished depending upon precisely what physiological processes are monitored and how feedback is administered.

Many physiological processes are involved directly in problems brought for treatment including hypertension, headaches, epileptic seizures, muscle spasms, cardiac arrhythmias (irregular heartbeat), anxiety, and others (see Blanchard & Epstein, 1977). Generally, biofeedback provides direct ongoing and immediate information to clients about various physiological processes. By providing feedback, the goal is to produce a change in the specific response focused upon. Biofeedback is included here as a self-control procedure because the goal of many of the procedures is to teach clients specific techniques to regulate their own responses in the natural environment. For example, biofeedback may be used to control blood pressure. In treatment sessions, the client may be connected to a device that monitors blood pressure and provides visual feedback (on a TV screen or digital counter) or auditory feedback (tone) when the pressure is above or below a specified criterion. The client can be instructed to decrease the pressure and receive immediate feedback on the extent to which this is successfully accomplished. Ideally, the client will learn to engage in responses (e.g., pleasant thoughts, relaxation) that are effective in decreasing blood pressure. These responses hopefully can be extended to everyday situations long after biofeedback training has been completed (Schwartz, 1977). Thus, biofeedback may begin with treatment sessions where the client learns how to control the response system of interest. However, after treatment, the client may be able to control the response system himself or herself without external feedback.

Epstein, Hersen, and Hemphill (1974) used biofeedback to control tension headaches of a 39-year-old adult who had a 16-year history of severe headaches. A neurological examination failed to reveal organic causes of the headaches. Apart from this case, research has shown that tension headaches often are associated with contractions of the frontalis (forehead) muscle. Hence, in this case, muscle relaxation of the frontalis was focused upon. To provide feedback, the client was attached to an electromyogram which measures muscle tension (by placing electrodes above the eyebrows). Feedback consisted of playing music to the client (recordings of his favorite music) whenever muscle tension was below a specified criterion. The client was instructed that the music was played whenever low levels of tension occurred and that he was to try to keep the music on as much as possible. In an ABAB design, baseline sessions (no feedback) were alternated with biofeedback sessions. As shown in Figure 10–4, biofeedback reduced overall muscle tension. In addition,

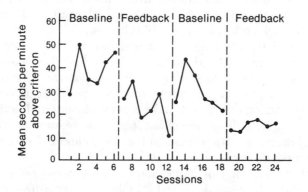

FIGURE 10–4 Mean seconds per minute that contained integrated responses above criterion microvolt level during baseline and feedback phases.

Source: Epstein, L. H., Hersen, M., & Hemphill, D. P. Music feedback in the treatment of tension headache: An experimental case study. *Journal of Behavior Therapy and Experimental Psychiatry*, 1974, **5**, 59–63.

the client reported a decrease in headaches. To ensure that relaxation would be maintained when the client returned to his normal routine, he was trained to engage in relaxation exercises he could perform on his own after treatment. Up to a 7-months follow-up, the client reported a low incidence of headaches.

Additional research has shown that clients' chronic tension headaches improve with biofeedback training of electromyographic muscle tension of the frontailis (Epstein & Abel, 1977). Although clients are less able to control tension by themselves without external feedback, headaches often are reduced after treatment. Other studies have shown that electromyographic feedback of the frontalis muscles can produce general relaxation that affects other responses than headaches (Surwit & Keefe, 1978). Relaxation training through electromyographic feedback has been associated with improved respiratory flow among asthmatics, reduced blood pressure among hypertensive patients, reduced sleep latency among clients with insomnia, and reduced tension among individuals suffering phobias or chronic anxiety.

Blanchard, Young, and Haynes (1975) provided feedback to two hospitalized patients who were referred for their elevated blood pressure. Feedback was provided while clients were connected to a sphygmomanometer (blood pressure apparatus) that automatically recorded pressure. The clients viewed a television monitor which displayed their pressure readings on a graph. The clients were asked to reduce their blood pressure using the feedback information. Feedback was consistently associated with reductions in blood pressure and these effects were maintained up to two weeks of follow-up.

Varni (1973) reported the use of biofeedback with a woman who suffered vaginismus (painful spasms of the vagina). The spasms caused contractions so that even inserting a small tampon was extremely painful. The client was given auditory and visual feedback of the pressure from the contractions, as measured by a device inserted directly into the vagina. Through feedback, the client learned to reduce the pressure of the vaginal muscles. After treatment the client reported successful sexual intercourse without pain.

Clinical applications of biofeedback have focused on a variety of responses including cardiac arrhythmias, tachycardia (accelerated heart rate), hypertension, muscle paralysis and inactivity, seizure activity, sexual arousal, anxiety, and others. Feedback has been provided in many different ways that reflect muscle tension and blood pressure, as already illustrated, and skin temperature, heart rate, brain waves, blood volume and galvanic skin responses. Although biofeedback has been successful in many reports, several authors have raised questions about whether treatment effects can be more easily obtained with relaxation training, a technique that is easier to implement (because no equipment is required) and more readily extended to the natural environment (Blanchard & Epstein, 1977; Schwartz, 1977; Surwit & Keefe, 1978). Also, relaxation training can be more readily applied to a wider range of problems because the technology to assess various processes cannot be applied to measure selected clinical problems (e.g., obsessive thoughts).

Another issue has been whether the effects of feedback are sustained after training is completed. Several reports have shown that feedback does not invariably provide a technique that clients implement on their own. Nevertheless, biofeedback often has been shown to result in sustained treatment effects. However, as with other self-control methods, biofeedback techniques have developed to a greater extent than have the methods of ensuring that subjects apply skills they learn in treatment to their everyday lives (Schwartz, 1977).

Self-Help Manuals.   Many of the self-control techniques discussed to this point develop skills in clients during treatment sessions. After the skills are developed, the client can extend these to the environment to control his or her own behavior in a variety of situations. Recently, several self-help techniques have been developed that clients implement for themselves with minimal or no therapist assistance. The techniques occasionally have been referred to generally as *bibliotherapy* because the techniques are conveyed to potential clients in written form, usually self-help books or manuals that can readily be bought in the store or are made available at a clinic. Bibliotherapy or the use of self-help manuals has been applied to an extraordinary range of problems including fear reduction, overeating, cigarette smoking, social skills, toileting accidents, sexual dysfunction, excessive alcohol consumption, and others (Glasgow & Rosen, 1979). The techniques included in these manuals encompass a variety of procedures, alone and in combination. The purpose of manuals is to describe in a step-by-step fashion how the client should proceed to alter his or her own problem.

One of the most widely circulated self-help manuals has been written by Azrin and Foxx (1974) and is designed for parents who wish to toilet train their children quickly. The manual includes a series of procedures based upon many of the techniques that have been reviewed including prompting, positive practice, reinforcement, and so on. Instructions, edible rewards, praise, feedback, guidance and occasional punishment (positive practice) are intertwined to develop the child's self-initiation of toileting skills. The specific procedures on which the manual is based have been carefully researched in experimental studies in which trainers have implemented training (Azrin & Foxx, 1973). The method has been found to produce rapid results. Indeed, the manual suggests that toilet training can be conducted in "less than a day" (average time about 4 hours).

Investigations of how parents actually do with the manual in training their children have been generally positive. Butler (1976) found that parents quickly trained toileting skills as shown by a reduction of toileting accidents using the Azrin and Foxx (1974) manual. The procedure was not implemented entirely as a self-help program because parents attended classroom lectures to learn the procedures. Thus, whether the program would have worked by just reading the book and applying its contents was unclear. Subsequent research has shown that implementing the procedure from reading the book alone was not very effective in developing toileting skills unless the trainer was available to the parents to provide supervision (Matson & Ollendick, 1977).

Self-help manuals have been used in adult treatment for a variety of problems. One of the better investigated applications is the self-administration of systematic desensitization, a treatment designed to reduce anxiety. Rosen, Glasgow, and Barrera (1976, 1977) evaluated the extent to which clients who feared snakes could self-administer desensitization without therapist contact. Desensitization, as usually practiced, is administered by a therapist. The client is trained to relax deeply and to imagine situations related to the fear while relaxed. By imagining a series of situations related to the fear (such as snakes) while deeply relaxed, the client eventually is no longer anxious in the presence of the actual situations themselves. Rosen et al. provided a written manual to clients that explained how to conduct systematic desensitization. A record was included that trained clients in relaxation. Also, instructions were provided to develop scenes that could be imagined and paired with relaxation. The results indicated that completely self-administered desensitization was as effective as therapist-administered desensitization on self-report, overt behavior, and physiological measures of anxiety. Self- and therapist-administered groups were superior to subjects who received no treatment or a manual that simply described information about snakes. These results were maintained up to two years of follow-up.

Self-help manuals have been effectively applied to alter child behaviors. For example, McMahon and Forehand (1978) examined the effectiveness of a self-help brochure for parents in training appropriate mealtime behaviors in their children. Three normal preschool children from different families participated on the basis of parents' interest in changing such behaviors as playing with food, throwing or stealing food, leaving the table prior to the meal, and other inappropriate behaviors. An initial consultation in the parents' home explained the procedures. At this point, parents received a brief brochure (2½ pages) describing how to provide attention and praise for appropriate mealtime behavior and how to use time out from reinforcement (isolating the child in another room) for inappropriate behaviors that the child did not cease when asked. With only this brief description of reinforcement and time out, parents implemented training. The results of training were evaluated by observations of actual eating behaviors in the home. The program was very effective, as shown in the multiple-baseline design across different children, plotted in Figure 10–5. The effects of the program were maintained at follow-up assessment of eating approximately six weeks after treatment. These results are extremely impressive because of the ability of the parents to administer treatment completely on their own.

Combined Treatments. The self-control procedures discussed to this point have been presented as individual techniques that can be

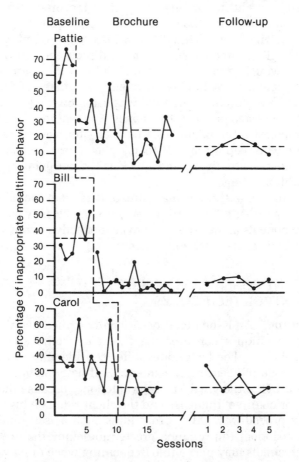

FIGURE 10–5 Percentage of intervals scored as inappropriate mealtime behavior. (Broken horizontal line in each phase indicates the mean percentage of intervals scored as inappropriate mealtime behavior across sessions for that phase.)

Source: McMahon, R. J., & Forehand, R. Nonprescription behavior therapy: Effectiveness of a brochure in teaching mothers to correct their children's inappropriate mealtime behaviors. *Behavior Therapy*, 1978, **9**, 814–20.

used in their own right. In many cases, various self-control techniques are combined to address the complexity of the problems that are brought to treatment. For example, treatment of obesity often has employed several self-control procedures in the same program. A case example illustrates the use of many different techniques for the same client. Coates (1978) used self-control treatment to manage nighttime eating. The client, a 30-year-old male, would wake in the middle of the night and eat an excessive amount of food. Several procedures were used to control nighttime eating. As part of the procedure, stimulus control was used in which the client tried to curb his eating by placing signs on the refrigerator ("Think"). Self-instruction training was used by having the client practice statements to discourage eating ("Its only food. Let me wait five minutes before I eat."). Self-reinforcement and punishment were used by having the client give money to a friend. The money would be refunded if no food was eaten on the previous night. If food had been eaten, some of the money was sent to support a politician whose policies the client disliked. Self-observation was used by having the client keep a diary of food eaten. These procedures along with a few others (actually putting a lock on the refrigerator) eventually led to control of eating.

Aside from case studies, many treatments often include multiple self-control ingredients. The multifaceted treatments may be used when specific components alone are shown to be ineffective or not sufficiently effective to achieve the desired changes.

■ IMPORTANT CONSIDERATIONS OF SELF-CONTROL TECHNIQUES

Self-Control. An issue that is occasionally argued pertaining to the self-control techniques concerns the extent to which clients control their own behavior. The techniques differ considerably in the role the client has in implementing treatment. Self-help manuals have attempted to provide the greatest client autonomy because the therapist exerts little or no direct influence and the client is left on his or her own to carry out procedures. Other procedures such as self-reinforcement and self-punishment imply much greater autonomy than often exists. Even though clients may play a role in deciding when or how to administer consequences to themselves, many external constraints may strongly influence how the consequences are administered and for what behaviors (Jones et al., 1977). For example, clients often are told *when* to administer consequences and *what* the standards for performance should be (e.g., Brownell, Colletti, Ersner-Hershfield, Hershfield, & Wilson, 1977). The client may be told he or she can deliver a reinforcer for performing *correctly* on a task (Felixbrod & O'Leary, 1973), for *los-*

ing weight (Mahoney et al., 1973) or for *interacting socially* (Rehm & Marston, 1968). Self-reinforcement and punishment usually require that a client be allowed to administer or not to administer the consequences at any time, and for any behaviors that he or she sees fit (Skinner, 1953). Programs usually have placed strong constraints on clients so they have less than complete control over the contingencies, for reasons that are clear below.

In general, self-control techniques might be viewed on a continuum in terms of the role clients have in changing their behavior. Clients exert obvious control to some extent in most techniques by being involved in selecting the problem focused upon in treatment. Beyond this, the client may have some role in implementing the techniques themselves. To the extent that the client can do this, perhaps self-control should be encouraged. One of the problems of treatment is ensuring that the gains extend to a variety of situations in the client's life and are maintained over time. The goal of treatment might be enhanced by training the individual to analyze the environmental influences that arise and to implement specific procedures that sustain performance. Hence, self-control may be useful as a technique to maintain behaviors once change has been achieved (see Chapter 11).

The different degrees of involvement that clients can play in their own treatment is an important consideration that needs to be raised in deciding the technique that will be used. Obviously, limits on the amount of control that therapy can delegate to the client may vary according to such variables as the age of the client, the type of problem focused upon, and the setting in which treatment is conducted. One would not expect young children to control their own hyperactivity with a self-help manual nor prisoners who are repeated sex offenders to alter their behavior with a few trials of self-instruction training. Problems occasionally arise with various self-control procedures, discussed below, that need to be used to determine in part whether the self-control technique should be applied or expected to accomplish the desired goal. As a general rule, involving the client in treatment probably is advisable whenever possible. Yet, guidelines for situations and problems in which clients should be responsible for their treatment remain to be elaborated.

Adherence to Treatment. An issue that arises in any treatment technique is the extent to which clients will adhere to or carry out the procedures. Even simple medical treatments (e.g., taking antibiotics in capsule form over a period of several days) do not have perfect adherence. Clients routinely stop taking drugs before they should or omit taking the requisite number prescribed. In the context of self-control behavioral treatments, adherence in various forms has arisen as a problem depending upon the specific technique.

Self-reinforcement and self-punishment techniques have provided problems in adherence. If an individual is completely free to deliver rewarding or punishing consequences for behavior, will these consequences be administered contingently? The natural contingencies, i.e., what might normally be fostered by the environment, could discourage adherence to self-reinforcement and self-punishment contingencies. For example, if a client does not meet a self-imposed performance criterion for self-reward (e.g., studying for two hours), he or she can still take the reward (e.g., going out with friends). If the standards are lowered for self-reinforcement, no immediate penalty will result from an external agent. Essentially, the client might be rewarded for ignoring the performance standard and the entire self-reinforcement contingency. Adherence to self-imposed contingencies may be difficult because delivering rewards to oneself or avoiding the delivery of punishing events might be expected whether or not the desired or undesired behaviors are performed.

In many self-reinforcement studies, the contingencies have not been adhered to consistently over time. For example, McReynolds and Church (1973) developed study skills of college students with low grades. Students devised "self-contracts" where they specified small response requirements (e.g., study for a few minutes each day) to acquire reinforcers (e.g., cigarettes or attending a sports event). A new contract was drawn up at the end of a few days as behavior met the previously specified criteria. Despite the fact that students devised the response criteria themselves—or perhaps because of it—many subjects rewarded themselves even though the requirements for the behavioral contract had not been met. These subjects did not adhere to the contingencies and hence, behavior change should not be expected.

Self-reinforcement has been most extensively used in classroom settings where students are permitted to provide reinforcing consequences to themselves for studying and paying attention to the lesson (Rosenbaum & Drabman, 1979). When students are allowed to determine the number of reinforcers or to decide when they have earned a given number of reinforcers, their standards often diminish. Children have been shown to become increasingly lenient over time and eventually provide reinforcing consequences to themselves for relatively disruptive behavior (Felixbrod & O'Leary, 1973, 1974; Santogrossi, O'Leary, Romanczyk, & Kaufman, 1973).

In classroom studies, several different procedures have been applied to decrease the tendency of children to administer consequences to themselves noncontingently or leniently. To maintain contingent self-reinforcement, external reinforcers (points or praise from the teacher) have been given when children do provide consequences for appropriate behavior; children have been instructed only to give themselves reinforcers for meeting stringent criteria; and teachers have checked the self-administered points to see that the children self-reward correctly and threaten punishment if they do not (Drabman et al., 1973; Hundert & Bastone, 1978; Santogrossi et al., 1973). Although providing externally-controlled reinforcing or punishing events or setting the standards for self-reward effectively control student behavior, the use of such procedures challenges the notion of "self-control."

Delivering aversive events to oneself also introduces the problem of leniency. As mentioned earlier, an aversive event administered by an external agent may result in escape or avoidance. There is no reason to believe that a similar phenomenon will not take place with self-administered aversive events. The individual may avoid applying the aversive event to himself. The client can avoid the self-administered aversive event in one of two ways. The aversive event can be avoided either by not performing the undesirable behavior or by simply performing the behavior but not applying the aversive event afterwards. Programs using self-administered punishment have reported that clients do not administer the consequences to themselves as they should (Wilson et al., 1975) or drop out of the program (Powell & Azrin, 1968). Hence, self-punishment alone is not likely to be widely adhered to by the client.

With both self-reinforcement and self-punishment, the clients may discontinue the contingency at any time because it is under their complete control. If the client suspends the contingency, even temporarily, he or she will be reinforced (obtain the positive reinforcer or avoid the aversive event). Hence, a concern with self-control procedures is what will maintain adherence to the contingency. Hopefully, the delayed reinforcing consequences or intended goal of the program (e.g., being thin to a previously obese individual) will sustain self-control. Everyday experience suggests that delayed consequences are not sufficient to maintain adherence to self-imposed contingencies. More often than not, individuals appear to go off diets, resume cigarette smoking, or give up some other contingency they originally designed. It may be important to provide individuals with some external reinforcement (perhaps delivered by friend, relative, or spouse) for adherence to the "self-control" contingency. Gradually, external reinforcement might be delivered increasingly intermittently, and eventually be eliminated altogether.

Adherence to treatment has been somewhat of a problem in bibliotherapy where clients are given self-help manuals and left to their own devices to implement treatment. First, persons left entirely on their own to conduct treatment have relatively high rates of attrition (dropping out of treatment), a finding shown in self-help training for such problems as anxiety associated with public speaking, fear of snakes, and sexual dysfunction (Kass & Strauss, 1975; Marshall, Preese, & Andrews, 1976; Rosen et al., 1976; Zeiss, 1978).

Second, clients who stay in treatment often do not carry out the specific procedures they are supposed to when left on their own with a self-help manual. For example, for the treatment of anxiety, investigators have reported that 50 percent or more of the clients failed to complete the procedures they were instructed to perform (Marshall et al., 1976; Rosen et al., 1976). In a study for the treatment of problem drinkers, a self-help manual was used to help maintain treatment gains (Miller, 1977, Exp. 2). Approximately one-third of the clients said they did not even read the manual. (Interestingly, these clients did not show greater drinking in up to 12 weeks of follow-up than did those who read the manual.) For many problems and clients, self-control may provide an adjunct to treatment. Therapist contact or supervision may be necessary to ensure that the program is carried out. At this point, research has not determined which problems or clients are most likely to benefit from self-control strategies.

Use of Self-Control Procedures.   Self-control procedures are relatively new in behavior therapy and have already achieved important accomplishments for a variety of problems. Diverse populations have been included encompassing children and adolescents in classroom settings, inpatient and outpatient clients treated for anxiety, overeating, alcohol consumption, parents interested in altering a variety of behaviors of their children at home, and so on. Several advantages accrue from the development of self-control procedures. First, such procedures permit various techniques to be more widely extended to the public than would ordinarily be the case with techniques completely carried out by trained professional therapists. In self-control techniques such as stimulus control, self-monitoring, and alternate response training, clients have initial contact with a therapist but carry out the procedures on their own. The initial contact means that little professional time and client expense are involved in beginning and carrying out treatment. With self-help manuals, the potential for widespread dissemination of treatment is even greater than with other self-control techniques. If techniques can be put into the form of a manual and carried out by readers, a large number of people who ordinarily might not even seek out treatment to begin with could be reached. Occasional checks can be made by having the therapist call the client to handle problems that arise, to provide encouragement, or to ensure that the program is carried out correctly.

Another possible advantage of self-control procedures is that they may be preferred by clients over a therapist-administered treatment. People might prefer implementing a treatment on their own not only because of the possible implications that self-administered treatment may have for cost and efficiency but also because they have a more direct role in their own treatment. Many clients might be more apt to undergo treatment if they could self-administer the procedures. For example, a Gallup Opinion Survey has indicated that among cigarette smokers, only about 34 percent would come for treatment at a clinic; most of the smokers would prefer self-help methods (Glasgow & Rosen, 1979). The preference for self-help procedures may extend to a variety of problems. The application of self-control techniques raises important questions that remain to be resolved. To begin with, the range of clients for whom self-control procedures can be applied has not been elaborated. Perhaps, self-control techniques are readily applied to clients who have enough control already to initiate the procedures. Many of the self-control procedures have been carried out on an adult outpatient basis. Inpatient populations such as retardates, psychiatric patients, delinquents, and prisoners, warrant further study in relation to self-control. For many of these groups treatment is not self-initiated but imposed by the agency or setting. The incentives to carry out self-control procedures may be reduced.

The range of problems for which self-control procedures is effective needs to be evaluated. Currently, applications of self-control procedures have encompassed a variety of problems including anxiety, sexual dysfunction, overeating, cigarette smoking, excessive alcohol consumption, studying, physical fitness, and others. At this early stage of research, demonstrations have simply assessed whether changes can be achieved. Additional work will need to examine whether some problems are more amenable than others to various self-control techniques.

At this point, many of the self-control techniques vary in the extent to which the therapist or some other external agent plays a role in treatment. In some techniques clients have initial contact with a therapist but then conduct treatment on their own with only minimal further contact (e.g., by phone). In other techniques, the clients may meet repeatedly with therapists to check up on how they are doing during the week (e.g., to control their eating habits). Finally, with other techniques, notably self-help manuals, therapists often are not included at all. An important issue will be to evaluate the role of therapist contact. Contact with the therapist may be important to ensure that treatment is conducted properly, to encourage the client when problems arise and when it would be easy to discontinue the procedures, and to help decide when other procedures should be tried.

Although many questions about self-control remain to be resolved, the accomplishments that already have been achieved are impressive. The range of techniques available provide several alternatives to clients to implement treatment for themselves. Although techniques to control one's own behavior have been advocated throughout the history of psychotherapy, only recently have such techniques been evaluated experimentally to establish their effectiveness. The results for many applications have demonstrated several procedures to help people gain control over their own behavior.

■ SUMMARY AND CONCLUSION

Self-control refers to those behaviors an individual deliberately undertakes to achieve self-selected outcomes. Behavioral techniques are applied by the individual rather than by an external agent. Laboratory work has shown that patterns of self-reinforcement and punishment can be developed according to the principles which control other behaviors. Direct reinforcement and modeling can convey performance standards by which an individual evaluates his or her own behavior and provides reinforcing and punishing consequences.

Several self-control techniques were discussed. *Stimulus control* allows an individual to control his or her own behavior by altering environmental and situational events which serve as cues for behaviors. The client can design the environment so that certain cues increase the likelihood that specific behaviors are performed and that other cues which have an unwanted controlling effect no longer influence behavior. *Self-observation* requires that an individual keep a careful record of the target response. Often merely observing one's behavior leads to a systematic change. *Self-reinforcement and self-punishment* require that a person apply certain events to himself or herself following behavior. The crucial aspect of self-reinforcement or punishment is that the individual is entirely free to partake of the reinforcer or not apply the punishing event but does so of his or her own accord. *Self-instructional training* develops patterns of instructing oneself how to perform. The self-statements allow an individual to analyze a situation and specify the requirements for his or her own performance. Once the instructional set is learned, the individual can apply the technique across a variety of situations. *Alternate response training* requires that an individual engage in a response which interferes with or replaces the response the client wishes to control.

Imagery-based procedures usually consist of having clients imagine various behaviors and consequences associated with these behaviors. As a self-control technique, clients can imagine various events in everyday life as needed to reduce or develop particular target behaviors. *Biofeedback procedures* provide information to people about their physiological processes. Ideally, clients can learn to control the bodily processes related to the problem for which they sought change. *Self-help manuals* consist of a large set of techniques that have in common the manner in which they are presented to the client. Clients receive written material in a brochure or book form that conveys how they are to conduct treatment for themselves. Clients can conduct treatment on their own with minimal or no contact with a therapist or consultant. In many of the self-control techniques, some preliminary training may be needed to convey the principle behind the technique and the requirements for effective application. However, once the basic principle is understood and initial training is completed, the client can implement the treatment intervention and determine the range of behaviors or situations to which it will be applied.

Three major issues pertaining to self-control techniques were discussed. First, in some applications, questions can be raised about the extent to which the client is permitted to *self*-control. Some techniques are embedded in strong external contingencies from a therapist or teacher. Other techniques, such as self-help manuals, often provide complete autonomy to the client with no extraneous sources of control from the therapist. Second, adherence to treatment has been an issue in various self-control techniques. Often clients do not carry out the procedures on their own. Over time the contingencies may deteriorate. Also, subjects have dropped out of some self-control techniques and perhaps consequently have a lower success rate than with therapist-administered treatment. Finally, several advantages are associated with self-control techniques. The techniques allow for the widespread extension of treatment to the public in ways that could not be readily accomplished with traditional therapist-administered treatment. The costs of treatment are minimal (as in the case of self-help manuals). Contact with a therapist, if present at all, is very brief. Hence, self-control techniques provide an opportunity for changing behavior on a large scale that would not be easily achieved with other techniques.

Response Maintenance and Transfer of Training

The techniques discussed in previous chapters frequently have produced marked increases in socially desirable behavior and decreases in deviant behavior. The accomplishments have been especially dramatic when the range of clients and problems is considered. Yet, the significance of the accomplishments is minor, if the changes in behavior do not last. What happens when the program is discontinued? Further, if the clients leave the setting where the behavior modification program has been conducted, will the changes carry over to the new setting? The issues raised by these questions have been referred to as *generalization*, and constitute the topic of the present chapter.

The term "generalization" has been applied very loosely to raise the question of whether behavior changes carry over (or generalize) to conditions other than those included in training. However, generalization can include a variety of phenomena. Generalization can refer to changes that carry over to other situations, time periods, or settings than those in which the behavior modification program was implemented. Changes that extend over time usually are referred to as *response maintenance* or resistance to extinction. The question addressed by response maintenance is whether behavior is maintained even after the program is terminated. Changes in behavior that extend across situations and settings usually are referred to as *transfer of training*. The question addressed by transfer is whether behavior extends to situations that are not included in the program (e.g., to the home when a program is conducted in the classroom). Transfer of training also can mean extension of behavior changes to other persons. For example, behaviors trained in the presence of parents may not carry over to other adults (guests, teachers, or peers).

Response maintenance and transfer of training are important issues for any enterprise that is interested in changing behavior, not just for behavior modification. For example, a major issue in psychotherapy is whether positive changes made in the office in the presence of a therapist (e.g., reduced guilt or anxiety in talking about a particular topic) are maintained after the client completes therapy and interacts with others in everyday situations. Similarly, in education, a major hope is that people may continue to read and educate themselves after they complete their formal education (maintenance) and continue these behaviors in everyday life outside of the classroom (transfer). Government and law also are interested in citizens maintaining their law-abiding behaviors (e.g., traveling at the speed limit) even when the contingencies (e.g., surveillance by police officers) are not in effect.

Response maintenance is an obvious issue in behavior modification programs. When the reversal design is used to demonstrate a causal effect of the program, appropriate behavior usually declines. As discussed earlier, the effects of a program can be demonstrated by returning to baseline conditions, after the program has been in effect. If desirable behavior declines when the program is withdrawn and improves when the program is introduced, a causal relationship is demonstrated. Withdrawing the program to show a reversal in behavior provides a preview of the conditions the individual will face once the program is completely terminated. If behavior reverses and the program is withdrawn or altered in some way, behavior change must be transient. This conclusion seems warranted in light of the frequent successful demonstrations using the reversal design.

Transfer of training represents another concern. Do the behaviors altered in one situation transfer to other situations in which the program has never been in effect? For example, does administration of reinforcement for cooperative behavior in the home transfer to behavior in the classroom, on the playground, at camp, and other situations? Since behavior is often situation specific, transfer of training should be as much a problem as response maintenance. Indeed, this is reflected in the use of the multiple-baseline design across situations. As discussed at length earlier, in this version of the multiple-baseline design the contingency is introduced to control a particular behavior across different situations. The contingency is introduced in the situations at different points in time. The design relies upon the failure of behavior change in one situation to generalize to other situations. The contingency can only be considered responsible for change, if behavior does not change in a given situation, until the contingency is introduced.

Response maintenance and transfer of training can readily be distinguished in the abstract but in practice they often go together. For example, if a psychiatric patient leaves a token reinforcement program in the hospital and returns home, both response maintenance and transfer of training are important. Reinforcement for the specific target behaviors is no longer forthcoming (i.e., extinction) and the setting is different from the hospital (i.e., transfer). Whether the behaviors will be maintained and transfer are important concerns that will determine the success of the patient's return to the community.

Response maintenance and transfer need not always go together. For example, reinforcement programs often are implemented in classroom situations at one time of the day (e.g., morning). Transfer of training can refer to whether behavior changes during other periods of the day (e.g., afternoon) or to other situations (e.g., the playground rather than the classroom) where the program has not been implemented. Response maintenance or resistance to extinction is not relevant here because the target behaviors are still reinforced in the morning. The issue is whether the reinforced behaviors transfer or generalize to other situations while the program is in effect.

The present chapter will focus on the evidence bearing on both response maintenance and transfer of training. Techniques to increase the likelihood that behaviors are maintained and carry over to new situations will also be discussed.

■ RESPONSE MAINTENANCE

At the outset, it is important to note that behaviors do not always revert to preprogram or baseline levels when the contingencies are withdrawn. Responses often are maintained after a behavior modification program is terminated. For example, in one program, speech was developed in two withdrawn chronic schizophrenic patients (Thomson, Fraser, & McDougall, 1976). Praise and food were delivered for intelligible words and later for complete sentences, which led to dramatic increases in verbal behavior. A year later, verbal behavior was maintained at the level close to that achieved in treatment even though the contingency had been eliminated. Similarly, Berkowitz, Sherry, and Davis (1971) trained institutionalized retarded boys to spoonfeed themselves rather than be fed by someone else. Prompts and reinforcement successfully developed self-feeding. After training, boys were returned to their cottage settings where they ate family style at large tables with little supervision. Yet, follow-up assessment up to over three years revealed that most of the boys had maintained their appropriate eating behaviors. Several other examples can be cited across a variety of settings and populations showing treatment effects that are maintained, even up to a number of years after the contingencies have been terminated (e.g., Griffin, Locke, & Landers, 1975; Rekers & Lovaas, 1974).

When responses are maintained after consequences have been withdrawn, the precise reason is usually unclear. A behavior should reflect the contingencies which operate in the environment. When the contingencies are withdrawn, one can only speculate why the response is maintained. Various explanations have been offered. First, it is possible that behaviors developed through a reinforcement program may come under control of other reinforcers in the setting. Events associated with the delivery of reinforcement acquire reinforcement value (Medland & Stachnik, 1972). Even though the programmed reinforcers are withdrawn, behavior may be maintained by other reinforcers. For example, behaviors may be maintained in a classroom in which token reinforcers were previously used because the teacher has been consistently associated with token reinforcement. The teacher may be a more powerful reinforcer after the program and maintain performance of the students without using other reinforcers such as tokens (Chadwick & Day, 1971).

A second and related explanation of response maintenance is that after reinforcers are withdrawn, reinforcers which result directly from the activities themselves maintain behavior. Many behaviors result in their own reinforcement. For example, reading, social interaction, or eating skills may be maintained once they are developed. Each of these behaviors can be reinforced by the consequences that naturally follow their execution. (More will be said about the natural contingencies and how they support or fail to support behaviors after they are developed.)

A final explanation of response maintenance is that even though the program is terminated and reinforcers are withdrawn, the agents administering the program (parents, teachers, and staff) have changed in their behavior in some permanent fashion. The agents may continue to use the principles of behavior modification even though a specific program has been withdrawn. For example, if a contingency contract system in the home is withdrawn, a child's desirable behavior may still be maintained at a high level. Although the contract is terminated, the parents may provide reinforcement (allowance and praise) and punishment (loss of privileges) more systematically than they had prior to the contract system. Unfortunately, very little evidence shows that the behavior of those who administer a behavior modification program is permanently altered (see Kazdin & Moyer, 1976). As soon as a program is withdrawn, the agents who administer the program frequently revert to behaviors previously used to control client behavior (e.g., Cooper et al., 1970; Katz et al., 1972).

Each of the above explanations of response maintenance is usually offered *post hoc.* After behavior fails to reverse when the program is withdrawn, an investigator may speculate why this occurred. Any of the explanations may be correct in a given instance. Yet, maintenance of behavior is more clearly understood when it is *predicted* in advance on the basis of using procedures to develop resistance to extinction, rather than when extinction does not occur and has to be explained.

In spite of the above examples and explanations of response maintenance, removal of the contingencies usually results in a decline of performance to or near baseline levels. Indeed, for many years, the most widely used experimental design to evaluate reinforcement, punishment, and extinction procedures has been the reversal design (Kazdin, 1975) that depends upon showing transient changes in performance. In demonstrations across a large range of populations and treatment settings, behaviors are shown to revert to preprogram levels when the contingencies are withdrawn (Kazdin, 1977e). This has led authors to state that if response maintenance is the goal of the program, it has to be programmed systematically into the contingencies rather than merely hoped for as a desirable side effect (Baer et al., 1968; Stokes & Baer, 1977).

■ TRANSFER OF TRAINING

Transfer of training can refer to different phenomena depending upon whether one is speaking of transfer across situations, settings, or trainers who implement the contingencies. In most programs, alteration of behavior in one situation does not result in a transfer of those changes to other situations or settings either while the program is in effect or after it has been withdrawn. Indeed, the stimulus conditions controlling behavior often are quite narrow, so that behavior changes are restricted to the specific setting in which training has taken place and even to those persons who administered the program. Although transfer of training across situations and settings is the exception rather than the rule, many examples are available. For example, Fichter et al. (1976) improved the social interaction behaviors of a chronic psychiatric patient in a hospital setting. Interestingly, the behaviors transferred to day treatment and residential home-care settings after the contingencies had been terminated.

In the classroom, programs altering behavior during one part of the day such as the morning or afternoon period, sometimes demonstrate behavior change at other periods of the day even though performance during these other periods is not reinforced (Kazdin, 1973e; Walker et al., 1971). Additionally, in programs for predelinquents, altering speech behavior in one situation has resulted in behavior change in situations in which the program has not been carried out (Bailey et al.,

1971). Finally, Page Iwata, and Neef (1976) trained physically handicapped and mentally retarded persons to engage in appropriate pedestrian skills (e.g., approaching and crossing intersections safely). Although training was conducted in a classroom situation, the skills transferred to actual performance in the city streets.

Despite many encouraging reports, transfer of training to situations or settings in which the program has not been conducted usually does not occur unless the program is continued across settings (Russo & Koegel, 1977; Walker & Buckley, 1972). Even when some transfer of the behavior occurs, it may be restricted to new situations which bear only very close resemblance to the training sessions. For example, Liberman et al. (1973) found that training psychiatric patients to speak rationally rather than to engage in delusional speech transferred from training sessions to similar sessions in which the contingencies were not in effect. However, treatment effects did not generalize to the ward in everyday interactions that patients had with the staff. As is the case with response maintenance, transfer of training usually has to be programmed directly to ensure that changes extend beyond the conditions of training.

■ PROGRAMMING RESPONSE MAINTENANCE AND TRANSFER

A number of authors have examined research over several years and noted that relatively little attention has been given to the assessment of maintenance and transfer (Cochrane & Sobel, 1976; Keeley, Shemberg, & Carbonell, 1976). Hence, the technology needed to develop maintenance and transfer has lagged behind the considerably better developed technology of behavior change. However, tremendous progress has been made, especially in recent years, in identifying techniques to ensure that behaviors will be maintained and will transfer to new situations (Marholin, Siegel, & Phillips, 1976; Stokes & Baer, 1977). The present section will review major techniques to achieve these ends. Techniques to achieve maintenance and transfer will be treated together because they often are focused upon simultaneously in a given program and also because the techniques that accomplish one often affects the other. Procedures that are more suited to maintenance or transfer, or vice versa, will be noted as such.

Bringing Behavior Under Control of the Natural Contingencies

Perhaps the most obvious procedure to ensure that behavior will be maintained and will transfer to new situations is to bring behavior under control of the consequences that naturally occur in the environment. Reinforcing and punishing consequences that ordinarily follow behavior in everyday life may be sufficient to *maintain* behavior once behavior has been well established. Also, if behavior comes under control of the natural contingencies, *transfer* of training will not be a problem because the consequences in the new situations may sustain the behavior. For example, praise and attention from others as well as consequences that follow from the behavior itself, as in the case of eating and reading, may sustain performance.

Bringing behavior under control of the natural contingencies has been advocated as a procedure to achieve maintenance and transfer for several years in applied behavior analysis. One suggestion has been to select a behavior in treatment that is likely to be maintained by the natural consequences (Ayllon & Azrin, 1968b). For example, behaviors important in everyday living such as grooming oneself, eating appropriately, and conversing with others should be maintained by the consequences that normally are delivered for such behaviors.

Baer (Baer, Rowbury, & Goetz, 1976; Baer & Wolf, 1970; Stokes & Baer, 1977) has introduced the notion of "behavioral traps" to convey the rationale behind maintenance and transfer that results from the natural contingencies. A *behavioral trap* refers to the idea that once a client's behavior is developed, it should be "trapped" into the system of reinforcers that is available in the environment. The purpose of behavioral interventions should be to bring a person's behavior up to the level that is sustained by the natural consequences. Behavior initially may be controlled by extraneous reinforcers (e.g., tokens, food and other consumables, or praise) that normally are not provided. However, after behavior is increased, other reinforcers (e.g., contact with peers) may sustain its high level.

Baer et al. (1976) provided an example of a program in a preschool classroom in which the target behavior appeared to be maintained by the natural reinforcers. The program focused on the behavior of a socially withdrawn boy. To develop social interaction, the teacher provided social reinforcement (attention, expressions of interest) when the boy interacted with his peers. As might be expected, teacher reinforcement increased the boy's interactions, and withdrawal of the teacher attention led to a reduction of his interaction. In fact, among several different phases, teacher praise was alternately delivered and withdrawn in the usual ABAB design. Two results were clear from the program. First, the teacher's praise was responsible for the child's increased interaction. Second, over time, the boy's interactions were maintained even when the teacher did not deliver praise. Apparently, the reinforcement resulting for peer interaction tended to maintain behavior after the social behavior had been well developed. The boy's social behavior was, as it were, trapped into the network of peer interaction that no longer required the behavior modification program. Other research has shown that training social behaviors such as smiling, sharing, and providing positive physical contact among children changes social behaviors of their peers (Cooke & Apolloni, 1978). Thus, behaviors may be maintained by mutual social reinforcement among peers and target subjects even when contingencies administered by the adult staff are withdrawn.

Developing behaviors to the level that they come into contact with the naturally available reinforcers is one of the many strategies that can be used to maintain behavior. Indeed, some authors believe that this strategy may be the most dependable among the available procedures (Stokes & Baer, 1977). Yet, there are several problems with the strategy for ensuring that behaviors will be maintained and carry over to a variety of situations.

First, behaviors that appear to be the kind that will be maintained by the natural environment very often are not maintained at all. For example, even social interaction, included in the above example of "trapping," usually is not maintained in children or adults after the contingencies are withdrawn (Buell et al., 1968; Kazdin & Polster, 1973; Strain et al., 1976, 1977). Similarly other behaviors that are followed by immediate reinforcement from engaging in the response such as appropriate eating skills are not automatically maintained by the natural environment (O'Brien et al., 1972). Behaviors such as paying attention to the lesson in classroom settings have been maintained in some classrooms (e.g., Kazdin, 1973e) but not in others (e.g., Kazdin & Klock, 1973); similarly, smiling among persons who appear depressed may be maintained after reinforcement is withdrawn (Hopkins, 1968) or it may decline (Reisinger, 1972). Thus, there is little consistency, at the present, in identifying the *behaviors* that will be maintained by naturally occurring events in environment.

Another difficulty in relying on natural reinforcers pertains to how the social environment operates. The natural network of reinforcers does not necessarily promote or maintain appropriate behavior. Behaviors that are deviant or disruptive are likely to receive attention or notice in everyday situations such as the home or at school (Allen et al., 1964; Wahler, 1969). Bizarre behaviors may be reinforced rather than extinguished in the natural environment because of the attention they receive. In addition, a number of studies, alluded to in the last chapter, pointed out how parents, teachers, hospital staff, and peers may actually reinforce inappropriate behavior as a matter of course. In fact, the natural contingencies often seem to operate against maintenance and transfer of behavior. For example, a delinquent who leaves an institutional setting where many behaviors have been altered goes home where parental and peer contingencies precipitate or support deviant behavior.

Perhaps the major obstacle in using the natural contingencies as a way to support desirable behavior is the lack of clear guidelines as to how this should be done. The procedures for improving behaviors are well developed. However, the ways to devise the situation so that the target behaviors are trapped by the social environment have not been developed.

For individuals functioning normally in society, many adaptive behaviors are maintained by the natural environment. Yet, most individuals have received extensive social training and respond to a variety of subtle external and self-imposed influences. In contrast, individuals in treatment, rehabilitation, and educational settings for whom most behavior modification programs are conducted are trained to respond to external consequences in carefully programmed situations. It is no surprise that their behaviors are not maintained when the consequences are withdrawn and they are placed in a social situation for which they have not been prepared. If the natural contingencies do not support or maintain the behaviors that have been developed, specific procedures can be implemented to achieve response maintenance and transfer of training after a behavior modification program has been withdrawn.

Programming "Naturally Occurring" Reinforcers

In many programs, the events and staff used to alter behavior are not ordinarily available in the setting where clients will eventually function. For example, tokens or candy usually do not follow behavior in the classroom or on the ward of a hospital. However, consequences that normally are available can replace those extraneous events that were used to alter behavior initially. Programming naturally occurring consequences, as the technique mentioned earlier, tries to utilize available events in the environment to maintain behavior or to achieve transfer. However, rather than depending upon the natural contingencies to support or to "trap" the behavior, naturally occurring events are programmed systematically to sustain performance. This procedure essentially consists of developing a program that takes advantage of events and resources in the client's natural environment.

Programming of naturally occurring reinforcers has been used successfully in many programs that are concerned with both response maintenance and transfer. For example, Kallman, Hersen, and O'Toole (1975) treated a male patient who complained that he could not walk. The patient had no organic problem but was hospitalized and confined to a wheel chair. Social reinforcement was used to develop standing and walking in daily sessions. Eventually the patient walked by himself. He returned home and treatment effects were maintained for about one month. However, he later said he could not walk again and returned to the hospital. Walking was developed and the patient again returned home. Videotaped interactions of the patient and the family revealed that the family had previously supported the patient's disability and ignored attempts to walk. Hence, to maintain walking, the patient's family was trained to reinforce walking and to ignore (extinguish) complaints of being unable to walk. Follow-up after training the relatives indicated the behavior was maintained up to 12 weeks after treatment. Hence, in this program, social consequences in the natural environment were used to sustain the gains that had been achieved in treatment.

The importance of training relatives to ensure response maintenance and transfer has been emphasized in the treatment of autistic children (Lovaas, Koegel, Simmons, & Long, 1973). In this report, follow-up assessment of the behavior of autistic children 1 to 4 years after treatment showed that the children whose parents were trained to carry out the behavioral procedures maintained their gains outside of the treatment facility and indeed improved slightly. On the other hand, children who had been institutionalized where the contingencies were not continued lost the gains that had been achieved in treatment.

Walker, Hops, and Johnson (1975) trained teachers to continue the contingencies initiated in a special setting to achieve both transfer and maintenance. Highly disruptive children participated in a token economy in a special education classroom to develop appropriate classroom behavior. After improvements were achieved, children were returned to their regular classes. Some of the children were returned to their regular classrooms where teachers conducted a behavioral program to sustain the gains achieved in the special classroom. Children who returned to a classroom where some of the contingencies were continued maintained their behavior in the new settings to a much greater extent than others who returned to a class with no program in effect. Perhaps even more interesting, when all programmed contingencies in the regular classrooms had been terminated, behavioral gains were maintained among students who had continued the program in their regular classrooms. Thus, the substitution of one program for another helped behavior transfer to the new setting and be maintained even though the program was eventually discontinued.

In general, behaviors may need to be developed with special contingencies to achieve high and consistent levels of performance. However, after behavior is developed, additional contingencies can be substituted that utilize sources of influence available in the natural environment. The natural contingencies, when unprogrammed, may not sustain appropriate behavior. However, if naturally occurring consequences are altered to support behavior, they provide a useful transition between highly programmed contingencies and the haphazard and often counterproductive contingencies of the natural environment.

Gradually Removing or Fading the Contingencies

Losses of behavioral gains following a behavior modification program may result from abruptly withdrawing the reinforcing and punishing consequences. Gradually removing or fading the program is less likely to be as discriminable to the client as is the abrupt withdrawal of consequences. Eventually, the consequences can be eliminated entirely without a return of behavior to its baseline rate.

Fading of the contingencies can be done in many different ways. One of the most frequently used methods has been reported in token economies in institutional settings. For example, with psychiatric patients, token economies often are divided into steps or levels. Patients pass through the various levels of the program depending upon their progress. As patients perform the target behaviors consistently, they move up in the system and more reinforcers may be available (to encourage further progress). At the highest level, few or no contingencies may actually be in effect so that the clients can learn to function without direct and immediate consequences.

Paul and Lentz (1977) used a leveled token economy to fade the contingencies for chronic psychiatric patients. At the first level, patients needed to perform only minimal levels of behavior such as attending activities to earn tokens. As they moved up to other levels, they could earn more tokens and had access to a larger range of back-up reinforcers. At the highest level, the patients could buy themselves off the system. They purchased a credit card instead of using tokens and had access to all of the reinforcers available as long as they continued to perform adequately.

Leveled systems have also been used for predelinquent boys at Achievement Place (Phillips et al., 1971). The boys initially were placed in a token economy where specific behaviors in the setting were followed by specific point rewards. After performance of desirable behavior in the setting was consistently high for several weeks, the client was advanced to a merit system where privileges and activities were "free" as long as the appropriate behaviors were maintained at a high level.

The purpose of using levels is to develop higher levels of performance over time and to reduce the highly structured contingencies that maintain performance. Ideally, the highest level in the program will resemble the contingencies that one is likely to encounter outside of the setting. If client performance continues at a high level with few or no contingencies, behavior is more likely to be maintained when the client leaves the setting.

The contingencies can be faded in other ways than using levels in a program. For example, Turkewitz, O'Leary, and Ironsmith (1975) used token reinforcement in a classroom to develop appropriate attentive behavior. Initially, the teacher provided points but eventually the children provided their own points. The teacher checked these to ensure that they matched her ratings. If the teacher and student agreed on the number of points earned, the child received a bonus. To fade the contingencies, the teacher checked only some of the students. In addition, to reduce reliance upon back-up reinforcers, a progressively lower percentage (50%, 33.3%, 12.5%) of the randomly selected students was allowed to exchange points for back-up events on a given day. Eventually, none of the students exchanged their points for consequences. Even though all back-up reinforcers were eliminated and the contingencies were essentially self-administered, disruptive behavior remained low. Maintenance was only assessed for a 5-day period but the results suggested that the program could be faded without an immediate loss of the desired behavior.

Gradually withdrawing the contingencies may be very useful because it prepares clients for the conditions under which they must normally function. In everyday living the contingencies often are unsystematic, and the consequences for performance may be delayed, if delivered at all. The gradual withdrawal of contingencies provides a transition between a highly programmed environment and one that is less well programmed with regard to given target behaviors. At present, the contribution of fading contingencies on long-term maintenance is not well established. Although programs using leveled systems that fade the contingencies have produced effects that last years after clients leave the setting (e.g., Paul & Lentz, 1977), research has not shown that maintenance and transfer are due specifically to the fading procedures. Nevertheless, at this point, fading represents an alternative maintenance and transfer strategy that can readily be incorporated into behavioral programs.

Expanding Stimulus Control

One reason that behaviors may not be maintained and do not transfer to new settings is that clients readily form a discrimination between the conditions in which reinforcement (or punishment) is and is not delivered. Behavior becomes associated with a narrow range of cues that may include specific staff members (e.g., teachers) who administer the program and the specific setting in which the contingencies are in effect (e.g., classroom rather than playground or at home). As soon as the program is withdrawn or the setting changes, clients discriminate that the desirable behavior is no longer associated with certain consequences. Thus, responses are not maintained and do not transfer to new situations.

Maintenance and transfer can be developed by expanding the breadth of stimuli that exert control over behavior. The procedures used to expand stimulus control may vary as a function of the type of transfer that is of interest. For example, in some programs client behavior may be restricted to the presence of specific persons who conduct training and implement the contingencies. In these cases, the narrow control exerted by the staff may be expanded by introducing more staff into training. For example, Stokes et al. (1974) trained four severely and profoundly retarded children to engage in greeting responses (handwaving). One staff member in the institution served as the trainer in special experimental sessions. Although the behaviors were developed, observations revealed that the children usually did not greet other staff members who approached them. The stimulus control was expanded by having a second staff member also conduct training. The effect of this additional training was not only to increase greeting responses to this staff member but also resulted in the greeting response in the presence of several other staff members who had not been associated with training. Thus, the behavior was no longer under the narrow stimulus control of the trainer.

Usually, it is of interest to ensure that the behavior transfers across several dimensions at the same time including staff members, trainers, and even situations. For example, Emshoff, Redd, and Davidson (1976) used praise and points (exchangeable for money) to develop positive interpersonal comments among four delinquent adolescents. To develop behavior that would transfer across a variety of stimulus conditions, two clients were trained under conditions that varied across activities (e.g., during games and discussions), trainers, locations in the facility, and time of the day. Clients who received this highly varied training showed more positive comments under several tests for generalization when tokens were delivered noncontingently, when a new trainer was introduced, and when the activity, setting, and trainer all varied as compared with clients who were trained under constant training conditions. Not only was transfer of training improved by the procedure, but clients who had the varied training conditions showed superior maintenance of the behavior 3 weeks after training was terminated.

As another example, Koegel and Rincover (1974, Exp. 1) developed such behaviors as attending to a task, imitating, speaking, and recognizing words among autistic children. Although these behaviors were increased, performance did not transfer beyond the one-to-one situation used in the training sessions. When a child was placed with others in a group situation, the trained behaviors decreased. To develop transfer to the classroom situation, various stimulus conditions of the classroom were gradually introduced into training (Koegel & Rincover, 1974, Exp. 2). Other children, the classroom teacher, and teacher aides were included into training situation to associate performance of the target behavior with a variety of stimuli. Expanding the stimulus conditions of training led to transfer of the behavior to the classroom.

Jackson and Wallace (1974) increased the voice volume of a mentally retarded adolescent girl by using token reinforcement. The procedures were carried out in a laboratory situation, but performance was measured in the classroom to measure transfer. Although the girl's voice volume increased, her behavior did not transfer to the other situations. To promote transfer to the classroom, the environmental stimuli associated with training were expanded. Some of the girl's classmates were included in the training sessions, classroom events were scheduled in the training situation for all students, and the teacher temporarily led the group of students in class while the girl was trained in full view of the class activities. After these added procedures were included in training, plus increasing the loudness requirements for reinforcement, behavior transferred to the classroom setting.

The above studies illustrate that transfer of training, and in some cases response maintenance as well, can be established by introducing various components of the situation in which transfer is desired or by expanding the range of individuals who administer the contingencies. From these examples it appears that the stimulus conditions of the transfer setting need to be introduced into training while training is still in effect. As the stimuli that exert control over behavior broaden, the likelihood that the behaviors will be performed in new situations and in the presence of a variety of others is markedly increased.

It is important to note that all of the conditions across which transfer is desired need not necessarily be introduced into training. For example, if it is desirable to have the target response extend across several settings or several people (trainers), not all of the settings or people need to be introduced into the training situation. Research suggests that only few of the new stimulus conditions need to be introduced into training after which transfer extends to new settings and people who have had no association with training (e.g., Murdock, Garcia, & Hardman, 1977; Stokes et al., 1974).

Schedules of Reinforcement

As mentioned earlier, resistance to extinction can be enhanced by using intermittent reinforcement. After behavior is well established, reinforcing consequences can be delivered intermittently. The intermittency of the reinforcement can be increased so that very little reinforcement is provided for behavior. Resistance of behavior to extinction once reinforcement is withdrawn is a function of the intermittency of the reinforcement. The more intermittent or thinner the reinforcement schedule, the greater the resistance to extinction.

Intermittent reinforcement has been used to maintain behavior in several projects. Kale et al. (1968) trained three schizophrenic patients to greet staff on the ward. Whenever patients greeted a staff member (e.g., "Hello, Mr. _____," or "Hi!"), they were given cigarettes and praised. After greetings were performed at a high rate, reinforcement was thinned so that not all responses were reinforced. For example, for one patient a variable ratio schedule was used so that on the average every second response was reinforced. The ratio was gradually increased so that many responses (e.g., on the average 20) were required for a cigarette. After reinforcement had been delivered intermittently for a few weeks, reinforcement was withdrawn completely. Yet, behavior was maintained at its reinforced level. A follow-up conducted approximately three months after treatment showed that greeting responses were maintained at the high level which was developed during treatment.

Kazdin and Polster (1973) used intermittent reinforcement to maintain social behavior. In a sheltered workshop two male adult retardates who engaged in little social interaction received tokens for talking to peers. During three work breaks the clients were told that they would receive tokens for each person they interacted with socially. An interaction was defined as a verbal exchange in which the client and a peer each made at least one statement to the other person. The statement had to reflect some content area such as information in the news, sports, television, and weather, rather than general greeting statements and and replies such as "Hi, how are you?" "Fine!" Peers were queried after each break to ensure that the client reported the conversation accurately. If a peer noted that the client had not spoken with him, or if the peer forgot the conversation, the client did not receive a token. Each of the two clients received a token for each peer they had spoken with during each break. Every interaction was reinforced. Figure 11–1 shows that during the first phase in which reinforcement was given, the daily average number of interactions gradually increased for both clients. Yet, during a reversal phase in which tokens were withdrawn, interactions decreased. When reinforcement was reinstated, one client (S_1) received reinforcement as he had before (i.e., continuous reinforcement). The other client (S_2) was told that he would receive tokens only once in a while (i.e., intermittent reinforcement). At first, the client received tokens at two of the work breaks, and after three weeks at only one of the three daily breaks. The client never knew for sure which break would be reinforced since the scheduled reinforcement varied each day. Eventually, all token reinforcement was withdrawn. As Figure 11–1 shows, the client who had been reinforced continuously showed an immediate decline in social interaction. However, the client who had been reinforced intermittently maintained a high rate of interaction for the final five weeks of the project. Thus, intermittent reinforcement appeared to help maintain behavior.

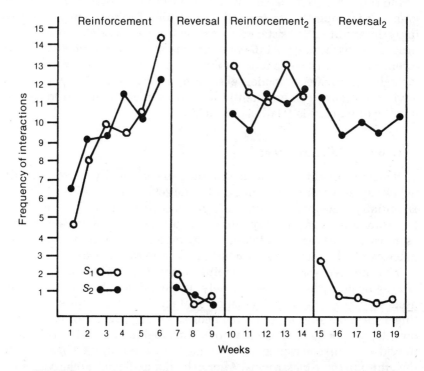

FIGURE 11–1   Mean frequency of interactions per day during reinforcement, reversal, reinforcement$_2$, and reversal$_2$ for subject 1 (S_1) and subject 2 (S_2).

Source: Kazdin, A. E., & Polster, R. Intermittent token reinforcement and response maintenance in extinction. *Behavior Therapy*, 1973, **4**, 386–91.

Some investigators continue the use of intermittent reinforcement to maintain behavior at a high level rather than eliminate all reinforcement. Intermittent reinforcement is quite effective, of course, while the reinforcement is still in effect. For example, Phillips et al. (1971) gave or withdrew points on the basis of the degree to which predelinquents cleaned their rooms. When the points were given, daily room cleaning was maintained at a high level. After the behavior was well established the reinforcing and punishing consequences became increasingly intermittent. The rooms were checked daily but reinforcement or punishment occurred only once in a while. When the consequences were delivered, the number of points given (or lost) on the basis of that day's performance was multiplied by the number of previous days that consequences had not been given. Although the consequences were delivered on only 8 percent of the days checked, behavior was maintained at a high level. The consequences were not completely withdrawn so the effect of intermittent reinforcement on extinction was not evaluated.

Intermittent reinforcement can be readily incorporated into all programs. It is important to make the schedule of reinforcement increasingly intermittent. Resistance to extinction can be delayed after the program is withdrawn. At the present time, it is unclear whether highly intermittent reinforcement only forestalls extinction temporarily or can virtually eliminate extinction even after a long extinction period. Behaviors reinforced intermittently have been maintained up to several months of extinction (Hall et al., 1977).

Delay of Reinforcement

Behavior might also be maintained by gradually increasing the delay between reinforcement and the target behavior. When behavior is initially developed, immediate reinforcement usually is essential to ensure a high rate of responding. As behavior stabilizes and is well established, the delay between behavior and the reinforcing consequences can be increased without a loss in performance.

The effectiveness of delaying reinforcement after a response in maintaining behavior has not been widely studied although it often has been used as part of other maintenance strategies such as fading the contingencies and altering reinforcement schedules. As an illustration of how delays can be used, Greenwood, Hops, Delquadri, and Guild (1974) provided group consequences contingent upon appropriate behavior for the group in three classrooms. After behavior achieved a relatively high level, a delay was introduced in earning the group consequences. The classes were required to perform high levels of behavior for an increasing number of consecutive sessions before the reinforcer was delivered. A maximum delay of 10 sessions was attained before earning the reinforcer. Follow-up data 3 weeks after the program was terminated revealed that appropriate classroom behaviors were maintained.

In a classroom program devised by Turkewitz et al. (1975), mentioned earlier, the delay between token reinforcement delivery and the exchange of tokens for back-up events was included as part of a more elaborate procedure to fade the contingencies. The procedure involved delayed reinforcement because only some of the children, determined on a random basis, were allowed to exchange their tokens for back-up events. Hence, for many children actual performance of the desired classroom behaviors and receipt of back-up events was delayed. Indeed, at the end of the program children behaved appropriately for several days even though none received back-up events.

Most reinforcers available in the social environment are delayed. Hence, it is important to wean a client from immediate reinforcement. Behaviors should be well established prior to invoking long delays. And, when delayed reinforcement is introduced, performance should be observed closely to ensure that there is no loss of behavior gains. Eventually, reinforcement might be withdrawn entirely or delivered only after long delays without a loss in performance.

Peer Facilitators

Peers have been discussed earlier as behavior-change agents. In addition, peers may be utilized to help maintain behavior and to develop transfer across a variety of situations. If behavior comes under the stimulus control of persons who implement the contingencies, it may be important to involve peers in the administration of various consequences. After the specific contingencies are terminated, peers still may influence the client's behavior. Because peers have contact with the client across a variety of situations, their presence may provide cues to the client to continue the target behavior across these situations.

Most of the programs utilizing peers as behavior-change agents have been conducted in classroom settings. Only a few of these programs have evaluated the extent to which peers may enhance maintenance or transfer. As one illustration, Johnston and Johnston (1972) developed correct speaking in two girls in a classroom setting. The girls were trained to monitor each other's pronunciation. Peer correction of the other child for inappropriate speaking and feedback for correct speech were reinforced with tokens. The behavior appeared to come under stimulus control of the peer who administered the program. When the children were in the presence of each other, their rates of correct speech were much higher than when they were in the presence of children who never monitored their speech. When token reinforcement for peer monitoring of the other child's speech was stopped, the children continued to monitor behavior and correct speech tended to be maintained. In short, the target behavior was maintained by the presence of the peer who previously administered the contingencies.

Stokes and Baer (1976) took advantage of the stimulus control that peers can exert over behavior to attain transfer. In a preschool classroom, children having difficulties in preacademic skills were taught a word-recognition task. One child taught the task to another by presenting the cards with the words and by praising correct responses. Both the target child and peer tutor improved in the word recognition task but the performance did not transfer from the work area of the class with the peer present to other situations unless the peer tutor was present. Thus, the behavior appeared to come under control of the presence of the peer. This report suggests that peers can be used to extend behaviors to new situations.

Other investigations have shown that peer-administered contingencies sometimes lead to maintenance and transfer of behavior to situations other than those in which training is conducted (Bailey et al., 1971). However, the use of peers as facilitators of transfer and maintenance remains to be exploited. In many situations in which behavioral programs are conducted, peers, siblings, other inmates or residents of the institution might be involved in monitoring behavior of a target subject.

Self-Control Procedures

As noted earlier, one reason that changes in behavior are not maintained and do not transfer is that behavior comes under the stimulus control of external agents (e.g., staff, teachers, parents) and restricted situations (e.g., classroom, ward) in which training is conducted. Performance might not be restricted to a narrow set of stimulus conditions if clients can be trained to control their own behavior. Specifically, clients can be trained to administer prompts and to deliver reinforcing and punishing consequences to themselves. If clients can be trained to control their own behavior, perhaps behavior changes will not be lost when a program is withdrawn. Also, because the client implements the contingencies, the self-administered program can be executed across situations.

Research has shown that clients can evaluate their own behavior, set criteria for reinforcement, and determine the amount of reinforcement they should receive (e.g., Felixbrod & O'Leary, 1974; Fixsen, Phillips, & Wolf, 1973). These promising results raise the possibility that clients might be able to continue the program to sustain and improve their performance across a variety of new settings. Actually, few programs have provided a stringent test of self-control strategies in long-term maintenance of behavior in applied settings. However, promising results have been suggested in selected instances.

Wood and Flynn (1978) demonstrated the potential effects of self-reinforcement on maintaining behaviors among six male predelinquents who lived in a family-style residential facility. The youths participated in a token economy where points for appropriate social, academic, and self-care behaviors could be exchanged for various privileges in the setting. Self-reinforcement was employed to develop room cleaning for each boy's room (e.g., having the bed made, shoes and clothes away, no objects on the bedspread or dresser, clothes folded and in drawers). Some of the boys first received tokens administered by the staff for keeping their room clean. Other boys were instructed to administer points to themselves for their room-cleaning behaviors. Self-administered points were monitored by the staff to ensure that the boys evaluated their behaviors accurately. Indeed, at first points were given for accuracy. When the boys were highly accurate (agreement on 80 percent of the behaviors), their self-evaluations completely determined how many points they would receive. High levels of accuracy were maintained by random spot checks for accuracy. Eventually, all boys were placed on a self-evaluation and self-reinforcement system.

Interestingly, at the end of the program, all contingencies were withdrawn to assess whether room-cleaning behaviors were maintained. The results, which appear in Figure 11–2, show that instructing the

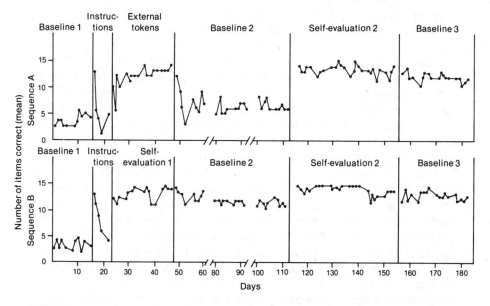

FIGURE 11–2 The mean number of room-cleaning behaviors correctly completed for two groups of youths receiving the conditions in a slightly different sequence. During the self-evaluation phases, the youths self-administered the reinforcing consequences based on evaluations of their own behavior.

Source: Wood, R., & Flynn, J. M. A self-evaluation token system versus an external evaluation token system alone in a residential setting with predelinquent youths. *Journal of Applied Behavior Analysis*, 1978, **11**, 503–12.

boys to clean their rooms had little effect on the behavior. However, in the third phase points administered by the staff (top portion of the Figure) or by the boys themselves (bottom portion) improved room cleaning. For each set of boys, self-evaluation and self-reinforcement later led to high levels of room cleaning and this effect was maintained up to 22 days after the contingencies were terminated. Thus, the self-evaluation procedure appeared to maintain high rates of the target behavior.

Drabman et al. (1973) allowed students to evaluate their own performance in a token economy. Initially, the students received their points only if their estimates corresponded the teacher's evaluation of their performance. Eventually, the children administered points to themselves without the teacher monitoring their self-reward. The low levels of disruptive behavior had been obtained earlier in the program when the teacher was responsible for administering the contingencies. Low levels were maintained for a 12-day period in which the children had complete control over the contingncies. The program suggests that students might be able to maintain their own appropriate behavior. In this application, the self-reward procedures might be conceived as substituting one program (self-administered reinforcers) for another program (teacher-administered reinforcers).

Epstein and Goss (1978) trained a highly disruptive fifth-grade boy to administer points to himself for appropriate behavior. After a teacher-administered program, the boy self-administered points which were monitored by the teacher. Extra points were provided when the boy's ratings of himself matched those provided by the teacher. The boy continued the self-reinforcement program which sustained high levels of attentive behavior over a six-week period.

Self-reinforcement as a technique to achieve maintenance may have its limitations. To begin with, and as pointed out earlier, persons allowed to self-reward often become increasingly lenient over time so that reinforcers are delivered even though the desired behaviors are not performed. Second, behaviors often are not maintained after self-reinforcement contingencies are withdrawn. Indeed, studies have shown little or no difference in response maintenance depending upon whether an external agent or the client himself or herself previously administered the reinforcers (Bolstad & Johnson, 1972; Felixbrod & O'Leary, 1974; Johnson & Martin, 1972).

In classroom applications, self-control contingencies have sustained performance as long as the contingencies are in effect and they are monitored by others such as a teacher. Special incentives for accurate self-reward including points or praise and reprimands may be necessary to ensure that the contingencies are executed to promote appropriate behavior (Drabman et al., 1973; Epstein & Goss, 1978). However, this amounts to continuation of a program rather than maintenance of the behavior without a specific reinforcement program in effect. Thus, at present, only sparse evidence exists in applied settings showing that self-reinforcement can maintain behavior without careful monitoring of the contingencies by an external agent such as a teacher (cf. Anderson,

Fodor, & Alpert, 1976). However, self-reinforcement might be useful as a supplement to other procedures such as fading the contingencies.

Self-instruction training is another technique that may be useful in maintaining behavior or aiding in its transfer to other situations (Meichenbaum, 1977). For example, in one of the early studies discussed previously, impulsive children were trained to administer instructions to themselves to perform various tasks in a methodical and deliberate fashion (Meichenbaum & Goodman, 1971). Not only was the training program quite effective in improving their work, but also the gains made during training were maintained after one month. Similarly, when schizophrenic patients were trained to instruct themselves on verbal and motor tasks, their performance improved (Meichenbaum & Cameron, 1973). The behavioral gains resulting from training were maintained at a three-week follow-up assessment. Moreover, the effects of self-instructional training transferred to tasks not included in training. In a classroom setting, Bornstein and Quevillon (1976) trained disruptive children to administer self-instructions to develop appropriate classroom behavior. Attentive behavior markedly increased and these effects were maintained several weeks after training.

Several studies have shown that behaviors developed through self-instruction are maintained and transfer to new stimulus conditions, although exceptions can be cited. For example, Robin et al. (1975) used self-instruction to develop writing skills among children with writing deficiencies. Although writing improved, the skills did not transfer across tasks that served as a measure of generalization. Interestingly, some of the children gave themselves the correct instructions on the new tasks, but these instructions did not help performance. In general, while self-reinforcement and self-instruction have been active areas of research within behavior modification, relatively little work has been completed evaluating these as strategies to maintain behavior and to promote transfer.

General Comments

The procedures discussed above are not mutually exclusive. They can be used independently or in conjunction with each other. For example, programs in treatment facilities can begin to wean a client from reinforcement programs by applying increasingly delayed and intermittent reinforcement. Also, additional persons in the setting or in the home environment can be trained to continue the contingencies to maximize the likelihood of transfer. The contingencies can be faded by allowing the client to self-evaluate his or her performance and to self-administer reinforcers. Depending upon the situation, other maintenance and transfer strategies, discussed above, may be incorporated into the situation.

Investigators frequently have used several procedures simultaneously to maximize the likelihood that responses are maintained and transfer to new situations. For example, Ayllon and Kelly (1974) restored speech of an 11-year old retarded girl who had not spoken in class for over eight months. Training consisted of providing candy and social reinforcement for components of speech (e.g., opening her mouth, blowing air out of her lips, making a sound, and eventually verbally responding to questions). To ensure that behaviors would be maintained and transfer from the sessions in the counselor's office to the classroom, several techniques were used simultaneously.

First, over the course of training the schedule of reinforcement was made increasingly intermittent. Second, praise was substituted for primary reinforcement (candy) so that the behavior would come under control of naturally occurring reinforcers in the environment. Third, stimuli associated with the classroom were introduced into the counselor's office so that the training situation would increasingly resemble the classroom. Thus, other children, a blackboard, and desks were added to the training situation. In fact, the trainer stood in front of the children to simulate the teacher's interaction with students that would occur in the classroom. Fourth, to maximize the occurrence of verbal responses in the presence of her peers, a group contingency was introduced. Candy was provided to the group if each of the children brought into the training session, including the target child, answered questions asked by the trainer. Fifth, training was continued for a brief period in the classroom in which the trainer and later the teacher administered reinforcement. Overall, training consisted of eight sessions outside of the classroom followed by seven more sessions in the classroom. The child's verbal responses increased markedly over the course of treatment. A follow-up assessment one year after training had been terminated indicated that the responses were maintained at a level achieved during training and transferred across three new teachers and settings within the school.

Many other behavior modification programs have combined various techniques to promote response maintenance and transfer such as expanding the stimulus control and scheduling intermittent reinforcement (Jackson & Wallace, 1974; Koegel & Rincover, 1974), fading the contingencies, self-reinforcement, and delayed reinforcement (Turkewitz et al., 1975), substituting one program for another and expanding stimulus control (Walker et al., 1975), and using peers, delayed reinforcement, and peer-administered consequences (Jones & Kazdin, 1975). Additional work is needed to develop other techniques and to look at those aspects of existing techniques that maximize maintenance and transfer.

Some of the problems in developing behaviors that are maintained and that transfer to a variety of situations or conditions may relate to the manner in which behavior-modification programs are conducted. In many programs, behaviors are reinforced or punished by parents, teachers, or other behavior-change agents who closely monitor performance. In such programs, stimulus control is automatically built into the contingencies because the consequences are very closely tied to specific staff, situations, and tasks. The use of peers as behavior-change agents or self-administered contingencies help remove the specific stimulus control often associated with staff. However, it might be possible to focus on certain *responses* that are less likely to lead to narrow stimulus control.

For example, Marholin and Steinman (1977) developed attentive behaviors and performance on arithmetic assignments in a special elementary school class for children who were behind in academic skills and exhibited disruptive classroom behavior. When the teacher administered tokens (points exchangeable for free time) for attentive behavior, the children improved. However, during periods in which the teacher and aides left the room, disruptive behavior increased. The reductions in disruptive behavior tended to require the teacher's presence. On the other hand, when correct completion of academic performance rather than attentive behavior was reinforced with tokens, the teacher's presence or absence made much less of a difference. Gains in arithmetic task completion *and* attentive behavior were maintained even when the teacher was not in the room. The authors noted that reinforcing a response that can be evaluated by completion of a product (such as academic assignments) does not require the close, constant monitoring that attentive behavior does. Hence, behavior may be less likely to come under stimulus control of the teacher. Additional work is needed to evaluate what aspects of a reinforcement program can be altered to promote maintenance and transfer.

In general, each of the procedures designed to promote maintenance and transfer emphasizes a different aspect of the contingencies that control behavior. The focus on any single factor such as the stimuli that exert control over the response, the scheduling of consequences, fading the contingencies, and other procedures may be limited when applied individually. In many situations in which maintenance and transfer are required, it is likely that several different procedures would have to be programmed systematically. For example, a delinquent might leave an institution to return to the home living situation with his or her parents. The environment into which the child will return represents a complex system of antecedents and consequences involving parents, peers, and the child. The complexity of the situation suggests that focusing on large changes within this behavioral system may be necessary to maintain behavior and ensure its transfer (Wahler et al., 1979). The interaction of the family may need to be altered significantly to help the child. Specific contingency changes might be useful to wean the child from specific consequences. However, explicit procedures may be needed to ensure that the contingencies that support or precipitate the undesired behaviors are not operative. Current research represents an important beginning by looking at specific techniques to achieve maintenance and transfer, but additional work is needed to examine the systems in which individuals function and the factors within these systems that can contribute to maintenance and transfer.

■ SUMMARY AND CONCLUSION

Two major issues in evaluating behavior modification programs are the degree to which behaviors are maintained once the program has been withdrawn and the degree to which behaviors transfer to other situations and settings than those in which training has taken place. These issues are referred to as response maintenance and transfer of training, respectively. In many applications, behaviors have been maintained after a program was withdrawn and have transferred to new settings. However, these occurrences are exceptions. Response maintenance and transfer are not automatic by-products of a program. Rather they have to be programmed directly by including specific procedures in the program.

Recently, advances have been made developing the techniques to help maintain behavior and to ensure its transfer. Major techniques include: (1) bringing behavior under the control of the natural contingencies, (2) programming naturally occurring reinforcers, (3) gradually removing or fading the contingencies, (4) expanding stimulus control over behavior, (5) altering the schedules of reinforcement, (6) increasing the delay of reinforcement, (7) using peer facilitators, and (8) using self-control procedures. These techniques vary in the extent to which they have been thoroughly evaluated and to which they achieve maintenance, transfer, or both. Also, the techniques often are combined in many programs to maximize the likelihood that durable and broad changes in performance will be attained. Hence, the effectiveness of individual techniques often is difficult to determine. Nevertheless, present work suggests that several procedures can be implemented to maintain high levels of performance and to extend these levels to new situations in which the client will function.

Ethical and Legal Issues

$\mathbf{B}$ehavioral techniques offer promise for a variety of client populations for whom traditional treatments have made only minor advances. Yet, the techniques raise major concerns over the misuse of a behavioral technology. The use of behavior modification to restructure institutional living of psychiatric patients, retarded residents, and prison inmates, for example, raises concerns about client rights and the potential abuses that may be associated with treatment (e.g., Martin, 1975; Mental Health Law Project, 1973). Occasionally authors have extrapolated behavioral principles to the design of society in general (Skinner, 1948, 1971), which may lead to even greater ethical concerns (London, 1969; Wheeler, 1973).

Even though behavioral techniques have only developed rather recently, a sufficient technology already exists that might be misused against individuals or groups of individuals. Thus, discussion of ethical and legal issues raised by applications of a behavioral technology is not academic. Ethical and legal issues raise questions about the focus of behavioral interventions, how treatments should be implemented, and the restricted conditions under which they should be applied. The ethical issues to be addressed include concerns about behavioral control, the purposes for which behavior is controlled, the individuals who exert control, and individual freedom. The legal issues to be addressed include infringements of individual rights, informed consent, and the use of aversive techniques.[1]

■ ETHICAL ISSUES

Behavior Control

Behavior control refers to exerting power over people by manipulating environmental conditions to which individuals are exposed to achieve a definite end such as developing new behavior and maintaining or eliminating already existing behaviors (Ulrich, 1967). The concern over behavioral control is that behaviors, attitudes, thoughts, and feelings of individuals will be regulated, perhaps for despotic ends (London, 1969). The fear that advances in behavioral technology will lead to behavior control encompasses three related issues, namely, the *purpose* for which behavior is to be controlled, *who* will decide the ultimate purpose and exert control, and whether behavior control entails an abridgment of individual *freedom*.

The concerns over behavior control have become especially evident to the public for a number of reasons. As the technology of behavior change has developed, more information about its application has been disseminated to the public. Often lay books present dramatic accounts of "control" and "manipulation" of behavior that often extend the technology well beyond the current level of development and suggest practices that even conflict with how the techniques really are applied (e.g., Burgess, 1963). Another reason that concern has increased is the tendency to view all techniques that can change behavior as "behavior modification." For example, medical interventions such as psychosurgery, which are *not* part of behavior modification, occasionally have been grouped inaccurately with behavior modification techniques (Subcommittee on Constitutional Rights, 1974). Proponents of behavior modification have carefully distinguished behavior modification techniques as those based primarily upon psychological principles of behavior and social and environmental interventions, as discussed in previous chapters, rather than upon biological principles and physiological interventions (Davison & Stuart, 1975; Kazdin, 1978b; Stolz, Wienckowski, & Brown, 1975). Nevertheless, concerns about surgical interventions reflect an increased awareness of recognition of individual client rights and the ethical issues involved in all interventions.

The concerns of behavior control are neither new nor peculiar to behavior modification. In areas of science other than psychology, the ethics of behavior control also arise. For example, research in psychopharmacology has led to the use of drugs to control behavior. Drugs have had undeniable benefits in, for example, altering anxiety and depression. Yet, there is a major concern with drug abuse in society at large and its potentially deleterious consequences. Similarly, work in genetics and biochemistry has sought means to detect physiological anomalies so that at least in some cases disorders can be controlled. Yet, the prospect of genetic manipulation and eugenics has become increasingly threatening in light of recent advances. Also, biochemically controlled behavior may be evident in warfare where entire cities are immobilized and made readily amenable to military invasion. Similarly, advances in electronics and brain research suggest techniques that can ameliorate intractable pain. Yet, electrical stimulation resulting from brain implantations can influence social interaction patterns and conceivably can be used to control society (London, 1969). Most of the problems of behavior control are similar among the various technologies (e.g., behavior modification, psychopharmacology, medicine).

Control of behavior is socially institutionalized in government and law, business, education, religion, psychotherapy, and the military. Each of these institutions explicitly attempts to alter behavior and supports specific procedures to achieve its ends. Indeed, some authors have commented upon the elaborate technology which uses systems of rewards and punishment already widely in evidence in government and organized crime (London, 1969). The behavior of everyone who interacts socially is controlled in some way. Controlling agents include parents, teachers, employers, peers, spouses, siblings, and so on. These agents by design or accident provide consequences or fail to provide consequences for behavior. As discussed earlier, presenting consequences (e.g., reinforcement or punishment) or failing to present them (extinction) influence behavior. Thus, behavior is always modified whether or not a particular behavioral program is specifically designed for this purpose.

The sources of behavioral control in everyday life often do not evoke major concern because they are part of the existing social structure and are considered essential for social functioning. Perhaps another reason there is little concern with many pervasive sources of behavioral control is that there is somewhat of a balance of influences and counterinfluences on behavior. The influences exerted on people conflict. For example, cigarette smokers are enticed with advertisements of new brands of cigarettes and even receive token reinforcement (redeemable coupons) for smoking. The attempt of advertising to control behavior is obvious. However, there also are counterinfluences which discourage smoking such as warnings by the American Cancer Society. Analogously, advertisements display tempting vacation sights to entice the consumer. At the same time, banks and savings and loan associations provide incentives for investing and saving money for protracted periods. The attempts of behavior control in society are simplified here. There are not merely two opposing influences on behavior. Rather, there are diverse influences representing various positions with regard to the performance of a particular behavior. Each influence contributes to the final behavior. For example, sexual expression is influenced by biological determinants, the mass media, the clergy, parental training, and peer influences, as well as other factors. Each influence is a source of control over behavior. Yet, the relative weight of each influence is different for each individual and even for the same individual at different points in time. Thus, the influences compete and exert "pull" in different directions. The final outcome is varied across individuals and contributes to vast differences in behavior patterns. All the influences attempt to control people. Each one attempts to do so in a fairly systematic fashion. Yet, because there are conflicting sources of control, the net effect varies across individuals. The control is no less behavior control because there are variations in the final success.

Of course, it would not be quite fair to equate behavior modification with sources of control evident in everyday life. Behavior modification represents very explicit attempts to alter specific behaviors. The behaviors focused upon, the techniques, and the goals that are sought raise ethical and legal issues that may not be evident in the mundane and relatively haphazard contingencies operative in everyday life. The very term "behavior modification" may raise special concerns in the minds of people in general. Behavior modification has drawn heavily upon research from laboratory experiments often with infrahuman species. Terms such as "control," "manipulation," and even "modification" may evoke visions of "mad scientists" experimenting with human behavior (Goldiamond, 1974). Indeed, the term "behavior modification" and the way in which behavioral techniques are described often evoke negative reactions (Cole & Kazdin, 1979; Woolfolk, Woolfolk, & Wilson, 1977). The reactions in part may stem from the concerns that people have about their behavior being manipulated, perhaps against their will.

As Skinner (1974) has noted, the major issue is not whether behavior *should* be altered or "controlled." Conditions that alter and control behavior are constantly present. Rather, the major issue is whether certain techniques rather than others should be used and whether the goals to which society is committed could be more efficiently attained. For example, in classroom settings, many of the attempts of teachers to "control" student behavior are based upon corporal and verbal punishment. The issue usually is not whether child behavior should be influenced (controlled) to achieve certain goals. Teachers use all sorts of methods to achieve these goals. Yet, if the goals are to be pursued, research in behavior modification has suggested a number of alternatives to some of the aversive techniques currently in use.

Control for What Purposes and by Whom?

Behavioral technology, as any other technology, has the potential for both use and abuse. The concern of behavioral technology is not so much with the technology per se but rather with the *purposes* for which the technology is used and the person(s) who have the power to misuse the techniques.

Behavior modification techniques only specify how to attain goals (i.e., develop certain behaviors) and not what the goals or purposes should be. Setting goals for society represents value judgments for which scientific training does not prepare a professional. Indeed, philosophers have argued, without resolution, the doctrines by which societal goals should be selected. Social goals can be determined by the people themselves as expressed in their political choices. A scientist might well be able to predict where a preselected goal will lead, make recommendations to avert undesirable consequences, or investigate the actual effects of pursuing certain goals. Yet the initial selection of the goal is out of the scientist's hands.

The effective use of a behavioral technology to achieve social goals requires that these goals be clearly specified in advance. Yet agreeing upon goals in society and the implications of selecting certain courses of action is extremely difficult, to say the least. What the goals should be remains an issue which has not changed throughout history and which reduces to questions of the good life and human values. A concern that misdirected goals or purposes will be selected by society or a given leader is not raised by behavior modification. However, the problem of vague or misdirected purposes is aggravated by the potent technology. If there is no efficient means to achieve a goal, it is academic to debate the desirability of different goals. If such a means exists in a technology of social change, discussions about desirable ends become more meaningful and the hazards of selecting deleterious goals more treacherous.

In most applications of behavioral principles the issue of purpose or goal is not raised because the psychologist or psychiatrist who uses the techniques is employed in a setting where the goals have been determined in advance. Behavior modification programs in hospitals and institutions, schools, day-care treatment facilities, and prisons have established goals already endorsed by society, such as returning the individual to the community, accelerating academic performance, developing self-help, communication, and social and vocational skills, alleviating bizarre behaviors, and so on.

In outpatient therapy and counseling, the client comes to treatment with a goal, namely, to develop some adaptive skill or to alleviate a problem which interferes with effective living. The primary role of the behavior modifier is to provide a means to obtain the goal insofar as the goal is consistent with generally accepted social standards. In virtually all cases, the goals of a client are compatible with generally accepted social values. If an individual is free from some behavior which impedes his or her functioning, the community is either enhanced or is not deleteriously affected. Such functioning is consistent with the social value that, within limits, an individual should freely pursue his or her own objectives.

The scientific study and practice of behavior change is *not* value free (Krasner, 1966; Rogers & Skinner, 1956; Szasz, 1960). There is no neutral or value-free position in implementing a technology of behavior change although the technology itself may not embrace a particular value position. Endorsing an individual client's goal, the goals of a treatment institution, or the "treatment" of particular "disorders" (e.g., sexual deviance) reflects a definite stance. Leaving the selection of goals to others such as a client or institution is an attempt to hide from the issue of values but still represents a definite position as to those behaviors which are change-worthy, deviant, or socially desirable. Thus, the position to which the therapist adheres with respect to desirable and undesirable behavior represents a definite value stance (London, 1964). The values of the individual therapist do influence the course of therapy and the values of the client (Rosenthal, 1955). While values enter into the process of behavior change, specialists in science and technology are not trained to dictate the social ends for which their specialties should be used. Indeed, it is unclear what training could serve as a basis for selecting the values of others.

An issue directly related to determining the purposes for which behavioral techniques are used is *who* shall be in control of society. The issue assumes that one individual or a small number of individuals (presumably psychologists) will be in charge of society and misuse behavioral techniques. Who should control society is not an issue raised by behavior modification or advances in technology. Countries differ philosophically in conceptions of how leaders should come to power. A behavioral technology is compatible with various philosophies. Indeed, the citizenry can be completely in charge of leadership and, in this sense, exert ultimate control. A behavioral technology can help the citizenry achieve goals (e.g., ameliorate social ills and improve education) with no actual change in who "controls" society. Society can determine the goals to be achieved relying on technological advances to obtain them.

Individual Freedom

Another aspect of behavior control is the widespread concern that a behavioral technology will necessarily mean an abridgment of individual freedom. Will the deliberate control of human behavior reduce an individual's ability to make choices and freely select his or her own goals? Whether or not an individual ever is free to behave counter to existing environmental forces has been actively discussed by philosophers, scientists, and theologians (Wheeler,•1973). However, a source of agreement among those who posit or disclaim the existence of freedom is that it is exceedingly important for individuals to feel they are free independently of whether in fact they are (Kanfer & Phillips, 1970; Krasner & Ullmann, 1973). In any case, the question is whether a behavioral technology will decrease the extent to which an individual can exert control over his or her environment or to which the individual can feel free to make his or her own choices.

The fear that behavioral technology threatens to eliminate or reduce freedom and choice ignores most of the applied work in behavior modification. Applied work usually is conducted with individuals whose behaviors have been identified as problematic or ineffective in some way. The responses may include deficits or behaviors which are not under socially accepted stimulus control. Such clients ordinarily have a limited number of opportunities to obtain reinforcers in their life as a function of their deficient or "abnormal" behavior. Individuals who differ from those who normally function in society are confined by their behavioral deficit which delimits those areas of social functioning from which they might choose. An alcoholic or drug addict is not free to fulfill himself or herself in a personally desired fashion because of a single but all encompassing behavioral obstacle. An alcoholic who goes untreated is "free" only in the weakest sense of the term.

Behavior modification is used to increase an individual's skills so that the number of response alternatives or options is increased. By overcoming debilitating or delimiting behaviors which restrict opportunities, the individual is freer to select from alternatives which were not previously available (Ball, 1968). For individuals whose behavior is considered "normal," and even for those who are gifted, behavioral techniques can increase performance or develop competencies beyond those achieved with current practices. As improved levels of performance are achieved, whether or not an individual initially was deficient in some way, response opportunities and choices increase. Thus, behavior modification, as typically applied, increases rather than stifles individual freedom.

Despite the potential of behavior modification to increase a person's freedom and choice, cases exist in which individual rights have been abridged. For example, in cases where persons are confined for treatment or incarcerated, legal issues have been raised about the abridgment of constitutional rights. These issues, discussed below, point to the need to define and protect rights of individuals who may be subjected to abuses under the guise of treatment. Once the rights of individuals are defined, behavioral interventions can work within this framework.

On a larger social scale than treatment, there is little question that individual freedom can be abridged by a dictatorial ruler. Yet, the undesirable control of a ruler may not raise special questions for behavior modification. It is unclear whether a behavioral technology would enhance despotic rule. Governments already control strong reinforcers such as food, water, and money and effectively deliver aversive consequences such as imprisonment and execution. There is no counterpart that the individual has to overcome many governmental control procedures. Hence, in the case of a despotic government, the possiblity of behavior control is a problem. Yet, this is by no means a new problem or one that is raised by a behavioral technology. The fear introduced by behavior modification is that an unreasonable leader will have even more means at his or her disposal to control the people. Yet, the techniques utilized in behavior modification are weak compared with the kinds of events dictators can use to control behavior.

Sources of protection against large-scale social control exist that stem in part from the behavioral technology itself. While a behavioral technology may provide would-be controllers with special powers, it also gives individuals who are controlled greater power over their own behavior (London, 1969; Mahoney & Thoresen, 1974). Persons can use the principles derived from a behavioral technology to achieve their own goals. Thus, self-control is a partial deterrent against control by others.

In addition, the methods of control that can be used against the people can be applied for countercontrol against the controllers (Platt, 1973; Skinner,1973). It might be possible to train people to utilize the principles of behavior modification to control the behavior of the "controllers." For example, the behaviors of people in the role of controllers (e.g., legislators, therapists, and parents) might be modified by others who ordinarily are not especially effective in exerting their own goals (e.g., citizens, clients, and children). Indeed, research was illustrated earlier where children in a classroom and institutionalized retarded residents were trained to modify the behaviors of the teachers and staff (Graubard et al., 1974; Seymour & Stokes, 1976). This research suggests, at least on a small scale, that persons whose behaviors usually are controlled by others can influence the behavior of controllers.

A final defense against coercive behavior control and manipulation may be awareness of potential techniques and abuses. Individuals who are unaware of those factors that control behavior may be more easily controlled by others. Thus, people need to be informed about factors controlling their behavior and the principles upon which such control is based. Increased knowledge about the existing technology may help people identify the situations where their behavior might be controlled to achieve purposes they do not wish to endorse.

■ LEGAL ISSUES

The increased feasibility of altering behavior raises legal as well as ethical issues. Behavioral and nonbehavioral treatments alike seek to control and to modify some facets of a person's behavior. It is quite possible that the goals as well as the means used to achieve behavior change in any given instance may conflict with the rights and values of the individual or the institution and society. Recently, the courts have entered increasingly into matters related to treatment, rehabilitation, and education where an individual's rights may be infringed upon. Generally, the courts have addressed conflicts that may rise between the personal freedoms granted to an individual under the United States Constitution and the state's right to treat or restrict individual freedoms in the interests or the welfare of society. Several legal issues have arisen especially with institutionalized populations such as psychiatric patients, prisoners, and the retarded who may be involuntarily confined. Questions arise pertaining to the extent to which treatment can abridge rights normally granted outside of institutional life. The present discussion reviews a few major issues and court cases that pertain directly to the implementation of behavior modification techniques discussed in previous chapters.

Contingent Consequences and Environmental Restraint

A basic feature of behavior modification programs is the contingent delivery of reinforcing events to alter behavior. A wide variety of reinforcers often are included. For example, in token economies for psychiatric patients, delinquents, and the mentally retarded, back-up reinforcers may include such basic items as access to a room, clothes, meals, a bed or, more commonly, to facilities that surpass minimal institutional conditions in each of these areas. Other events less essential to basic subsistence may be used as well, such as engaging in recreational activities, walking on the institutional grounds, and visiting home. In most institutional programs where token economies are not in effect, these events may be provided on a noncontingent basis. In behavior modification programs, the constitutionality of withholding positive events such as those listed above has been challenged.

In a landmark decision (*Wyatt* v. *Stickney*), the court ruled on the conditions for adequate care that encompassed institutionalized psychiatric patients and mentally retarded persons. Among other things, the court's decision specified that residents are entitled to a variety of events and activities such as the right to receive a nutritionally balanced meal, to receive visitors, and to have a comfortable bed, a place for one's own clothes, and a closet or locker for personal belongings. Patients also are entitled to regular exercise, interaction with the opposite sex, and television privileges. Court rulings for other treatment populations such as delinquents have specified similar privileges as part of the basic rights (*Morales* v. *Turman*).

Decisions specifying the basic amenities to which institutionalized populations are entitled have obvious implications for behavioral programs. In many programs, particularly prior to the relevent court rulings, basic amenities had been used as *privileges* (i.e., benefits provided to individuals who earn them). The rulings make these amenities *rights* (i.e., conditions of institutional living to which all are entitled). Occasional exceptions can be made, if, for example, the patient or resident agrees to participate in a program to earn events contingently. However, the legal rulings specify the limitations within which incentive systems can operate. Reinforcement programs for involuntarily confined individuals need to provide back-up events beyond those normally provided in the setting to which individuals are entitled by right.

Court rulings that specify basic amenities to which patients are entitled are part of a broader guarantee that the environment to which a person is committed will be the *least restrictive alternative* that is necessary (Ennis & Friedman, 1973). An involuntarily confined individual is entitled to the least restrictive conditions that achieve the purposes of confinement so that the interests of the public (confining someone of potential danger) and the individual (personal liberty) are balanced. Thus, hospitalizing individuals who might function adequately without such confinement can be challenged because institutionalization may be more restrictive than is necessary.

The least-restrictive-conditions doctrine specified by the courts requires an institution to justify its actions with respect to care given a patient. The restrictions placed on a patient must be shown to be necessary. In many programs, deprivation of access to the hospital grounds or restrictions on patient movement on the ward may serve as a basis for providing reinforcing back-up events. Many aspects of reinforcement programs may be restrictive because individuals may have limited access to various privileges and activities. Indeed, operating under a set of contingencies may in some sense be restrictive and in need of justification. Behavior modification programs need to justify explicitly whether any restrictive conditions placed upon institutionalized populations in fact are necessary or promise benefits that might warrant temporary deprivation of rights. (The issue of deprivation is discussed later.)

Use of Aversive Techniques

Behavior modification tends to rely much more heavily on positive reinforcement than on negative reinforcement and punishment. Yet, techniques involving aversive stimuli have been used for a variety of populations and have come under judicial review. Actually, the courts have a long history of evaluating punishment before the development of behavior modification, because physical restraint, corporal punishment, and inhumane conditions often have been used under the guise of treatment or rehabilitation. The courts seek to protect individuals from "cruel and unusual" punishments, as specified by the Constitution.

Many of the rulings do not apply to the procedures used in behavior modification because more dramatic and intrusive forms of punishment such as chaining individuals or beating them are not part of the behavioral techniques. Judicial rulings of punishment procedures that may be a part of behavior modification are important to consider. Decisions reached about punishment, of course, depend heavily upon the specific procedures that are used. Obviously, considerations governing a few minutes of isolation (one form of time out) differ from those governing very long isolation or electric shock. Indeed, the courts have ruled that extended periods of isolation are not permissible and that during brief periods of seclusion the clients must have adequate access to food, lighting, and sanitation facilities (*Hancock v. Avery*). The courts also have specified that brief periods of isolation are allowed only for severe target behaviors such as those leading to physical harm or to destruction of property and only when the procedures are closely supervised by professional staff (*Morales v. Turman*; *Wyatt v. Stickney*). Yet, in some rulings, the courts have ruled out isolation as a technique (*New York State Association for Retarded Children v. Rockefeller*). Clear and consistent guidelines are not yet available for the use of time out and isolation. The implications of rulings, as they continue to be made, may only affect time out from reinforcement when that consists of isolation. As noted in the chapter on punishment, a variety of alternative time-out procedures are available that do not involve isolation and are less restrictive to the client.

Electric shock as a punishing event is used infrequently. With such a severe form of punishment, the courts have delineated rather clear restrictions for its use. For example, in the *Wyatt v. Stickney* decision, shock was restricted to extraordinary circumstances such as when a client is engaging in self-destructive behavior that is likely to inflict physical damage. Moreover, shock should only be applied when another procedure had been used unsuccessfully, when a committee on human rights within the institution approved of the treatment, and when the client or a close relative provided consent.

The courts have not addressed many forms of punishment that currently are used in behavior modification. For example, overcorrection, positive practice, and response cost, relatively commonly used techniques, have not been ruled upon. Indeed, these procedures may be relatively mild forms of punishment considering the types of aversive interventions that have come before the courts. In general, a major obstacle in using aversive techniques can be resolved by obtaining informed consent from the client or a guardian or relative, if the client is not able to provide consent.

Informed Consent

Some of the problems raised in implementing programs with involuntarily confined clients can be alleviated if clients provide their consent about receiving treatment. For example, the client can agree to waive rights of access to various aspects of hospital life (e.g., taking walks on the grounds) as part of a reinforcement program in order to achieve some therapeutic goal. Essentially, the client can consent to the restrictions imposed by the intervention. Obtaining informed consent would seem to resolve many of the legal problems about infringements of client rights. In fact, there are many ambiguities about informed consent and the precise role it can occupy in treatment of involuntarily confined populations (Kassirer, 1974; Wexler, 1975a).

Consent includes at least three elements, namely, competence, knowledge, and volition (Friedman, 1975; Martin, 1975; Wexler, 1975a). Competence refers to the individual's ability to make a well reasoned decision, to understand the nature of the choice presented, and to give consent meaningfully. There is some question whether many individuals exposed to treatment programs (e.g., some psychiatric patients, children, and retardates) have the capacity to provide truly informed consent. In these cases, of course, parents or guardians can provide consent.

Even in cases where client consent is sought and obtained, it is unclear whether this provides an adequate means of client protection. This was illustrated in a study of the adequacy of informed consent which queried patients in a psychiatric hospital (Palmer & Wohl, 1972). Sixty percent of the patients who were asked about their status were unable to recall signing the admission form within 10 days after admission. Thirty-three percent of the patients did not recall the content of the form or could only inaccurately recall the contents. Some of the patients even denied having signed the form! These results call into question either the competence of the patients to give consent or the procedures employed to secure it.

The second element of consent is knowledge, which includes understanding the nature of treatment, the alternatives available, and the potential benefits and risks involved. It is difficult, if not impossible, to provide complete information to meet the requirements for a knowledgeable decision given that so little is known about many of the available treatments. An extremely important feature of consent is that the individual is aware that he or she does not have to give consent and that once given, consent can be revoked.

The third element of consent is *volition*. The client must agree to participate in treatment. Agreement to participate must not be given under duress. Thus, giving a patient a "choice" between undergoing a particular treatment or suffering some sort of deprivation if he or she does not choose treatment is not an adequate base from which consent can be provided. It is difficult to ensure that individuals involuntarily confined to an institutional setting can provide consent to participate in a program without some duress. In prisons and psychiatric hospitals, inmates may feel compelled to participate in a program because of anticipated long-term gains from favorable evaluation by staff and administration whose opinions play an important role in release.

The issue of consent raises a host of problems for treatment in general and for reinforcement practices in particular. Even if the client initially gives consent for a particular treatment, it appears that he or she may be allowed to withdraw consent at will (*Knecht* v. *Gillman*). For example, in a token economy, a hospitalized patient may waive the right for various events such as meals, adequate sleeping quarters, and ground privileges. With the patient's consent these may be delivered contingently. Yet, if the patient does not earn sufficient tokens to purchase the events which he consented to waive as rights, he may withdraw consent and terminate the program. Withdrawing consent may be easier than performing the token earning behaviors that would allow purchase of the back-up events (Wexler, 1975b). From the standpoint of implementing effective programs, obtaining consent does not guarantee that the contingencies could be adequately applied given that consent can be revoked. Reinforcement programs for institutionalized populations will have to rely heavily on highly attractive incentives that do not require consent of the client.

■ PROTECTION OF CLIENT RIGHTS

Because of the many ethical and legal issues that arise in any form of treatment, particularly for clients who are involuntarily confined, a number of safeguards have been suggested to protect client rights. Many different safeguards have been proposed including international codes and national guidelines to cover clinically relevant research (see Kazdin, 1978b). In addition, organizations for professionals involved in

ETHICAL ISSUES FOR HUMAN SERVICES

The questions related to each issue have deliberately been cast in a general manner that applies to all types of interventions, and not solely or specifically to the practice of behavior therapy. Issues directed specifically to behavior therapists might imply erroneously that behavior therapy was in some way more in need of ethical concern than non-behaviorally-oriented therapies.

In the list of issues, the term "client" is used to describe the person whose behavior is to be changed, "therapist" is used to describe the professional in charge of the intervention; "treatment" and "problem," although used in the singular, refer to any and all treatments and problems being formulated with this checklist. The issues are formulated so as to be relevant across as many settings and populations as possible. Thus, they need to be qualified when someone other than the person whose behavior is to be changed is paying the therapist, or when that person's competence or the voluntary nature of that person's consent is questioned. For example, if the therapist has found that the client does not understand the goals or methods being considered, the therapist should substitute the client's guardian or other responsible person for "client," when reviewing the issues below.

A. **Have the goals of treatment been adequately considered?**
   1. To insure that the goals are explicit, are they written?
   2. Has the client's understanding of the goals been assured by having the client restate them orally or in writing?
   3. Have the therapist and client agreed on the goals of therapy?
   4. Will serving the client's interests be contrary to the interests of other persons?
   5. Will serving the client's immediate interests be contrary to the client's long-term interest?

B. **Has the choice of treatment methods been adequately considered?**
   1. Does the published literature show the procedure to be the best one available for that problem?
   2. If no literature exists regarding the treatment method, is the method consistent with generally accepted practice?
   3. Has the client been told of alternative procedures that might be preferred by the client on the basis of significant differences in discomfort, treatment time, cost, or degree of demonstrated effectiveness?
   4. If a treatment procedure is publicly, legally, or professionally controversial, has formal professional consultation been obtained, has the reaction of the affected segment of the public been adequately considered, and have the alternative treatment methods been more closely reexamined and reconsidered?

FIGURE 12–1 Ethical Issues for Human Services.

Source: Association for Advancement of Behavior Therapy. Ethical issues for human services. *Behavior Therapy*, 1977, **8**, v–vi.

clinical and behavioral research in general have provided guidelines. Although the range of regulations, codes, and guidelines are too extensive to review here, a few of the sources of protection warrant mention.

One set of guidelines that has been offered raises a number of questions that therapists (or staff who design and implement the program) should adequately address prior to implementing therapy. The questions, which appear in Figure 12–1, raise a number of issues to ensure that the procedures are appropriate and that the client (or guardian) is fully aware of the intervention. The questions address some of the con-

FIGURE 12–1 (*Continued*)

C. **Is the client's participation voluntary?**
   1. Have possible sources of coercion on the client's participation been considered?
   2. If treatment is legally mandated, has the available range of treatments and therapists been offered?
   3. Can the client withdraw from treatment without a penalty or financial loss that exceeds actual clinical costs?
D. **When another person or an agency is empowered to arrange for therapy, have the interests of the subordinated client been sufficiently considered?**
   1. Has the subordinated client been informed of the treatment objectives and participated in the choice of treatment procedures?
   2. Where the subordinated client's competence to decide is limited, have the client as well as the guardian participated in the treatment discussions to the extent that the client's abilities permit?
   3. If the interests of the subordinated person and the superordinate persons or agency conflict, have attempts been made to reduce the conflict by dealing with both interests?
E. **Has the adequacy of treatment been evaluated?**
   1. Have quantitative measures of the problem and its progress been obtained?
   2. Have the measures of the problem and its progress been made available to the client during treatment?
F. **Has the confidentiality of the treatment relationship been protected?**
   1. Has the client been told who has access to the records?
   2. Are records available only to authorized persons?
G. **Does the therapist refer the clients to other therapists when necessary?**
   1. If treatment is unsuccessful, is the client referred to other therapists?
   2. Has the client been told that if dissatisfied with the treatment, referral will be made?
H. **Is the therapist qualified to provide treatment?**
   1. Has the therapist had training or experience in treating problems like the client's?
   2. If deficits exist in the therapist's qualifications, has the client been informed?
   3. If the therapist is not adequately qualified, is the client referred to other therapists, or has supervision by a qualified therapist been provided? Is the client informed of the supervisory relation?
   4. If the treatment is administered by mediators, have the mediators been adequately supervised by a qualified therapist?

cerns raised in the discussion of legal issues such as informed consent. It should be noted that these guidelines are *not* directed specifically toward behavior modification procedures because behavior-change procedures in general, whether behavioral or not, raise similar ethical issues. The questions are suggested to guide those who implement any form of psychological treatment.

A variety of other sources of protection have been suggested. A well known proposal was developed in Florida in response to a program that engaged in several abuses in a token economy for mentally retarded, delinquent, and disturbed boys. The abuses, many of which were inappropriately viewed as behavior modification, included severe physical punishment, forced sexual acts, and deprivation, all in the form of several specific consequences for undesirable behavior.

The abuses led to formation of a Task Force to develop guidelines based upon psychological and legal principles against which programs subsequently could be evaluated (May, Risley, Twardosz, Friedman, Bijou, & Wexler, 1976). The guidelines included recommendations that emphasized the need for informed consent and the least-restrictive-treatment doctrine. Perhaps the most unique feature was setting guidelines for selecting and approving of various treatment methods.

Basically, a three-level schema was devised based upon the treatment procedures that would be considered for the client and the behaviors that were to be changed. Treatments at the *first* level would be relatively routine techniques applied to behaviors that raise no special controversy. For example, positive reinforcement using praise, feedback, and other events that do not threaten the rights of the clients to alter such behaviors as self-help skills or self-stimulation might be included in this first level. The procedures and behaviors at this level are standard, conventional, widely practiced, and do not seem to pose a serious threat to the client.

At the *second* level, procedures that are more controversial might be considered for the client. These procedures would only be justified if procedures in the first level did not produce change and include such mildly aversive techniques as time out or response cost. The behaviors to which these techniques would be applied would be conventional treatment aimed at the behaviors included in the previous level.

The *third* and final level includes behaviors and techniques that may be controversial. Behaviors focused upon might include patterns of sexual deviance where the direction of behavior change or whether change should be sought at all can be questioned. The procedures at this level would consist of last-resort interventions such as electric shock or drugs. Because of the severity of the techniques, the possibility of their abuse, and the nature of the behaviors altered, the Florida guidelines recommended that committees closely review treatment applications falling into the third level. The committee would help ensure that the client's rights are fully taken into account. To this end, a review committee should include legal counsel, a behavioral scientist, a lay person, and others who would represent different interests on the part of the client.

A final means of protecting clients against the potential abuses of treatment to be discussed here involves developing a contractual arrangement between the therapist and client (Schwitzgebel, 1975; Stuart, 1977). A contract can make explicit the goals of treatment, the procedures that will be used, as well as the risks and benefits that are likely to result. A useful feature of a contract is that the client and his or her guardians can negotiate the final goals of treatment. Active participation in the design of treatment in addition to other sources of protection such as informed consent are likely to make treatment more fair than is a treatment imposed on the client without any input on his or her part.

An excellent example of the contractual arrangement in practice was reported by Ayllon and Skuban (1973) who treated an 8-year-old boy who engaged in tantrums and did not comply with instructions. Treatment consisted of the therapist taking the client to a variety of settings in everyday life such as a zoo, parks, swimming pool, and shopping centers where he could receive token reinforcement (money) for compliance with requests. The purpose was to train the child to comply without engaging in tantrums or screaming, his usual responses to requests for him to do something.

A contract was devised similar to a contingency contract. The contract specified the overall goal of treatment, namely to reduce or eliminate tantrums. In fact, specific criteria to assess the effectiveness of treatment were included in the contract (e.g., compliance with at least 80–100 percent of the requests given by adults in a test session at the end of treatment). Also, the duration of treatment, the number of sessions per week, and the fees by the therapist were all specified in the contract so the most aspects of treatment that are usually unmentioned were included into the treatment program.

The contractual arrangement mentioned above is only one of the possible methods for protecting client rights. The advantage of the contract is the explicitness with which the conditions, goals, and procedures can be spelled out. At present, relatively little use has been made of the contractual model for using behavioral or other forms of treatment.

■ GUIDELINES FOR AVERSIVE TECHNIQUES

Guidelines designed to protect client rights encompass a variety of treatment procedures based upon behavioral and nonbehavioral treatments. In addition to guidelines that apply to treatment in general, it may be useful to consider practical issues that might guide the use of controversial techniques within behavior modification. Among the available techniques, the use of aversive methods within behavior modification is likely to be of greatest concern to the public.

The concern over the use of aversive techniques in behavior modification revolves around two techniques, namely, the use of painful stimuli and deprivation. Prior to discussing these controversial techniques, it is important to reiterate that behavior modification deemphasizes the use of aversive techniques in applied settings. Most of the reasons for this deemphasis were presented in the discussion of punishment and negative reinforcement. Potential side effects and the ineffectiveness of mildly aversive events when not combined with positive reinforcement militate against the widespread application of punishment. The ethical concerns and emotional social reactions associated with aversive stimuli also have limited the use of punishment. Positive reinforcement and not aversive techniques constitutes the major application of behavior modification. Nevertheless, the use of aversive events evokes concern and requires serious consideration of a number of issues.

Painful Stimuli. The concern with aversive techniques in behavior modification is raised when painful stimuli are used. Among studies using aversive techniques, painful stimuli are rarely employed. Yet the attention painful stimuli receive is so great, it is worth elaborating the rationale behind their use.

Initially, it is important to distinguish types of aversive techniques of behavior modification. Aversive events are not necessarily painful or demeaning. They do not require a violation of rights or deprivation of essential human needs. Many events which serve as punishing stimuli are not at all painful, such as withdrawing slips of paper with a child's name on it (Hall et al., 1971), taking brief pauses during a meal (Barton et al., 1970), pausing while listening to music (Barrett, 1962), hearing one's voice played back immediately after speaking (Goldiamond, 1965), and numerous others reviewed earlier. As noted earlier, in some behavior therapy techniques, the aversive events (e.g., nausea) are *imagined* so that nothing is actually done to the client. Thus, the objection to aversive techniques rarely acknowledges that the majority of aversive events employed are not painful.

Painful aversive stimuli sometimes appear to be useful when the behavior to be changed is already under control of strong positive reinforcers. For example, sexual deviance, drug addiction, and alcohol consumption frequently are treated with aversive events such as shock or nausea-inducing drugs (Hallam & Rachman, 1976). Aversive techniques in these contexts attempt to accomplish two related goals. First, an attempt is made to change the valence of a highly desirable stimulus (e.g., alcohol), through classical conditioning. A painful or intense aversive stimulus which elicits an anxiety and escape reflex sometimes is required. A strong aversive event is needed so that a reflex reaction is elicited. Eventually, by repeatedly pairing the desirable stimulus (e.g., alcohol) with the strong aversive event (e.g., shock), the escape reaction is elicited in the presence of the previously desirable stimulus alone. Thus, the previously desirable stimulus loses its attraction because of its association with an aversive event.

A second goal in treating behaviors which are maintained by strong positive reinforcers is to suppress approach responses to obtain the desired stimulus. A painful stimulus is needed to overcome the highly reinforcing properties of the attractive stimulus. Obviously, fining an individual ten cents for engaging in a sexually deviant behavior is not likely to be effective. A response maintained by a powerful reinforcer is less easily suppressed than one maintained by a weak reinforcer. The aversive event may need to be commensurate with the attraction of the positive reinforcer to suppress behavior. Thus, in cases where maladaptive behavior is maintained by strong reinforcers, strong and sometimes painful aversive events are used.

Painful stimuli, such as shock, have been used in a number of outpatient cases (Hallam & Rachman, 1976). However, ethical concerns have not been strongly voiced for outpatient applications of aversive techniques. The client who seeks outpatient treatment gives his or her consent for the use of such procedures and usually may leave treatment at any time.

Deprivation.   One aversive technique which evokes strong emotional responses is the use of deprivation. The main thrust of the objection is directed toward deprivation of primary reinforcers which are essential for human existence including food, water, shelter, and human contact. The argument against depriving an individual is that this is a violation of basic human rights and dignity. Aside from the deprivation of primary reinforcers, secondary reinforcers such as activities, privileges, and attention may also be withheld. If the objection to deprivation includes these secondary reinforcers, it has much wider application because an exceedingly small number of programs withhold food and shelter.

Deprivation, in a variety of forms, plays a major role in ordinary social existence. For example, normal social living requires deprivation in areas such as sexual expression and free speech. Moreover, different social groups (e.g., minorities) undergo diverse types of deprivation. Individuals who experience poverty are deprived of essential materials such as food and shelter. Finally, certain social institutions which actually serve or operate under the guise of treatment and rehabilitation (e.g., psychiatric hospitals and prisons), by their very design, deprive individuals of rights and privileges. The conditions which "justify" or require deprivation normally imposed in society are ambiguous at best, even without the advent of behavior modification in treatment settings.

In behavior modification programs the alternatives are rarely as simple as deciding whether or not to deprive the client of something. The majority of individuals for whom behavior modification techniques are used are deprived in some significant way by virtue of their failure to perform certain behaviors. Institutionalized clients are deprived of "normal" community living, friends, and freedom to choose where and how they would like to live. Students in educational settings who are having academic difficulties may at some point be deprived of access to employment, additional academic work, and economic opportunities as a function of their behavior. Delinquents are deprived of some desirable features of social living because of their antisocial acts.

For individuals who are functioning normally in society, a lack of specific behaviors or the presence of mildly debilitating problems also constitute a deprivation of some kind. For example, an individual may decry his or her "shyness" because of the deprivation of social experiences with which these may be associated. Children and adults with debilitating, albeit circumscribed, problems are deprived of moving about in life freely because of some behavior which presents obstacles.

The social deprivation that individuals normally experience as a function of their behavioral problems or deficits has to be weighed against any other deprivation temporarily resulting from treatment. The issue of deprivation versus no deprivation would be relatively easy to decide. Yet, weighing the relative disadvantages of different types of deprivation and the duration of each type makes the issue more complex (Baer, 1970).

■ CONSIDERATIONS FOR JUSTIFYING USE OF PAINFUL STIMULI OR DEPRIVATION

The decision to use painful stimuli, deprivation, or any other controversial technique requires consideration of at least four issues: the kind of painful stimuli or deprivation, the duration of the program, availability of alternative treatment strategies, and demonstrable benefits resulting from their use. These issues determine, in part, whether use of the aversive technique might be justified.

Kind of Painful Stimuli or Deprivation. Certainly, the aversiveness of the stimulus or deprivation has to be carefully weighed. Cruel or unusual events should not be employed for behavior change nor could their use be readily justified. When painful events such as shock are used, the stimuli are not immobilizing, usually have no after-effects, and are not permanently damaging (Tanner, 1973). For example, the pain associated with shock typically is described as resembling an injection, a sting, or feeling as if an unanesthetized tooth were being drilled (Lovaas & Simmons, 1969; Miron, 1968). In some cases, such as outpatient treatment with alcoholics, the "painful" or rather uncomfortable aversive event is drug-induced nausea. Thus, it should be readily apparent that those relatively infrequent uses of painful stimuli bear no resemblance to torture, misery, and agony.

When deprivation is used, it is usually deprivation of secondary reinforcers such as activities or privileges rather than primary reinforcers. Indeed, according to legal restrictions, various populations must be assured several amenities of everyday life. Many programs currently provide previously unavailable reinforcers (e.g., special activities such as fishing trips, dances) or increase the availability of reinforcers already available in the setting (e.g., extra time off the ward or in the community). Programs employing this approach avoid deprivation, as usually conceived. Nevertheless, an objection sometimes voiced is that extra privileges or activities which are introduced as reinforcers should be given to all individuals noncontingently to improve their existence. If the events are not provided, the clients may be deprived of the most desirable conditions that treatment settings could provide. Yet, if the goal of a program or treatment facility is therapeutic behavior change, the noncontingent delivery of all available reinforcers is not likely to advance this goal.

There are infrequent exceptions which report deprivation of basic needs. As mentioned earlier, in one program hospitalized patients were told they would not receive food unless they worked (Cotter, 1967). This kind of deprivation represents a misuse of behavior modification for a variety of reasons. Food was withdrawn without making any provisions for a client's basic needs or ensuring that less drastic procedures would achieve the same end.

Even when primary reinforcers such as food are used, an individual should not be completely deprived. For example, in a reinforcement program the clients may not respond to candy, tokens, praise, or activities. Deprivation may be used to increase the reinforcing value of food. Yet the deprivation can be mild such as temporarily reducing or eliminating dessert after a meal rather than omitting the meal itself. As mentioned earlier, small meals are sometimes used so that the client never is satiated and food will be reinforcing over a long period throughout the day (O'Brien et al., 1972). In programs where deprivation of complete meals is used as a last resort, patients are normally given a concentrated nutritive substance daily or are placed on a special diet to ensure that their survival is not in jeopardy. Even so, deprivation of meals certainly is objectionable and probably does not meet some other conditions (see below) which might justify the use of controversial techniques. In the actual practice of behavior modification in applied settings, the kind of aversive events employed, in part, dictates whether the program is justified. Of course, other conditions which might justify the use of aversive techniques are important to consider.

Duration of the Program. An important consideration in justifying the use of painful stimuli or deprivation is the duration of the program. The program should have reasonably well specified limits as to how long it can be in effect and the conditions which will lead to its termination or continuation. Most individuals in treatment facilities already undergo aversive conditions which stem directly from their behavioral deficits or socially censured responses. For example, retarded children are deprived of possibilities for a variety of reinforcers thoughout their lives. To invoke further hardship such as subjecting them to any aversive event or further deprivation as part of a behavior modification program must be for a limited time only. Otherwise adverse conditions of the program are merely superimposed upon social deprivation that is constantly experienced. It might be better not to intervene unless the aversive consequences are scheduled for a relatively short period and promise to result in improved conditions.

The duration of the aversive techniques used as part of the program needs to be weighed against the aversive conditions resulting from the client's deficits or aberrant behaviors. Since punishment usually shows rapid effects, aversive consequences can be withdrawn in a relatively short period. For example, the elimination of self-injurious behavior in autistic and retarded children may take only a few sessions. In many cases, self-destructive behavior has been ongoing for years. Thus, the duration of the program is exceedingly short relative to the length of time that self-imposed aversive conditions have been in effect. Independent of the history of the client's behavior, the duration of any punishment program should be limited. If the effects of punishment are not immediate, the program should be altered or discontinued whether or not painful stimuli or deprivation are employed.

Availability of Alternative Treatment Strategies. Perhaps the most important single consideration in selecting painful stimuli or deprivation is the lack of availability of other techniques to change behavior for a given individual. Generally, programs attempt to alter behavior using only reinforcement or reinforcement with a relatively limited amount of punishment. When positive reinforcement is used, mildly aversive events or nonpainful aversive consequences (e.g., time out or fines) usually are effective in suppressing behavior. If these approaches fail, there may be some justification for turning to painful stimuli or deprivation. For example, in one case, shock was used to suppress chronic sneezing of a female high school student. Shock was used only after numerous other procedures (e.g., psychotherapy, hypnosis, hospitalization, medication) had been unsuccessful (Kushner, 1968). However, in most programs procedures which are less objectionable than painful stimuli and deprivation are readily available.

Somtimes other techniques are available but they are inefficient or have undesirable consequences. For example, withholding attention from individuals who perform self-destructive behavior effectively reduces the rate of such behavior (Lovaas & Simmons, 1969). Yet, as the slow process of extinction unfolds, there is danger that the individual will mutilate himself. Electric shock, when used briefly, can eliminate the behavior quickly. Institutions ordinarily may use physical restraint (e.g., straitjackets or tying residents to benches) to reduce self-destructive behavior or aggressive tantrums. Indeed, restraint may be continued for a period of months or even years (Lovaas et al., 1965; Miron, 1968). Brief punishment is seen as an alternative to a life of physical restraint. (This is an interesting example because physical restraint, which deprives an individual of interaction with the physical and social environment, can be obviated by briefly using painful stimuli to eliminate the behavior that led to restraint.)

Programs considering aversive techniques, particularly the use of painful stimuli or deprivation, need as one basis of justification some assurance that less objectionable techniques do not work. At least some attempt is needed to determine whether a reinforcement program using a variety of different reinforcers is sufficient to change behavior. Since the evidence is vast that reinforcement techniques will work across a variety of settings and treatment populations (Kazdin 1977e), only the unambiguous lack of their efficacy might justify relying on aversive events. Even when a reinforcement program has not altered client behavior sufficiently, a number of techniques are available to increase the effect of reinforcement rather than turning to aversive events. Using aversive techniques such as shock or deprivation, without trying other procedures first, including mildly aversive events, is ethically objectionable.

Demonstrable Benefits of Aversive Techniques.   A final consideration in determining whether the use of painful stimuli or deprivation is justified is whether there are clear benefits which result. Unfortunately, this is not the criterion for use of painful stimuli or deprivation in society. Deprivation and pain are inherent in many social institutions which are not clearly justified by their efficacy in changing behavior. For example, criminals are obviously deprived of individual rights when incarcerated. A rationale for this procedure is to protect society. Yet, such deprivation does not always appear to be in the best interest of the criminals (i.e., increase their subsequent noncriminal behavior) or society (i.e., prevent or reduce further crimes). Indeed, it is likely that the overall frequency of crimes is augmented by the "training" one receives while in prison. If there are favorable effects resulting from deprivation and pain to which criminals are exposed, they are not clear and rarely carefully demonstrated.

Similarly, psychiatric patients represent a group for whom social deprivation has dubious demonstrable effects. Supposedly, individuals are hospitalized to protect them from endangering others or themselves. Unfortunately, rarely is there evidence that individuals are hospitalized because they present an actual danger (Scheff, 1966). Hospitalized patients are deprived of a variety of rights, varying across states and countries, which include the right to vote, to obtain a marriage or driver's license, to convey property, and to procreate children. Social deprivation might be justified, if clear beneficial effects are derived from its use. However, the benefits derived from hospitalization both for the patient himself and society have been seriously questioned. Indeed, evidence suggests that the patient becomes more bizarre and withdrawn after hospitalization (e.g., Wing, 1962).

The justification for deprivation in behavior modification depends upon producing a demonstrable change in behavior, in addition to the other conditions discussed above. If behavior does not change or show a trend in the direction of change, continuation of deprivation, and indeed of *any* program, is not justified. The experimental stance of evaluating effectiveness of the techniques is particularly important when those techniques are a source of ethical concern.

Use of Aversive Techniques: Summary.   The four considerations for using controversial aversive techniques to change behavior represent minimum requirements. They provide guidelines rather than definitive ethical imperatives. Yet it is not readily conceivable that a program would fail to meet these minimal requirements and still be justified. There are basic rights to which all individuals should be entitled. Certainly one of these rights is to not be deprived of those events which are required for existence. It is unclear precisely under what conditions deprivation of those things not essential to life would be justified. As mentioned earlier, social institutions invoke deprivation such as prison confinement. Yet the ethics of deprivation in society are not explicit. What is socially approved as suitable for "punishment" is not approved under the guise of "treatment."

Probably the ethically least undesirable use of deprivation of any kind is part of a self-control regimen or contingency contract system where the client selects the deprivation (e.g., of a privilege) as an appropriate means to achieve a self-selected or agreed upon outcome. In many cases in society, individuals voluntarily submit to aversive events to eradicate discomfort or portending problems such as when one attends a dentist to repair a tooth or a surgeon to perform an operation (Tanner, 1973). In these instances, as with outpatient treatment in aversion therapy, the individual consents to undergo some aversive condition to achieve a beneficial (self-selected) gain. Providing consent helps reduce but does not eliminate the problems of using aversive conditions because of the difficulties of obtaining truly informed consent.

■ SUMMARY AND CONCLUSION

Implementation of behavior-change techniques raises a variety of ethical and legal issues. These issues are not necessarily unique to behavior modification. However, advances in the technology of behavior change and increased public awareness in general of individual rights make salient the need to consider the means and ends of treatment. Ethical issues often raised in considering a technology of behavior change consist of who will be in the position to control behavior, the purposes for which behavioral control techniques will be used, and whether individual freedom will be abridged in the process. Recent developments in behavior modification do not necessarily increase the threats that exist to one's freedom. Indeed, a case can be made for the increased opportunities for individual choice and freedom because of the possibilities for self-control that behavioral techniques provide.

Several legal issues have arisen in the context of treatment, many of which are directly relevant to behavior modification. The courts have provided clear guidelines that restrict the use of certain sorts of reinforcers for institutionalized treatment populations. Also, some of the aversive procedures that might be used or abused (e.g., prolonged seclusion and electric shock) have been examined by the courts. The conditions under which such procedures might be used have been limited. Understandably, the courts have been concerned primarily with aversive techniques that are most amenable to abuse. Techniques most commonly used in behavior modification have not received attention.

Many of the legal questions can be partially resolved if clients can provide their informed consent. For many institutionalized populations and in many of the settings in which they are confined, whether the conditions of truly informed consent are met is a major issue.

The increased concern over ethical and legal issues has been associated with a variety of recommendations designed to protect individual rights. Codes, guidelines, and specific procedures have been recommended to increase the input of the client and to ensure that the least intrusive treatments are used. In general, examination of treatments and their effects by the courts and review committees who oversee treatment plans for institutionalized clients might make treatment increasingly more accountable. Historically, psychological and behavioral treatments have received relatively little legal and public scrutiny. Closer scrutiny is to be actively encouraged to develop techniques that at once are effective, consistent with the goals of treatment, and acceptable to potential clients.

■ NOTE

[1] The ethical and legal issues raised by behavior modification can only be highlighted here. Several other sources are available that provide extended discussions of the issues (Budd & Baer, 1976; Friedman, 1975; Krapfl & Vargas, 1977; Wexler, 1975b).

Contemporary Issues and Future Directions

Behavioral techniques have been applied to a large variety of settings and treatment populations. No doubt work will continue to develop in clinical, educational, and rehabilitation settings. It is always difficult to predict future directions the field will take. However, two areas of contemporary work seem especially important as possible guides to future emphases. First, behavior modification techniques are increasingly applied to diverse areas of behavior change. The techniques have moved beyond the usual problems included in clinical practice in such areas as clinical psychology, psychiatry, education, and "mental-health" related fields. Second, behavior modification techniques are becoming more responsive to the social context in which treatment must be implemented. If behavioral techniques are to be utilized, they must begin to take into account the interests of people in everyday life who are responsible for identifying problem behaviors and who ultimately determine whether treatment has been successful. The opinions of people in everyday life are relied upon increasingly to help determine the behaviors that are developed in treatment, to evaluate whether treatment techniques are acceptable to those who use them, and to assess whether the gains in treatment really make a difference in the client's everyday life. The present chapter reviews major areas that illustrate the extension of behavioral techniques and the social issues raised in implementing and evaluating treatment.

■ EXTENSIONS OF BEHAVIORAL TECHNIQUES

Behavioral techniques based upon operant conditioning have been extended to a variety of clients and behaviors that traditionally have been regarded as abnormal, deviant, or deficient. Most programs have been conducted in institutions and hospitals, school classrooms, facilities for delinquents, and in the homes of children who are considered to have "problems." In general, behavioral techniques have been applied most extensively to persons whose behavior traditionally would be included in the domain of "mental health."

The success of behavioral techniques in altering a variety of behaviors within traditional domains of treatment and education has led to their extension to several other areas. And, new disciplines and areas of research have emerged, as illustrated below. It is important to sample some of the innovative lines of application in current use not only to provide a perspective of the range of applications but to point to areas where further work is likely to accelerate in the future. Major areas of innovative applications can only be sampled here because of the range of areas that are being explored and developed.

Socially and Environmentally Relevant Problems

Behavioral techniques have been extended to a variety of behaviors that can be distinguished by their special relevance to contemporary social concerns. Applications have extended to such problems as energy conservation, littering, recycling, employment, job performance, community self-government, and racial integration (see Kazdin, 1977c; Nietzel, Winett, MacDonald, & Davidson, 1977).

Energy Conservation. Consumption of electricity, gasoline, and home heating oil and gas obviously is a current concern with major implications pertaining to the economy and personal life styles. The limited energy resources provided from useable fossil fuel and the increased demand for energy have created worldwide concern. Several investigations have examined whether behavioral techniques can be used to curb energy consumption.

For example, Seaver and Patterson (1976) studied 180 homes randomly drawn from rural communities in a four-month project designed to reduce fuel-oil consumption in the home. Homes were assigned randomly to one of three conditions: feedback, feedback plus social commendations, and no treatment. In the feedback condition, households received information at the time of fuel delivery about the amount of consumed fuel relative to the same period in the previous year and the dollars saved or lost. In the feedback plus commendation condition, households received the above feedback plus social recognition (in the form of a decal saying "We are saving oil.") if they reduced their fuel consumption. The feedback plus commendation homes used significantly less fuel than did the other homes. Feedback alone and no-treatment control groups were not different from each other.

Many other studies have shown that feedback and monetary reinforcement can be effective in reducing home energy consumption (see Kazdin, 1977c). Behavioral applications can be implemented because home fuel consumption often can be readily monitored by meter readings and by records of utility companies. Thus, energy use can be monitored by consumers as well as by agents who could provide incentives for performance.

A major source of fuel consumption is the use of automobile gasoline. A few applications have suggested that behavior modification techniques can curb use of the automobile. For example, Foxx and Hake (1977) reduced the driving of college students who volunteered to participate in the project. Subjects in the behavioral group received monetary rewards (e.g., $5 or $10) plus special events (e.g., free oil change, refund for the cost of their parking permit) based upon the extent of their mileage reduction at the end of four weeks. Students in the behavioral group were compared with others assigned to the control condition that did not receive the incentive system. The effects of contingent consequences for reduced driving were dramatic, as illustrated in Figure 13–1. Subjects in the experimental group were slightly higher than control subjects in the mileage driven in baseline (before treatment) but were markedly lower in the reinforcement phase. In a return to baseline phase, the effects of the incentive system were not maintained. However, the initial demonstration suggests that relatively simple techniques might have promise in reducing driving, and hence gas consumption.

Other energy conservation research has attempted to decrease the use of automobile fuel by encouraging people to use mass transit. The use of mass transit not only conserves fuel but also can reduce the amount of pollutants in the air. In a demonstration project, Everett, Hayward, and Meyers (1974) used token reinforcement (tickets worth from 5¢ to 10¢ that could be exchanged for items available at local stores in the community to increase bus riding). On a university campus, students who rode the bus received tokens during the reinforcement phase. Bus ridership increased when the contingency was in effect and returned to baseline levels when the contingency was withdrawn.

Littering. Littering in public places is a matter of great concern not only because it is unsightly but also because of the tremendous expense of removing it. Estimates suggest that millions of dollars are required to clean major highways alone (Keep America Beautiful, 1968). Campaigns and public appeals have not been especially effective

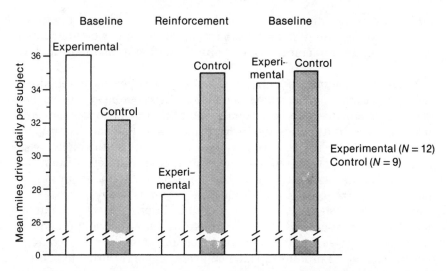

FIGURE 13–1 The mean miles driven daily per subject by the experimental and control groups. During the two baseline conditions, no contingencies were in effect for mileage reduction. In the reinforcement condition, the experimental group's mileage reductions were reinforced; the control group remained under baseline conditions.

Source: Foxx, R. M., & Hake, D. F. Gasoline conservation: A procedure for measuring and reducing the driving of college students. *Journal of Applied Behavior Analysis*, 1977, **10**, 61–74.

in reducing littering. Incentive systems have effectively reduced littering or increased the removal of existing litter in such settings as national forests, schools, movie theaters, and athletic stadiums.

A few projects have shown that prompts delivered prior to littering are effective. For example, Geller (1975) provided handbills to people entering a movie theater (announcing the show for the coming weekend) or entering a grocery store (announcing shopping "specials of the week"). On some occasions the handbills provided the prompt typed at the bottom saying, "please dispose of properly." When the antilitter message was included, more of the handbills were properly disposed (e.g., in trash cans, in ashtrays) than when the message was omitted.

Providing instructions or prompts usually has been only mildly effective, so several projects have focused on incentive systems. For example, Chapman and Risley (1974) decreased litter in an urban-housing area with over 390 low-income families living in a 15-square-block area. Litter was collected in residential yards, public yard areas, streets, sidewalks, and other areas. Providing small monetary incentives (10¢ for filling up a litter bag, or for making yards clean rather than merely for turning in filled litter bags) reduced the amount of litter observed in the neighborhood, as measured by sampling 25 randomly selected yards. Paying children for clean yards was more effective than was paying them for full litter bags. Both incentive conditions demonstrated the utility of reinforcement in a community setting in maintaining low levels of litter.

Many applications reducing the amount of litter have relied on monetary incentives. Yet, such interventions need not be expensive. For example, in one program individuals who picked up litter were given a ticket to win an attractive monetary prize ($20) (Powers, Osborne, & Anderson, 1973). Tickets were drawn from a lottery so the money was not provided to each individual who participated. A lottery system is a useful way to sustain high levels of the behavior without providing money or a prize to each individual who performs the response.

Recycling Wastes. A concern related to littering is the accumulation of waste products in the environment. An alternative approach to litter control, at least with some items that are littered, is to encourage recycling. If waste products (e.g., metal cans, paper, returnable bottles) can be recycled in some form, they become a resource rather than an accumulated waste.

Geller, Chaffee, and Ingram (1975) increased the recycling of paper on a university campus. Several dormitories had collected waste paper from the students to be sold at a paper mill at $15 per ton and eventually recycled. Over a six-week period, each of six dormitories received different phases. During baseline, no special contingencies were invoked and students who brought paper to the collection room were merely thanked. One experimental intervention involved making a contest between a men's and women's dormitory. "Recycling contest" rules were posted on the collection-room door of each dorm and specified that the dorm with more paper would receive a $15 bonus. Another experimental intervention consisted of making a raffle in which each student who brought paper to the collection room received a ticket. Tickets were drawn each week and earned prizes including monetary certificates redeemable at clothing or grocery stores or for a piece of furniture, sleeping bag, and other items varying in monetary value. Both contest and raffle contingencies increased the amount of paper brought to the collection rooms of the dormitories. The raffle contingency was superior to the contest contingency in the total amount of paper received and in the number of individuals who brought paper.

Extrinsic reinforcers are not always necessary to increase recycling. In one project, residents of three apartment complexes were merely informed of the location of recycling containers to be used to collect newspapers (Reid, Luyben, Rawers, & Bailey, 1976). Near the containers, which were placed in the laundry rooms of the apartments, were instructions explaining the use of containers. Also, residents were interviewed briefly and prompted about the use of the containers prior to the program. Over a several week period, the amount of newspapers collected increased relative to baseline levels.

Employment and Job-Related Skills.   Obtaining and keeping a job entail problems of obvious social significance. Aside from the economic implications, lack of employment is associated with a number of social ills including crime, "mental illness," alcoholism, racial discrimination, medical neglect, and family desertion (see Jones & Azrin, 1973). Behavior modification has focused on job-interview performance, obtaining employment, and on-the-job performance.

A few studies have examined procedures to help individuals obtain employment (e.g., Jones & Azrin, 1973). For example, Azrin, Flores, and Kaplin (1975) developed a job-finding club for unemployed persons to train skills that would enhance the opportunities for obtaining a job. Members were paired into dyads so that each member would have someone to provide support and encouragement. Also, members were trained to search for jobs through various sources (e.g., former employers, relatives), role-played job interviews, received instructions in dress and grooming, learned to prepare a résumé, and expanded their job interests. Job seekers who participated in the club found employment within a shorter time period and received higher wages than persons who had not participated. Three months after participation in the program, 92 percent of the clients in the program obtained employment compared with 60 percent of persons who had not participated.

Engaging in appropriate job-interview behaviors also has been improved using behavioral techniques. For example, Furman, Geller, Simon, and Kelly (1979) trained formerly hospitalized psychiatric patients in interview skills. In individual sessions over a four to six-week period, clients were trained to provide positive information about themselves and their experiences, to make appropriate arm and hand gestures while speaking, to express interest and enthusiasm for the potential position, and to ask appropriate questions of the job interviewer. Training used role-playing, practice, videotaped feedback, prompts, and praise for appropriate behavior. The effects of training are illustrated in Figure 13–2, where the changes in the behavior of one subject are evident in a multiple-baseline design. At the end of training, and experienced job interviewer unfamiliar with the training program rated interview skills as improved.

On-the-job performance has been improved in several behavior-modification programs. A well known example of the use of reinforcement in industry was conducted at the Emery Air Freight Corporation (*Business Week*, 1971). To improve many aspects of company operations, feedback, praise, and social recognition were used to reinforce job performance. For example, in one application, the cost of delivering air freight was reduced by shipping several smaller packages in a large

338

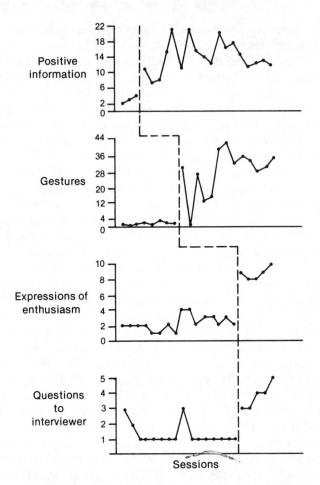

FIGURE 13–2 Job interview training for subject 1: Multiple baseline introduction of giving positive information, gesturing, asking questions and expressing enthusiasm in the position.

Source: Furman, W., Geller, M., Simon, S. J., & Kelly, J. A. The use of a behavioral rehearsal procedure for teaching job-interviewing skills to psychiatric patients. *Behavior Therapy*, 1979, **10,** 157–67.

single shipment rather than separately. Employees who worked on the loading dock received feedback using a checklist and praise for shipping packages in larger containers, thus saving money. Use of the containers increased 95 percent and remained at a high level for almost two years saving the company approximately $650,000 per year.

Other applications within behavior modification have improved performance. For example, Pierce and Risley (1974) used wages to improve performance of adolescents in a youth employment program. The individuals worked as aides at a community recreation center where they supervised play activities. Pay was delivered contingent upon the number of tasks that were correctly completed (e.g., operating a snack bar, monitoring the number of individuals engaged in activities, preparing the game rooms). When wages were contingent upon task completion, performance increased markedly.

Several studies in industry have focused upon absenteeism and tardiness, two problems that have important economic implications. For example, Pedalino and Gamboa (1974) provided a playing card to each employee who came to work in order to reduce absenteeism. At the end of the week, the employees who had the best poker hands received a $20 cash prize. This reinforcement system markedly reduced absenteeism. Similarly, token reinforcement (slips of paper that could be exchanged for a maximum of 80¢ each week) were used to reinforce and increase punctuality in an industrial setting (Hermann, deMontes, Dominguez, Montes, & Hopkins, 1973).

Community Self-Government.   A few projects have attempted to increase the involvement of persons in decisions that affect their community living situations. For example, several years ago, one project used reinforcement techniques to increase the attendance of welfare recipients to self-help group meetings (Miller & Miller, 1970). A wide variety of skills might be useful to help community members exert influence in their communities. As one example, Briscoe, Hoffman, and Bailey (1975) developed problem-solving skills in lower socioeconomic adolescents and adults who participated in a self-help project. The participants attended weekly board meetings that focused upon identifying and solving community problems such as arranging to have repairs made at the community center, organizing social and educational events, discovering and distributing social welfare resources, and providing medical care. Problem-solving skills were developed that included identifying problems for discussion, stating, evaluating, and selecting alternative solutions, and making decisions. Role-playing, modeling, and social reinforcement successfully trained these behaviors and improved participants' skills in solving problems.

Behavioral techniques have been used for broader community living behaviors. For example, a small community-living project has been conducted at a major university based upon operant principles (Miller, 1976). College students lived in the large house in which the program was conducted and received credit for performing various jobs needed to run the house (e.g., preparing food, cleaning). The credits were exchanged for reductions in monthly rent. The house was self-governed so that job assignments were carefully coordinated and credits were given for serving in one of the many administrative–coordinating positions. Investigations have been completed demonstrating the influence of contingent reinforcement on the amounts of work completed in the facility. Interestingly, participants have indicated relatively high satisfaction with the self-governed living facility relative to alternative housing arrangements.

Racial Integration. Racial integration represents a complex social issue that has received little direct intervention from behavior modification techniques. The precise targets for resolving segregation are multiple and encompass diverse behaviors across a range of settings and target groups. Procedures to facilitate racial integration usually have been directed at changing attitudes. However, changes in attitudes toward racial groups does not necessarily result in corresponding behavior change (Mann, 1959).

Some research has focused upon changing how individuals describe and evaluate others against whom they show racial bias. For example, Best, Smith, Graves, and Williams (1975, Exp. 1) used reinforcement techniques to alter the tendency of children to evaluate light-skinned (Euro-American) persons positively and dark-skinned (Afro-American) persons negatively. This racial bias has been demonstrated in a large number of studies with both Euro- and Afro-American children. Preschool children were trained with a teaching machine in which selection of light- or dark-skinned figures were differentially reinforced in the context of stories in which positive and negative descriptions were presented. Responses associating Afro-American characters with positive adjectives and Euro-American characters with negative adjectives were reinforced either with an advance of the machine to the next story or by tokens (pennies exchangeable for candy). Racial bias was altered by the reinforcement procedures. The changes in bias were maintained up to one week and, to a lesser extent, up to one year after training. These results, and similar findings from other studies, show that operant techniques can alter children's tendencies to associate negative adjectives with Afro-American children (Edwards & Williams, 1970; McMurtry & Williams, 1972). Although these studies clearly demonstrate the change of attitudinal and laboratory-based responses involving racial bias, they do not reflect whether interracial social behaviors would vary. Additional research is necessary to more clearly show that behaviors in nonlaboratory settings can be altered.

An initial attempt to alter overt interracial social behavior was reported by Hauserman, Walen, and Behling (1973) who developed a program to integrate five black children in a predominantly white first-grade classroom. The students in the class isolated themselves along racial lines for all activities of a social nature. To increase interracial interaction, all students in the class received tokens and praise for sitting with "new friends" during lunch. Sitting with new friends included interracial combinations of students although this was not specified to the students. Tokens were redeemable for a snack after lunch. Interracial interactions increased during the token- and social-reinforcement phase. Interestingly, interaction transferred to a free-play period immediately after lunch even though reinforcers were never provided for interracial socialization during this period. Although the effects were not maintained, this study suggests the amenability of interracial interaction to change as a function of consequences. Positively reinforcing racial interaction might provide another alternative to public appeals and forced integration.

Medical Applications

Behavior modification techniques increasingly are applied to problems that relate to physical health and illness. Applications of behavioral science to the prevention, diagnosis, treatment, and rehabilitation of problems of physical health recently have emerged as an area referred to as *behavioral medicine* (Schwartz & Weiss, 1978; Williams & Gentry, 1977). The domain of behavioral medicine is large and encompasses a wide range of problems including adherence to medical regimens such as exercising, following a special diet, or taking medicine, the treatment of a variety of disorders including cardiac arrhythmias, hypertension, seizures, headaches, pain, muscle spasms, and many others, and behaviors such as overeating, drug abuse, cigarette smoking, and excessive alcohol consumption that can lead to impairment of physical health.

Although examples throughout previous chapters have illustrated applications of behavioral medicine, it is important to highlight the area here. Behavioral medicine is a rapidly developing area. Only a few of the many problems treated in behavioral medicine can be illustrated.

Adherence and Compliance.   Adherence to medical regimens is an important area of concern because many forms of medical and psychological treatment depend upon client compliance with treatment recommendations. Yet, estimates have suggested that up to 50% of medical patients do not comply with their prescribed regimens (Gillum & Barsky, 1974). Behavior modification has been used to increase adherence to a variety of treatment procedures (e.g., Epstein & Masek, 1978).

For example, Lowe and Lutzker (1979) treated a juvenile diabetic, named Amy, who had been hospitalized repeatedly as a result of not adhering to the medical regimen that her physician had prescribed. The physician had prescribed a special diet to ensure a blood-sugar balance, insulin injections, and exercise. Amy was instructed to conduct urine tests several times daily to indicate the success in balancing diet, insulin, and exercise. Also, she was told to maintain personal hygiene,

342

especially foot care because of the poor circulation to the feet, loss of sensation in her feet, and possible injuries that might become infected if not detected. Unfortunately, Amy did not follow the appropriate diet, nor conduct urine tests or engage in foot care (wash and inspect for cuts and bruises).

To increase compliance with this medical regimen at home, the experimenter gave a "memo" (written instructions) to Amy that told her how to complete the desired behaviors and at what times each day. After several days of the memo, a token economy was devised in which Amy earned points (exchangeable for rewards daily or at the end of the week) for engaging in the tasks to manage her diabetes. The effects of the program are presented in Figure 13–3 where the percentage of completion of the desired tasks of the many opportunities available each day are graphed. Introducing the memo increased adherence to the diet (bottom portion of the figure) but did not affect the other behaviors. The

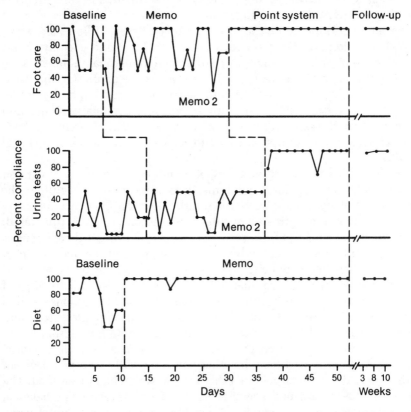

FIGURE 13–3 Percentage compliance to foot care, urine testing, and diet.

Source: Lowe, K., & Lutzker, J. R. Increasing compliance to a medical regimen with a juvenile diabetic. *Behavior Therapy*, 1979, **10**, 57–64.

token system, however, markedly improved foot care and urine tests that were conducted each day. During the follow-up period, the experimenter no longer was formally involved in the program. Yet, the parents continued the program and behaviors were maintained at a high rate.

Other applications have shown techniques useful for adherence to a special diet. For example, Green (1978) monitored urine sugar levels in a diabetic psychiatric patient. The patient frequently ate candy and potato chips and drank soda instead of her specially prepared meals. Her high sugar levels led to dizziness and inactivity. When access to the hospital grounds was made contingent upon low sugar levels in her urine, her levels decreased.

Seizure Control. A variety of seizure disorders are routinely treated with various medications. However, seizures may still occur relatively frequently even with medication. Seizure activity may involve sudden tension or flexion in the muscles, staring into space, jerking or shaking of various muscles, idiosyncratic facial expressions or grimacing, falling to the ground, dizziness, and lack of consciousness.

Several behavioral procedures have been applied to reduce the frequency of seizure activity. Zlutnick et al. (1975) used behavioral techniques to modify seizures in several children. The treatment was based upon interrupting preseizure activity that led eventually to the seizure. For example, one subject was a 7-year-old boy who had a 2-year history of seizures and had been diagnosed at various points as autistic, brain damaged, and learning disabled. His seizures consisted of various components beginning with a fixed stare, followed by body rigidity, violent shaking, and ending with a fall to the floor. Because staring always was preceded by the fixed stare, an attempt was made to interrupt the chain of behaviors leading to a seizure. In a special education classroom where the program was conducted, a staff member observed the child and was instructed to interrupt the preseizure activity. Specifically, when the child began the fixed stare, the staff member was to go over to the child and shout "no" loudly and sharply and to grasp the child by the shoulders with both hands and shake him once. The results of this relatively simple interruption procedure for one boy were evaluated in an ABAB design, as shown in Figure 13–4. The procedure markedly reduced the number of seizures per week. At the end of a 6-month follow-up, only one seizure had been observed. The interruption procedure was effective in controlling seizures in other children, demonstrating that the impressive results were not unique to one particular child.

Wells, Turner, Bellack, and Hersen (1978) treated a retarded adult patient who had repeated seizures. Although the patient was on several

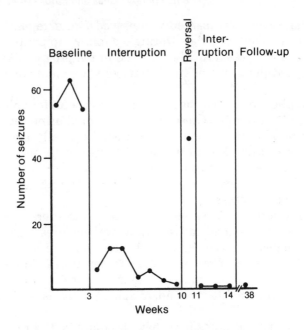

FIGURE 13-4 The number of minor motor seizures per week for Subject 1. The reversal is prorated for a five-day week. Follow-up data represent the absolute number of seizures for the next six months.

Source: Zlutnick, S., Mayville, W. J., & Moffat, S. Modification of seizure disorders: The interruption of behavioral chains. *Journal of Applied Behavior Analysis*, 1975, **8**, 1–12.

medications designed to control her seizures, she continued to have several seizures on the ward each day. The seizures were characterized by a fixed stare, dilated pupils, and muscle rigidity followed by falling to the floor. The patient reported that she felt a "tight queasy feeling" in her stomach prior to her seizures. The patient was trained in deep muscle relaxation. The patient was instructed to use the cue word "relax," which had been paired with relaxation and to relax herself when she felt preseizure behavior. In an ABAB design, both the seizures and the client's overall anxiety level decreased as a function of the relaxation procedure. The patient was discharged to a group home-living situation and was monitored for three months. Control of the seizures continued throughout the follow-up period after discharge.

Other reports have suggested the effectiveness of behavioral techniques to alter seizure activity. Reinforcement for periods of nonseizure activity, time out from reinforcement for the onset of seizure activity, thought stopping, biofeedback, and other procedures alone or in combination have reduced seizures (see Lubar & Shouse, 1977; Masur, 1977).

Anorexia Nervosa. Behavioral techniques have been applied to a variety of eating disorders that can lead to or reflect physical disease including obesity, ruminative vomiting, and anorexia nervosa. Anorexia nervosa involves reduced food consumption that results in extreme loss of weight. The disorder invariably is found in young women who lose at least 20% of their normal body weight, have a marked fear of becoming obese, and resist gaining any weight. Physical consequences of significant weight loss include an emaciated appearance, cessation of menstration, and, in severe cases, death.

Pertschuk, Edwards, and Pomerleau (1978) treated several anorexia nervosa patients using a contingency contract system. Hospitalized patients were told that they would require a daily weight gain of one-half pound in order to earn certain privileges on the ward. The privileges depended upon the particular activities in which the subjects engaged during baseline observations. Individualized contracts were drawn up in writing and signed by the therapist and patient. The patients were told they were responsible for gaining weight and that they could request nutritional counseling if they wished assistance. During baseline, patients had generally continued to lose weight. However, during the contact period (about 2 weeks), the patients showed an average weight gain of about 4.2 kg. (9.3 lbs.). Follow-up assessment ranging from 3 to 28 months indicated that the patients had continued to gain weight after discharge from the hospital. Other reports have suggested successful treatment of anorexia nervosa with reinforcement and feedback techniques, contingency contracting, desensitization, and other behavioral procedures alone or in combination (e.g., Agras, Barlow, Chapin, Abel, & Leitenberg, 1974; Hauserman & Lavin, 1977; Monti, McCrady, & Barlow, 1977).

Pain. Behavioral techniques have been applied to treat pain associated with a variety of disorders. The techniques usually are applied to alter many of the behaviors associated with pain such as time out of one's bed, grimacing, moaning, complaining, walking in a guarded or protective manner, and relying heavily upon medication.

Pioneering work applying behavioral techniques to chronic pain was reported by Fordyce and his colleagues (Fordyce et al., 1968, 1973). In one of the studies, patients suffering back pain due to a variety of diagnosed disorders participated in a treatment program for approximately seven weeks within the hospital. During treatment, patients received social reinforcement from their family and from the staff for engaging in increased activity in the hospital such as going on walks. Complaints, moaning, inactivity, and grimacing were ignored. After treatment, patients reported less intense pain, reduced their intake of medication, and increased the amount of time spent out of bed. Similarly, Cairns and Pasino (1977) utilized reinforcement procedures for hospitalized patients diagnosed with chronic low back pain. Verbal praise from the staff was used to increase activities (e.g., walking, riding an exercycle).

As a final example, Miller and Kratochwill (1979) used time out from reinforcement to reduce the frequency of stomachache complaints in a 10-year-old girl, named Karen. Karen had no evidence of organic impairment, and the complaints had not been eliminated through medication. Analysis of the home environment suggested strong reinforcement for complaints (staying home from school, watching television, playing with toys, being waited on with food, drink, and social attention). The mother was instructed to use a time out whenever Karen complained. When Karen complained about her stomach, she was told to rest in her room. Although some reinforcers were available (books), television, toys, and games were not included. The curtains were drawn and the door was almost closed so she could rest quietly. The main feature of time out appeared to be a reduction of attention for complaining on the part of the mother. The effects of the program at home are illustrated in Figure 13–5. In the third phase, there was an accidental return to

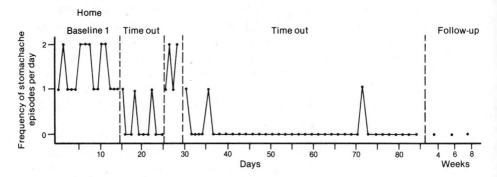

FIGURE 13–5   The frequency of stomach pain complaint episodes at home during the time-out program.

Source: Miller, A. J., & Kratochwill, T. R. Reduction of frequent stomachache complaints by time out. *Behavior Therapy*, 1979, **10**, 211–18.

baseline when Karen vomited and received extra attention for a four-day period. The treatment plan was again implemented which reduced complaints again. Follow-up several weeks and one year after treatment indicated no further problem with complaints of pain.

Other reports have suggested that behavioral techniques including biofeedback, relaxation training, self-statements, and several combined procedures can treat pain associated with menstruation, intercourse, localized pain of the masserter area of the face, and others (e.g., Stenn, Mothersill, & Brooke, 1979; Tasto & Chesney, 1974; Varni, 1973). Also, work on specific disorders such as headaches represents an area where several techniques have been applied (Blanchard & Epstein, 1977; Williams, 1977).

Additional Applications

Extensions of behavior modification to social, environmental, and health-related problems represent only a few of the innovative directions that the field has taken. Each of the areas where interesting applications have been conducted cannot begin to be elaborated within a brief space. Consider just a few of the other areas where work is being done and is likely to increase in the future.

Behavioral techniques have been applied to alter the behavior of the elderly such as nursing-home residents and geriatric patients. Programs have focused upon improving social interaction, physical activity, and recovery from physical illness (e.g., Libb & Clements, 1969; Sachs, 1975). In extensions of behavioral techniques to crime, programs have identified prompting techniques that can reduce shoplifting in department stores and police patrol techniques that can reduce city-wide rates of burglary (e.g., McNees et al., 1976; Schnelle et al., 1975, 1978). Community-based research has used incentive systems successfully to increase the frequency that low-income parents seek dental care for their children (Reiss, Piotrowski, & Bailey, 1976). Related work has improved the diets of economically-impoverished children and of senior citizens by providing prompts and incentives for eating well balanced meals (Bunck & Iwata, 1978; Madsen, Madsen, & Thompson, 1974). Behavioral techniques have been applied to improve athletic performance (e.g., Rushall & Siedentop, 1972), to reinforce appropriate behaviors during basic training in the army (e.g., Datel & Legters, 1970), and a variety of other behaviors. Increasingly, behavioral techniques are branching out to areas that traditionally have not been actively included in psychological interventions.

General Comments

Behavioral techniques have been widely extended to a variety of problem areas. It is important to note that the results in most of these areas are quite preliminary. The major problems to which extensions of behavior modification have been applied have not been resolved either on a large or small scale. For example, reinforcement programs have reduced energy consumption in several projects. However, applications still have not reached the point where energy consumption is significantly reduced for a large number of people over a prolonged period. Current research suggests that the technology of behavior change can contribute to the problems of energy conservation, but as yet the contributions remain to be made. Similarly, applications of behavioral techniques to problems of physical health such as hypertension have shown very promising demonstrations. However, the magnitude of changes that have been achieved and the short-term periods of follow-up assessed leave important questions remaining about whether specific techniques will be effective and for large-scale use. In general, the extensions of behavior modification to many new areas offer considerable promise. Yet, the enthusiasm that such promise may engender should be tempered with a careful evaluation of the specific accomplishments reached at this particular point in time.

■ THE SOCIAL CONTEXT OF BEHAVIOR MODIFICATION

Increasingly, the social context in which behavioral interventions have been conducted has played a role in treatment. The social context refers to a variety of considerations that pertain to concerns of society that must be taken into account in any treatment program. For example, many of the ethical and legal issues discussed in the last chapter suggest concerns that people have about behavioral and other interventions. These concerns are directly relevant to the implementation of interventions in the many different situations in which behavior change might be desired. Although it is extremely important to develop an effective technology, the techniques must take into account the concerns of society at large or of consumers of treatment to ensure that the treatments that are developed will be implemented. Three areas of social concern seem to be especially relevant in light of recent developments in the field, namely, the focus of behavioral treatments, the social acceptability of the treatments that are used, and the utility of the outcomes that are achieved.

Focus of Treatment

The focus on various problems and behaviors in treatment illustrated in previous chapters usually reflects consensus. Thus, considerable agreement exists that behavior-change techniques should be applied to improve academic behaviors of children doing poorly in school, to increase coherent speech among psychiatric patients who might be delusional, to eliminate self-destructive behavior among autistic or retarded children, and to decrease antisocial behavior among delinquents. In most instances the focus of treatment does not raise major questions. However, situations have arisen and no doubt will continue to arise that pose fundamental questions about the focus of treatment and the social implications of treatment.

Social and moral questions about the focus of treatments can be illustrated in the controversy associated with the application of behavioral techniques to a boy, named Kraig, who engaged in cross-gender behaviors (Rekers & Lovaas, 1974). As noted in an earlier chapter, Kraig was almost five years old and engaged in several feminine behaviors including dressing up as a girl, playing with cosmetics, and showing severe pronounced feminine mannerisms, gestures, and gait. He mimicked subtle feminine behaviors of an adult woman. Also, he seemed to avoid masculine behaviors and constantly played with girls. The cross-gender behaviors appeared very severe and led to Kraig's social isolation and to ridicule. Also, because cross-gender behaviors in childhood sometimes are associated with sexual deviance in adulthood (Green & Money, 1969), the need to intervene seemed especially urgent. In any case, Kraig's parents sought treatment.

Rekers and Lovaas developed masculine behaviors such as playing with toys typical of little boys (e.g., soldiers, gun, airplanes), engaging in aggressive behaviors (e.g., playing cowboys and Indians, playing with a dart gun, rubber knife), and dressing in masculine-typed clothes (e.g., army shirt, football helmet). Behaviors such as dressing in girls' clothes, playing with dolls, taking the role of the girl in games, and showing feminine gestures were decreased. In therapy sessions, the mother attended to masculine behaviors and ignored feminine behaviors; at home, the parents used token reinforcement to develop gender behaviors considered appropriate. The program was very effective in altering these behaviors, and 26 months after treatment sex-typed behaviors were considered to have become "normalized." Indeed, follow-up not only revealed the absence of pretreatment feminine behaviors but expanded sex-role activities characteristic of boys (e.g., more rough-and-tumble play, interest in camping out).

Fundamental questions have been raised about the focus of this study (Nordyke et al., 1977; Rekers, 1977; Winkler, 1977). Developing masculine behaviors explicitly adheres to social stereotypes about how little boys and girls, and later, men and women, *should* behave. Yet, traditional sex-role behaviors may be questioned—they are not necessarily psychologically "healthy" or natural. Indeed, females who are high in femininity and males who are high in masculinity often show characteristics such as high anxiety, low self-esteem, and low social acceptance (Bem, 1975). Similarly, children who show high sex-typed behaviors have been found to have lower intelligence than those who are less sex-typed. The important point is merely to show that fostering sex-typed behavior reflects a value stance and that the adjustment of the individual or society may not necessarily be enhanced by stronger sex-typed behavior.

On the other side of the issue, Rekers and Lovaas (1974; Rekers, 1977) noted that the severity of Kraig's cross-gender behavior, the possibility of sexual deviance in adulthood, and the parents' concern with Kraig's social adjustment suggested the need to intervene. The issue extends beyond any particular case and raises questions about areas of treatment that are controversial and value-laden. Scientific research cannot resolve the many issues that arise. For example, it is not known that children with cross-gender behaviors in fact later become deviant. If it were, additional questions might be raised about whether the deviance (e.g., transvestism) would necessarily harm the individual or society. And, issues such as informed consent in applying treatment do not resolve the problem because neither the therapist nor the client (or his parents) could be truly *informed*. Insufficient information exists about what the consequences are of treating or failing to treat the problem and so the risks and benefits of treatment cannot be known.

In other, albeit related areas of clinical interventions, issues have been raised about whether some behaviors should be treated at all. For example, Davison (1976) argued that treating homosexuality explicitly acknowledges sexual preferences for the same sex as a "problem." Yet, sexual preferences per se may not be the problem but rather adjusting to a world that has strong biases against homosexuality. Many homosexuals may be driven to treatment because of the tremendous pressures associated with staying in the "closet." Therapists are not apt to treat heterosexuals who might wish to be homosexual or to expand their sexuality to include homosexual relations. So, it has been argued, perhaps homosexuals should not be "treated" for their sexual preferences. Independently of the stand that a particular person may take on this issue, the issue clearly illustrates the role that values may play in selecting target behaviors.

The social value of target behaviors selected in behavioral and other forms of treatment arises with behaviors that may evoke fewer emotional responses than sex-role behaviors and sexual preferences. For example classroom applications of behavioral techniques frequently focus on making children well behaved so that they remain in their seats, do not speak without permission, and attend to their lessons (Winett & Winkler, 1972). Most of the programs have not included especially deviant children who engaged in severely disruptive or dangerous behavior (e.g., as hyperactivity, aggression). Yet, for many years, the focus on attentive behavior among mildly disruptive or inattentive children had gone unchallenged. However, with very few exceptions, a large number of investigations have shown that improving attentiveness among students in the classroom does not improve academic performance. Perhaps, proponents of behavior modification have been too apt to embrace the goals selected by others—having "well behaved and quiet children"—while neglecting major goals of education such as improved academic performance. A shift in research focus in educational settings has shown that improving academic performance frequently has as a side effect improved classroom attentiveness and reduced disruptive behavior (e.g., Ayllon & Roberts, 1974; Marholin, Steinman, McInnis, & Heads, 1975; Winett & Roach, 1973). Thus, concerns that many teachers have about discipline can be remedied by improving academic behaviors. And, unless severe behaviors are apparent, the focus of most classrooms might be appropriately directed to academic accomplishment.

In general, the focus of treatment needs to be given careful consideration. In fact, the focus may reflect priorities that are not necessarily in the best interests of the client or society at large. Thus, although the techniques that can be used for altering behavior may be ethically neutral—in the sense that by themselves they do not necessarily dictate target focus—these techniques are invariably applied in situations where a definite value structure is implicit. Recognition of the social context in which behaviors need to be developed is an important step in deciding how the technology should be applied.

The value questions of changing particular target behaviors, of course, have not been resolved. Yet, some attention has been given to the selection of target behaviors and whether they are important from the standpoint of the social context in which the individual functions. For example, Minkin et al. (1976) were interested in developing conversational skills in predelinquent girls at Achievement Place for Girls. Any of a large number of skills might be trained to improve social interaction. What precisely should be taught that people in the community normally would regard as important skills for improved relationships? To answer this question, the investigators first asked "normal" junior high school and college girls to converse to see how people without social skills problems interacted. Videotaped recordings of the conversations were made so that observers could examine the social interaction. The investigators identified behaviors that seemed important in conversation including providing positive feedback to another person, indicating that one understands what was said, asking a question or clarification, and the total amount of time talked. Other college students and people from the community (e.g., gas-station attendant, homemakers) rated the tapes on the basis of how well they reflected overall conversational skills. The judges' ratings were correlated with the specific behaviors identified as important by the investigators. Higher rates of performing the above behaviors led to more positive evaluations of overall conversational skills.

The above procedures were completed to select the behaviors that might be relevant to teach the predelinquent girls whose conversational skills were deficient. The girls were trained using instructions, practice, feedback, and token reinforcement. At the end of training the girls improved on the specific skills and judges' ratings of conversation was up to the average level of university and junior high school students in overall conversational ability.

Identifying behaviors that people in everyday life regard as important is referred to as *social validation* (Wolf, 1978). Social validation can refer to selecting behaviors that the social community regards as important or evaluating whether the changes that are achieved in treatment are important. In either case, the social context consisting of evaluations of lay persons or others who may be in contact with the client help determine whether the focus or accomplishments of treatment are really important. Behavior modification techniques may be able to change a variety of behaviors, but which behaviors should be changed is a function of what people in everyday life identify as important. Increasingly, investigators are utilizing the evaluations of people in everyday life to determine the behaviors that need to be trained. While people in everyday life are not in a position to say what behaviors are "correct," or "healthy," their opinions often reflect behaviors that determine who is considered to be deviant or abnormal. With many populations, the goal is to return clients to the community. Adequate functioning of the community may mean developing behaviors that enable the person to fit into his or her social situation.

Treatment Outcomes

Behavioral interventions have effectively produced dramatic changes in performance as evident throughout previous chapters. However, it is still appropriate to ask whether the changes are really important and make a difference in the lives of the clients. As noted above, social validation considers whether the amount of change achieved in treatment is important. One way to evaluate the importance of the change is to determine whether improvements bring the client to the levels of his or her peers who have not been identified as showing problems that warrant treatment. For example, O'Brien and Azrin (1972a) developed appropriate eating behaviors in mentally retarded residents of a state hospital who seldom used utensils, constantly spilled food on themselves, stole food from others, and ate food previously spilled on the floor. Using prompts, verbal praise, and food reinforcement, training increased appropriate behaviors (as illustrated in the discussion of Control Group Designs in Chapter 5). Although training increased appropriate eating behaviors, one can still raise the question of whether the improvements really are very important and approach eating skills of people who are regarded as "normal" in this regard. To address these questions, O'Brien and Azrin (1972a) compared the group that received training with the eating habits of "normals." Customers in a local restaurant were watched by observers who recorded eating behavior. The level of inappropriate eating behaviors is illustrated by the dashed line in Figure 13–6. As is evident, the level of

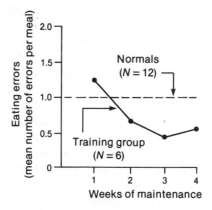

FIGURE 13–6 The mean number of improper responses per meal performed by the training group of retardates and the mean number of improper responses performed by normals.

Source: O'Brien, F., & Azrin, N. H. Developing proper mealtime behaviors of the institutionalized retarded. *Journal of Applied Behavior Analysis*, 1972, **5**, 389–99.

inappropriate mealtime behaviors among the retarded residents was even lower than the normal rate of inappropriate eating behavior of people eating in a restaurant. These results suggest that the magnitude of changes achieved with training brought behavior of the residents to acceptable levels of people functioning in everyday life.

Several reports have evaluated whether the behavior of deviant, socially disruptive, or withdrawn children, inassertive or shy adults, and the speech of psychiatric patients all come up to the level of normative behaviors by individuals functioning adequately in everyday life (Kazdin, 1977b). By evaluating the amount of changes relative to the level of behavior associated with adequate functioning, behavior modification has relied increasingly on the social context to help determine whether treatment effects are beneficial.

Another method for evaluating whether the changes achieved are important is asking people in contact with the client or in a position of expertise whether behavior change has made a difference. For example, Werner et al. (1975) trained predelinquent boys to interact appropriately with the police. Behaviors that the police had identified as important behaviors in situations where police and youths interact were focused upon in treatment such as facing the officer, responding politely, and showing cooperation, understanding, and interest in reforming. After these target behaviors were increased, the investigators were interested in whether the results made a difference in how the youths' behaviors would be evaluated. So, police, citizens from the community, and college students evaluated videotapes of the youths interacting with police in simulated situations. The boys who had been trained were rated more appropriately on ratings of suspiciousness and cooperativeness than boys who had not been trained.

Subjective evaluations of treatment effects have been used to assess whether improvements in writing skills of children are reflected in ratings of creativity or interest value of the compositions, whether individuals who are trained in public speaking skills are evaluated more positively by the audience, and whether people in contact with deviant children see their behaviors differently after treatment (see Kazdin, 1977b). The opinions of others in contact with the clients do not necessarily reflect actual changes in performance. However, subjective opinions of people in contact with the client are important as a criterion in their own right because they often reflect the evaluations the client will encounter after he or she leaves treatment.

Treatment Techniques

The selection of target behaviors and evaluation of treatment outcome is not the only place that the social context is relevant. The techniques that can be used to alter behavior must consider people's opinions about what is appropriate and what should be done. It may be of little use to develop effective treatments if the procedures are highly objectionable to people who need them (e.g., parents, teachers, clients) or to those for whom they will be used (e.g., children, patients).

Recently, attention has been given to the public reaction to the procedures that are to be used in treatment and whether the treatments are really acceptable ways of changing behavior. Part of the reasons for looking at the acceptability of the procedures stems from the ethical and legal issues discussed in the last chapter. As mentioned earlier, one of the recommended procedures for ensuring that client rights are protected is to have lay people evaluate whether the procedures that are recommended for treatment really are acceptable or reasonable in light of the client's problem. The ethical and legal issues make it increasingly important to design procedures that not only are effective but also desirable, preferred, or acceptable.

There are other reasons than ethical and legal considerations for developing procedures that are highly acceptable to possible consumers. Clients and therapists are more likely to carry out treatments they view as highly acceptable. In outpatient treatment, clients are more likely to remain in treatment rather than drop out of treatment if the procedures that are used are palatable or positive. Indeed, as noted earlier, aversion techniques often have high drop-out rates presumably because the techniques, even if effective, are not very acceptable.

Research has begun to look at how people evaluate treatment and whether the treatment procedures used are acceptable. For example, investigators have developed time out from reinforcement procedures that do not take the person out of the situation. The variations of time out that differ on whether the individual is or is not removed from the situation may be just as effective as isolation. However, people tend to view time out without isolation as much more acceptable treatment procedures (see Foxx & Shapiro, 1977; Porterfield et al., 1976).

Kazdin (1979a) asked college students to evaluate several different punishment procedures that were applied to children for highly deviant and disruptive behavior in the home and at school. The procedures were described in detail, and subjects rated the extent to which the different treatments were consistent with commonly held notions of what treatment should be, whether treatment was fair or cruel, whether treatment was appropriate for clients who could not give consent, and similar questions. The measure, considered to reflect the overall acceptability of treatment, showed marked differences among the treatments. The results of the ratings on the acceptability scale appear in Figure 13–7. A reinforcement technique (in which appropriate behaviors were reinforced as a way of reducing inappropriate behavior) was viewed as much more acceptable than alternative treatments. Electric shock was viewed as the most unacceptable. Drug therapy to reduce disruptive behavior, commonly used in the treatment of hyperactivity, for example, and time out from reinforcement (isolating the child) were intermediate in acceptability value. Interestingly, time out was viewed as much more acceptable than drugs in treating disruptive child behavior.

The above information about alternative treatments represents a very preliminary step in evaluating treatment acceptability. It is likely that people's views of treatment depend upon how it is applied, who applies it, the severity of the problem, the number of alternative treat-

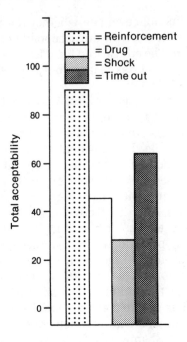

FIGURE 13–7 Acceptability of alternative treatments including reinforcement of appropriate behavior, drug treatment, electric shock, and time out from reinforcement. Higher scores indicated that a treatment was rated as more acceptable.

ments that have been tried without success, and so on. Also, it may make a difference who is asked to evaluate treatment. Hence, one procedure might not always be more acceptable than another and results from one or a few studies should not be taken as any more than suggestive. Yet, the concerns about how people evaluate treatment and their preferences among alternative treatments is an important new dimension in developing behavior modification procedures.

General Comments

Traditionally, treatment techniques have been evaluated by looking at how effective they are on various measures of personality and behavior. Obviously, the effectiveness of a technique is extremely important and the measures of outcome will continue to be used. However, treatments, behavioral or nonbehavioral in orientation, need to be evaluated along many dimensions (Kazdin & Wilson, 1978a; Strupp & Hadley, 1977). Many of the dimensions reflect broader concerns than the extent of therapeutic improvement for a particular client. Client evaluations of the procedures, the ease of implementing the techniques, the costs of treatment, and similar considerations illustrate the expanded criteria to evaluate treatment. Within behavior modification, the criteria include concerns about the importance of the changes achieved as well as the consumer satisfaction with the techniques themselves and how they are conducted.

■ SUMMARY AND CONCLUSION

Behavioral techniques have been applied to areas that greatly expand the usual clinical, educational, and rehabilitation focus. Programs have altered socially and environmentally relevant problems such as energy conservation, littering, recycling, employment and job performance, community self-government, and racial integration. Medical applications have addressed a variety of problems, as illustrated by research on adherence, seizure control, anorexia nervosa, and pain. Extensions of behavior modification, only sampled in the present chapter, include promising areas of work that could have significant impact on social and personal problems in the future.

Increasingly, behavioral techniques consider the social context in which treatment is administered. Specifically, work has begun to examine critically the behaviors that are focused upon in treatment and the social and value questions raised by treatment. Also, work has examined the behaviors that should be altered to have implications for how the client is viewed by others and the magnitude of change needed to produce a clinically important change. The acceptability of alternative treatment techniques also has begun to receive attention. In general, if behavioral techniques are to be widely practiced, they need to consider the interests of those who will ultimately utilize the techniques or who are in a position to evaluate whether the behavior changes made in treatment are important. Extending the focus of behavior modification to new areas of work and recognizing the social context in which treatment is performed should be two major areas of continued work in the future.

Glossary

ABAB Design—See Reversal Design.

Alternate Response Training—A technique used in therapy (as desensitization) and as a self-control strategy in which the individual is trained to engage in a response (e.g., relaxation) which interferes with or replaces another response which is to be controlled or eliminated.

Aversive Event—A stimulus which suppresses a behavior it follows or increases a behavior which results in its termination.

Avoidance—Performance of a behavior which postpones or averts the presentation of an aversive event.

Back-Up Reinforcer—An object, activity, or event (primary or secondary reinforcer) that can be purchased with tokens. Those reinforcers which "back up" the value of the tokens.

Baseline—The frequency that behavior is performed prior to initiating a behavior modification program. The rate of performance used to evaluate the effect of the program. Operant rate of behavior. Initial phase of reversal, multiple-baseline, changing-criterion, and simultaneous-treatment designs.

Behavior—Any observable and measurable response or act. (The terms "behavior" and "response" are used synonymously.)

Behavior Control—Exerting power or influence over others by altering the environmental contingencies to achieve a definite end.

Behavioral Medicine—The application of behavioral procedures to problems of physical health and illness. Applications focus on problems related to prevention, diagnosis, treatment, and rehabilitation of physical disorders or behaviors with consequences related to health and illness.

Behavioral Trap—Refers to the notion that once a client's behavior is developed it may become entrenched and maintained (i.e., trapped) into the social system of available reinforcers in the client's everyday environment. Behaviors may initially be developed through special contingency arrangements but be maintained by ordinary naturally occurring contingencies after the program is withdrawn.

Biofeedback—Procedures that provide information to persons about their ongoing physiological processes. The information is displayed to the client so that the moment-to-moment changes in these processes can be monitored.

Chain—A sequence of behaviors that occurs in a fixed order. Each behavior in the chain serves as a discriminative stimulus (S^D) for the next response. Also each behavior in the chain (except the first behavior) serves as a conditioned reinforcer which reinforces the previous response.

Chaining—Developing a sequence of responses in a backward order. The terminal response in the chain is developed first. The next to the last response is trained second. Remaining responses are trained in the reverse order of their performance once the chain is finally performed. Developing a complex behavior by training individual components of the behavior in a backward fashion.

Changing-Criterion Design—An experimental design in which the effect of the program is evaluated by repeatedly altering the criterion for reinforcement or punishment. If behavior matches the criterion as the criterion is repeatedly altered, this suggests that the contingency is responsible for behavior change.

Classical (or Respondent) Conditioning—A type of learning in which a neutral (conditioned) stimulus is paired with an unconditioned stimulus which automatically elicits a reflex response. After repeatedly following the conditioned stimulus with the unconditioned stimulus, the conditioned stimulus alone will elicit a reflex response. In classical conditioning new stimuli gain the power to elicit respondent behavior.

Conditioned Aversive Stimulus—An event which is initially neutral may acquire aversive properties by virtue of being paired with other aversive events or a signal that no reinforcement will be forthcoming.

Conditioned Reinforcer—See Secondary Reinforcer.

Conditioned Response—A reflex response elicited by a conditioned stimulus alone in the absence of the unconditioned stimulus. It resembles, but is not identical to, the unconditioned response. See Classical Conditioning.

Conditioned Stimulus—A previously neutral stimulus which through repeated associations with an unconditioned stimulus elicits a reflex response. See Classical Conditioning.

Consequence Sharing—A contingency arrangement in which the consequences earned by one person are provided to that person as well as his or her peers.

Contingency—The relationship between a behavior (the response to be changed) and the events (consequences) which follow behavior. Sometimes events which precede the behavior are also specified by a contingency.

Contingency Contracts—A behavior modification program in which an agreement or contract is made between the persons who wish behavior to change (e.g., parents) and those whose behavior is to be changed (e.g., their children). The contract specifies the relationship between behavior and the consequences that follow.

Contingent Delivery of a Reinforcer—The delivery of a reinforcer only when a specified behavior has been performed. Contrast with Noncontingent Delivery of a Reinforcer.

Continuous Reinforcement—A schedule of reinforcement in which a response is reinforced each time it is performed.

Control Group Design—An experimental design in which the effect of the program is evaluated by comparing (at least) two groups, a group which receives the program and another group which does not receive the program.

Coverant—A private event such as a thought, fantasy, or image which is not "observable" to anyone other than the individual to whom it is occurring. Private events can be viewed as responses which can be altered by varying the consequences which follow them. "Coverant" is a contraction of "covert" and "operant."

Covert Event—A private event such as a thought, fantasy, or image. See Coverant.

Cue—See Discriminative Stimulus (S^D).

Delay of Reinforcement—The time interval between a response and delivery of the reinforcer.

Deprivation—Reducing the availability of or access to a reinforcer.

Differential Reinforcement—Reinforcing a response in the presence of one stimulus (S^D) and extinguishing the response in the presence of other stimuli (S^Δ). Eventually the response is consistently performed in the presence of the S^D but not in the presence of the S^Δ.

Differential Reinforcement of Low Rates (DRL)—Delivery of a reinforcer for reductions in performance of the target behavior. Reinforcers may be delivered for reduction in the overall frequency of a response within a particular time period or an increase in the amount of time that elapses between responses. A DRL schedule can reduce the frequency of a target response.

Differential Reinforcement of Other Behavior (DRO)—Delivery of a reinforcer after any response *except* the target response. The individual is reinforced only when he or she is not performing the target response. Behaviors other than the target response are reinforced. The effect of a DRO schedule is to decrease the target (unreinforced) response.

Discrimination—Responding differently in the presence of different cues or antecedent events. Control of behavior by discriminative stimuli. See Stimulus Control.

Discriminative Stimulus (S^D)—An antecedent event or stimulus which signals that a certain response will be reinforced. A response is reinforced in the presence of an S^D. After an event becomes an S^D by being paired with reinforcement, its presence can increase the probability that the response will occur.

Disease Model—A general approach in medicine in which symptoms (e.g., fever) are viewed as a result of some underlying disease or pathology (e.g., bacterial infection). Ideally, treatment is directed at the underlying disease. This general model was transferred to abnormal behavior by positing an underlying "psychological disease." The intrapsychic model in psychology is consistent with the disease approach within medicine.

Elicit—To automatically bring about a response. Respondent or reflex behaviors are elicited by unconditioned stimuli. Contrast with Emit and Operant Behavior. See Classical Conditioning.

Emit—To perform a response spontaneously. An emitted response is not automatically controlled by stimuli which precede it. Operant behaviors are emitted. They are controlled primarily by the consequences which follow them. Contrast with Elicit and Respondent. See Operant Conditioning.

Escape—Performance of a behavior which terminates an aversive event.

Experimental Design—The plan of the program which determines how the effect of the experimental contingency will be causally demonstrated. The plan to evaluate whether the behavior modification program rather than various extraneous factors was responsible for behavior change.

Extinction—A procedure in which the reinforcer is no longer delivered for a previously reinforced response.

Extinction Burst—An increase in the frequency and intensity of responding at the beginning of extinction.

Fading—The gradual removal of discriminative stimuli (S^D) including prompts such as instructions or physical guidance. Initially, developing behavior is often facilitated by prompts. Yet it is important in most situations to *fade* the prompt. Fading also can refer to the gradual removal of reinforcement as in the progressive thinning of a reinforcement schedule.

Fixed-Interval Schedule—A schedule of administering reinforcement. In an FI schedule, the first occurrence of the target response after a fixed time interval elapses is reinforced.

Fixed-Ratio Schedule—A schedule of administering reinforcement. In an FR schedule, an unvarying number of occurrences of the target response is required for reinforcement.

Functional Relationship—A relationship between the experimental condition or contingency and behavior. A functional relationship is demonstrated if behavior systematically changes when the contingency is applied, withdrawn, and reapplied.

Generalized Conditioned Reinforcer—A conditioned reinforcer that has acquired reinforcing value by being associated or paired with a variety of other reinforcers. Money is an example of a generalized conditioned reinforcer.

Group Contingencies—Contingencies in which the group participates. There are two major variations: (1) An individual's behavior can determine the consequences delivered to the group; (2) the behavior of a group as a whole determines the consequences that the group (each member) receives.

High Probability Behavior—A response which is performed with a relatively high frequency when the individual is given the opportunity to select among alternative behaviors. See Premack Principle.

Incompatible Behavior—Behavior that cannot be performed at the same time as or that interferes with another behavior.

Informed Consent—Agreeing to participate in a program with full knowledge about the nature of treatment, the risks, benefits, expected outcomes, and alternatives. Three elements are required for truly informed consent: competence, knowledge, and volition.

Intermittent Reinforcement—A schedule of reinforcement in which a response is not reinforced every time it is performed. Only some occurrences of the response are reinforced.

Interval Schedule of Reinforcement—A schedule in which reinforcement is delivered on the basis of the amount of time that passes before a response can be reinforced. Contrast with Ratio Schedule of Reinforcement.

Intrapsychic Model—The view that behavior, whether "normal" or "abnormal" is a result of underlying psychological processes. The underlying process must be treated before the overt behavior can be changed.

Modeling—See Observational Learning.

Multiple-Baseline Designs—Experimental designs which demonstrate the effect of a contingency by introducing the contingency across different behaviors, individuals, or situations at different points in time. The effect of the contingency is demonstrated without a reversal phase.

Multiple-Baseline Design Across Behaviors—An experimental design in which baseline data are gathered across two or more behaviors. The experimental contingency is applied to the first behavior while baseline conditions are continued for the other behaviors. After all behaviors have stabilized, the contingency is introduced for the second behavior. This is continued until the experimental contingency is applied to all target behaviors at different points in time. A causal relationship between the experimental contingency and behavior is demonstrated, if each behavior changes when and only when the contingency is introduced.

Multiple-Baseline Design Across Individuals—An experimental design in which baseline data are gathered across two or more individuals. The experimental contingency is applied to the first individual while baseline conditions are continued for the other individuals. After behavior has stabilized for all individuals, the contingency is introduced for the second individual. This is continued until the experimental contingency is applied to all individuals at different points in time. A causal relationship between the experimental contingency and behavior is demonstrated, if each individual's behavior changes when and only when the contingency is introduced.

Multiple-Baseline Design Across Situations—An experimental design in which baseline data are gathered across two or more situations. The experimental contingency is applied to behavior in the first situation while baseline conditions are continued for the behavior in the other situations. After behavior has stabilized in each situation, the contingency is introduced for behavior in the second situation. This is continued until the contingency is applied to all situations at different points in time. A causal relationship between the experimental contingency and behavior is demonstrated, if behavior in each situation changes when and only when the contingency is introduced.

"Naturally Occurring" Reinforcers—Those reinforcing events in the environment which are not contrived but are usually available as part of the setting. Attention, praise, completion of an activity, and mastery of a task are some events which are "naturally occurring" reinforcers.

Negative Reinforcement—An increase in the frequency of a response which is followed by termination or removal of a negative reinforcer. See Negative Reinforcer.

Negative Reinforcer—An aversive event or stimulus which when terminated increases the frequency of the preceding response. The increase in frequency of the response which terminates or removes the aversive event is called negative reinforcement.

Noncontingent Delivery of a Reinforcer—The delivery of a reinforcer independently of behavior. The reinforcer is delivered without reference to how the individual is behaving. Contrast with Contingent Delivery of a Reinforcer.

Observational Learning—Learning by observing another individual (a model) engage in a behavior. To learn from a model, the observer need not perform the behavior nor receive direct consequences for his or her performance.

Observer Drift—Refers to gradually departing from the definitions that observers may use when they record behavior. The definitions that observers use can change over time. Changes in the target behavior may reflect changes in how responses are scored rather than the effects of the program.

Occasion—To increase the likelihood that a response is performed by presenting an S^D. Certain cues in the environment (e.g., music) occasion certain responses (e.g., singing).

Operant Behavior—Emitted behavior that is controlled by its consequences.

Operant Conditioning—A type of learning in which behaviors are altered primarily by regulating the consequences which follow them. The frequency of operant behaviors is altered by the consequences which they produce.

Operant Rate—See Baseline.

Overcorrection—A punishment procedure which consists of two components. First, the environmental consequences of the undesirable behavior must be corrected (e.g., cleaning up a mess). Second, correct forms of desirable behavior must be thoroughly rehearsed or practiced (e.g., cleaning up messes made by several other people).

Overt Behavior—Behavior that is publicly observable and measurable. Contrast with Covert Event.

Positive Practice—Repeatedly practicing appropriate responses or responses that are incompatible with an undesirable response that is to be suppressed. This is a component of overcorrection but often is used alone as a punishment technique when the behavior that is to be suppressed (e.g., self-stimulatory behaviors such as rocking) has no clear environmental consequence that can be corrected.

Positive Reinforcement—An increase in the frequency of a response which is followed by a positive reinforcer. See Positive Reinforcer.

Positive Reinforcer—An event which, when presented, increases the probability of a response it follows.

Premack Principle—A principle that states that of any pair of responses or activities in which an individual freely engages, the more frequent one will reinforce the less frequent one.

Primary Reinforcer—A reinforcing event which does not depend on learning to achieve its reinforcing properties. Food, water, and sex are primary reinforcers. Contrast with Secondary Reinforcer.

Prompt—An antecedent event which helps initiate a response. A discriminative stimulus which occasions a response. Instructions, gestures, physical guidance, and modeling cues serve as prompts.

Psychodynamic View—An explanation of personality which accounts for behavior by positing underlying psychological forces. The behavior of an individual is traced to psychological drives, impulses, or personality dynamics.

Punishment—Presentation of an aversive event or removal of a positive event contingent upon a response which decreases the probability of that response.

Ratio Schedule of Reinforcement—A schedule in which reinforcement is delivered on the basis of the number of responses which are performed. Contrast with Interval Schedule of Reinforcement.

Reinforcement—An increase in the frequency of a response when the response is immediately followed by a particular consequence. The consequence can be either the presentation of a positive reinforcer or removal of a negative reinforcer.

Reinforcer Sampling—A case of response priming where the purpose is to develop or increase utilization of an event as a reinforcer. The client is provided with a sample or small portion of the event which increases the likelihood that the entire event can serve as a reinforcer.

Reliability of Assessment—The consistency with which different observers working independently score a target response. Reliability can be calculated with different methods depending upon the method used to assess behavior (e.g., frequency, interval, or duration methods). The calculation of reliability yields a percentage of agreement between observers.

Resistance to Extinction—The extent to which a response is maintained once reinforcement is no longer provided.

Respondent—Behavior that is elicited or automatically controlled by antecedent stimuli. Reflexes are respondents because their performance automatically follows certain stimuli. The connection between unconditioned respondents and antecedent events which control them is unlearned. Respondents may come under the control of otherwise neutral stimuli through classical conditioning.

Response Cost—A punishment procedure in which a positive reinforcer is lost or some penalty is invoked contingent upon behavior.

Unlike timeout, there is no specified time limit to the withdrawal of the reinforcer. Fines represent a common form of response cost.

Response Generalization—Reinforcement of one response increases the probability of other responses which are similar to and resemble the target response. Contrast with Stimulus Generalization.

Response Priming—Any procedure which initiates early steps in a sequence of responses. Response priming increases the likelihood that the terminal behavior in a sequence of responses will be performed by initiating early responses in the sequence.

Reversal Design—An experimental design where the target behavior of a subject or group of subjects is assessed to determine baseline performance. After a stable rate of behavior is shown, the experimental condition is introduced until behavior changes. A reversal phase follows where the program is withdrawn. Finally, the experimental condition is reintroduced. A functional relationship is demonstrated if behavior changes in each phase in which the experimental condition is presented and reverts to baseline or near baseline levels when it is withdrawn. Also called an ABAB design.

Reversal Phase—A phase in the reversal design in which the program is withdrawn or altered to determine whether behavior reverts to baseline or near baseline levels. During a reversal phase one of three changes usually is made: (1) the program is withdrawn, (2) the consequences are delivered noncontingently, or (3) the consequences follow a DRO schedule.

Satiation—Providing an excessive amount of the reinforcer. A loss of effectiveness that occurs after a large amount of the reinforcer has been delivered.

Schedule of Reinforcement—The rule denoting how many responses or which responses will be reinforced.

S^D—See Discriminative Stimulus.

S^Δ—An antecedent event or stimulus which signals that a certain response will not be reinforced.

Secondary (or Conditioned) Reinforcer—An event which becomes reinforcing through learning. An event becomes a secondary reinforcer by being paired with other events (primary or conditioned) which are already reinforcing. Praise and attention are examples of secondary reinforcers. Contrast with Primary Reinforcer.

Self-Administered Reinforcement—Refers to the client delivering the reinforcer to himself.

Self-Control—Refers to those behaviors an individual deliberately undertakes to achieve self-selected outcomes by manipulating antecedent and consequent events.

Self-Determined Reinforcement—Refers to the client specifying the criteria for reinforcement.

Self-Help Manuals—Written materials in the form of books, manuals, or brochures that are designed to teach clients how to implement treatments for themselves. Little or no therapist contact usually is required as the client applies the techniques in a step-by-step fashion, as specified by the manual.

Self-Instruction—A self-control technique in which an individual prompts his or her own behavior by providing covert self-instructions or statements which direct and guide performance.

Self-Observation—Assessing or recording one's own behavior. Sometimes used as a self-control technique.

Self-Punishment—Providing oneself with punishing consequences contingent upon behavior.

Self-Reinforcement—Providing oneself with reinforcing consequences contingent upon behavior. To qualify as self-reinforcement, the client must be free to partake of the reinforcer at any time whether or not a particular response is performed.

Shaping—Developing a new behavior by reinforcing successive approximations toward the terminal response. See Successive Approximations.

Simultaneous-Treatment Design—An experimental design in which two or more interventions are implemented concurrently in the same treatment phase. The interventions are balanced (varied across) different conditions such as the time period of the day in which treatment is implemented. The design is useful for comparing the relative effectiveness of two or more interventions.

Social Reinforcers—Reinforcers which result from interpersonal interaction such as attention, praise and approval, smiles, and physical contact.

Social Validation—Refers to the evaluation of the social importance of the behavior that is focused upon in treatment or the importance of the changes that are achieved. The applied or clinical significance of behavioral programs often is evaluated after treatment by comparing the behavior of the target subject with others who perform adaptively or by soliciting opinions of persons in the community with whom the client interacts.

Spontaneous Recovery—The temporary recurrence of a behavior during extinction. Even though the response has not been reinforced, it may suddenly reappear during the course of extinction. The magnitude of a response which temporarily recovers spontaneously is usually lower than its magnitude prior to extinction.

Stimulus—A measurable event that may have an effect upon the behavior.

Stimulus Control—The presence of a particular stimulus serves as an occasion for a particular response. A response is performed when in the presence of a particular stimulus but not in its absence. See Discriminative Stimulus.

Stimulus Generalization—Transfer of a trained response to situations or stimulus conditions other than those in which training has taken place. The behavior generalizes to other situations. Contrast with Response Generalization.

Successive Approximations—Responses which increasingly resemble the terminal behavior which is being shaped. See Shaping.

Symptom Substitution—The view stemming from the psychodynamic model that if maladaptive behavior is treated without focusing on the underlying psychological problem, a substitute symptom may develop in place of the one which was treated.

Target Behavior—The behavior to be altered or focused upon during a behavior modification program. The behavior assessed and to be changed.

Team-Based Contingency—A group contingency in which members earn reinforcers on the basis of performance of the group. In addition, subgroups or teams are used so that there is competition to earn the reinforcers between the teams.

Terminal Response—The final goal or behavior that is achieved at the end of shaping. See Shaping.

Time-Out from Reinforcement—A punishment procedure in which access to positive reinforcement is withdrawn for a certain period of time. The opportunity to receive reinforcement is removed contingent upon behavior. Isolation from a group exemplifies time-out from reinforcement.

Token—A tangible object which serves as a generalized conditioned reinforcer. It can be exchanged for back-up reinforcers from which it derives its value. Poker chips, coins, tickets, stars, points, and checkmarks are commonly used as tokens. See Token Economy.

Token Economy—A reinforcement system where tokens are earned for a variety of behaviors and purchase a variety of back-up reinforcers. A token economy represents a system analogous to a national economy where money serves as a medium of exchange, and can be earned and spent in several ways.

Traits—Patterns of behavior which are enduring over time and across situations.

Transfer of Training—The extent to which responses trained in one setting transfer to settings other than those in which training takes place. See Stimulus Generalization.

Unconditioned Response—A reflex response elicited by an unconditioned stimulus. See Classical Conditioning and Respondent.

Unconditioned Stimulus—A stimulus which elicits a reflex response.

The response is automatically evoked by the unconditioned stimulus. See Classical Conditioning.

Variable-Interval Schedule—A schedule of administering reinforcement. In a VI schedule, the first occurrence of the target response after a given time interval has elapsed is reinforced. However, the time interval changes each time, that is, it is variable. The schedule is denoted by the average time which must elapse before a response can be reinforced.

Variable-Ratio Schedule—A schedule of administering reinforcement. In a VR schedule, a number of occurrences of the target response is required for reinforcement. The number of responses required varies each time reinforcement is delivered. The schedule is denoted by the average number of occurrences of the response required before reinforcement is delivered.

Vicarious Reinforcement—Reinforcement of one individual sometimes increases performance of the reinforced behavior in other individuals who are not directly reinforced. A spread of reinforcement effects to other individuals whose behaviors are not directly reinforced.

References

Aaron, B. A., & Bostow, D. E. Indirect facilitation of on-task behavior produced by contingent free-time for academic productivity. *Journal of Applied Behavior Analysis*, 1978, *11*, 197.

Abrams, L., Hines, D., Pollack, D., Ross, M., Stubbs, D. A., & Polyot, C. J. Transferable tokens: Increasing social interaction in a token economy. *Psychological Reports*, 1974, *35*, 447–452.

Adams, M. R., & Popelka, G. The influence of "time-out" on stutterers and their dysfluency. *Behavior Therapy*, 1971, *2*, 334–339.

Agras, W. S., Barlow, D. H., Chapin, H. W., Abel, G. G., & Leitenberg, H. Behavior modification of anorexia nervosa. *Archives of General Psychiatry*, 1974, *30*, 279–286.

Agras, W. S., Kazdin, A. E., & Wilson, G. T. *Behavior therapy: Toward an applied clinical science*. San Francisco: W. H. Freeman, 1979.

Alford, G. S., Blanchard, E. B., & Buckley, T. M. Treatment of hysterical vomiting by modification of social contingencies: A case study. *Journal of Behavior Therapy and Experimental Psychiatry*, 1972, *3*, 209–212.

Allen, G. J. Case study: Implementation of behavior modification techniques in summer camp settings. *Behavior Therapy*, 1973, *4*, 570–575.

Allen, K. E., & Harris, F. R. Elimination of a child's excessive scratching by training the mother in reinforcement procedures. *Behaviour Research and Therapy*, 1966, *4*, 79–84.

Allen, K. E., Hart, B. M., Buell, J. S., Harris, F. R., & Wolf, M. M. Effects of social reinforcement on isolate behavior of a nursery school child. *Child Development*, 1964, *35*, 511–518.

Allen, K. E., Turner, K. D., & Everett, P. M. A behavior modification classroom for Head Start children with problem behaviors. *Exceptional Children*, 1970, *37*, 119–127.

Altman, K., Haavik, S., & Cook, J. W. Punishment of self-injurious behavior in natural settings using contingent aromatic ammonia. *Behaviour Research and Therapy*, 1978, *16*, 85–96.

Anderson, L., Foder, I., & Alpert, M. A comparison of methods for training self-control. *Behavior Therapy*, 1976, *7*, 649–658.

Aragona, J., Cassady, J., & Drabman, R. S. Treating overweight children through parental training and contingency contracting. *Journal of Applied Behavior Analysis*, 1975, *8*, 269–278.

Aronfreed, J., & Reber, A. Internalized behavioral suppression and the timing of social punishment. *Journal of Personality and Social Psychology*, 1965, *1*, 3–16

Arthur, A. Z. Diagnostic testing and the new alternatives. *Psychological Bulletin*, 1969, *72*, 183–192.

Association for Advancement of Behavior Therapy, Ethical issues for human services. *Behavior Therapy*, 1977, *8*, v–vi.

Axelrod, S. Comparison of individual and group contingencies in two special classes. *Behavior Therapy*, 1973, *4*, 83–90.

Axelrod, S., Brantner, J. P., & Meddock, T. D. Overcorrection: A review and critical analysis. *Journal of Special Education*, 1978, *12*, 367–391.

Ayllon, T. Intensive treatment of psychotic behavior by stimulus satiation and food reinforcement. *Behaviour Research and Therapy*, 1963, *1*, 53–61.

Ayllon, T., & Azrin, N. H., Reinforcer sampling: A technique for increasing the behavior of mental patients. *Journal of Applied Behavior Analysis*, 1968, *1*, 13–20. (a)

Ayllon, T., & Azrin, N. H. *The token economy: A motivational system for therapy and rehabilitation.* New York: Appleton-Century-Crofts, 1968. (b)

Ayllon, T., & Haughton, E. Modification of symptomatic verbal behavior of mental patients. *Behaviour Research and Therapy*, 1964, *2*, 87–97.

Ayllon, T., & Kelly, K. Reinstating verbal behavior in a functionally mute retardate. *Professional Psychology*, 1974, *5*, 385–393.

Ayllon, T., Layman, D., & Kandel, H. J. A behavioral-educational alternative to drug control of hyperactive children. *Journal of Applied Behavior Analysis*, 1975, *8*, 137–146.

Ayllon, T., & Michael, J. The psychiatric nurse as a behavioral engineer. *Journal of the Experimental Analysis of Behavior*, 1959, *2*, 323–334.

Ayllon, T., & Roberts, M. D. Eliminating discipline problems by strengthening academic performance. *Journal of Applied Behavior Analysis*, 1974, *7*, 71–76.

Ayllon, T., & Rosenbaum, M. S. The behavioral treatment of disruption and hyperactivity in school settings. In B. B. Lahey & A. E. Kazdin (Eds.), *Advances in clinical child psychology, Volume 1.* New York: Plenum, 1977.

Ayllon, T., & Skuban, W. Accountability in psychotherapy: A test case. *Journal of Behavior Therapy and Experimental Psychiatry*, 1973, *4*, 19–30.

Azrin, N. H., Flores, T., & Kaplan, S. J. Job-finding club: A group-assisted program for obtaining employment. *Behaviour Research and Therapy*, 1975, *13*, 17–27.

Azrin, N. H., & Foxx, R. M. A rapid method of toilet training the institutionalized retarded. *Journal of Applied Behavior Analysis*, 1971, *4*, 89–99.

Azrin, N. H., & Foxx, R. M. *Toilet training in less than a day.* New York: Simon & Schuster, 1974.

Azrin, H. H., Gottlieb, L., Hughart, L., Wesolowski, M. D., & Rahn, T. Eliminating self-injurious behavior by educative prodecures. *Behaviour Research and Therapy*, 1975, *13*, 101–111.

Azrin, N. H., & Holz, W. C. Punishment. In W. K. Honig (Ed.), *Operant behavior: Areas of research and application.* New York: Appleton-Century-Crofts, 1966.

Azrin, N. H., & Powers, M. A. Eliminating classroom disturbances of emotionally disturbed children by positive practice procedures. *Behavior Therapy*, 1975, *6*, 525–534.

Azrin, N. H., & Wesolowski, M. D. Theft reversal: An overcorrection procedure for eliminating stealing by retarded persons, *Journal of Applied Behavior Analysis*, 1974, *7*, 577–581.

Azrin, N. H., & Wesolowski, M. D. Eliminating habitual vomiting in a retarded adult by positive practice and self-correction. *Journal of Behavior Therapy and Experimental Psychiatry*, 1975, *6*, 145–148.

Baer, D. M. A case for the selective reinforcement of punishment. In C. Neuringer & J. L. Michael (Eds.), *Behavior modification in clinical psychology.* New York: Appleton-Century-Crofts, 1970.

Baer, D. M., Rowbury, T. G., & Goetz, E. M. Behavioral traps in the preschool: A proposal for research. *Minnesota Symposia on Child Psychology,* 1976, *10,* 3–27.

Baer, D. M., & Wolf, M. M. The entry into natural communities of reinforcement. In R. Ulrich, T. Stachnik, & J. Mabry (Eds.), *Control of human behavior, Volume 2.* Glenview, Illinois: Scott, Foresman and Company, 1970.

Baer, D. M., Wolf, M. M., & Risley, T. R. Some current dimensions of applied behavior analysis. *Journal of Applied Behavior Analysis,* 1968, *1,* 91–97.

Bailey, J. S., Timbers, G. D., Phillips, E. L., & Wolf, M. M. Modification of articulation errors of pre-delinquents by their peers. *Journal of Applied Behavior Analysis,* 1971, *4,* 265–281.

Ball, T. S. Issues and implications of operant conditioning: The reestablishment of social behavior. *Hospital & Community Psychiatry,* 1968, *19,* 230–232.

Ballard, K. D., & Glynn, T. Behavioral self-management in story writing with elementary school children. *Journal of Applied Behavior Analysis,* 1975, *8,* 387–398.

Bandura, A. Influence of models' reinforcement contingencies on the acquisition of imitative responses. *Journal of Personality and Social Psychology,* 1965, *1,* 589–595.

Bandura, A. Psychotherapy based upon modeling principles. In A. E. Bergin, & S. L. Garfield (Eds.), *Handbook of psychotherapy and behavior change: An empirical analysis.* New York: Wiley, 1971. (a)

Bandura, A. Vicarious and self-reinforcement processes. In R. Glaser (Ed.), *The nature of reinforcement.* New York: Academic Press, 1971. (b)

Bandura, A. Self-reinforcement: Theoretical and methodological considerations. *Behaviorism,* 1976, *4,* 135–155.

Bandura, A. *Social learning theory.* Englewood Cliffs, New Jersey: Prentice-Hall, 1977.

Bandura, A., Grusec, J., & Menlove, F. Some social determinants of self-monitoring reinforcement systems.

Journal of Personality and Social Psychology, 1967, *5,* 449–455.

Bandura, A., & Kupers, C. J. Transmission of patterns of self-reinforcement through modeling. *Journal of Abnormal and Social Psychology,* 1964, *69,* 1–9.

Bandura, A., & Walters, R. H. *Adolescent aggression.* New York: Ronald Press, 1959.

Barrett, B. H. Reduction in rate of multiple tics by free operant conditioning methods. *Journal of Nervous and Mental Disease,* 1962, *135,* 187–195.

Barton, E. J., & Osborne, J. G. The development of classroom sharing by a teacher using positive practice. *Behavior Modification,* 1978, *2,* 231–250.

Barton, E. S., Guess, D., Garcia, E., & Baer, D. M. Improvements of retardates' mealtime behaviors by timeout procedures using multiple-baseline techniques. *Journal of Applied Behavior Analysis,* 1970, *3,* 77–84.

Bassett, J. E., & Blanchard, E. B. The effect of the absence of close supervision on the use of response cost in a prison token economy. *Journal of Applied Behavior Analysis,* 1977, *10,* 375–379.

Bateman, S. Application of Premack's generalization on reinforcement to modify occupational behavior in two severely retarded individuals. *American Journal of Mental Deficiency,* 1975, *79,* 604–610.

Beck, A. T. *Cognitive therapy and emotional disorders.* New York: International Universities Press, 1976.

Becker, J. V., Turner, S. M., & Sajwaj, T. E. Multiple behavioral effects of the use of lemon juice with a ruminating toddler-age child. *Behavior Modification,* 1978, *2,* 267–278.

Beiman, I., Graham, L. E., & Ciminero, A. R. Self-control progressive relaxation training as an alternative nonpharmacological treatment for essential hypertension: Therapeutic effects in the natural environment. *Behaviour Research and Therapy,* 1978, *16,* 371–375.

Bellack, A. S. A comparison of self-reinforcement and self-monitoring in a weight reduction program. *Behavior Therapy,* 1976, *7,* 68–75.

Bem, S. L. Sex-role adaptability: One consequence of psychological androgyny. *Journal of Personality and Social Psychology,* 1975, *31,* 634–643.

Bergin, A. E. The evaluation of therapeutic outcomes. In A. E. Bergin & S. L. Garfield (Eds.), *Handbook of psychotherapy and behavior change: An empirical analysis.* New York: Wiley, 1971.

Bergin, A. E., & Lambert, M. J. The evaluation of therapeutic outcomes. In S. L. Garfield & A. E. Bergin (Eds.), *Handbook of psychotherapy and behavior change: An empirical analysis* (second edition). New York: Wiley, 1978.

Berkowitz, S., Sherry, P. J., & Davis, B. A. Teaching self-feeding skills to profound retardates using reinforcement and fading procedures. *Behavior Therapy,* 1971, *2,* 62–67.

Best, D. L., Smith, S. C., Graves, D. J., & Williams, J. E. The modification of racial bias in preschool children. *Journal of Experimental Child Psychology,* 1975, *20,* 193–205.

Bigelow, G., Liebson, I., & Griffiths, R. Alcoholic drinking: Suppression by a brief time-out procedure. *Behaviour Research and Therapy,* 1974, *12,* 107–115.

Bijou, S. W., Peterson, R. F., & Ault, M. H. A method to integrate descriptive and experimental field studies at the level of data and empirical concepts. *Journal of Applied Behavior Analysis.* 1968, *1,* 175–191.

Bijou, S. W., Peterson, R. F., Harris, F. R. Allen, K. E., & Johnston, M. S. Methodology for experimental studies of young children in natural settings. *Psychological Record,* 1969, *19,* 177–210.

Birnbrauer, J. S. Generalization of punishment effects: A case study. *Journal of Applied Behavior Analysis,* 1968, *1,* 201–211.

Blanchard, E. B., & Epstein, L. H. The clinical usefulness of biofeedback. In M. Hersen, R. M. Eisler, & P. M. Miller (Eds.), *Progress in behavior modification, Volume 4.* New York: Academic Press, 1977.

Blanchard, E. B., Young, L. D., & Haynes, M. R. A simple feedback system for the treatment of elevated blood pressure. *Behavior Therapy,* 1975, *6,* 241–245.

Blanco, R. F. Fifty recommendations to aid exceptional children. *Psychology in the Schools,* 1970, *7,* 29–37.

Bolstad, O. D., & Johnson, S. M. Self-regulation in the modification of disruptive behavior. *Journal of Applied Behavior Analysis,* 1972, *5,* 443–454.

Bootzin, R. R. Stimulus control treatment for insomnia. *Proceedings, 80th Annual Convention, American Psychological Association,* 1972, *7,* 395–396.

Bootzin, R. R., & Nicassio, P. M. Behavioral treatments for insomnia. In M. Hersen, R. M. Eisler, & P. M. Miller (Eds.), *Progress in behavior modification, Volume 6.* New York: Academic Press, 1978.

Boren, J. J., & Colman, A. D. Some experiments on reinforcement principles within a psychiatric ward for delinquent soldiers. *Journal of Applied Behavior Analysis,* 1970, *3,* 29–37.

Bornstein, M. T., Bellack, A. S., & Hersen, M. Social-skills training for unassertive children: A multiple-baseline analysis. *Journal of Applied Behavior Analysis,* 1977, *10,* 183–195.

Bornstein, P. H., Hamilton, S. B., & Quevillon, R. P. Behavior modification by long-distance: Disruptive behavior in a rural classroom setting. *Behavior Modification,* 1977, *1,* 369–380.

Bornstein, P. H., & Quevillon, R. P. The effects of a self-instructional package on overactive preschool boys. *Journal of Applied Behavior Analysis,* 1976, *9,* 179–188.

Breyer, N. L., & Allen, G. J. Effects of implementing a token economy on teacher attending behavior. *Journal of Applied Behavior Analysis,* 1975, *8,* 373–380.

Briscoe, R. V., Hoffman, D. B., & Bailey, J. S. Behavioral community psychology: Training a community board to problem solve. *Journal of Applied Behavior Analysis,* 1975, *8,* 157–168.

Bristol, M. M. Control of physical aggression through school- and home-based reinforcement. In J. D. Krumboltz & C. E. Thoresen (Eds.), *Counseling methods.* New York: Holt, Rinehart & Winston, 1976.

Bristol, M. M., & Sloane, H. N. Effects of contingency contracting on study rate and test performance. *Journal of*

Applied Behavior Analysis, 1974, 7, 271–285.

Brownell, K. D., Colletti, G., Ersner-Hersfield, R., Hershfield, S. M., & Wilson, G. T. Self-control in school children: Stringency and leniency in self-determined and externally imposed performance standards. *Behavior Therapy*, 1977, 8, 442–455.

Brush, R. F. (Ed.), *Aversive conditioning and learning*. New York: Academic Press, 1971.

Bucher, B., & King, L. W. Generalization of punishment effects in the deviant behavior of a psychotic child. *Behavior Therapy*, 1971, 2, 68–77.

Budd, K. S., & Baer, D. M. Behavior modification and the law: Implications of recent judicial decisions. *Journal of Psychiatry and Law*, 1976, 4, 171–244.

Budd, K. S., & Stokes, T. F. Cue properties of praise in vicarious reinforcement with preschoolers. Paper presented at meeting of the American Psychological Association, San Francisco, August 1977.

Buehler, R. E., Patterson, G. R., & Furniss, J. M. The reinforcement of behaviour in institutional settings. *Behaviour Research and Therapy*, 1966, 4, 157–167.

Buell, J., Stoddard, P., Harris, F., & Baer, D. M. Collateral social development accompanying reinforcement of outdoor play in a preschool child. *Journal of Applied Behavior Analysis*, 1968, 1, 167–173.

Bunck, T. J., & Iwata, B. A. Increasing senior citizen participation in a community-based nutritious meal program. *Journal of Applied Behavior Analysis*, 1978, 11, 75–86.

Burchard, J. D., & Barrera, F. An analysis of timeout and response cost in a programmed environment. *Journal of Applied Behavior Analysis*, 1972, 5, 271–282.

Burgess, A. *A clockwork orange*. New York: W. W. Norton, 1963.

Bushell, D., Jr. The design of classroom contingencies. In F. S. Keller & E. Ribes-Inesta (Eds.), *Behavior modification: Applications to education*. New York: Academic Press, 1974.

Business Week, New tool: "Reinforcement" for good work. December 18, 1971, 76–77.

Butler, J. F. The toilet training success of parents after reading *Toilet Training in Less Than a Day. Behavior Therapy*, 1976, 7, 185–191.

Cahoon, D. D. Symptom substitution and the behavior therapies: Reappraisal. *Psychological Bulletin*, 1968, 69, 149–156.

Cairns, D., & Pasino, J. A. Comparison of verbal reinforcement and feedback in the operant treatment of disability due to chronic low back pain. *Behavior Therapy*, 1977, 8, 621–630.

Calhoun, K. S., & Lima, P. P. Effects of varying schedules of timeout on high- and low-rate behaviors. *Journal of Behavior Therapy and Experimental Psychiatry*, 1977, 8, 189–194.

Campbell, D. T., & Stanley, J. C. Experimental and quasi-experimental designs for research and teaching. In N. L. Gage (Ed.), *Handbook of research on teaching*. Chicago: Rand McNally, 1963.

Carlson, C. S., Arnold, C. R., Becker, W. C., & Madsen, C. H. The elimination of tantrum behavior of a child in an elementary classroom. *Behaviour Research and Therapy*, 1968, 6, 117–119.

Catania, A. C. The myth of self-reinforcement. *Behaviorism*, 1975, 3, 192–199.

Cautela, J. R. Covert sensitization. *Psychological Reports*, 1967, 20, 459–468.

Cautela, J. R. The present status of covert modeling. *Journal of Behavior Therapy and Experimental Psychiatry*, 1976, 7, 323–326.

Chadwick, B. A., & Day, R. C. Systematic reinforcement: Academic performance of underachieving students. *Journal of Applied Behavior Analysis*, 1971, 4, 311–319.

Chapman, C., & Risley, T. R. Anti-litter procedures in an urban high-density area. *Journal of Applied Behavior Analysis*, 1974, 7, 377–384.

Christopherson, E. R., Arnold, C. M., Hill, D. W., & Quilitch, H. R. The home point system: Token reinforcement procedures for application by parents of children with behavior problems. *Journal of Applied Behavior Analysis*, 1972, 5, 485–497.

Christy, P. R. Does use of tangible rewards with individual children affect peer observers? *Journal of Applied Behavior Analysis*, 1975, *8*, 187–196.

Clark, H. B., Rowbury, T., Baer, A. M., & Baer, D. M. Timeout as a punishing stimulus in continuous and intermittent schedules. *Journal of Applied Behavior Analysis*, 1973, *6*, 443–455.

Clark, H. B., Greene, B. F., Macrae, J. W., McNees, M. P., Davis, J. L., & Risley, T. R. A parent advice package for family shopping trips: Development and evaluation. *Journal of Applied Behavor Analysis*, 1977, *10*, 605–624.

Clark, H. B., Boyd, S. B., & Macrae, J. W. A classroom program teaching disadvantaged youths to write biographic information. *Journal of Applied Behavior Analysis*, 1975, *8*, 67–75.

Coates, T. J. Successive self-management strategies towards coping with night eating. *Journal of Behavior Therapy and Experimental Psychiatry*, 1978, *9*, 181–183.

Cochrane, R., & Sobol, M. P. Myth and methodology in behaviour therapy research. In M. P. Feldman & A. Broadhurst (Eds.), *Theoretical and empirical bases of the behaviour therapies*. London: Wiley, 1976.

Cole, P. M., & Kazdin, A. E. Role of label and content in negative attitudes toward behavior modification. Unpublished manuscript, The Pennsylvania State University, 1979.

Cook, J. W., Altman, K., Shaw, J., & Blaylock, M. Use of contingent lemon juice to eliminate public masturbation by a severely retarded boy. *Behaviour Research and Therapy*, 1978, *16*, 131–134.

Cooke, T. P., & Apolloni, T. Developing positive social-emotional behaviors: A study of training and generalization effects. *Journal of Applied Behavior Analysis*, 1976, *9*, 65–78.

Cooper, M. L., Thomson, C. L., & Baer, D. M. The experimental modification of teacher attending behavior. *Journal of Applied Behavior Analysis*, 1970, *3*, 153–157.

Copeland, R., & Hall, R. V. Behavior modification in the classroom. In M. Hersen, R. M. Eisler, & P. M. Miller (Eds.), *Prog-ress in behavior modification*, Volume 3. New York: Academic Press, 1976.

Cossairt, A., Hall, R. V., & Hopkins, B. L. The effects of experimenter's instructions, feedback, and praise on teacher praise and student attending behavior. *Journal of Applied Behavior Analysis*, 1973, *6*, 89–100.

Cotter, L. H. Operant conditioning in a Vietnamese mental hospital. *American Journal of Psychiatry*, 1967, *124*, 23–28.

Coughlin, R. C. The aversive properties of withdrawing positive reinforcement: A review of the recent literature. *Psychological Record*, 1972, *22*, 333–354.

Creer, T. L., Chai, H., & Hoffman, A. A single application of an aversive stimulus to eliminate chronic cough. *Journal of Behavior Therapy and Experimental Psychiatry*, 1977, *8*, 107–109.

Danaher, B. G. Theoretical foundations and clinical applications of the Premack Principle: Review and critique. *Behavior Therapy*, 1974, *5*, 307–324.

Dapcich-Miura, E., & Hovell, M. F. Contingency management of adherence to a complex medical regimen in an elderly heart patient. *Behavior Therapy*, 1979, *10*, 193–201.

Datel, W. E., & Legters, L. J. The psychology of the army recruit. Paper presented at the American Medical Association. Chicago, June, 1970.

Davison, G. C. Homosexuality: The ethical challenge. *Journal of Consulting and Clinical Psychology*, 1976, *44*, 157–162.

Davison, G. C. & Stuart, R. B. Behavior therapy and civil liberties. *American Psychologist*, 1975, *7*, 755–763.

Deitz, S. M. An analysis of programming DRL schedules in educational settings. *Behaviour Research and Therapy*, 1977, *15*, 103–111.

Deitz, S. M., & Repp, A. C. Decreasing classroom misbehavior through the use of DRL schedules of reinforcement. *Journal of Applied Behavior Analysis*, 1973, *6*, 457–463.

Deitz, S. M., Slack, D. J., Schwarzmueller, E. B., Wilander, A. P., Weatherly, T. J., & Hilliard, G. Reducing inappropriate behavior in special classrooms by reinforcing average interresponse times: Interval DRL. *Behavior Therapy*, 1978, *9*, 37–46.

DeMaster, B., Reid, J., & Twentyman, C. The effects of different amounts of feedback on observer's reliability. *Behavior Therapy*, 1977, *8*, 317–329.

Dericco, D. A., Brigham, T. A., & Garlington, W. K. Development and evaluation of treatment paradigms for the suppression of smoking behavior. *Journal of Applied Behavior Analysis*, 1977, *10*, 173–181.

DeRisi, W. J., & Butz, G. *Writing behavioral contracts: A case simulation practice manual.* Champaign, Illinois: Research Press, 1975.

Dineen, J. P., Clark, H. B., & Risley, T. R. Peer tutoring among elementary students: Educational benefits to the tutor. *Journal of Applied Behavior Analysis*, 1977, *10*, 231–238.

Dittes, J. E. Extinction during psychotherapy or GSR accompanying "embarrassing" statements. *Journal of Abnormal and Social Psychology*, 1957, *54*, 187–191.

Doleys, D. M., & Arnold, S. Treatment of childhood encopresis: Full cleanliness training. *Mental Retardation*, 1975, *13*, 14–16.

Doleys, D. M., & Slapion, M. J. The reduction of verbal repetitions by response cost controlled by a sibling. *Journal of Behavior Therapy and Experimental Psychiatry*, 1975, *6*, 61–63.

Doleys, D. M., Wells, K. C., Hobbs, S. A., Roberts, M. W., & Cartelli, L. M. The effects of social punishment on noncompliance: A comparison with timeout and positive practice. *Journal of Applied Behavior Analysis*, 1976, *9*, 471–482.

Dornbusch, S. M., Hastorf, A. H., Richardson, S. A., Muzzy, R. E., & Vreeland, R. S. The perceiver and the perceived: Their relative influence on the categories of interpersonal cognition. *Journal of Personality and Social Psychology*, 1965, *1*, 434–440.

Drabman, R. S., Spitalnik, R., & O'Leary, K. D. Teaching self-control to disruptive children. *Journal of Abnormal Psychology*, 1973, *82*, 10–16.

Drabman, R., Spitalnik, R., & Spitalnik, K. Sociometric and disruptive behavior as a function of four types of token reinforcement programs. *Journal of Applied Behavior Analysis*, 1974, *7*, 93–101.

Dunn, L. M. Special education for the mildly retarded—is much of it justifiable? In W. C. Becker (Ed.), *An empirical basis for change in education*. Chicago: Science Research Associates, 1971.

Edwards, C. D., & Williams, J. E. Generalization between evaluative words associated with racial figures in preschool children. *Journal of Experimental Research in Personality*, 1970, *4*, 144–155.

Eitzen, D. S. The effects of behavior modification on the attitudes of delinquents. *Behaviour Research and Therapy*, 1975, *13*, 295–299.

Ellis, A. *The essence of rational psychotherapy: A comprehensive approach to treatment.* New York: Institute for Rational Living, 1970.

Emshofff, J. G., Redd, W. H., & Davidson, W. S. Generalization training and the transfer of treatment effects with delinquent adolescents. *Journal of Behavior Therapy and Experimental Psychiatry*, 1976, *7*, 141–144.

Ennis, B. J., & Friedman, P. R. (Eds.), *Legal rights of the mentally handicapped, Volumes 1 & 2.* Practicing Law Institute, The Mental Health Law Project, 1973.

Epstein, L. H., & Abel, G. G. An analysis of biofeedback training effects for tension headache patients. *Behavior Therapy*, 1977, *8*, 37–47.

Epstein, L. H., Hersen, M., & Hemphill, D. P. Music feedback in the treatment of tension headache: An experimental case study. *Journal of Behavior Therapy and Experimental Psychiatry*, 1974, *5*, 59–63.

Epstein, L. H., & Masek, B. J. Behavioral control of medicine compliance. *Journal of Applied Behavior Analysis*, 1978, *11*, 1–9.

Epstein, R., & Goss, C. M. A self-control procedure for the maintenance of nondisruptive behavior in an elementary school child. *Behavior Therapy*, 1978, *9*, 109–117.

Everett, P. B., Hayward, S. C., & Meyers, A. W. The effects of a token reinforcement procedure on bus ridership, *Journal of Applied Behavior Analysis*, 1974, *7*, 1–9.

Eysenck, H. J. *The effects of psychotherapy.* New York: International Science Press, 1966.

Fairweather, G. W., & Simon, R. A further follow-up of psychotherapeutic programs. *Journal of Consulting Psychology,* 1963, *27,* 186.

Feingold, L., & Migler, B. The use of experimental dependency relationships as a motivating procedure on a token economy ward. In R. D. Rubin, H Fensterheim, J. D., Henderson, & L. P. Ullmann (Eds.), *Advances in behavior therapy.* New York: Academic Press, 1972.

Felixbrod, J. J., & O'Leary, K. D. Effects of reinforcement on children's academic behavior as a function of self-determined and externally imposed contingencies. *Journal of Applied Behavior Analysis,* 1973, *6,* 241–250.

Felixbrod, J. J., & O'Leary, K. D. Self-determination of academic standards by children: Toward freedom from external control. *Journal of Educational Psychology,* 1974, *66,* 845–850.

Ferster, C. B. Positive reinforcement and behavioral deficits of autistic children. *Child Development,* 1961, *32,* 437–456.

Ferster, C. B., Nurnberger, J. I., & Levitt, E. B. The control of eating. *Journal of Mathetics,* 1962, *1,* 87–109.

Ferster, C. B., & Skinner, B. F. *Schedules of reinforcement.* New York: Appleton-Century-Crofts, 1957.

Fichter, M. M., Wallace, C. J., Liberman, R. P., & Davis, J. R. Improving social interaction in a chronic psychotic using discriminated avoidance ("nagging"): Experimental analysis and generalization. *Journal of Applied Behavior Analysis,* 1976, *9,* 337–386.

Fink, W. T., & Carnine, D. W. Control of arithmetic errors using informational feedback and graphing. *Journal of Applied Behavior Analysis,* 1975, *8,* 461.

Fischer, J., & Nehs, R. Use of a commonly available chore to reduce a boy's rate of swearing. *Journal of Behavior Therapy and Experimental Psychiatry,* 1978, *9,* 81–83.

Fixsen, D. L., Phillips, E. L., & Wolf, M. M. Achievement Place: Experiments in self-government with pre-delinquents. *Journal of Applied Behavior Analysis,* 1973, *6,* 31–47.

Fixsen, D. L., Phillips, E. L., Phillips, E. A., & Wolf, M. M. The teaching-family model of group home treatment. In W. E. Craighead, A. E. Kazdin, & M. J. Mahoney (Eds.), *Behavior modification: Principles, issues, and applications.* Boston: Houghton Mifflin, 1976.

Fjellstedt, N., & Sulzer–Azaroff, B. Reducing the latency of a child's responding to instructions by means of a token system. *Journal of Applied Behavior Analysis,* 1973, *6,* 125–130.

Flavell, J. E., McGimsey, J. F., & Jones, M. L. The use of physical restraint in the treatment of self-injury and as positive reinforcement. *Journal of Applied Behavior Analysis,* 1978, *11,* 225–241.

Fo, W. S. O., & O'Donnell, C. R. The buddy system: Relationship and contingency conditions in a community intervention program for youth with nonprofessionals as behavior change agents. *Journal of Consulting and Clinical Psychology,* 1974, *42,* 163–169.

Fordyce, W., Fowler, R., Lehmann, J., & DeLateur, B. Some implications of learning in problems of chronic pain. *Journal of Chronic Diseases,* 1968, *21,* 179–190.

Fordyce, W. E., Fowler, R. S., Lehmann, J. F., DeLateur, B. J., Sand, P. L., & Trieschmann, R. B. Operant conditioning in the treatment of chronic pain. *Archives of Physical Medicine and Rehabilitation,* 1973, *54,* 399–408.

Forehand, R., Roberts, M. W., Doleys, D. M., Hobbs, S. A., & Resick, P. A. An examination of disciplinary procedures with children. *Journal of Experimental Child Psychology,* 1976, *21,* 109–120.

Fox, L. Effecting the use of efficient study habits. *Journal of Mathetics,* 1962, *1,* 75–86.

Foxx, R. M., & Azrin, N. H. Restitution: A method of eliminating aggressive-disruptive behavior of retarded and brain damaged patients. *Behaviour Research and Therapy,* 1972, *10,* 15–27.

Foxx, R. M., & Hake, D. F. Gasoline conservation: A procedure for measuring and reducing the driving of college students. *Journal of Applied Behavior Analysis*, 1977, *10*, 61–74.

Foxx, R. M., & Martin, E. D. Treatment of scavenging behavior (coprophagy and pica) by overcorrection. *Behaviour Research and Therapy*, 1975, *13*, 153–162.

Foxx, R. M., & Shapiro, S. T. The time-out ribbon: A nonexclusionary timeout procedure. *Journal of Applied Behavior Analysis*, 1978, *11*, 125–136.

Frank, G. *Psychiatric diagnosis: A review of research*. Oxford: Pergamon, 1975.

Frederiksen, L. W. Treatment of ruminative thinking by self-monitoring. *Journal of Behavior Therapy and Experimental Psychiatry*, 1975, *6*, 258–259.

Frederiksen, L. W., Jenkins, J. O., Foy, D. W., & Eisler, R. M. Social skills training to modify abusive verbal outbursts in adults. *Journal of Applied Behavior Analysis*, 1976, *9*, 117–125.

Freeman, H. E., & Simmons, O. G. *The mental patient comes home*. New York: Wiley, 1963.

Friedman, P. R. Legal regulation of applied behavior analysis in mental institutionalized and prisons. *Arizona Law Review*, 1975, *17*, 39–104.

Furman, W., Geller, M., Simon, S. J., & Kelly, J. A. The use of a behavioral rehearsal procedure for teaching job-interviewing skills to psychiatric patients. *Behavior Therapy*, 1979, *10*, 157–167.

Gardner, J. M. Teaching behavior modification to nonprofessionals. *Journal of Applied Behavior Analysis*, 1972, *5*, 517–521.

Gelfand, D. M., Elton, R. H., & Harman, R. E. A videotape-feedback training method to teach behavior modification skills to nonprofessionals. *Research in Education*, 1972, *7*, 15.

Gelfand, D. M., Gelfand, S., & Dobson, W. R. Unprogrammed reinforcement of patients' behaviour in a mental hospital. *Behaviour Research and Therapy*, 1967, *5*, 201–207.

Gelfand, D. M., & Hartmann, D. P. *Child behavior analysis and therapy*. New York: Pergamon, 1975.

Geller, E. S. Prompting anti-litter behaviors. *Proceedings of the 81st Annual Convention of the American Psychological Association*, 1973, *8*, 901–902.

Geller, E. S., Chaffee, J. L., & Ingram, R. E. Promoting paper recycling on a university campus. *Journal of Environmental Systems*, 1975, *5*, 39–57.

Gewirtz, J. L., & Baer, D. M. Deprivation and satiation of social reinforcers as drive conditions. *Journal of Abnormal and Social Psychology*, 1958, *57*, 165–172.

Gillum, R. R., & Barsky, A. J. Diagnosis and management of patient noncompliance. *Journal of the American Medical Association*, 1974, *12*, 1563–1567.

Gladstone, B. W., & Sherman, J. A. Developing generalized behavior-modification skills in high-school students working with retarded children. *Journal of Applied Behavior Analysis*, 1975, *8*, 169–180.

Gladstone, B. W., & Spencer, C. J. The effects of modeling on the contingent praise of mental retardation counsellors. *Journal of Applied Behavior Analysis*, 1977, *10*, 75–84.

Glasgow, R. E., & Rosen, G. M. Self-help behavior therapy manuals: Recent developments and clinical usage. *Clinical Behavior Therapy Review*, 1979, *1*, 1–20.

Glynn, E. L. Classroom applications of self-determined reinforcement. *Journal of Applied Behavior Analysis*, 1970, *3*, 123–132.

Goetz, E. M., Holmberg, M. C., & LeBlanc, J. M. Differential reinforcement of other behavior and noncontingent reinforcement as control procedures during the modification of a preschooler's compliance. *Journal of Applied Behavior Analysis*, 1975, *8*, 77–82.

Goldfried, M. R. The use of relaxation and cognitive relabeling as coping skills. In R. B. Stuart (Ed.), *Behavioral self-management: Strategies, techniques and outcomes*. New York: Brunner/Mazel, 1977.

Goldfried, M. R., & Kent, R. N. Traditional vs. behavioral personality assessment: A comparison of methodological and theoretical assumptions. *Psychological Bulletin*, 1972, *77*, 409–420.

Goldfried, M. R., & Linehan, M. M. Basic issues in behavioral assessment. In A. R. Ciminero, K. S. Calhoun, & H. E. Adams (Eds.), *Handbook of behavioral assessment*. New York: Wiley, 1977.

Goldfried, M. R., & Merbaum, M. (Eds.), *Behavior change through self-control*. New York: Holt, Rinehart & Winston, 1973.

Goldiamond, I. Self-control procedures in personal behavior problems. *Psychological Reports*, 1965, 17, 851–868.

Graubard, P. S., Rosenberg, H., & Miller, M. B. Student applications of behavior modification to teachers and environments or ecological approaches to social deviancy. In R. Ulrich, T. Stachnik, & J. Mabry, (Eds.), *Control of human behavior, Volume 3*. Glenview, Illinois: Scott, Foresman, 1974.

Gray, F., Graubard, P. S., & Rosenberg, H. Little brother is changing you. *Psychology Today*, 1974, 7, March, 42–46.

Graziano, A. M. Parents as behavior therapists. In M. Hersen, R. M. Eisler, & P. M. Miller (Eds.), *Progress in behavior modification*, Volume 4. New York: Academic Press, 1977.

Green, R., & Money, J. *Transsexualism and sex assignment*. Baltimore: Johns Hopkins University Press, 1969.

Green, R. J., & Hoats, D. L. Reinforcing capabilities of television distortion. *Journal of Applied Behavior Analysis*, 1969, 2, 139–141.

Green, R. W. Self-regulated eating behaviors in a diabetic mental patient. *Behavior Therapy*, 1978, 9, 521–525.

Greenberg, D. J., Scott, S. B., Pisa, A., & Friesen, D. D. Beyond the token economy: A comparison of two contingency programs. *Journal of Consulting and Clinical Psychology*, 1975, 43, 498–503.

Greene, B. F., Willis, B. S., Levy, R. & Bailey, J. S. Measuring client gains from staff-implemented programs. *Journal of Applied Behavior Analysis*, 1978, 11, 395–412.

Greenwood, C. R., Hops, H., Delquadri, J., & Guild, J. Group contingencies for group consequences in classroom management: A further analysis. *Jour-nal of Applied Behavior Analysis*, 1974, 7, 413–425.

Griffin, J. C., Locke, B. J., & Landers, W. F. Manipulation of potential punishment parameters in the treatment of self-injury. *Journal of Applied Behavior Analysis*, 1975, 8, 458.

Guerney, B. G., Jr. (Ed.), *Psychotherapeutic agents: New roles for nonprofessionals, parents, and teachers*. New York: Holt, Rinehart & Winston, 1969.

Hackmann, A., & McLean, C. A comparison of flooding and thought stopping in the treatment of obsessional neurosis. *Behaviour Research and Therapy*, 1975, 13, 263–269.

Hall, C. S., & Lindzey, G. *Theories of personality*. (third edition). New York: Wiley, 1978.

Hall, R. V., Axelrod, S., Foundopoulos, M., Shellman, J., Campbell, R. A., & Cranston, S. The effective use of punishment to modify behavior in the classroom. *Educational Technology*, 1971, 11, 24–26.

Hall, R. V., Axelrod, S., Tyler, L., Grief, E., Jones, F. C., & Robertson, R. Modification of behavior problems in the home with a parent as observer and experimenter. *Journal of Applied Behavior Analysis*, 1972, 5, 53–64.

Hall, R. V., Fox, R., Willard, D., Goldsmith, L., Emerson, M., Owen, M., Davis, F., & Porcia, E. The teacher as observer and experimenter in the modification of disputing and talking-out behaviors. *Journal of Applied Behavior Analysis*, 1971, 4, 141–149.

Hall, S. M., Cooper, J. L., Burmaster, S., & Polk, A. Contingency contracting as a therapeutic tool with methadone maintenance clients: Six single subject studies. *Behaviour Research and Therapy*, 1977, 15, 438–441.

Hallam, R. S. Extinction of ruminations: A case study. *Behavior Therapy*, 1974, 5, 565–568.

Hallam, R. S., & Rachman, S. Current status of aversion therapy. In M. Hersen, R. M. Eisler, & P. M. Miller (Eds.), *Progress in behavior modification*, Volume 2. New York: Academic Press, 1976.

Hamblin, R. L., Hathaway, C., & Wodarski, J. Group contingencies, peer tutoring, and accelerating academic achievement. In R. Ulrich, T.

Stachnik, & J. Mabry, *Control of human behavior, Volume 3*. Glenview, Illinois: Scott, Foresman and Company, 1974.

Hancock v. Avery, 301 F. Supp. (M.D. Tenn. 1969).

Hardiman, S. A., Goetz, E. M., Reuter, E., & LeBlanc, J. M. Primes, contingent attention, and training: Effects on a child's motor behavior. *Journal of Applied Behavior Analysis*, 1975, *8*, 399–409.

Harris, F. C., & Lahey, B. B. A method for combining occurrence and nonoccurrence interobserver agreement scores. *Journal of Applied Behavior Analysis*, 1978, *11*, 523–527.

Harris, M. B. Self-directed program for weight control: A pilot study. *Journal of Abnormal Psychology*, 1969, *74*, 263–270.

Harris, S. L., & Romanczyk, R. G. Treating self-injurious behavior of a retarded child by overcorrection. *Behavior Therapy*, 1976, *7*, 235–239.

Harris, V. W., & Sherman, J. A. Use and analysis of the "good behavior game" to reduce disruptive classroom behavior. *Journal of Applied Behavior Analysis*, 1973, *6*, 405–417.

Hartmann, D. P., & Hall, R. V. The changing criterion design. *Journal of Applied Behavior Analysis*, 1976, *9*, 527–532.

Hauserman, N., & Lavin, P. Post-hospitalization continuation treatment of anorexia nervosa. *Journal of Behavior Therapy and Experimental Psychiatry*, 1977, *8*, 309–313.

Hauserman, N., Walen, S. R., & Behling, M. Reinforced racial integration in the first grade: A study in generalization. *Journal of Applied Behavior Analysis*, 1973, *6*, 193–200.

Hawkins, R. P., & Dobes, R. W. Behavioral definitions in applied behavior analysis: Explicit or implicit. In B. C. Etzel, J. M. LeBlanc, & D. M. Baer (Eds.), *New developments in behavioral research: Theory, methods, and applications. In honor of Sidney W. Bijou*. Hillsdale, New Jersey: Lawrence Erlbaum Associates, 1975.

Hawkins, R. P., & Dotson, V. A. Reliability scores that delude: An Alice in Wonderland trip through the misleading characteristics of inter-observer agreement scores in interval recording. In E. Ramp & G. Semb (Eds.), *Behavior analysis: Areas of research and application*. Englewood Cliffs, New Jersey: Prentice-Hall, 1975.

Hayes, S. C., Brownell, K. D., & Barlow, D. H. The use of self-administered covert sensitization in the treatment of exhibitionism and sadism. *Behavior Therapy*, 1978, *9*, 283–289.

Heckel, R. B., Wiggins, S. L., & Salzberg, H. C. Conditioning against silences in group therapy. *Journal of Clinical Psychology*, 1962, *18*, 216–217.

Henriksen, K., & Doughty, R. Decelerating undesired mealtime behavior in a group of profoundly retarded boys. *American Journal of Mental Deficiency*, 1967, *72*, 40–44.

Herbert, E. W., & Baer, D. M. Training parents as behavior modifiers: Self-recording of contingent attention. *Journal of Applied Behavior Analysis*, 1972, *5*, 139–149.

Hermann, J. A., de Montes, A. I., Dominguez, B., Montes, F., & Hopkins, B. L. Effects of bonuses for punctuality on the tardiness of industrial workers. *Journal of Applied Behavior Analysis*, 1973, *6*, 563–570.

Hersen, M. Historical perspectives in behavioral assessment. In M. Hersen & A. S. Bellack (Eds.), *Behavioral assessment: A practical handbook*. Oxford: Pergamon, 1976.

Hersen, M., & Barlow, D. H. *Single-case experimental designs: Strategies for studying behavior change*. New York: Pergamon, 1976.

Hersen, M., Eisler, R. M., Alford, G. S., & Agras, W. S. Effects of token economy on neurotic depression: An experimental analysis. *Behavior Therapy*, 1973, *4*, 392–397.

Hewett, F. M. *The emotionally disturbed child in the classroom*. Boston: Allyn and Bacon, 1968.

Hilgard, E. R., & Marquis, P. G. *Conditioning and learning*. New York: Appleton-Century, 1940.

Hineline, P. N. Negative reinforcement and avoidance. In W. K. Honig & J. E. R. Staddon (Eds.), *Handbook of operant behavior*. Englewood Cliffs, NJ: Prentice-Hall, 1977.

Hobbs, S. A., & Forehand, R. Important

parameters in the use of timeout with children: A re-examination. *Journal of Behavior Therapy and Experimental Psychiatry*, 1977, *8*, 365–370.

Hobbs, S. A., Forehand, R., & Murray, R. G. Effects of various durations of timeout on the noncompliant behavior of children. *Behavior Therapy*, 1978, *9*, 652–656.

Hoffman, M. L. Power assertion by the parent and its impact on the child. *Child Development*, 1960, *31*, 129–143.

Hollander, M. A., & Plutchik, R. A reinforcement program for psychiatric attendants. *Journal of Behavior Therapy and Experimental Psychiatry*, 1972, *3*, 297–300.

Hollander, M., Plutchik, R., & Horner, V. Interaction of patient and attendant reinforcement programs: The "piggyback" effect. *Journal of Consulting and Clinical Psychology*, 1973, *41*, 43–47.

Hollandsworth, J. G., Glazeski, R. C., & Dressel, M. E. Use of social-skills training in the treatment of extreme anxiety and deficient verbal skills in the job-interview setting. *Journal of Applied Behavior Analysis*, 1978, *11*, 259–269.

Holroyd, K. A., Andrasik, F., & Westbrook, T. Cognitive control of tension headache. *Cognitive Therapy and Research*, 1977, *1*, 121–133.

Homme, L. E. Perspectives in psychology: XXIV. Control of coverants, the operants of the mind. *Psychological Record*, 1965, *15*, 501–511.

Homme, L. E., Csanyi, A., Gonzales, M., & Rechs, J. *How to use contingency contracting in the classroom.* Champaign, Illinois: Research Press, 1969.

Hopkins, B. L. Effects of candy and social reinforcement, instructions, and reinforcement schedule learning on the modification and maintenance of smiling. *Journal of Applied Behavior Analysis*, 1968, *1*, 121–129.

Hopkins, B. L., & Hermann, J. A. Evaluating interobserver reliability of interval data. *Journal of Applied Behavior Analysis*, 1977, *10*, 121–126.

Horner, R. D., & Keilitz, I. Training mentally retarded adolescents to brush their teeth. *Journal of Applied Behavior Analysis*, 1975, *8*, 301–309.

Hundert, J., & Bastone, D. A practical procedure to maintain pupils' accurate self-rating in a classroom token program. *Behavior Modification*, 1978, *2*, 93–112.

Hunt, J. G., & Zimmerman, J. Stimulating productivity in a simulated sheltered workshop setting. *American Journal of Mental Deficiency*, 1969, *74*, 43–49.

Hutchinson, R. R. By-products of aversive control. In W. K. Honig & J. E. R. Staddon (Eds.), *Handbook of operant behavior.* Englewood Cliffs, NJ: Prentice-Hall, 1977.

Hutchinson, R. R., Azrin, N. H., & Hunt, G. M. Attack produced by intermittent reinforcement of a concurrent operant response. *Journal of the Experimental Analysis of Behavior*, 1968, *11*, 489–495.

Hutt, P. J. Rate of bar pressing as a function of quality and quantity of food reward. *Journal of Comparative and Physiological Psychology*, 1954, *47*, 235–239.

Iwata, B. A., Bailey, J. S., Brown, K. M., Foshee, T. J., & Alpern, M. A performance-based lottery to improve residential care and training by institutional staff. *Journal of Applied Behavior Analysis*, 1976, *9*, 417–431.

Jackson, D. A., & Wallace, R. F. The modification and generalization of voice loudness in a fifteen-year-old retarded girl. *Journal of Applied Behavior Analysis*, 1974, *7*, 461–471.

Jackson, J. L., & Calhoun, K. S. Effects of two variable-ratio schedules of timeout: Changes in target and non-target behaviors. *Journal of Behavior Therapy and Experimental Psychiatry*, 1977, *8*, 195–199.

Jacobson, E. *Progressive relaxation.* Chicago: University of Chicago Press, 1938.

Johnson, M. S., & Bailey, J. S. The modification of leisure behavior in a halfway house for retarded women. *Journal of Applied Behavior Analysis*, 1977, *10*, 273–282.

Johnson, S. M. & Martin, S. Developing self-evaluation as a conditioned reinforcer. In B. Ashem, & E. G. Poser (Eds.), *Behavior modification with children.* New York: Pergamon, 1972.

Johnston, J. M., & Johnston, G. T. Modification of consonant speech–sound articulation in young children. *Journal of Applied Behavior Analysis*, 1972, *5*, 233–246.

Jones, F. H., & Eimers, R. C. Role-playing to train elementary teachers to use a classroom management "skill package." *Journal of Applied Behavior Analysis*, 1975, *8*, 421–433.

Jones, M. C. A laboratory study of fear: The case of Peter. *Pedagogical Seminary*, 1924, *31*, 308–315.

Jones, R. J., & Azrin, N. H. An experimental application of a social reinforcement approach to the problem of job-finding. *Journal of Applied Behavior Analysis*, 1973, *6*, 345–353.

Jones, R. R., Vaught, R. S., & Weinrott, M. Time-series analysis in operant research. *Journal of Applied Behavior Analysis*, 1977, *10*, 151–166.

Jones, R. T., & Kazdin, A. E. Programming response maintenance after withdrawing token reinforcement. *Behavior Therapy*, 1975, *6*, 153–164.

Jones, R. T., Nelson, R. E., & Kazdin, A. E. The role of external variables in self-reinforcement: A review. *Behavior Modification*, 1977, *1*, 147–178.

Kale, R. J., Kaye, J. H., Whelan, P. A., & Hopkins, B. L. The effects of reinforcement on the modification, maintenance, and generalization of social responses of mental patients. *Journal of Applied Behavior Analysis*, 1968, *1*, 307–314.

Kallman, W. H., Hersen, M., & O'Toole, D. H. The use of social reinforcement in a case of conversion reaction. *Behavior Therapy*, 1975, *6*, 411–413.

Kanfer, F. H. The many faces of self-control, or behavior modification changes its focus. In R. B. Stuart (Ed.), *Behavioral self-management: Strategies, techniques and outcomes*. New York: Brunner/Mazel, 1977.

Kanfer, F. H., Karoly, P., & Newman, A. Reduction of children's fear of the dark by competence-related and situational threat-related verbal cues. *Journal of Consulting and Clinical Psychology*, 1975, *43*, 251–258.

Kanfer, F. H., & Phillips, J. S. *Learning foundations of behavior therapy*. New York: Wiley, 1970

Karoly, P. Behavioral self-management in children: Concepts, methods, issues, and directions. In M. Hersen, R. M. Eisler, & P. M. Miller (Eds.), *Progress in behavior modification, Volume 5*. New York: Academic Press, 1977.

Kass, D. J., & Stauss, F. *Sex therapy at home*. New York: Simon & Schuster, 1975.

Kassirer, L. B. Behavior modification for patients and prisoners: Constitutional ramifications of enforced therapy. *Journal of Psychiatry and Law*, 1974, *2*, 245–302.

Katz, R. C., Johnson, C. A., & Gelfand, S. Modifying the dispensing of reinforcers: Some implications for behavior modification with hospitalized patients. *Behavior Therapy*, 1972, *3*, 579–588.

Kaufman, K. F., & O'Leary, K. D. Reward, cost and self-evaluation procedures for disruptive adolescents in a psychiatric hospital. *Journal of Applied Behavior Analysis*, 1972, *5*, 293–309.

Kaufman, M. E. The effects of institutionalization on development of stereotyped and social behaviors in mental defectives. *American Journal of Mental Deficiency*, 1967, *71*, 581–585.

Kazdin, A. E. The effect of response cost in suppressing behavior in a pre-psychotic retardate. *Journal of Behavior Therapy and Experimental Psychiatry*, 1971, *2*, 137–140.

Kazdin, A. E. Response cost: The removal of conditioned reinforcers for therapeutic change. *Behavior Therapy*, 1972, *3*, 533–546.

Kazdin, A. E. The effect of response cost and aversive stimulation in suppressing punished and nonpunished speech disfluencies. *Behavior Therapy*, 1973, *4*, 73–82. (a)

Kazdin, A. E. The effect of vicarious reinforcement on attentive behavior in the classroom. *Journal of Applied Behavior Analysis*, 1973, *6*, 71–78. (b)

Kazdin, A. E. The effect of vicarious reinforcement on performance in a rehabilitation setting. *Education and Training of the Mentally Retarded*, 1973, *8*, 4–11. (c)

Kazdin, A. E. The failure of some patients to respond to token programs. *Journal of Behavior Therapy and Experimental Psychiatry*, 1973, *4*, 7–14. (d)

Kazdin, A. E. Role of instructions and reinforcement in behavior changes in token reinforcement programs. *Journal of Educational Psychology*, 1973, *64*, 63–71. (e)

Kazdin, A. E. Time out for some considerations on punishment. *American Psychologist*, 1973, *28*, 939–941.(f)

Kazdin, A. E. The assessment of teacher training in a reinforcement program. *Journal of Teacher Education*, 1974, *25*, 266–270. (a)

Kazdin, A. E. Self-monitoring and behavior change. In M. J. Mahoney & C. E. Thoresen (Eds.), *Self-control: Power to the person*. Monterey, California: Brooks/Cole, 1974. (b)

Kazdin, A. E. Characteristics and trends in applied behavior analysis. *Journal of Applied Behavior Analysis*, 1975, *8*, 332.

Kazdin, A. E. Statistical analyses for single-case experimental designs. In M. Hersen & D. H. Barlow, *Single-case experimental designs: Strategies for studying behavior change*. New York: Pergamon, 1976.

Kazdin, A. E. Artifact, bias, and complexity of assessment: The ABC's of reliability. *Journal of Applied Behavior Analysis*, 1977, *10*, 141–150. (a)

Kazdin, A. E. Assessing the clinical or applied significance of behavior change through social validation. *Behavior Modification*, 1977, *1*, 427–452. (b)

Kazdin, A. E. Extensions of reinforcement techniques to socially and environmentally relevant behaviors. In M. Hersen, R. M. Eisler, & P. M. Miller (Eds.), *Progress in behavior modification, Volume 4*. New York: Academic Press, 1977. (c)

Kazdin, A. E. The influence of behavior preceding a reinforced response on behavior change in the classroom. *Journal of Applied Behavior Analysis*, 1977, *10*, 299–310. (d)

Kazdin, A. E. *The token economy: A review and evaluation*. New York: Plenum, 1977. (e)

Kazdin, A. E. Vicarious reinforcement and direction of behavior change in the classroom. *Behavior Therapy*, 1977, *8*, 57–63. (f)

Kazdin, A. E. Covert modeling: The therapeutic application of imagined rehearsal. In J. L. Singer & K. Pope (Eds.), *The power of human imagination: New techniques of psychotherapy*. New York: Plenum, 1978. (a)

Kazdin, A. E. *History of behavior modification: Experimental foundations of contemporary research*. Baltimore: University Park Press, 1978. (b)

Kazdin, A. E. Methodological and interpretive problems of single-case experimental designs. *Journal of Consulting and Clinical Psychology*, 1978, *46*, 629–642. (c)

Kazdin, A. E. Methodology of applied behavior analysis. In A. C. Catania & T. A. Brigham (Eds.), *Handbook of applied behavior analysis: Social and instructional processes*. New York: Irvington, 1978. (d)

Kazdin, A. E. Acceptability of alternative treatments for deviant child behavior. *Journal of Applied Behavior Analysis*, 1979, in press. (a)

Kazdin, A. E. Unobtrusive measures in behavioral assessment. *Journal of Applied Behavior Analysis*, 1979, in press. (b)

Kazdin, A. E. Vicarious reinforcement and punishment in operant programs for children. *Child Behavior Therapy*, 1979, *1*, 13–36. (c)

Kazdin, A. E. *Research design in clinical psychology*. New York: Harper & Row, 1980.

Kazdin, A. E., & Geesey, S. Simultaneous-treatment design comparisons of the effects of earning reinforcers for one's peers versus for oneself. *Behavior Therapy*, 1977, *8*, 682–693.

Kazdin, A. E., & Hartmann, D. P. The simultaneous-treatment design. *Behavior Therapy*, 1978, *9*, 912–922.

Kazdin, A. E., & Klock, J. The effect of nonverbal teacher approval on student attentive behavior. *Journal of Applied Behavior Analysis*, 1973, *6*, 643–654.

Kazdin, A. E., & Moyer, W. Training teachers to use behavior modification. In S. Yen & R. McIntire (Eds.), *Teaching behavior modification*. Kalamazoo, Michigan: Behaviordelia, 1976.

Kazdin, A. E., & Polster, R. Intermittent token reinforcement and response maintenance in extinction. *Behavior Therapy*, 1973, *4*, 386–391.

Kazdin, A. E., & Pulaski, J. L. Joseph Lancaster and behavior modification in education. *Journal of the History of the Behavioral Sciences*, 1977, *13*, 261–266.

Kazdin, A. E., Silverman, N. A., & Sittler, J. L. The use of prompts to enhance vicarious effects of nonverbal approval. *Journal of Applied Behavior Analysis*, 1975, *8*, 279–286.

Kazdin, A. E., & Smith, G. M. Covert conditioning: A review and evaluation. *Advances in Behaviour Research and Therapy*, 1979, *2*, 57–98.

Kazdin, A. E., & Wilson, G. T. Criteria for evaluating psychotherapy. *Archives of General Psychiatry*, 1978, *35*, 407–416. (a)

Kazdin, A. E., & Wilson, G. T. *Evaluation of behavior therapy: Issues, evidence, and research strategies.* Cambridge, Massachusetts: Ballinger, 1978. (b)

Keeley, S. M., Shemberg, K. M., & Carbonell, J. Operant clinical intervention: Behavior management or beyond? Where are the data? *Behavior Therapy*, 1976, *7*, 292–305.

Keep America Beautiful, Inc. *Who litters and why?* 99 Park Avenue, New York, New York, 1968.

Kelly, J. A., & Drabman, R. S. Overcorrection: An effective procedure that failed. *Journal of Clinical Child Psychology*, 1977, *6*, 38–40.

Kendall, P. C. On the efficacious use of verbal self-instructional procedures with children. *Cognitive Therapy and Research*, 1977, *1*, 331–341.

Kent, R. N., & Foster, S. L. Direct observational procedures: Methodological issues in naturalistic settings. In A. R. Ciminero, K. S. Calhoun, & H. E. Adams (Eds.), *Handbook of behavioral assessment.* New York: Wiley, 1977.

Kent, R. N., Kanowitz, J., O'Leary, K. D., & Cheiken, M. Observer reliability as a function of circumstances of assessment. *Journal of Applied Behavior Analysis*, 1977, *10*, 317–324.

Kent, R. N., O'Leary, K. D., Diament, C., & Dietz. A. Expectation biases in observational evaluation of therapeutic change. *Journal of Consulting and Clinical Psychology*, 1974, *42*, 774–780.

Kimble, G. A. *Hilgard and Marquis'*

conditioning and learning. New York: Appleton-Century-Crofts, 1961.

Kimmel, H. D. Instrumental conditioning of autonomically mediated responses in human beings, *American Psychologist*, 1974, *29*, 325–335.

Kirby, F. D., & Shields, F. Modification of arithmetic response rate and attending behavior in a seventh-grade student. *Journal of Applied Behavior Analysis*, 1972, *5*, 79–84.

Kircher, A. S., Pear, J. J., & Martin, G. L. Shock as punishment in a picture-naming task with retarded children. *Journal of Applied Behavior Analysis*, 1971, *4*, 227–233.

Kirigin, K. A., Wolf, M. M., Braukmann, C. J., Fixsen, D. L., & Phillips, E. L. Achievement Place: A preliminary outcome evaluation. In J. S. Stumphauzer (Ed.), *Progress in behavior therapy with delinquents.* Springfield, Illinois: Charles C Thomas, 1979.

Kirkland, K. D., & Thelen, M. H. Uses of modeling in child treatment. In B. B. Lahey & A. E. Kazdin (Eds.), *Advances in clinical child psychology, Volume 1.* New York: Plenum, 1977.

Knapp, T. J. The Premack principle in human experimental and applied settings. *Behaviour Research and Therapy*, 1976, *14*, 133–147.

Knecht v. Gillman, 488· F.2d 1136 (8th Cir. 1973).

Knight, M. F., & McKenzie, H. S. Elimination of bedtime thumbsucking in home settings through contingent reading. *Journal of Applied Behavior Analysis*, 1974, *7*, 33–38.

Koegel, R. L., Glahn, T. J., & Nieminen, G. S. Generalization of parent-training results. *Journal of Applied Behavior Analysis*, 1978, *11*, 95–109.

Koegel, R. L., & Rincover, A. Treatment of psychotic children in a classroom environment: I. Learning in a large group. *Journal of Applied Behavior Analysis*, 1974, *7*, 45–59.

Koegel, R. L., Russo, D. C., & Rincover, A. Assessing and training teachers in the generalized use of behavior modification with autistic children. *Journal of Applied Behavior Analysis*, 1977, *10*, 197–205.

Komaki, J., & Barnett, F. T. A behavioral

approach to coaching football: Improving the play execution of the offensive backfield on a youth football team. *Journal of Applied Behavior Analysis*, 1977, *10*, 657–664.

Kounin, J. S. *Discipline and group management in classrooms*. New York: Holt, Rinehart & Winston, 1970.

Krapfl, J., & Vargas, E. (Eds.). *Behaviorism and ethics*. Kalamazoo, Michigan: Behaviordelia, 1977.

Krasner, L. The behavioral scientist and social responsibility: No place to hide. *Journal of Social Issues*, 1966, *21*, 9–30.

Krasner, L., & Ullmann, L. P. *Behavior influence and personality: The social matrix of human action*. New York: Holt, Rinehart & Winston, 1973.

Kratochwill, T. R. (Ed.), *Single-subject research: Strategies for evaluating change*. New York: Academic Press, 1978.

Krumboltz, J. D., & Thoresen, C. E. (Eds.), *Counseling methods*. New York: Holt, Rinehart & Winston, 1976.

Kubany, E. S., Weiss, L. E., & Sloggett, B. B. The good behavior clock: A reinforcement/time out procedure for reducing disruptive classroom behavior. *Journal of Behavior Therapy and Experimental Psychiatry*, 1971, *2*, 173–179.

Kushner, M. The operant control of intractable sneezing. In C. D. Spielberger, R. Fox, & B. Masterson (Eds.), *Contributions to general psychology*. New York: Ronald Press, 1968.

Lahey, B. B., McNees, P. M., & McNees, M. C. Control of an obscene "verbal tic" through timeout in an elementary school classroom. *Journal of Applied Behavior Analysis*, 1973, *6*, 101–104.

Lattal, K. A. Contingency management of toothbrushing behavior in a summer camp for children. *Journal of Applied Behavior Analysis*, 1969, *2*, 195–198.

Lawson, R. *Frustration*. New York: MacMillan, 1965.

LeBlanc, J. M., Busby, K. H., & Thomson, C. L. The functions of time out for changing the aggressive behaviors of a preschool child: A multiple-baseline analysis. In R. Ulrich, T. Stachnik, & J. Mabry (Eds.), *Control of human behavior, Volume 3*. Glenview, Illinois: Scott, Foresman, 1974.

Leitenberg, H. (Ed.), *Handbook of behavior modification and behavior therapy*. Englewood Cliffs, New Jersey: Prentice-Hall, 1976.

Leitenberg, H., Agras, W. S., Allen, R., Butz, R., & Edwards, J. Feedback and therapist praise during treatment of phobia. *Journal of Consulting and Clinical Psychology*, 1975, *43*, 396–404.

Leitenberg, H., Agras, W. S., Thompson, L. D., & Wright, D. E. Feedback in behavior modification: An experimental analysis in two phobic cases. *Journal of Applied Behavior Analysis*, 1968, *1*, 131–137.

Levin, G., & Simmons, J. Response to food and praise by emotionally disturbed boys. *Psychological Reports*, 1962, *2*, 539–546.

Levitt, E. E. Research on psychotherapy with children. In A. E. Bergin & S. L. Garfield (Eds.), *Handbook of psychotherapy and behavior change: An empirical analysis*. New York: Wiley, 1971.

Libb, J. W., & Clements, C. B. Token reinforcement in an exercise program for hospitalized geriatric patients. *Perceptual and Motor Skills*, 1969, *28*, 957–958.

Liberman, R. D., Teigen, J. Patterson, R., & Baker, V. Reducing delusional speech in chronic, paranoid schizophrenics. *Journal of Applied Behavior Analysis*, 1973, *6*, 57–64.

Liebert, R. M., & Allen, M. K. The effects of the rule structure and reward magnitude on the acquisition and adoption of self-reward criteria. *Psychological Reports*, 1967, *21*, 445–452.

Lindsay, W. R., & Stoffelmayr, B. E. A comparison of the differential effects of three different baseline conditions within an ABA_1B_1 experimental design. *Behaviour Research and Therapy*, 1976, *14*, 169–173.

Linscheid, T. R., & Cunningham, C. E. A controlled demonstration of the effectiveness of electric shock in the elimination of chronic infant rumination. *Journal of Applied Behavior Analysis*, 1977, *10*, 500.

Linscheid, T. R., Malosky, P., & Zimmerman, J. Discharge as the major consequence in a hospitalized patient's behavior management program: A case study. *Behavior Therapy*, 1974, 5, 559–564.

Litow, L., & Pumroy, D. K. A brief review of classroom group-oriented contingencies. *Journal of Applied Behavior Analysis*, 1975, 8, 341–347.

Locke, E. A., Cartledge, N., & Koeppel, J. Motivational effects of knowledge of results. *Psychological Bulletin*, 1968, 70, 474–485.

Loeber, R. Engineering the behavioral engineer. *Journal of Applied Behavior Analysis*, 1971, 4, 321–326.

Lombardo, T. W., & Turner, S. M. Thought-stopping in the control of obsessive ruminations. *Behavior Modification*, 1979, 3, 267–272.

London, P. *The modes and morals of psychotherapy.* New York: Holt, Rinehart and Winston, 1964.

London, P. *Behavior control.* New York: Harper & Row, 1969.

Lovaas, O. I., & Bucher, B. D. (Eds.), *Perspectives in behavior modification with deviant children.* Englewood Cliffs, New Jersey: Prentice-Hall, 1974.

Lovaas, O. I., Koegel, R., Simmons, J. Q., & Long, J. S. Some generalization and follow-up measures on autistic children in behavior therapy. *Journal of Applied Behavior Analysis*, 1973, 6, 131–166.

Lovaas, O. I., Schaeffer, B., & Simmons, J. Q. Building social behavior in autistic children by use of electric shock. *Journal of Experimental Research in Personality*, 1965, 1, 99–109.

Lovaas, O. I., & Simmons, J. Q. Manipulation of self-destruction in three retarded children. *Journal of Applied Behavior Analysis*, 1969, 2, 143–157.

Lovibond, S. H. *Conditioning and enuresis.* New York: Pergamon, 1964.

Lovitt, T. C., & Curtiss, K. Academic response rate as a function of teacher-and self-imposed contingencies. *Journal of Applied Behavior Analysis*, 1969, 2, 49–53.

Lowe, K., & Lutzker, J. R. Increasing compliance to a medical regimen with a juvenile diabetic. *Behavior Therapy*, 1979, 10, 57–64.

Lowitz, G. H., & Suib, M. R. Generalized control of persistent thumbsucking by differential reinforcement of other behaviors. *Journal of Behavior Therapy and Experimental Psychiatry*, 1978, 9, 343–346.

Lubar, J. F., & Shouse, M. N. Use of biofeedback in the treatment of seizure disorders and hyperactivity. In B. B. Lahey & A. E. Kazdin (Eds.), *Advances in clinical child psychology, Volume 1.* New York: Plenum, 1977.

Luria, A. *The role of speech in the regulation of normal and abnormal behavior.* New York: Liveright, 1961.

MacDonald, W. S., Gallimore, R., & MacDonald, G. Contingency counseling by school personnel: An economical model of intervention. *Journal of Applied Behavior Analysis*, 1970, 3, 175–182.

Madsen, C. H., Becker, W. C., & Thomas, D. R. Rules, praise and ignoring: Elements of elementary classroom control. *Journal of Applied Behavior Analysis*, 1968, 1, 139–150.

Madsen, C. H., Becker, W. C., Thomas, D.R., Koser, L., & Plager, E. An analysis of the reinforcing function of "sit down" commands. In R. K. Parker (Ed.), *Readings in educational psychology.* Boston: Allyn & Bacon, 1970.

Madsen, C. H., Madsen, C. K., & Thompson, F. Increasing rural Head Start children's consumption of middle-clsss meals. *Journal of Applied Behavior Analysis*, 1974, 7, 257–262.

Mahoney, K., Van Wagenen, R. K., & Meyerson, L. Toilet training of normal and retarded children. *Journal of Applied Behavior Analysis*, 1971, 4, 173–181.

Mahoney, M. J. The self-management of covert behavior: A case study. *Behavior Therapy*, 1971, 2, 575–578.

Mahoney, M. J. *Cognition and behavior modification.* Cambridge, Massachusetts: Ballinger, 1974.

Mahoney, M. J., & Arnkoff, D. Cognitive and self-control therapies. In S. L. Garfield & A. E. Bergin (Eds.), *Handbook of psychotherapy and behavior change: An empirical analysis* (second edition). New York: Wiley, 1978.

Mahoney, M. J., Moura, N. G., & Wade,

T. C. The relative efficacy of self-reward, self-punishment, and self-monitoring techniques for weight loss. *Journal of Consulting and Clinical Psychology*, 1973, *40*, 404–407.

Mahoney, M. J., & Thoresen, C. E. (Eds.), *Self-control: Power to the person*. Monterey, California: Brooks/Cole, 1974.

Maley, R. F., Feldman, G. L., & Ruskin, R. S. Evaluation of patient improvement in a token economy treatment program. *Journal of Abnormal Psychology*, 1973, *82*, 141–144.

Maloney, K. B., & Hopkins, B. L. The modification of sentence structure and its relationship to subjective judgments of creativity in writing. *Journal of Applied Behavior Analysis*, 1973, *6*, 425–433.

Mandelker, A. V., Brigham, T. A., & Bushell, D. The effects of token procedures on a teacher's social contacts with her students. *Journal of Applied Behavior Analysis*, 1970, *3*, 169–174.

Mann, J. H. The effect of inter-racial contact on sociometric choices and perceptions. *Journal of Social Psychology*, 1959, *50*, 143–152.

Mansdorf, I. J. Reinforcer isolation: An alternative to subject isolation in time-out from positive reinforcement. *Journal of Behavior Therapy and Experimental Psychiatry*, 1977, *8*, 391–393.

Margolis, R. B., & Shemberg, K. M. Cognitive self-instruction in process and reactive schizophrenics: A failure to replicate. *Behavior Therapy*, 1976, *7*, 668–671.

Marholin, D., II, & Gray, D. Effects of group response cost procedures on cash shortages in a small business. *Journal of Applied Behavior Analysis*, 1976, *9*, 25–30.

Marholin, D., II, Siegel, L. J., & Phillips, D. Treatment and transfer: A search for empirical procedures. In M. Hersen, R. M. Eisler, & P. M. Miller (Eds.), *Progress in behavior modification, Volume 3*. New York: Academic Press, 1976.

Marholin, D., II, & Steinman, W. M. Stimulus control in the classroom as a function of the behavior reinforced. *Journal of Applied Behavior Analysis*, 1977, *10*, 465–478.

Marholin, D., II, Steinman, W. M., McIn-

nis, E. T., & Heads, T. B. The effect of a teacher's presence on the classroom behavior of conduct-problem children. *Journal of Abnormal Child Psychology*, 1975, *3*, 11–25.

Marholin, D., II, & Townsend, N. M. An experimental analysis of side effects and response maintenance of a modified overcorrection procedure: The case of a persistent twiddler. *Behavior Therapy*, 1978, *9*, 383–390.

Marks, I. Behavioral psychotherapy of adult neuroses. In S. L. Garfield & A. E. Bergin (Eds.), *Handbook of psychotherapy and behavior change: An empirical analysis (second edition)*. New York: Wiley, 1978.

Marshall, W. L., Presse, L., & Andrews, W. R. A self-administered program for public speaking anxiety. *Behaviour Research and Therapy*, 1976, *14*, 33–40.

Martin, R. *Legal challenges to behavior modification: Trends in schools, corrections and mental health*. Champaign, Illinois: Research Press, 1975.

Masur, F. T. Assorted physical disorders. In R. B. Williams, Jr. & W. D. Gentry (Eds.), *Behavioral approaches to medical treatment*. Cambridge, Massachusetts: Ballinger, 1977.

Matson, J. L., & Ollendick, T. H. Issues in toilet training normal children. *Behavior Therapy*, 1977, *8*, 549–553.

May, J. G., Risley, T. R., Twardosz, S., Friedman, P., Bijou, S. W., & Wexler, D. *Guidelines for the use of behavioral procedures in state programs for retarded persons*. Arlington, Texas: National Association for Retarded Citizens, 1976.

Mayhew, G. L., & Harris, F. C. Some negative side effects of a punishment procedure for stereotyped behavior. *Journal of Behavior Therapy and Experimental Psychiatry*, 1978, *9*, 245–251.

McCarty, T., Griffin, S., Apolloni, T., & Shores, R. E. Increased peer-teaching with group-oriented contingencies for arithmetic performance in behavior-disordered adolescents. *Journal of Applied Behavior Analysis*, 1977, *10*, 313.

McClannahan, L. E., & Risley, T. R. Design of living environments for nursing-home residents: Increasing participation in recreation activities. *Journal of Applied Behavior Analysis*, 1975, *8*, 261–268.

McFall, R. M., & Twentyman, C. T. Four experiments on the relative contributions of rehearsal, modeling, and coaching to assertion training. *Journal of Abnormal Psychology*, 1973, *81*, 199–218.

McGee, C. S., Kauffman, J. M., & Nussen, J. L. Children as therapeutic change agents: Reinforcement intervention paradigms. *Review of Educational Research*, 1977, *47*, 451–477.

McKenzie, T. L., & Rushall, B. S. Effects of self-recording on attendance and performance in a competitive swimming training environment. *Journal of Applied Behavior Analysis*, 1974, *7*, 199–206.

McMahon, R. J., & Forehand, R. Nonprescription behavior therapy: Effectiveness of a brochure in teaching mothers to correct their children's inappropriate mealtime behaviors. *Behavior Therapy*, 1978, *9*, 814–820.

McMurtry, C. A., & Williams, J. E. The evaluation dimension of the affective meaning system of the preschool child. *Developmental Psychology*, 1972, *6*, 238–246.

McNamara, J. R. Teacher and students as a source for behavior modification in the classroom. *Behavior Therapy*, 1971, *2*, 205–213.

McNees, M. P., Egli, D. S., Marshall, D. S., Schnelle, R. S., Schnelle, J. F., & Risley, T. R. Shoplifting prevention: Providing information through signs. *Journal of Applied Behavior Analysis*, 1976, *9*, 399–405.

McReynolds, W. T., & Church, A. Self-control study skills development and counseling approaches to the improvement of study behavior. *Behaviour Research and Therapy*, 1973, *11*, 233–235.

McSweeny, A. J. Effects of response cost on the behavior of a million persons. Charging for directory assistance in Cincinnati. *Journal of Applied Behavior Analysis*, 1978, *11*, 47–51.

Medland, M. B., & Stachnik, T. J. Good-behavior game: A replication and systematic analysis. *Journal of Applied Behavior Analysis*, 1972, *5*, 45–51.

Meehl, P. E. The cognitive activity of the clinician. *American Psychologist*, 1960, *15*, 19–27.

Meichenbaum, D. H. Examination of model characteristics in reducing avoidance behavior. *Journal of Personality and Social Psychology*, 1971, *17*, 298–307.

Meichenbaum, D. H. *Cognitive behavior modification*. New York: Plenum Press, 1977.

Meichenbaum, D. Teaching self-control. In B. B. Lahey & A. E. Kazdin (Eds.), *Advances in clinical child psychology, Volume 2*. New York: Plenum, 1979.

Meichenbaum, D. H., Bowers, K., & Ross, R. R. Modification of classroom behavior of institutionalized female adolescent offenders. *Behaviour Research and Therapy*, 1968, *6*, 343–353.

Meichenbaum, D. H., & Cameron, R. Training schizophrenics to talk to themselves: A means of developing attentional controls. *Behavior Therapy*, 1973, *4*, 515–534.

Meichenbaum, D. H., & Goodman, J. Training impulsive children to talk to themselves: A means of developing self-control. *Journal of Abnormal Psychology*, 1971, *77*, 115–126.

Meltzoff, J., & Kornreich, M. *Research in psychotherapy*. New York: Atherton, 1970.

Mental Health Law Projects. *Basic rights of the mentally handicapped*. Washington, D.C.: Mental Health Law Project, 1973.

Mercatoris, M., & Craighead, W. E. Effects of nonparticipant observation on teacher and pupil classroom behavior. *Journal of Educational Psychology*, 1974, *66*, 512–519.

Meyers, A., Mercatoris, M., & Sirota, A. Use of covert self-instruction for the elimination of psychotic speech. *Journal of Consulting and Clinical Psychology*, 1976, *44*, 480–482.

Milby, J. B. Modification of extreme social isolation by contingent social reinforcement. *Journal of Applied Behavior Analysis*, 1970, *3*, 149–152.

Miller, A. J., & Kratochwill, T. R.   Reduction of frequent stomachache complaints by time out. *Behavior Therapy*, 1979, *10*, 211–218.

Miller, D.   Retrospective analysis of posthospital mental patient's worlds. *Journal of Health and Social Behavior*, 1967, *8*, 136–140.

Miller, L. K.   Behavioral principles and experimental communities. In W. E. Craighead, A. E. Kazdin, & M. J. Mahoney (Eds.), *Behavior modification: Principles, issues, and applications*. Boston: Houghton Mifflin, 1976.

Miller, L. K., & Miller, O. L.   Reinforcing self-help group activities of welfare recipients. *Journal of Applied Behavior Analysis*, 1970, *3*, 57–64.

Miller, P. M.   The use of behavioral contracting in the treatment of alcoholism: A case report. *Behavior Therapy*, 1972, *3*, 593–596.

Miller, P. M., & Drennen, W. T.   Establishment of social reinforcement as an effective modifier of verbal behavior in chronic psychiatric patients. *Journal of Abnormal Psychology*, 1970, *76*, 392–395.

Miller, S. J., & Sloane, H. N., Jr.   The generalization effects of parent training across stimulus settings. *Journal of Applied Behavior Analysis*, 1976, *9*, 355–370.

Miller, W. R.   Behavioral self-control training in the treatment of problem drinkers. In R. B. Stuart (Ed.), *Behavioral self-management: Strategies, techniques and outcomes*. New York: Brunner/Mazel, 1977.

Minkin, N., Braukmann, C. J., Minkin, B. L., Timbers, G. D., Timbers, B. J., Fixsen, D. L., Phillips, E. L., & Wolf, M. M.   The social validation and training of conversational skills. *Journal of Applied Behavior Analysis*, 1976, *9*, 127–139.

Miron, N. B.,   Issues and implications of operant conditioning: The primary ethical consideration. *Hospital and Community Psychiatry*, 1968, *19*, 226–228.

Mischel, W.   *Personality and assessment*. New York: Wiley, 1968.

Mischel, W.   *Introduction to personality*. New York: Holt, Rinehart and Winston, 1971.

Mitchell, W. S., & Stoffelmayr, B. E.   Application of the Premack principle to the behavioral control of extremely inactive schizophrenics. *Journal of Applied Behavior Analysis*, 1973, *6*, 419–423.

Montegar, C. A., Reid, D. H., Madsen, C. H., & Ewell, M. D.   Increasing institutional staff to resident interactions through in-service training and supervisor approval. *Behavior Therapy*, 1977, *8*, 533–540.

Monti, P. M., McCrady, B. S., & Barlow, D. H.   Effect of positive reinforcement, informational feedback, and contingency contracting on a bulimic anorexic female. *Behavior Therapy*, 1977, *8*, 258–263.

Moore, B. L., & Bailey, J. S.   Social punishment in the modification of a preschool child's "autistic-like" behavior with a mother as therapist. *Journal of Applied Behavior Analysis*, 1973, *6*, 497–507.

Morales v. Turman, 383 F. Supp. 53 (E.D. Tex. 1974).

Morris, E. K., & Redd, W. H.   Children's performance and social preference for positive, negative, and mixed adult-child interactions. *Child Development*, 1975, *46*, 525–531.

Morse, W. H., & Kelleher, R. T.   Determinants of reinforcement and punishment. In W. K. Honig & J. E. R. Staddon (Eds.), *Handbook of operant behavior*. Englewood Cliffs, New Jersey: Prentice-Hall, 1977.

Mowrer, O. H., & Mowrer, W. M.   Enuresis: A method for its study and treatment. *American Journal of Orthopsychiatry*, 1938, *8*, 436–459.

Murdock, J. Y., Garcia, E. E., & Hardman, M. L.   Generalizing articulation training with trainable mentally retarded subjects. *Journal of Applied Behavior Analysis*, 1977, *10*, 717–733.

Murray, E. J., & Jacobson, L. I.   Cognition and learning in traditional and behavioral therapy. In S. L. Garfield & A. E. Bergin (Eds.), *Handbook of psychotherapy and behavior change: An empirical analysis (second edition)*. New York: Wiley, 1978.

Nay, W. R.   A systematic comparison of instructional techniques for parents. *Behavior Therapy*, 1975, *6*, 14–21.

Neef, N. A., Iwata, B. A., & Page, T. J. Public transportation training: In vivo versus classroom instruction. Journal of Applied Behavior Analysis, 1978, 11, 331–344.

Neisworth, J. T., & Moore, F. Operant treatment of asthmatic responding with the parent as therapist. Behavior Therapy, 1972, 3, 95–99.

Nelson, R. O. Assessment and therapeutic functions of self-monitoring. In M. Hersen, R. M. Eisler, & P. N. Miller (Eds.), Progress in behavior modification, Volume 5. New York: Academic Press, 1977.

Nelson, R. O., Kapust, J. A., & Dorsey, B. L. Minimal reactivity of overt classroom observations on student and teacher behaviors. Behavior Therapy, 1978, 9, 695–702.

New York State Association for Retarded Children v. Rockefeller, 357 F. Supp. 752 (EDNY 1973).

Nietzel, M. T., Winett, R. A., MacDonald, M. L., & Davidson, W. S. Behavioral approaches to community psychology. New York: Pergamon, 1977.

Nordyke, N. S., Baer, D. M., Etzel, B. C., & LeBlanc J. M. Implications of the stereotyping and modification of sex role. Journal of Applied Behavior Analysis, 1977, 10, 553–557.

Nunes, D. L., Murphy, R. J., & Ruprecht, M. L. Reducing self-injurious behavior of severely retarded individuals through withdrawal of reinforcement procedures. Behavior Modification, 1977, 1, 499–516.

O'Brien, F., & Azrin, N. H. Developing proper mealtime behaviors of the institutionalized retarded. Journal of Applied Behavior Analysis. 1972, 5, 389–399. (a)

O'Brien, F., & Azrin, N. H. Symptom reduction by functional displacement in a token economy: A case study. Journal of Behavior Therapy and Experimental Psychiatry, 1972, 3, 205–207. (b)

O'Brien, F., & Azrin, N. H. Interaction-priming: A method of reinstating patient-family relationships. Behaviour Research and Therapy, 1973, 11, 133–136.

O'Brien, F., Azrin, N. H., & Bugle, C. Training profoundly retarded children to stop crawling. Journal of Applied Behavior Analysis, 1972, 5, 131–137.

O'Brien, F., Azrin, N. H., & Henson, K. Increased communications of chronic mental patients by reinforcement and response priming. Journal of Applied Behavior Analysis, 1969, 2, 23–29.

O'Brien, F., Bugle, C., & Azrin, N. H. Training and maintaining a retarded child's proper eating. Journal of Applied Behavior Analysis, 1972, 5, 67–72.

O'Brien, J. S., Raynes, A. E., & Patch, V. D. An operant reinforcement system to improve ward behavior in inpatient drug addicts. Journal of Behavior Therapy and Experimental Psychiatry, 1971, 239–242.

O'Connor, R. D. Modification of social withdrawal through symbolic modeling. Journal of Applied Behavior Analysis, 1969, 2, 15–22.

O'Leary, K. D. The operant and social psychology of token systems. In A. C. Catania & T. A. Brigham (Eds.), Handbook of applied behavior analysis: Social and instructional processes. New York: Irvington, 1978.

O'Leary, K. D., Kaufman, K. F., Kass, R., & Drabman, R. The effects of loud and soft reprimands on the behavior of disruptive students. Exceptional Children, 1970, 37, 145–155.

O'Leary, K. D., Kent, R. N., & Kanowitz, J. Shaping data collection congruent with experimental hypotheses. Journal of Applied Behavior Analysis, 1975, 8, 43–51.

Ollendick, T. H., & Matson, J. L. Overcorrection: An overview. Behavior Therapy, 1978, 9, 830–842.

Olson, R. P., & Greenberg, D. J. Effects of contingency-contracting and decision-making groups with chronic mental patients. Journal of Consulting and Clinical Psychology, 1972, 38, 376–383.

Osborne, J. B. Free-time as a reinforcer in the management of classroom behavior. Journal of Applied Behavior Analysis, 1969, 2, 113–118.

Page, T. J., Iwata, B. A., & Neef, N. A. Teaching pedestrian skills to retarded persons: Generalization from the classroom to the natural environment.

Journal of Applied Behavior Analysis, 1976, 9, 433–444.

Palmer, A. B., & Wohl, J. Voluntary-admission forms: Does the patient know what he's signing? *Hospital and Community Psychiatry*, 1972, 23, 250–252.

Palmer, M. H., Lloyd, M. E., & Lloyd, D. E. An experimental analysis of electricity conservation procedures. *Journal of Applied Behavior Analysis*, 1977, 10, 665–671.

Parsonson, B. S., Baer, A. M., & Baer, D. M. The application of generalized correct social contingencies by institutional staff: An evaluation of the effectiveness and durability of a training program. *Journal of Applied Behavior Analysis*, 1974, 7, 427–437.

Parsonson, B. S., & Baer, D. M. The analysis and presentation of graphic data. In T. R. Kratochwill (Ed.), *Single-subject research: Strategies for evaluating change*. New York: Academic Press, 1978.

Patterson, G. R., & Reid, J. B. Reciprocity and coercion: Two facets of social systems. In C. Neuringer & J. L. Michael (Eds.), *Behavior modification in clinical psychology*. New York: Appleton-Century-Crofts, 1970.

Paul, G. L., & Lentz, R. J. *Psychosocial treatment of chronic mental patients: Milieu versus social-learning programs*. Cambridge, Massachusetts: Harvard University Press, 1977.

Peacock, R., Lyman, R. D., & Rickard, H. C. Correspondence between self-report and observer-report as a function of task difficulty. *Behavior Therapy*, 1978, 9, 578–583.

Pedalino, E., & Gamboa, V. U. Behavior modification and absenteeism: Intervention in one industrial setting. *Journal of Applied Psychology*, 1974, 59, 694–698.

Pertschuk, M. J., Edwards, N., & Pomerleau, O. F. A multiple-baseline approach to behavioral intervention in anorexia nervosa. *Behavior Therapy*, 1978, 9, 368–376.

Peterson, D. R. *The clinical study of social behavior*. New York: Appleton-Century-Crofts, 1968.

Phillips, D. L. Rejection: A possible consequence of seeking help for mental disorders. *American Sociological Review*, 1963, 28, 963–972.

Phillips, E. L. Achievement Place: Token reinforcement procedures in a home-style rehabilitation setting for "pre-delinquent" boys. *Journal of Applied Behavior Analysis*, 1968, 1, 213–223.

Phillips, E. L., Phillips, E. A., Fixsen, D. L., & Wolf, M. M. Achievement Place: Modification of the behaviors of pre-delinquent boys within a token economy. *Journal of Applied Behavior Analysis*, 1971, 4, 45–59.

Phillips, E. L., Phillips E. A., Wolf, M. M., & Fixsen, D. L. Achievement Place: Development of the elected manager system. *Journal of Applied Behavior Analysis*, 1973, 6, 541–561.

Pierce, C. H., & Risley, T. R. Improving job performance of Neighborhood Youths Corps aides in an urban recreation program. *Journal of Applied Behavior Analysis*, 1974, 7, 207–215.

Pierce, M. L. A behavior modification approach to facilitating a disturbed child's school re-entry by teaching time-out procedures to the child's classmates. *School Applications of Learning Theory*, 1971, 3, 1–6.

Pinkston, E. M., Reese, N. M., LeBlanc, J. M., & Baer, D. M. Independent control of a pre-school child's aggression and peer interaction by contingent teacher attention. *Journal of Applied Behavior Analysis*, 1973, 6, 115–124.

Platt, J. R. The Skinnerian revolution. In H. Wheeler (Ed.), *Beyond the punitive society*. San Francisco: W. H. Freeman, 1973.

Plummer, S., Baer, D. M., & LeBlanc, J. M. Functional considerations in the use of procedural timeout and an effective alternative. *Journal of Applied Behavior Analysis*, 1973, 6, 115–124. 705.

Polirstok, S. R., & Greer, R. D. Remediation of mutually aversive interactions between a problem student and four teachers by training the student in reinforcement techniques. *Journal of Applied Behavior Analysis*, 1977, 10, 707–716.

Pomerleau, O. F., Bobrove, P. H., & Smith, R. H. Rewarding psychiatric aides for the behavioral improvement of assigned patients. *Journal of Applied Behavior Analysis*, 1973, 6, 383–390.

Pommer, D. A., & Streedbeck, D. Motivating staff performance in an operant learning program for children. *Journal of Applied Behavior Analysis*, 1974, 7, 217–221.

Porterfield, J. K., Herbert-Jackson, E., & Risley, R. R. Contingent observation: An effective and acceptable procedure for reducing disruptive behavior of young children in a group setting. *Journal of Applied Behavior Analysis*. 1976, 9, 55–64.

Powell, J., & Azrin, N. The effects of shock as a punisher for cigarette smoking. *Journal of Applied Behavior Analysis*, 1968, 1, 63–71.

Powers, R. B., Osborne, J. G., & Anderson, E. G. Positive reinforcement of litter removal in the natural environment. *Journal of Applied Behavior Analysis*, 1973, 6, 579–586.

Premack, D. Reinforcement theory. In D. Levine (Ed.), *Nebraska symposium on motivation*. Lincoln: University of Nebraska Press, 1965.

Quilitch, H. R. A comparison of three staff-management procedures. *Journal of Applied Behavior Analysis*, 1975, 8, 59–66.

Rachlin, H. Self-control: Part I. In A. C. Catania & T. A. Brigham (Eds.), *Handbook of applied behavior analysis: Social and instructional processes*. New York: Irvington, 1978.

Rachman, S. *The effects of psychotherapy*. New York: Pergamon, 1971.

Rachman, S. Clinical applications of observational learning, imitation and modeling. *Behavior Therapy*, 1972, 3, 379–397.

Rachman, S., & Teasdale, J. *Aversion therapy and behaviour disorders: An analysis*. Coral Gables: University of Miami Press, 1969.

Redd, W. H. Effects of mixed reinforcement contingencies on adults' control of children's behavior. *Journal of Applied Behavior Analysis*, 1968, 2, 249–254.

Redd, W. H., & Birnbrauer, J. S. Adults as discriminative stimuli for different reinforcement contingencies with retarded children. *Journal of Experimental Child Psychology*, 1969, 7, 440–447.

Redd, W. H., Morris, E. K., & Martin, J. A. Effects of positive and negative adult-child interactions on children's social preference. *Journal of Experimental Child Psychology*, 1975, 19, 153–164.

Rehm, L. P., & Marston, A. R. Reduction of social anxiety through modification of self-reinforcement: An instigation therapy technique. *Journal of Consulting and Clinical Psychology*, 1968, 32, 565–574.

Reid, D. H., Luyben, P. L., Rawers, F. A., & Bailey, J. S. The effects of prompting and proximity of containers on newspaper recycling behavior. *Environment and Behavior*, 1976, 8, 471–482.

Reid, D. H., Schuh-Wear, C. L., & Brannon, M. E. Use of a group contingency to decrease staff absenteeism in a state institution. *Behavior Modification*, 1978, 2, 251–266.

Reid, J. B. Reliability assessment of observation data: A possible methodological problem. *Child Development*, 1970, 41, 1143–1150.

Reisinger, J. J. Treatment of "anxiety depression" via positive reinforcement and response cost. *Journal of Applied Behavior Analysis*, 1972, 5, 125–130.

Reiss, M. L., Piotrowski, W. D., & Bailey, J. S. Behavioral community psychology: Encouraging low-income parents to seek dental care for their children. *Journal of Applied Behavior Analysis*, 1976, 9, 387–397.

Rekers, G. A. Atypical gender development and psychosocial adjustment. *Journal of Applied Behavior Analysis*, 1977, 10, 559–571.

Rekers, G. A., & Lovaas, O. I. Behavioral treatment of deviant sex-role behaviors in a male child. *Journal of Applied Behavior Analysis*, 1974, 7, 173–190.

Repp, A. C., & Deitz, S. M. Reducing aggressive and self-injurious behavior of institutionalized retarded children through reinforcement of other behaviors. *Journal of Applied Behavior Analysis*, 1974, 7, 313–325.

Resick, P. A., Forehand. R., & McWhorter, A. Q. The effect of parental treatment with one child on an untreated sibling. *Behavior Therapy*, 1976, 7, 544–548.

Resick, P. A., Forehand, R., & Peed, S. Prestatement of contingencies: The effects on acquisition maintenance of behavior. *Behavior Therapy*, 1974, 5, 642–647.

Reynolds, G. S. *A primer of operant conditioning.* Glenview, Illinois: Scott, Foresman, 1968.

Rilling, M. Stimulus control and inhibitory processes. In W. K. Honig & J. E. R. Staddon (Eds.), *Handbook of operant behavior.* Englewood Cliffs, NJ: Prentice-Hall, 1977.

Rimm, D. C., & Masters, J. C. *Behavior therapy: Techniques and empirical findings* (second edition). New York: Academic Press, 1979.

Ringer, V. M. The use of a "token helper" in the management of classroom behavior problems and in teacher training. *Journal of Applied Behavior Analysis*, 1973, 6, 671–677.

Rioch, M. J., Elkes, E., Flint, A. A., Usdansky, B. C., Newman, R. G., & Silber, E. National Institute of Mental Health pilot study in training mental health counselors. *American Journal of Orthopsychiatry*, 1963, 33, 678–689.

Risley, T. R. The effects and side effects of punishing the autistic behaviors of a deviant child. *Journal of Applied Behavior Analysis*, 1968, 1, 21–34.

Risley, T. R. Behavior modification: An experimental–therapeutic endeavor. In L. A. Hamerlynck, P. O. Davidson, & L. E. Acker (Eds.), *Behavior modification and ideal mental health services.* Calgary, Alberta, Canada: University of Calgary Press, 1970.

Robertson, S. J., DeReus, D. M., & Drabman, R. S. Peer and college-student tutoring as reinforcement in a token economy. *Journal of Applied Behavior Analysis*, 1976, 9, 169–177.

Robin, A. L., Armel, S., & O'Leary, K. D. The effects of self-instruction on writing deficiencies. *Behavior Therapy*, 1975, 6, 178–187.

Rogers, C. R. *Client-centered therapy.* Boston: Houghton-Mifflin, 1951.

Rogers, C. R., & Skinner, B. F. Some issues concerning the control of human behavior: A symposium. *Science*, 1956, 124, 1057–1066.

Rollings, J. P., Baumeister, A. A., & Baumeister, A. A. The use of overcorrection procedures to eliminate the stereotyped behaviors of retarded individuals: An analysis of collateral behaviors and generalization of suppressive effects. *Behavior Modification*, 1977, 1, 29–46.

Romanczyk, R. G., Kent, R. N., Diament, C., & O'Leary, K. D. Measuring the reliability of observational data: A reactive process. *Journal of Applied Behavior Analysis*, 1973, 6, 175–184.

Rosen, G. M., Glasgow, R. E., & Barrera, M. Jr. A controlled study to assess the clinical efficacy of totally self-administered systematic desensitization. *Journal of Consulting and Clinical Psychology*, 1976, 44, 208–217.

Rosen, G. M., Glasgow, R. E., & Barrera, M., Jr. A two-year follow-up on systematic desensitization with data pertaining to the external validity of laboratory, fear assessment. *Journal of Consulting and Clinical Psychology*, 1977, 45, 1188–1189.

Rosenbaum, A., O'Leary, K. D., & Jacob, R. G. Behavioral intervention with hyperactive children: Group consequences as a supplement to individual contingencies. *Behavior Therapy*, 1975, 6, 315–323.

Rosenbaum, M. S., & Drabman, R. S. Self-control training in the classroom: A review and critique. *Journal of Applied Behavior Analysis*, 1979, 12, 467–485.

Rosenthal, D. Changes in some moral values following psychotherapy. *Journal of Consulting Psychology*, 1955, 19, 431–436.

Rosenthal, T. L., & Bandura, A. Psychological modeling: Theory and practice. In S. L. Garfield and A. E. Bergin (Eds.), *Handbook of psychotherapy and behavior change: An empirical analysis* (second edition). New York: Wiley, 1978.

Rotter, J. B. *Social learning and clincial psychology.* New York: Prentice-Hall, 1954.

Rowbury, T. G., Baer, A. M., & Baer, D. M. Interactions between teacher guidance and contingent access to play in developing preacademic skills of deviant preschool children. *Journal of Applied Behavior Analysis*, 1976, 9, 85–104.

Rule, S. A comparison of three different types of feedback on teachers' performance. In G. Semb (Ed.), *Behavior analysis and education.* Lawrence, Kansas: University of Kansas, 1972.

Rushall, B. S., & Siedentop, D. *The development and control of behavior in sport and physical education.* Philadelphia: Lea & Febiger, 1972.

Russo, D. C., & Koegel, R. L. A method for integrating an autistic child into a normal public school classroom. *Journal of Applied Behavior Analysis*, 1977, 10, 579–590.

Sachs, D. A. Behavioral techniques in a residential nursing home facility. *Journal of Behavior Therapy and Experimental Psychiatry*, 1975, 26, 123–127.

Sajwaj, T., Libert, J., & Agras, W. S. Lemon-juice therapy: The control of life-threatening rumination in a six-month-old infant. *Journal of Applied Behavior Analysis*, 1974, 7, 557–563.

Sajwaj, T., Twardosz, S., & Burke, M. Side effects of extinction procedures in a remedial preschool *Journal of Applied Behavior Analysis*, 1972, 5, 163–175.

Salter, A. *The case against psychoanalysis.* New York: Henry Holt, 1952.

Salzberg, B. H., Wheeler, A. A., Devar, L. T., & Hopkins, B. L. The effect of intermittent feedback and intermittent contingent access to play on printing of kindergarten children. *Journal of Applied Behavior Analysis*, 1971, 4, 163–171.

Sanders, M. R., & Glynn, T. Functional analysis of a program for training high and low preference peers to modify disruptive classroom behavior. *Journal of Applied Behavior Analysis*, 1977, 10, 503.

Sanson-Fisher, B., & Jenkins, H. J. Interaction patterns between inmates and staff in a maximum security institution for delinquents. *Behavior Therapy*, 1978, 9, 703–716.

Santogrossi, D. A., O'Leary, K. D., Romanczyk, R. G., & Kaufman, K. F. Self-evaluation by adolescents in a psychiatric hospital school token program. *Journal of Applied Behavior Analysis*, 1973, 6, 277–287.

Scheff, T. J. *Being mentally ill: A sociological theory.* Chicago: Aldine, 1966.

Schnelle, J. F. A brief report on invalidity of parent evaluations of behavior change. *Journal of Applied Behavior Analysis*, 1974, 7, 341–343.

Schnelle, J. F., Kirchner, R. E., Macrae, J. W., McNees, M. P., Eck, R. H., Snodgrass, S., Casey, J. D., & Uselton, P. H. Police evaluation research: An experimental and cost-benefit analysis of a helicopter patrol in a high crime area. *Journal of Applied Behavior Analysis*, 1978, 11, 11–21.

Schnelle, J. F., Kirchner, R. E., McNees, R. M., & Lawler, J. M. Social evaluation research: The evaluation of two police patrolling strategies. *Journal of Applied Behavior Analysis*, 1975, 8, 353–365.

Schultz, J. H., & Luthe, W. *Autogenic training.* New York: Grune & Stratton, 1959.

Schwartz, B., & Gamzu, E. Pavlovian control of operant behavior. In W. K. Honig & J. E. R. Staddon (Eds.), *Handbook of operant behavior.* Englewood Cliffs, New Jersey: Prentice-Hall, 1977.

Schwartz, G. E. Biofeedback and the self-management of disregulation disorders. In R. B. Stuart (Ed.), *Behavioral self-management: Strategies, techniques and outcomes.* New York: Brunner/Mazel, 1977.

Schwartz, G. E., & Weiss, S. M. Yale Conference on Behavioral Medicine: A proposed definition and statement of goals. *Journal of Behavioral Medicine*, 1978, 1, 3–12.

Schwitzgebel, R. K. A contractual model for the protection of the rights of institutionalized mental patients. *American Psychologist*, 1975, 30, 815–820.

Seaver, W. B., & Patterson, A. H. Decreasing fuel oil consumption through feedback and social commendation. *Journal of Applied Behavior Analysis*, 1976, 9, 147–152.

Seymour, F. W., & Stokes, T. F. Self-recording in training girls to increase work and evoke staff praise in an institution for offenders. *Journal of Applied Behavior Analysis*, 1976, 9, 41–54.

Shafto, F., & Sulzbacher, S. Comparing

treatment tactics with a hyperactive preschool child: Stimulant medication and programmed teacher intervention. *Journal of Applied Behavior Analysis*, 1977, *10*, 13–20.

Shier, D. A. Applying systematic exclusion to a case of bizarre behavior. In J. D. Krumboltz & C. E. Thoresen (Eds.), *Behavioral counseling: Cases and techniques*. New York: Holt, Rinehart & Winston, 1969.

Silverman, P. J. The role of social reinforcement in maintaining an obsessive–compulsive neurosis. *Journal of Behavior Therapy and Experimental Psychiatry*, 1977, *8*, 325–326.

Skinner, B. F. *Walden Two*. New York: Macmillan, 1948.

Skinner, B. F. *Science and human behavior*. New York: Free Press, 1953.

Skinner, B. F. *Beyond freedom and dignity*. New York: Knopf, 1971.

Skinner, B. F. Answers for my critics. In H. Wheeler (Ed.), *Beyond the punitive society*, San Francisco: W. H. Freeman, 1973.

Skinner, B. F. *About behaviorism*. New York: Knopf, 1974.

Smith, M. L., & Glass, G. V. Meta-analysis of psychotherapy outcome studies. *American Psychologist*, 1977, *32*, 752–760.

Sobell, L. C., Schaefer, H. H., Sobell, M. B., & Kremer, M. E. Food priming: A therapeutic tool to increase the percentage of meals bought by chronic mental patients. *Behaviour Research and Therapy*, 1970, *8*, 339–345.

Sobey, F. *The nonprofessional revolution in mental health*. New York: Columbia University Press, 1970.

Solnick, J. V., Rincover, A., & Peterson, C. R. Some determinants of the reinforcing and punishing effects of timeout. *Journal of Applied Behavior Analysis*, 1977, *10*, 415–424.

Solomon, R. L., Kamin, L. J., & Wynne, L. C. Traumatic avoidance learning: The outcomes of several extinction procedures with dogs. *Journal of Abnormal and Social Psychology*, 1953, *48*, 291–302.

Speidel, G. E., & Tharp, R. G. Teacher-training workshop strategy: Instructions, discrimination training, modeling, guided practice, and video feedback. *Behavior Therapy*, 1978, *9*, 735–739.

Spring, F. L., Sipich, J. F., Trimble, R. W., & Goeckner, D. J. Effects of contingency and noncontingency contracts in the context of a self-control-oriented smoking modification program. *Behavior Therapy*, 1978, *9*, 967–968.

Staats, A. W. *Social behaviorism*. Homewood, Illinois: Dorsey, 1975.

Stenn, P. G., Motherskill, K. J., & Brooke, R. I. Biofeedback and a cognitive behavioral approach to treatment of myofascial pain dysfunction syndrome. *Behavior Therapy*, 1979, *10*, 29–36.

Stokes, T. F., & Baer, D. M. Preschool peers as mutual generalization-facilitating agents. *Behavior Therapy*, 1976, *7*, 549–556.

Stokes, T. F., & Baer, D. M. An implicit technology of generalization. *Journal of Applied Behavior Analysis*, 1977, *10*, 349–367.

Stokes, T. F., Baer, D. M., & Jackson, R. L. Programming the generalization of a greeting response in four retarded children. *Journal of Applied Behavior Analysis*, 1974, *7*, 599–610.

Stolz, S. B., Wienckowski, L. A., & Brown, B. S. Behavior modification: A perspective on critical issues. *American Psychologist*, 1975, *30*, 1027–1048.

Strain, P. S., Shores, R. E., & Kerr, M. M. An experimental analysis of "spillover" effects on the social interaction of behaviorally handicapped preschool children. *Journal of Applied Behavior Analysis*, 1976, *9*, 31–40.

Strain, P. S., Shores, R. E., & Timm, M. A. Effects of peer social initiations on the behavior of withdrawn preschool children. *Journal of Applied Behavior Analysis*, 1977, *10*, 289–298.

Strupp, H. H., & Hadley, S. W. A tripartite model of mental health and therapeutic outcomes. *American Psychologists*, 1977, *32*, 187–196.

Stuart, R. B. *Trick or treatment: How and when psychotherapy fails*. Champaign, Illinois: Research Press, 1970.

Stuart, R. B. Behavioral contracting with the families of delinquents. *Journal of Behavior Therapy and Experimental Psychiatry*, 1971, *2*, 1–11.

Stuart, R. B. (Ed.), *Behavioral self-management: Strategies, techniques, and outcomes.* New York: Brunner/Mazel, 1977. (a)

Stuart, R. B. *Client–therapist treatment contract.* Champaign, Illinois: Research Press, 1977. (b)

Stuart, R. B., & Lott, L. A., Jr. Behavioral contracting with delinquents: A cautionary note. *Journal of Behavior Therapy and Experimental Psychiatry,* 1972, *3,* 161–169.

Subcommittee on Constitutional Rights, Committee of the Judiciary, United States Senate, Ninety-Third Congress, *Individual rights and the federal role in behavior modification.* Washington, D. C.: U.S. Government Printing Office, 1974.

Surratt, P. R., Ulrich, R. E., & Hawkins, R. P. An elementary student as a behavioral engineer. *Journal of Applied Behavior Analysis,* 1969, *2,* 85–92.

Surwit, R. S., & Keefe, F. J. Frontalis EMG feedback training: An electronic panacea? *Behavior Therapy,* 1978, *9,* 779–792.

Switzer, E. B., Deal, T. E., & Bailey, J. S. The reduction of stealing in second graders using a group contingency. *Journal of Applied Behavior Analysis,* 1977, *10,* 267–272.

Szasz, T. S. The myth of mental illness. *American Psychologist,* 1960, *15,* 113–118.

Tanner, B. A. Aversive shock issues: Physical danger, emotional harm, effectiveness and "dehumanization." *Journal of Behavior Therapy and Experimental Psychiatry,* 1973, 4, 113–115.

Taplin, P. S., & Reid, J. B. Effects of instructional set and experimenter influence on observer reliability. *Child Development,* 1973, *44,* 547–554.

Tasto, D. L., & Chesney, M. A. Muscle relaxation treatment for primary dysmenorrhea. *Behavior Therapy,* 1974, *5,* 668–672.

Tate, B. G., & Baroff, G. S. Training the mentally retarded in the production of a complex product: A demonstration of work potential. *Exceptional Children,* 1967, *9,* 405–408.

Thomas, J. D., Presland, I. E., Grant, M. D., & Glynn, T. L. Natural rates of teacher approval and disapproval in grade-7 classrooms. *Journal of Applied Behavior Analysis,* 1978, *11,* 91–94.

Thomson, N., Fraser, D., & McDougall, A. The reinstatement of speech in near-mute chronic schizophrenics by instructions, imitative prompts, and reinforcement. *Journal of Behavior Therapy and Experimental Psychiatry,* 1974, *5,* 77–80.

Thoresen, C. E., & Mahoney, M. J. *Behavioral self-control.* New York: Holt, Rinehart and Winston, 1974.

Thorndike, E. L. *The fundamentals of learning.* New York: Teachers College, 1932.

Truax, C. B. Reinforcement and non-reinforcement in Rogerian psychotherapy. *Journal of Abnormal Psychology,* 1966, *71,* 1–9.

Trudel, G., Boisvert, J., Maruca, F., & Leroux, P. Unprogrammed reinforcement of patients' behaviors in wards with and without token economy. *Journal of Behavior Therapy and Experimental Psychiatry,* 1974, *5,* 147–149.

Turkewitz, H., O'Leary, K. D., & Ironsmith, M. Generalization and maintenance of appropriate behavior through self-control. *Journal of Consulting and Clinical Psychology,* 1975, *43,* 557–583.

Turner, A. J., & Vernon, J. C.. Prompts to increase attendance in a community mental-health center. *Journal of Applied Behavior Analysis,* 1976, *9,* 141–145.

Twardosz, S., & Baer, D. M. Training two severely retarded adolescents to ask questions. *Journal of Applied Behavior Analysis,* 1973, *6,* 655–661.

Ullmann, L. P., & Krasner, L. *A psychological approach to abnormal behavior* (second edition). Englewood Cliffs, New Jersey: Prentice-Hall, 1975.

Ulrich, R. Behavior control and public concern. *Psychological Record,* 1967, *17,* 229–234.

Upper, D. A "ticket" system for reducing ward rule violations on a token economy program. *Journal of Behavior Therapy and Experimental Psychiatry,* 1973, *4,* 137–140.

Upper, D., Lochman, J. E., & Aveni, C. A. Using contingency contracting to modify the problematic behaviors of foster home residents. *Behavior Modification*, 1977, *1*, 405–416.

VanDeventer, A. D., & Laws, D. R. Orgasmic reconditioning to redirect sexual arousal in pedophiles. *Behavior Therapy*, 1978, *9*, 748–765.

Van Houten, R., Hill, S., & Parsons, M. An analysis of a performance feedback system: The effects of timing and feedback, public posting, and praise upon academic performance and peer interaction. *Journal of Applied Behavior Analysis*, 1975, *8*, 449–457.

Varni, J. G. The use of biofeedback in the treatment of vaginismus. Paper presented at meeting of the Society for Psychophysiological Research, Galveston, Texas, 1973.

Wahler, R. G. Setting generality: Some specific and general effects of child behavior therapy. *Journal of Applied Behavior Analysis*, 1969, *2*, 239–246.

Wahler, R. G. Some ecological problems in child behavior modification. In S. W. Bijou & E. Ribes-Inesta (Eds.), *Behavior modification: Issues and extensions*, New York: Academic Press, 1972.

Wahler, R. G. Some structural aspects of deviant child behavior. *Journal of Applied Behavior Analysis*, 1975, *8*, 27–42.

Wahler, R. G. Deviant child behavior within the family: Developmental speculations and behavior change strategies. In H. Leitenberg (Ed.), *Handbook of behavior modification and behavior therapy*. Englewood Cliffs, New Jersey: Prentice-Hall, 1976.

Wahler, R. B., Berland, R. M., & Coe, T. D. Generalization processes in child behavior change. In B. B. Lahey & A. E. Kazdin (Eds.), *Advances in clinical child psychology, Volume 2*. New York: Plenum, 1979.

Wahler, R. G., Peterson, R. F., Winkel, G. H., & Morrison, D. C. Mothers as behavior therapists for their own children. *Behaviour Research and Therapy*, 1965, *3*, 113–124.

Walker, H. M., & Buckley, N. K. Programming generalization and maintenance of treatment effects across time and across settings. *Journal of Applied Behavior Analysis*, 1972, *5*, 209–224.

Walker, H. M., & Hops, H. Use of normative peer data as a standard for evaluating classroom treatment effects. *Journal of Applied Behavior Analysis*, 1976, *9*, 159–168.

Walker, H. M., Hops, H. & Fiegenbaum, E. Deviant classroom behavior as a function of combinations of social and token reinforcement and cost contingency. *Behavior Therapy*, 1976, *7*, 76–88.

Walker, H. M. Hops, H., & Johnson, S. M. Generalization and maintenance of classroom treatment effects. *Behavior Therapy*, 1975, *6*, 188–200.

Walker, H. M., Mattson, R. H., & Buckley, N. K. The functional analysis of behavior within an experimental class setting. In W. C. Becker (Ed.), *An empirical basis for change in education*. Chicago: Science Research Associates, 1971.

Warren, S. A., & Mondy, L. W. To what behaviors do attending adults respond? *American Journal of Mental Deficiency*, 1971, *75*, 449–455.

Watson, D. L., Tharp, R. G., & Krisberg, J. Case study in self-modification: Suppression of inflammatory scratching while awake and asleep. *Journal of Behavior Therapy and Experimental Psychiatry*, 1972, *3*, 213–215.

Watson, J. B., & Rayner, R. Conditioned emotional reactions. *Journal of Experimental Psychology*, 1920, *3*, 1–14.

Weil, G., & Goldfried, M. R. Treatment of insomnia in an eleven-year-old child through self-relaxation. *Behavior Therapy*, 1973, *4*, 282–284.

Weisberg, P., & Clements, P. Effects of direct, intermittent, and vicarious reinforcement procedures on the development and maintenance of instruction-following behaviors in a group of young children. *Journal of Applied Behavior Analysis*, 1977, *10*, 314.

Weisberg, P., & Waldrop, P. B. Fixed-interval work habits of Congress. *Journal of Applied Behavior Analysis*, 1972, *5*, 93–97.

Wells, K. C., Forehand, R., Hickey, K., & Green, K. D. Effects of a procedure derived from the overcorrection principle on manipulated and nonmanipulated behaviors. *Journal of Applied Behavior Analysis*, 1977, *10*, 679–687.

Wells, K. C., Turner, S. M., Bellack, A. S., & Hersen, M. Effects of cue-controlled relaxation on psychomotor seizures: An experimental analysis. *Behaviour Research and Therapy*, 1978, *16*, 51–53.

Werner, J. S., Minkin, N., Minkin, B. L., Fixsen, D. L., Phillips, E. L., & Wolf, M. M. "Intervention package": An analysis to prepare juvenile delinquents for encounters with police officers. *Criminal Justice and Behavior*, 1975, *2*, 55–83.

Wexler, D. B. Behavior modification and other behavior change procedures: The emerging law and the proposed Florida guidelines. *Criminal Law Bulletin*, 1975, *11*, 600–616. (a)

Wexler, D. B. Reflections on the legal regulation of behavior modification in institutional settings. *Arizona Law Review*, 1975, *17*, 132–143. (b)

Whaley, D. L., & Tough, J. Treatment of a self-injuring mongoloid with shock-induced suppression and avoidance. In R. Ulrich, T. Stachnik, & J. Mabry (Eds.), *Control of human behavior: From cure to prevention, Volume 2.* Glenview, Illinois: Scott, Foresman and Company, 1970.

Wheeler, H. (Ed.), *Beyond the punitive society.* San Francisco: W. H. Freeman, 1973.

White, C. D. The effects of observer presence on the activity level of families. *Journal of Applied Behavior Analysis*, 1977, *10*, 734.

White, G. D., Nielson, G., & Johnson, S. M. Timeout duration and the suppression of deviant behavior in children. *Journal of Applied Behavior Analysis*, 1972, *5*, 111–120.

White, M. A. Natural rates of teacher approval and disapproval in the classroom. *Journal of Applied Behavior Analysis*, 1975, *8*, 367–372.

White-Blackburn, G., Semb, S., & Semb, G. The effects of a good-behavior contract on the classroom behaviors of sixth-grade students. *Journal of Applied Behavior Analysis*, 1977, *10*, 312.

Whitman, T. L., Mercurio, J. R., &

Caponigri, V. Development of social responses in two severely retarded children. *Journal of Applied Behavior Analysis*, 1970, *3*, 133–138.

Williams, C. D. The elimination of tantrum behaviors by extinction procedures. *Journal of Abnormal and Social Psychology*, 1959, *59*, 269.

Williams. R. B., Jr. Headache. In R. B. Williams, Jr. & W. D. Gentry (Eds.), *Behavioral approaches to medical treatment.* Cambridge, Massachusetts: Ballinger, 1977.

Williams, R. B., Jr., & Gentry, W. D. (Eds), *Behavioral approaches to medical treatment.* Cambridge, Massachusetts: Ballinger, 1977.

Wilson, D. D., Robertson, S. J., Herlong, L. H., & Haynes, S. N. Vicarious effects of time-out in the modification of aggression in the classroom. *Behavior Modification*, 1979, *3*, 97–111.

Wilson, G. T., Leaf, R. C., & Nathan, P. E. The aversive control of excessive alcohol consumption by chronic alcoholics in the laboratory setting. *Journal of Applied Behavior Analysis*, 1975, *8*, 13–26.

Winett, R. A., & Roach, E. M. The effects of reinforcing academic performance on social behavior. *Psychological Record*, 1973, *23*, 391–396.

Winett, R. A. & Winkler, R. C. Current behavior modification in the classroom: Be still, be quiet, be docile. *Journal of Applied Behavior Analysis*, 1972, *5*, 499–504.

Wing, J. K. Institutionalism in mental hospitals. *British Journal of Social and Clinical Psychology*, 1962, *1*, 38–51.

Winkler, R. C. Reinforcement schedules for individual patients in a token economy. *Behavior Therapy*, 1971, *2*, 534–537. (a)

Winkler, R. C. The relevance of economic theory and technology of token reinforcement systems. *Behaviour Research and Therapy*, 1971, *9*, 81–88. (b)

Winkler, R. C. What types of sex-role behavior should behavior modifiers promote? *Journal of Applied Behavior Analysis*, 1977, *10*, 549–552.

Wolf, M. M. Social validity: The case for subjective measurement or how applied behavior analysis is finding its heart. *Journal of Applied Behavior Analysis*, 1978, *11*, 203–214.

Wolf, M. M., Birnbrauer, J. S., Williams, T., & Lawler, J. A note on apparent extinction of the vomiting behavior of a retarded child. In L. P. Ullmann & L. Krasner (Eds.), *Case studies in behavior modification*. New York: Holt, Rinehart and Winston, 1965.

Wolf, M. M., Hanley, E. L., King, L. A., Lachowicz, J., & Giles, D. K. The timer-game: A variable interval contingency for the management of out-of-seat behavior. *Exceptional Children*, 1970, *37*, 113–117.

Wolpe, J. *Psychotherapy by reciprocal inhibition*. Stanford: Stanford University Press, 1958.

Wood, R., & Flynn J. M. A self-evaluation token system *vs* an external evaluation token system alone in a residential setting with predelinquent youth. *Journal of Applied Behavior Analysis*, 1978, *11*, 503–512.

Woolfolk, A. E., Woolfolk, R. L., & Wilson, G. T. A rose by another name . . . .: Labeling bias and attitudes toward behavior modification. *Journal of Consulting and Clinical Psychology*, 1977, *45*, 184–191.

Wright, D. F., Brown, R. A., & Andrews, M. E. Remission of chronic ruminative vomiting through a reversal of social contingencies. *Behaviour Research and Therapy*, 1978, *16*, 134–136.

Wulbert, M., & Dries, R. The relative efficacy of methylphenidate (Ritalin) and behavior modification techniques in the treatment of a hyperactive child. *Journal of Applied Behavior Analysis*, 1977, *10*, 21–31.

Wyatt v. Stickney, 344 F. Supp, 373, 344 F. Supp. 387 (M.D. Ala. 1972); affirmed sub nom. *Wyatt v. Aderholt*, 503 F. 2d. 1305 (5th Cir. 1974).

Zeiss, R. A. Self-directed treatment for premature ejaculation. *Journal of Consulting and Clinical Psychology*, 1978, *46*, 1234–1241.

Zilboorg, G., & Henry, G. *A history of medical psychology*. New York: Norton, 1941.

Zimmerman, J., Overpeck, C., Eisenberg, H., & Garlick, B. Operant conditioning in a sheltered workshop. *Rehabilitation Literature*, 1969, *30*, 326–334.

Zlutnick, S., Mayville, W. J., & Moffat, S. Modification of seizure disorders: The interruption of behavioral chains. *Journal of Applied Behavior Analysis*, 1975, *8*, 1–12.

Author Index

Subject Index

411

This book has been set VIP in 10 and 9 point
Melior, leaded 2 points. Chapter numbers are
18 point Helvetica medium and chapter titles
are 24 point Melior. The size of the type is 27
by 45½ picas.

BEHAVIOR MODIFICATION
IN APPLIED SETTINGS